REFUGE LOST

As Europe deals with a so-called 'refugee crisis', Australia's harsh border control policies have been suggested as a possible model for Europe to copy. Key measures of this system such as long-term mandatory detention, intercepting and turning boats around at sea, and the extraterritorial processing of asylum claims were actually used in the United States long before they were adopted in Australia. The book examines the process through which these policies spread between the United States and Australia and the way the courts in each jurisdiction have dealt with the measures. Daniel Ghezelbash's innovative interdisciplinary analysis shows how policies and practices that 'work' in one country might not work in another. This timely book is a must-read for those interested in preserving the institution of asylum in a volatile international and domestic political climate.

DANIEL GHEZELBASH is a senior lecturer at Macquarie University, Sydney, Australia, where he teaches and researches in the areas of refugee and immigration law, human rights and administrative law. He is a practicing refugee lawyer and the director and founder of the Macquarie University Social Justice Law Clinic.

CAMBRIDGE ASYLUM AND MIGRATION STUDIES

At no time in modern history have so many people been on the move as at present. Migration facilitates critical social, economic, and humanitarian linkages. But it may also challenge prevailing notions of bounded political communities, of security, and of international law.

The political and legal systems that regulate the transborder movement of persons were largely devised in the mid-twentieth century, and are showing their strains. New challenges have arisen for policymakers, advocates, and decision-makers that require the adaptation and evolution of traditional models to meet emerging imperatives.

Edited by a world leader in refugee law, this new series aims to be a forum for innovative writing on all aspects of the transnational movement of people. It publishes single or coauthored works that may be legal, political, or cross-disciplinary in nature, and will be essential reading for anyone looking to understand one of the most important issues of the twenty-first century.

Series Editor
James Hathaway, James E. and Sarah A. Degan Professor of Law, and Director of Michigan Law's Program in Refugee and Asylum Law, University of Michigan, USA

Editorial Advisory Board
Alexander Betts, Leopold Muller Professor of Forced Migration and International Affairs, and the Director of the Refugee Studies Centre, University of Oxford, UK
Vincent Chetail, Professor of Public International Law, and Director of the Global Migration Centre, Graduate Institute of International and Development Studies, Switzerland
Thomas Gammeltoft-Hansen, Research Director, Raoul Wallenberg Institute of Human Rights and Humanitarian Law, Sweden
Audrey Macklin, Professor and Chair in Human Rights Law, University of Toronto, Canada
Saskia Sassen, Robert S. Lynd Professor of Sociology, and Chair of the Committee on Global Thought, Columbia University, USA

Books in the Series
The Child in International Refugee Law Jason Pobjoy
Refuge Lost: Asylum Law in an Interdependent World Daniel Ghezelbash

REFUGE LOST

Asylum Law in an Interdependent World

DANIEL GHEZELBASH
Macquarie University, Sydney

CAMBRIDGE
UNIVERSITY PRESS

CAMBRIDGE
UNIVERSITY PRESS

University Printing House, Cambridge CB2 8BS, United Kingdom

One Liberty Plaza, 20th Floor, New York, NY 10006, USA

477 Williamstown Road, Port Melbourne, VIC 3207, Australia

314–321, 3rd Floor, Plot 3, Splendor Forum, Jasola District Centre, New Delhi – 110025, India

79 Anson Road, #06-04/06, Singapore 079906

Cambridge University Press is part of the University of Cambridge.

It furthers the University's mission by disseminating knowledge in the pursuit of education, learning, and research at the highest international levels of excellence.

www.cambridge.org
Information on this title: www.cambridge.org/9781108425254
DOI: 10.1017/9781108349031

© Daniel Ghezelbash 2018

This publication is in copyright. Subject to statutory exception and to the provisions of relevant collective licensing agreements, no reproduction of any part may take place without the written permission of Cambridge University Press.

First published 2018

Printed in the United Kingdom by Clays, St Ives plc

A catalogue record for this publication is available from the British Library.

Library of Congress Cataloging-in-Publication Data
Names: Ghezelbash, Daniel, 1985–, author.
Title: Refuge lost : asylum law in an interdependent world / Daniel Ghezelbash.
Description: New York : Cambridge University Press, 2018. | Series: Cambridge asylum and migration studies | Includes bibliographical references and index.
Identifiers: LCCN 2017049384| ISBN 9781108425254 (hardback) | ISBN 9781108441414 (paperback)
Subjects: LCSH: Asylum, Right of. | Refugees–Legal status, laws, etc. | BISAC: LAW / Comparative.
Classification: LCC K3268.3 .G54 2018 | DDC 342.08/3–dc23 LC record available at https://lccn.loc.gov/2017049384

ISBN 978-1-108-42525-4 Hardback
ISBN 978-1-108-44141-4 Paperback

Cambridge University Press has no responsibility for the persistence or accuracy of URLs for external or third-party internet websites referred to in this publication and does not guarantee that any content on such websites is, or will remain, accurate or appropriate.

For all the refugees
particularly Azita and Jamal who nurtured me
and Anna who completed me

Farewell happy fields,
Where joy forever dwells: hail, horrors!

John Milton, *Paradise Lost*

CONTENTS

List of Figures	page x
List of Tables	xi
Series Editor's Preface	xiii
Acknowledgements	xiv
List of Abbreviations	xvi

1 Introduction   1
    1.1 Legal Transfer, Policy Transfer and Diffusion   4
    1.2 Identifying Transfers   7
    1.3 Measuring Success   11
    1.4 Definitions   17
    1.5 The Road Ahead   19

2 Managing Asylum-Seeker Flows in the Twenty-First Century   20
    2.1 Efficiency, Prestige and Coercion   21
    2.2 Cooperation and Competition   22
    2.3 The Quest for Control   28
    2.4 Impediments to Control   31

3 Long-Term Mandatory Immigration Detention   35
    3.1 United States   36
    3.2 Australia   43

  3.3 Identifying Transfers 46
    3.3.1 Phase One: United States → Australia (1989–1994) 48
    3.3.2 Phase Two: Australia → United States (1996–2003) 49
    3.3.3 Phase Three: Australia ↔ United States (2004–2016) 50
  3.4 Comparing the US and Australian Jurisprudence 53
    3.4.1 Mandatory Detention 58
    3.4.2 Indefinite Detention 62

4 Maritime Interdiction 74
  4.1 US Coast Guard Alien Migrant Interdiction Program 75
  4.2 Australia's Interdiction and 'Push-Back' Operations 81
  4.3 Comparing the US and Australian Jurisprudence 95

5 Extraterritorial Processing 100
  5.1 Extraterritorial Processing in the United States 101
    5.1.1 Processing at Sea 101
    5.1.2 Guantánamo Bay 103
    5.1.3 Third Country Processing and Transfers 110
  5.2 Extraterritorial Processing in Australia 111
    5.2.1 Pacific Solution Mark I 111
    5.2.2 Christmas Island 113
    5.2.3 The Malaysian Solution 117
    5.2.4 Return to Offshore Processing: Pacific Solution Mark II 120
    5.2.5 The Australia–United States Resettlement Deals 127
    5.2.6 Processing at Sea 129
  5.3 Comparing the US and Australian Jurisprudence 130

6 International Law 133
  6.1 Mandatory Detention 133
    6.1.1 Arbitrary Detention 133
    6.1.2 Right to Challenge Detention 136

6.1.3	Conditions of Detention	137
6.1.4	Duration of Detention	137
6.2	Maritime Interdiction	138
6.2.1	Stopping Boats	139
6.2.2	'Taking'	141
6.2.3	*Non-refoulement*	143
6.2.4	Collective Expulsion	149
6.2.5	'Place of Safety'	150
6.3	Extraterritorial Processing	150
6.3.1	Conditions in Extraterritorial Camps	151
6.3.2	Quality of RSD and Risk of *Refoulement*	157
6.3.3	State Responsibility	159
6.3.4	Transferring Asylum Seekers to Third Countries	162
6.4	Special Protections for Child Asylum Seekers	163
6.5	Non-Discrimination and Non-Penalisation	165

7 Lessons for Other Jurisdictions — 167

7.1	The 'Australian Solution' as a Model for Europe?	167
7.1.1	Maritime Interdiction	169
7.1.2	Extraterritorial Processing	171
7.2	Interdiction and Push-Back Operations in Thailand, Malaysia and Indonesia	174
7.3	Mandatory Detention in Canada and New Zealand	175
7.4	Lessons for Lawmakers	177
7.4.1	Legal Success	177
7.4.2	Programmatic Success	180
7.4.3	Process Success	183
7.4.4	Political Dimension	184
7.4.5	Ramifications for the International Refugee Protection Regime	184

Appendix: US and Australian Boat Migrant Statistics — 187

Index — 190

FIGURES

1.1 A framework for identifying contemporary legal transfers   *page 8*

TABLES

1.1	List of interview subjects	*page* 11
A.1	US Coast Guard migrant interdiction, 1982–2016	187
A.2	Asylum-seeker boat arrivals in Australia, 1991–2016	188
A.3	Known boat 'turnbacks' carried out by the Australian government, 2001–2016	189

SERIES EDITOR'S PREFACE

In *Refuge Lost: Asylum Law in an Interdependent World*, Daniel Ghezelbash warns that '[t]he protections set out in the Refugee Convention and other human rights treaties are only words. Their effectiveness in the real world is shaped by state practice'.

This conclusion is not, as might be thought, a restatement of the obvious. The enforcement deficit of international law is of course well documented, and is perhaps especially clear in the context of the Refugee Convention – the only UN human rights treaty that still lacks a system of independent oversight.

Ghezelbash's point is instead that developed countries *systematically learn from, and emulate* each other's national asylum-denying laws and policies. Looking primarily at policies of mandatory detention, interception and extraterritorial processing – perhaps the most critical ways in which powerful states presently seek to undermine the refugee treaty to which they have agreed – he shows that there is a global process of diffusion of tactics designed to enable treatment at odds with legal duties owed to refugees.

The argument in *Refuge Lost: Asylum Law in an Interdependent World* is grounded in a novel and painstakingly detailed analysis of the interdependence of asylum law and policy in Australia and the United States, which Ghezelbash shows is embedded in a broader global process of diffusion. Critically, this pervasive borrowing of domestic rights-denying asylum law and policy is possible despite important differences of constitutional and other legal culture among states: because migration is generally agreed to be a matter of near complete sovereign discretion, it is unusually well insulated from traditional modes of judicial control. Asylum law, in other words, is fertile ground for nefarious transnational learning.

This book could not be more timely. Even as the world debates whether to make changes to the global refugee regime, Ghezelbash reminds us that the formal structures of international refugee law and policy may sadly have become something of a sideshow. Dissatisfied with the ability of the Refugee Convention to serve their perceived needs yet unwilling to court the political costs of renouncing the treaty, powerful states increasingly choose simply to operate outside the bounds of the legal regime. As Daniel Ghezelbash shows us in these pages, states can – and do – achieve their coordination goals by means of legal and policy transfer, effectively setting up a parallel regime to the treaty-based system.

For those of us committed to the conduct of refugee protection under a truly global rule of law, the analysis here provides a sobering challenge.

James C. Hathaway
Editor, Cambridge Asylum and Migration Studies

ACKNOWLEDGEMENTS

This book is the product of a long academic and personal journey backed by numerous institutions and individuals. It is a substantially reworked version of my doctoral research carried out at Sydney Law School. The research on US law and policy was undertaken over an eighteen-month period during which I took up posts as a visiting scholar at Harvard Law School, Brooklyn Law School and New York Law School. The final product was weaved together during my tenure with my current employer, Macquarie Law School. The endeavour would not have been possible without the generous support and encouragement of my colleagues, friends and family, the lines between which have become increasingly blurred: my dear wife, Anna, without whose love and support (and countless hours of proofreading and editing) this project would not have been completed; my mother, Azita, who worked hard to instil in me a passion for learning and scholarship, and who, along with my father Jamal, sacrificed so much to provide me with the opportunity to pursue that passion; my dear friend and doctoral supervisor, Mary Crock, who sowed the first seeds for this entire endeavour when I was a student in her undergraduate Migration Law unit, and subsequently spent hundreds of hours nurturing it into fruition; Anna Boucher, for her supervision and advice and guidance on the social science aspects of this project; and colleagues who took the time to provide thoughtful feedback on my work, including Lenni Benson at New York Law School, Gerald Neuman and Holger Spamann at Harvard Law School, Maryellen Fullerton and Mark Noferi at Brooklyn Law School, Daniel Kanstroom at Boston College, Azadeh Dastyari at Monash Law School, Natalie Klein and Joel Harrison at Macquarie Law School and David Fitzgerald at University of California, San Diego. A big thank you also to Niels Frenzen at University of Southern California Gould School of Law for his assistance in obtaining up-to-date data on US Coast Guard migrant interdictions. A special acknowledgement to my research assistants, Rebekah Stevens, Laura Smith-Khan, Rhiannon Bell and Danielle Kroon, who humbled me with their hard work, ingenuity and attention to detail. I am grateful for the feedback and suggestions of audiences of earlier drafts of chapters presented at conferences of the American Society of Comparative Law: Younger Comparativists Committee, Harvard's Institute for Global Law and Policy, Emerging Immigration Law Scholars and Teachers Network, International Studies Association and Refugee Law Initiative. I would also like to thank the series editor, James Hathaway, and the anonymous reviewers for their comments and feedback.

Earlier versions of some of the themes and arguments explored in this book have been published elsewhere, including 'Legal Transfers of Restrictive Immigration Laws: A Historic Perspective' (2017) 66 *International and Comparative Law Quarterly* 235–55; 'Forces of Diffusion: What Drives the Transfer of Immigration Policy and Law Across Jurisdictions?' (2014) 1(2) *International Journal of Migration and Border Studies* 139–53; 'Lessons in

Exclusion: Interdiction and Extraterritorial Processing of Asylum Seekers in the United States and Australia' in Mariagiulia Guiffre, Lilian Tsourdi and Jean-Pierre Gauci (eds.), *Exploring the Boundaries of Refugee Law: Current Protection Challenges* (Brill, 2015) 89–116. I am indebted to the editors and anonymous reviewers who provided feedback on those works.

The topicality of the subject matter examined in this book means that law and policies examined are in a state of flux. My analysis reflects the law as it stood, to the best of my knowledge, on 23 June 2017.

ABBREVIATIONS

ATD	Alternatives to Detention
CAT	Convention against Torture and Other Cruel, Inhuman and Degrading Treatment or Punishment
CBP	Customs and Border Protection
CEAS	Common European Asylum System
CERD	Convention on the Elimination of all Forms of Racial Discrimination
CIA	Central Intelligence Agency
DIAC	Department of Immigration and Citizenship
DIBP	Department of Immigration and Border Protection
DIMIA	Department of Immigration and Multicultural and Indigenous Affairs
DHS	Department of Homeland Security
ECHR	European Convention on Human Rights
ECtHR	European Court of Human Rights
EU	European Union
ExCom	Executive Committee of the High Commissioner's Programme
FCA	Federal Court of Australia
FBI	Federal Bureau of Investigation
FRONTEX	European Agency for the Management of Operational Co-operation at the External Borders of the Member States of the European Union
HCA	High Court of Australia
HLD	High Level Dialogue
ICE	Immigration and Customs Enforcement
ICCPR	International Covenant on Civil and Political Rights
IGC	Intergovernmental Consultations on Migration, Asylum and Refugees
IIRIRA	Illegal Immigration Reform and Immigrant Responsibility Act
IMR	Independent Merits Review
IOM	International Organization for Migration
INA	Immigration and Nationality Act
INS	Immigration and Naturalization Service
ISAP	Intensive Supervision Appearance Program
MIAC	Minister for Immigration and Citizenship
MIBP	Minister for Immigration and Border Protection
MIEA	Minister for Immigration and Ethnic Affairs
MILGEA	Minister for Immigration, Local Government and Ethnic Affairs
MIMA	Minister for Immigration and Multicultural Affairs
MIMAC	Minister for Immigration and Multicultural Affairs and Citizenship

MIMIA	Minister for Immigration and Multicultural and Indigenous Affairs
MOC	Migrant Operations Centre
MOU	Memorandum of Understanding
MPA	Maritime Powers Act
NGO	Non-Governmental Organisation
NSC	National Security Committee
OEP	Offshore Entry Person
PNG	Papua New Guinea
PTA	Protection Transfer Arrangement
RCP	Regional Consultative Process
RPC	Regional Processing Centre
RSA	Refugee Status Assessment
RSD	Refugee Status Determination
SOLAS	International Convention for the Safety of Life at Sea
UMA	Unauthorised Maritime Arrival
UN	United Nations
UNCLOS	United Nations Convention of the Law of the Sea
UNHCR	United Nations High Commissioner for Refugees
UNTS	United Nations Treaty Series
UK	United Kingdom
US	United States of America
USCIS	United States Citizenship and Immigration Service

1

Introduction

> We are witnessing a paradigm change, an unchecked slide into an era in which the scale of global forced displacement as well as the response required is now clearly dwarfing anything seen before.
>
> UN High Commissioner for Refugees António Guterres, June 2015

As Europe deals with a so-called 'refugee crisis', Australia's harsh border control policies have been touted as a possible model to emulate. Former Australian Prime Minister, Tony Abbott has called on European leaders to regain control of their borders by implementing elements of the military-led operation introduced in Australia under his leadership to prevent asylum seekers reaching Australia by boat.[1] This call has been echoed in newspaper stories across Europe, particularly in Germany, Austria and the United Kingdom.[2] When President Donald Trump announced his travel ban for persons from specified Muslim-majority countries and tough border security reforms in January 2017, Australian politicians were quick to claim that Trump was emulating Australia's example.[3] The irony is that these policies, which form what has been dubbed the 'Australian solution', are not Australian innovations. Key measures such as long-term mandatory detention, intercepting and turning boats around at sea and the extraterritorial processing of asylum claims were used in the United States long before they were adopted in Australia. This book examines the process through which these policies were transferred between the United States and Australia and the way the courts in each jurisdiction have dealt with the measures. This is done with reference to an innovative framework of analysis which draws on scholarship from law, political science and sociology. The experience of the United States and Australia is used as an example from which to glean lessons for states which may be considering adopting these measures in the future, and to shed light on the broader interdependence of asylum and border control policymaking.

The international refugee protection regime is under unprecedented pressure. There are now more people fleeing their homes in search of asylum than at any other time since

---

[1] Tony Abbott, 'Second Annual Margaret Thatcher Lecture' (Speech delivered at the Margaret Thatcher Centre, London, 27 October 2015).
[2] David Wroe, 'Refugee Crisis: Europe Looks to Australia for Answers', *Sydney Morning Herald* (online), 24 April 2015 www.smh.com.au/national/refugee-crisis-europe-looks-to-australia-for-answers-20150424-1ms804.html.
[3] Katharine Murphy, 'Scott Morrison Says Trump Travel Ban Shows "World Is Catching Up" to Australia', *The Guardian* (online), 30 January 2017 www.theguardian.com/australia-news/2017/jan/30/scott-morrison-trump-travel-ban-world-is-catching-up-to-australia-border-protection.

records began. The United Nations High Commissioner for Refugees (UNHCR) reports that there were 65.6 million people forcibly displaced around the world in 2016.[4] This was up from 33.9 million two decades ago.[5] While most of these people remain in their region of origin, a growing number are choosing to travel further afield in search of protection. Visa requirements mean that most asylum seekers cannot make this journey legally. Travel by clandestine means is the only option. This is facilitated by increasingly sophisticated people-smuggling routes that link the refugee-producing regions in the developing world to wealthier and safer destinations in Europe, North America and Australia. Other migrants also utilise these routes, presenting themselves as asylum seekers in a bid to overcome immigration barriers. These complex flows of asylum seekers and economic migrants pose significant challenges for governments. The ability to distinguish persons who have a well-founded fear of persecution from people who are migrating for other reasons is essential to the integrity of the international refugee protection regime. But this distinction is becoming blurred as governments resort to blanket exclusion policies aimed at limiting and controlling access to their territories. In this context of securitisation of borders, asylum seekers have become stigmatised as persons attempting to break the law. The policy imperative is to deter and deflect all irregular migrants, asylum seekers or otherwise.

Governments have always been concerned about what other jurisdictions are doing when it comes to regulating asylum and irregular migration more broadly. This is because of the potential for changes in the policies of one state to influence migration flows to other nations. Rogers Brubaker describes the most direct manifestation of this influence: 'a person cannot be expelled from one territory without being expelled into another, cannot be denied entry into one territory without having to remain in another'.[6] This interdependence also operates at a more indirect level. A more permissive policy in one state can lead to a reduction of immigration flows in neighbouring states, while a more restrictive policy may increase the number of migrants seeking entry into other states.[7] The recent increase in the sophistication and proliferation of people-smuggling routes has further heightened this interdependence. Asylum seekers and other irregular migrants now have more choice in selecting their destinations and can travel further away from their home regions. The result is that changes in the policy of one jurisdiction no longer only just affect neighbouring countries, but can influence flows to nations on the other side of the globe. The longer journeys also mean asylum seekers are travelling through multiple jurisdictions to reach their final destination. Changes in the stringency of the asylum and border control policies of any of these transit states can have major ramifications for asylum flows to the final destination country, as well as other transit nations further along the route.

I explore this interdependence with reference to an in-depth analysis of measures adopted in the United States and Australia aimed at limiting asylum-seeker flows. I argue that the existence of similar policies in these jurisdictions is the result of a process of legal and policy transfer. The focus is on three measures: (1) long-term mandatory administrative detention of unauthorised arrivals; (2) maritime interdiction and deflection of

---

[4] UNHCR, *Global Trends: Forced Displacement in 2016* (UNHCR, 2017) 5.   [5] Ibid.
[6] Rogers Brubaker, *Citizenship and Nationhood in France and Germany* (Harvard University Press, 1992) 26.
[7] Sandra Lavenex and Emek Uçarer, 'The External Dimension of Europeanization: The Case of Immigration Policies' (2004) 39 *Cooperation and Conflict* 417, 425.

asylum-seeker vessels, which involves intercepting boats at sea and returning them to their point of departure or other locations and (3) the use of extraterritorial sites on external territories or third countries for the processing of asylum claims.

I utilise an original interdisciplinary framework for identifying transfers to document how policymakers in Australia and the United States have monitored developments in each other's asylum policies and have borrowed laws and policies they perceive as successful. I identify the motivations of the players involved, examine the multilateral and bilateral forums which facilitate the practice, and critically analyse the information sources on which policymakers rely when engaging in transfers.

I then turn my attention to assessing the *success* of the transfers that have taken place. This is done with a view to answering the question of why some transfers of restrictive measures succeed, while others fail. I begin with the assumption that transfers can be an effective tool for the development of law and policy. When faced with a problem, it makes sense to examine the practice of comparator jurisdictions. My concern, however, is that states may be adopting migration control measures devised by other countries, without effective evaluation and study of the laws and policies in question. Moreover, I explore the degree to which policymakers ought to consider differences in legal structures and systems when considering undertaking transfers. The restrictive policies examined in this book have pushed the boundaries of what is acceptable under both international and domestic law. They have been the subject of numerous judicial challenges in the highest courts in the United States and Australia. I undertake a detailed comparative analysis of the case law to determine the similarities and differences in the challenges made and the ways in which these have been treated by the respective judicial bodies. This is done with a view to evaluate how different legal structures and political contexts impact judicial decision-making.

The book concludes with an examination of the ramifications of my findings for policymakers considering adopting the case-study policies in other jurisdictions. I highlight the need to critically engage with claims made by politicians about the efficacy of the policies in reducing asylum-seeker flows. Any decision to adopt the US and Australian models would also have to factor in the high costs involved. These include exorbitant monetary costs, damage to the governments' international reputations and the devastating impact on the health and well-being of asylum seekers subject to the policies.

I outline how elements of the case-study policies may contravene the *Refugee Convention*, human rights treaties and the international law of the sea.[8] I caution that if other countries were to adopt harsh border protection mechanisms modelled on the US and Australian precedents, this would add further fuel to the competitive nature of the legal and policy transfers occurring in the asylum space. The result would be a 'race to the bottom' as states seek to outdo the deterrent measures introduced in comparator jurisdictions. I raise concerns that this competition has the potential to unravel the international refugee protection regime. I examine competing theories on why nations conform to international human rights norms. I argue that all these theories point to the conclusion that repeated non-compliance with international protection norms, particularly by wealthy liberal democracies, severely undermines the legitimacy of these norms.

---

[8] *Convention Relating to the Status of Refugees*, opened for signature 28 July 1951, 189 UNTS 137 (entered into force 22 April 1954) ('*Refugee Convention*').

1.1 Legal Transfer, Policy Transfer and Diffusion

The book utilises an interdisciplinary methodological framework which draws on the approaches taken in legal transfer/transplant scholarship, public policy work on policy transfer and international relations and sociology scholarship on diffusion. While rooted in different disciplinary frameworks, all these approaches focus on the spread of policy, law and other innovations across jurisdictional boundaries. While there have been studies comparing the policy transfer and diffusion literature and identifying lessons from each discipline,[9] to date the legal scholarship has developed in relative isolation.[10] Given the close similarity in the subject matter examined, the lack of dialogue is surprising. It is ironic that bodies of literature devoted to studying the transfer of ideas between governments have been resistant to the transfer of ideas across disciplines. This book aims to bridge this long-standing interdisciplinary gap.

Legal scholars examining the transfer of law across jurisdictions have given the process a number of different labels. Alan Watson coined the term 'legal transplant' to describe 'the moving of a rule ... from one country to another, or from one people to another'.[11] Other terms and metaphors used by legal scholars to refer to this phenomenon include 'diffusion',[12] 'reception',[13] 'circulation',[14] 'transposition',[15] 'borrowing',[16] 'migration',[17] 'transmigration',[18] 'translation'[19] and 'transfer'.[20] It is beyond the scope of this study to engage with the subtle differences in the meanings of these various terms and with the ongoing debate as to which metaphor/term best captures the characteristics of the transfer process. I adopt the term 'transfer' to describe the phenomenon, as it is comparatively neutral and aligns with the language used in policy transfer and diffusion scholarship.

---

[9] See, eg, David Marsh and JC Sharman, 'Policy Diffusion and Policy Transfer' (2009) 30 *Policy Studies* 269; Adam Newmark, 'An Integrated Approach to Policy Transfer and Diffusion' (2002) 19 *Review of Policy Research* 151.

[10] In fact, it is very rare to see legal scholars cite the policy transfer or diffusion literature at all. For a notable exception, see Mathias Siems, *Comparative Law* (Cambridge University Press, 2014) 193–4 (acknowledging the fact that political scientists are asking very similar questions to legal scholars in regard to interjurisdictional transfers).

[11] Alan Watson, *Legal Transplants: An Approach to Comparative Law* (Scottish Academic Press, 1974) 21.

[12] William Twining, 'Diffusion of Law: A Global Perspective' (2004) 49 *Journal of Legal Pluralism* 1; William Twining, 'Social Science and Diffusion of Law' (2005) 32 *Journal of Law and Society* 203.

[13] Wolfgang Wiegand, 'The Reception of American Law in Europe' (1991) 39 *American Journal of Comparative Law* 229. The 1970 International Academy of Comparative Law Congress dedicated a section to 'The global reception of foreign law': Michele Graziadei, 'Comparative Law as the Study of Transplants and Receptions' in Mathias Reimann and Reinhard Zimmermann (eds), *The Oxford Handbook of Comparative Law* (Oxford University Press, 2006) 441, 442.

[14] Edward Wise, 'The Transplant of Legal Patterns' (1990) 38 *American Journal of Comparative Law* 1.

[15] Esin Örücü, 'Law as Transposition' (2000) 51 *International and Comparative Law Quarterly* 205.

[16] Barry Friedman and Cheryl Saunders, 'Symposium: Constitutional Borrowing' (2003) 1 *International Journal of Constitutional Law* 177.

[17] Sujit Choudhry (ed) *The Migration of Constitutional Ideas* (Cambridge University Press, 2006).

[18] Nicholas Foster, 'Transmigration and Transferability of Commercial Law in a Globalised World' in Andrew Harding and Esin Örücü (eds), *Comparative Law in the 21st Century* (Kluwer Academic, 2002) 55.

[19] Maximo Langer, 'From Legal Transplants to Legal Translations: The Globalization of Plea Bargaining and the Americanization Thesis in Criminal Procedure' (2004) 45 *Harvard International Law Journal* 1.

[20] Graziadei, above n 13.

The study of legal transfers is currently in a state of flux, with long-standing assumptions being questioned. As William Twining notes, until relatively recently, legal scholars were focused on what he labels as the 'naïve model' of transfers based around the following paradigm example: '[A] bipolar relationship between two countries involving a direct one-way transfer of legal rules or institutions through the agency of governments involving formal enactment or adoption at a particular moment of time (a reception date) without major change.'[21]

These generally involved wholesale adoption of entire legal systems or codes. Typical case-studies included the imposition of legal systems by colonists in settled states and the more voluntary modernisation efforts of developing nations. Starting in the late 1980s, the focus shifted to the legal reforms of former socialist countries.

The contemporary legal scholarship has moved on from the assumptions which underpinned the 'naïve' model identified by Twining to better reflect the realities of the transfer process. The vast majority of contemporary legal transfers concern discrete legal rules (or fragments of such rules) rather than entire legal codes or systems.[22] Moreover, in addition to formal legal rules, transfers are also occurring at the level of policy, executive or administrative orders, or judicial decisions. Verbatim copying has become increasingly rare, with the laws more likely to be transferred in some degree of abstraction. A general idea may be borrowed and implemented using a completely different mechanism.[23] Lawmakers in the receiving country may deliberately tweak the imported legal rule to meet local needs and conditions. Changes may also be made inadvertently during the transfer process.[24] Contemporary transfers are usually multi-event interactions under which the original and transferred rules continue to interact after the initial transfer is made.[25] This gives rise to multi-directional transfers, with the original exporting country drawing lessons and implementing developments from the original importing country.[26] The actors involved in the transfer process are much broader than conceptualised in the old model. Transfers often include more than two jurisdictions and can be the product of interactions between several players.[27] This includes non-government agents, such as international institutions, international companies, global law firms and other private actors.[28] In an era of globalisation, importers may choose fragments of rules from various legal systems and integrate

---

[21] William Twining, *Globalisation and Legal Scholarship* (Wolf Legal Publishers, 2011) 51–2.

[22] Margit Cohn, 'Legal Transplant Chronicles: The Evolution of Unreasonableness and Proportionality Review of the Administration in the United Kingdom' (2010) 58 *American Journal of Comparative Law* 583, 596–7.

[23] Jörg Fedtke, 'Legal Transplants' in Jan Smits (ed), *Elgar Encyclopedia of Comparative Law* (Elgar, 2006) 434, 436.

[24] Langer, above n 19, 33 (setting out a typology of ways in which rules can change in the transfer process).

[25] Cohn, above n 22, 601–2 (identifying several models of long-term interaction); John Paterson and Gunther Teubner, 'Changing Maps: Empirical Legal Autopoiesis' (1998) 7 *Social & Legal Studies* 451 (drawing on autopoietic theory to identify modes of ongoing interaction).

[26] Twining, 'Diffusion of Law: A Global Perspective', above n 12, 20; Daniel Ghezelbash, 'Forces of Diffusion: What Drives the Transfer of Immigration Policy and Law across Jurisdictions?' (2014) 1(2) *International Journal of Migration and Border Studies* 139.

[27] Cohn, above n 22, 585.

[28] See Li-Wen Lin, 'Legal Transplants through Private Contracting: Codes of Vendor Conduct in Global Supply Chains as an Example' (2009) 57 *American Journal of Comparative Law* 711 (on legal transplants through private contracting).

them into a single law.[29] Esin Örücü's culinary metaphors of a mixing bowl, salad bowl, salad plate and purée are devised to capture the various forms of eclectic multi-source transfers.[30] Transfers are drawn not only horizontally from other municipal jurisdictions, but also from different levels of legal ordering such as international law or supranational law.[31] Examples of such vertical transfers include European harmonisation efforts,[32] as well as the domestic implementation of the *Refugee Convention* and *Protocol*.[33]

Legal scholars are still grappling with how to come to terms with this radical reconception of legal transfers and the new methodological issues to which they give rise. It is thus an opportune time to take stock of how the transfer of law and policy across jurisdictions has been conceptualised in other disciplines. Diffusion and policy transfer scholars are examining the same subject matter as contemporary legal transfer scholars: namely, the transfer of law, policy, programs, innovations and ideas across jurisdictional boundaries. The diffusion scholarship has been described as the study of 'chronological and geographic patterns of the adoption of a policy innovation across government units'.[34] It encompasses work done across a number of different disciplines, including sociology, international relations and economics. A central objective of the research is explaining why some states adopt policies and practices more readily than others. Examples of relevant factors identified include cultural similarities;[35] geographic proximity;[36] the role of policy networks;[37] and political, economic and social characteristics.[38] Diffusion scholars use quantitative techniques to analyse a large number of case-studies to produce generalisations about the reasons for, and the results of, the process.

Policy transfer scholars examine the 'process by which knowledge of policies, administrative arrangements, institutions and ideas in one political system (past or present) is used

---

[29] Ibid 712; Takao Tanase, 'Global Markets and the Evolution of Law in China and Japan' (2006) 27 *Michigan Journal of International Law* 873, 876.

[30] Esin Örücü, 'A Theoretical Framework for Transfrontier Mobility of Law' in Robert Jagtenberg, Esin Örücü and Annie J de Roo (eds), *Transfrontier Mobility of Law* (Kluwer Law International, 1995) 5.

[31] Twining, 'Diffusion of Law: A Global Perspective', above n 12, 19.

[32] See David Nelken, 'Comparatists and Transferability' in Pierre Legrand and Roderick Munday (eds), *Comparative Legal Studies: Traditions and Transitions* (Cambridge University Press, 2003) 437; Gunther Teubner, 'Legal Irritants: Good Faith in British Law or How Unifying Law Ends Up in New Divergences' (1998) 61 *Modern Law Review* 11 (analysing the transplant of the European continental principle of *bona fides* into British contract law through the EU Directive on Unfair Terms in Consumer Contracts).

[33] *Protocol Relating to the Status of Refugees*, opened for signature 31 January 1967, 606 UNTS 267 (entered into force 4 October 1967). See Chapter 2.

[34] Karen Mossberger and Harold Wolman, 'Policy Transfer as a Form of Prospective Policy Evaluation: Challenges and Recommendations' (2003) 63 *Public Administration Review* 428, 429.

[35] Beth Simmons and Zachary Elkins, 'The Globalisation of Liberalisation: Policy Diffusion in the International Political Economy' (2004) 98 *American Political Science Review* 171.

[36] Frances Stokes Berry and William D Berry, 'State Lottery Adoptions as Policy Innovations: An Event History Analysis' (1990) 84 *American Political Science Review* 395, 396.

[37] Everett M Rogers and F Floyd Shoemaker, *Communication of Innovations: A Cross-Cultural Approach* (Free Press, 1971); Robert L Savage, 'Diffusion Research Traditions and the Spread of Policy Innovations in a Federal System' (1985) 15 *Publius* 1; Everett M Rogers, *Diffusion of Innovations* (Free Press, 5th ed, 2003).

[38] Jack L Walker, 'The Diffusion of Innovations among the American States' (1969) 63 *American Political Science Review* 880 (identifying the following internal characteristics as facilitating innovation: per capita income; interparty competition; legislative professionalism; and percentage of urban population); Rogers and Shoemaker, above n 37 (emphasising the role of higher education levels, higher literacy rates and greater upward mobility).

in the development of policies, administrative arrangements, institutions and ideas in another political system'.[39] While diffusion is concerned with outcomes, policy transfer is more process-orientated. To this end, studies tend to employ small sample qualitative case-studies that focus on a detailed analysis of the transfer of a policy between two, or several, countries. Lesson-drawing refers to transfers based on the rational choice of policy-makers who identify a gap in policy knowledge and look for examples in other similarly situated jurisdiction.[40] However, the transfer process will not always involve this form of deliberate and rational policy choice. Policy transfer scholars recognise that transfers encompass both 'voluntary' and 'coercive' forms of practice. The latter can occur when 'one government or supra-national institution [is] pushing, or even forcing another' to adopt policy innovations.[41]

The different methodological approaches taken by legal transfer, policy transfer and diffusion scholars each have benefits and drawbacks. The large-sample, highly quantitative studies employed by diffusion scholars allow for generalisations to be made about the causes and consequences of the diffusion process. The downside of the large sample size is that the data is prone to oversimplification. For example, diffusion is generally presented as a dichotomous ('adopt'/'not adopt') variable. The policy transfer and legal transfer approaches recognise that there can be many degrees of transfer, with complete transfer being very rare. Their small-sample qualitative approach allows for a far more nuanced examination of reasons for and outcomes of the process. However, findings are less generalisable. The policy transfer approach is most suited to capturing the *process* underlying transfers, while the legal transfer methodology focuses on the detailed *content* of transfers. Finally, the diffusion literature takes for granted the fact that the diffusion process is inevitable and beneficial.[42] In contrast, the policy transfer and legal transfer literature recognise the possibility that transfers can result in failures and provide frameworks to test prerequisites for good policy-making and policy success.

Drawing on these strengths and weaknesses, I propose new interdisciplinary approaches to dealing with a number methodological issues that are central to this study. The first relates to how you identify whether a transfer has taken place. I propose a framework that combines the policy transfer focus on *process,* with rigorous doctrinal comparative law methods. The second relates to how you measure the success or failure of transfers. I survey the legal and public policy approaches to answering this question and propose a new measure I label *legal success.* In Chapter 2, I draw on the legal transfer, policy transfer and diffusion literature to identify the mechanisms driving the transfer of asylum and immigration law and policy across jurisdictions.

1.2 Identifying Transfers

The recent expansion of the focus of legal transfer scholarship has made it better equipped to capture the complexity and richness of the transfer phenomenon. However, the

---

[39] David Dolowitz and David Marsh, 'Who Learns What from Whom: A Review of the Policy Transfer Literature' (1996) 44 *Political Studies* 343, 344.
[40] Richard Rose, *Learning from Comparative Public Policy: A Practical Guide* (Routledge, 2005).
[41] Dolowitz and Marsh, 'Who Learns What from Whom', above n 39, 344.
[42] Simon Bulmer et al, *Policy Transfer in European Union Governance: Regulating the Utilities* (Routledge, 2007) 12.

> 1. Identify a policy problem (or *motive*)
> 2. Undertake a detailed comparative analysis of the suspected transferred law or policy in both the sending and receiving country
> 3. Search for physical evidence that a transfer has occurred (evidence of *opportunity*, and the *direct transfer* of information)
> 4. If necessary, identify and carry out interviews with key agents involved in the transfer process.

Figure 1.1 A framework for identifying contemporary legal transfers

acknowledgement of this complexity has given rise to a new challenge. Transfers that fit the 'naïve model' of legal transfer, as described by Twining above,[43] are easy to identify. A framework for identifying legal transfers was not necessary in the context of verbatim transfers of entire legal systems (or large parts thereof). The existence of the transfer in such a context was self-evident. As Holger Spamann notes, '[one] cannot but see diffusion in identical statutes'.[44] However, the identification of more subtle forms of transfers gives rise to evidentiary issues that cannot be overcome by a simple comparison of formal legal instruments and institutions.

While the problem of determining whether a legal transfer has taken place has been noted,[45] to date no solution has been proposed to tackle the issue. In Figure 1.1, I set out a framework for this task. It builds on the process-orientated approaches put forward in the policy transfer literature,[46] but incorporates the detailed legal comparison carried out by comparative lawyers. The identification of specific instances of transfers is not seen as an end in and of itself. Rather, such identification is an essential prerequisite for making observations about the processes and pathways of exchange, thereby gaining a deeper understanding of why transfers are occurring and identifying the factors that lead to their success or failure.

1 Identifying a Policy Problem

The first step involves identifying the *motive* for lawmakers to engage in legal transfer. In the case of voluntary transfers, this will be the common policy problem in the suspected source and importing country. The political climate in which the suspected transfer occurred may also be a relevant factor. The temptation to engage in legal borrowing may be more prevalent at times of crisis when a policy solution needs to be developed

---

[43] See Twining, *Globalisation and Legal Scholarship*, above n 21 and accompanying text.
[44] Holger Spamann, 'Contemporary Legal Transplants: Legal Families and the Diffusion of (Corporate) Law' (2009) 6 *Brigham Young University Law Review* 1813, 1823.
[45] Ibid 1852; Fedtke, above n 23, 436; Graziadei, above n 13, 454.
[46] See, in particular, the frameworks set out by Colin J Bennett, 'Understanding Ripple Effects: The Cross-National Adoption of Policy Instruments for Bureaucratic Accountability' (1997) 10 *Governance* 213; Mark Evans and Jonathan Davies, 'Understanding Policy Transfer: A Multi-Level, Multi-Disciplinary Perspective' (1999) 77 *Public Administration* 361.

quickly.[47] In the case of coercive transfers, the policy problem needs to be identified from the point of view of the agent or agents imposing the transfer.

2 Comparative Analysis of Legal and Policy Responses

The next step involves a detailed comparative analysis of the suspected source and imported laws or policies. Key documents examined at this stage include legislation, regulations, policy documents and government statements. This requires two distinct levels of analysis. The first is a doctrinal comparison of the sources outlined above to ascertain the degree of similarity in drafting and design. The existence of laws that are drafted in similar terms and language raise a presumption that a transfer has taken place. The more alike the laws and policies are in the suspected source and receiving country, the more likely it is that a transfer has taken place. The second is a functional analysis, where the focus is on examining whether, in practice, the suspected source and imported laws serve the same function in both legal systems. The existence of functionally equivalent laws also raises a presumption that a transfer has taken place. However, the existence of doctrinal or functional similarities are not conclusive evidence of transfer. Two jurisdictions may come up with similar innovations independently as a response to similar domestic pressures. This process is referred to as parallel path development.[48] Just as individuals collectively open their umbrellas simultaneously during a rainstorm, governments may decide to adopt the same policy in response to similar policy problems.[49]

3 Physical Evidence

The third stage involves examining sources in the receiving state for evidence that a transfer has taken place. The focus here is to find evidence that rebuts the alternative explanation that the doctrinally or functionally similar laws were the result of independent development. Two types of evidence are relevant in this context. The first relates to whether lawmakers from the suspected source and importing country had an *opportunity* to transfer information relating to the suspected imported law. Relevant evidence includes the existence of forums, meetings or avenues of communication which could be used to share information relating to the suspected imported rule. The second is *direct evidence* demonstrating that the source law was consulted, or formed the basis of the suspected imported law. Examples include government statements acknowledging the role the source law played in the development of the imported rule; government press releases or reports acknowledging discussions between the source and receiving country; or references to the

---

[47] Richard Rose, 'What Is Lesson-Drawing?' (1991) 11 *Journal of Public Policy* 3, 12 (stating '[a]doption is often contingent upon an exogenous crisis generating sufficient dissatisfaction to create a demand for doing something new').
[48] Randall Hansen and Patrick Weil, *Towards a European Nationality: Citizenship, Immigration, and Nationality Law in the EU* (Palgrave, 2001).
[49] This analogy is adapted from Katharina Holzinger and Christoph Knill, 'Causes and Conditions of Cross-National Policy Convergence' (2005) 12 *Journal of European Public Policy* 775, 786.

source law in the parliamentary debates, parliamentary hearings, explanatory memorandum, or policy material.

4 Interviews

The absence of physical evidence does not always mean that a transfer has not taken place. Interactions between policymakers often occur behind closed doors and are not always publicly acknowledged. Further, in this digital age, lawmakers can instantly access a wealth of material about the detail and operation of foreign law and practice without leaving their desks. Lessons drawn from such materials may not be documented. This stage of analysis goes beyond publicly available sources and involves identifying and interviewing key agents involved in the transfer process. This step takes the policy transfer focus on agents and processes of transfer to its logical conclusion. Transfers cannot occur without agents. Identifying and interviewing these agents provides the richest source of evidence about the existence and degree of the transfer which has occurred.

In the present study, I utilised a reputational snowballing approach to identify relevant policymakers involved in the development of mandatory detention, interdiction and extraterritorial processing policies in the United States and Australia. The method draws a purposive sample that includes the most important players who have participated in the event being studied.[50] The first stage of sample selection involved identifying a subset of relevant respondents through an examination of government press releases, media reports, conference proceedings, parliamentary speeches, explanatory memoranda and other parliamentary and departmental reports.[51] This initial sample was used to initiate a snowballing/chain-referral process whereby each interview respondent was asked to provide a list of people they felt were influential in the suspected transfer under study. This procedure was repeated with each round of new nominees, until respondents began repeating names. This method has the additional advantage of assessing the level of influence of each interview subject, as the number of nominations each person receives provides an indication of their stature within the law and policymaking process.[52]

A total of thirty-five Australian and twenty-five US policymakers were identified as being potentially involved in the case-study transfers. Of these, sixteen Australian and eight US policymakers agreed to be interviewed. The breakdown between politicians, bureaucrats, and others is set out in Table 1.1. Confidentiality for interview subjects was guaranteed so as to maximise participation and encourage full and frank disclosure. Each interview respondent is referred to in the study with reference to a codename. The first two letters of the code indicate which country the policymaker is from: AU (Australia) or US (United States). The third letter indicates if the policymaker is a politician (P), bureaucrat (B) or other (O). This latter category consists of NGO actors and academics who were directly involved in the policy development process. The last two digits are randomised numbers from 01–99 which are used to provide a unique identifier for each respondent.

---

[50] Oisín Tansey, 'Process Tracing and Elite Interviewing: A Case for Non-Probability Sampling' (2007) 40 *PS: Political Science and Politics* 765; Karen Farquharson, 'A Different Kind of Snowball: Identifying Key Policymakers' (2005) 8 *International Journal of Social Research Methodology* 345.

[51] These are what I identify as sources of 'physical evidence' in my framework for identifying transfers set out above.

[52] Farquharson, above n 50, 349–50.

Table 1.1 List of interview subjects

Australia		United States
AUB41	AUP50	USO62
AUO12	AUP49	USB19
AUP11	AUB67	USB21
AUB01	AUB30	USB79
AUB15	AUB80	USO82
AUB77	AUB27	USB98
AUP35	AUB96	USB33
AUB19	AUO40[53]	USO11

Politician (P), Bureaucrat (B), Other (O)

1.3 Measuring Success

Success is a notoriously slippery concept.[54] Substantial work has been carried out attempting to identify the factors that contribute to either the success or the failure of transfers. The trouble is that no consensus has emerged on the indicators of success and failure, either within or across legal and policy transfer literature. David Nelken writes that '[s]tudents of legal transfers do often talk confidently about what makes for success or failure. The trouble is that what they are looking for can be quite different'.[55] Before engaging in any assessment of the success or failure of a policy, it is important to articulate what type of success we are talking about.

Roger Cotterrell distinguishes three competing dimensions of success in the legal transfer literature.[56] Each reflects a different approach to the way law is conceptualised. For those who view law as 'culture', a transfer will be successful when it proves consistent with the legal culture of the receiving country. For scholars who view law as positive rules, the simple promulgation of a borrowed law can be viewed as a success, regardless of how it operates in practice. Those who view law as an instrument will only regard a transfer as successful when the law has its intended effect.[57]

The legal transfer literature on success has been dominated by a long-standing debate between proponents of 'law as culture' and advocates of 'law as positive rules'. At issue is the viability (and even possibility) of legal transfers. At one extreme, Pierre Legrand argues that law is a culturally determined construct that can never be transplanted fully into another

---

[53] This interview subject subsequently agreed to be named as a source and is thus referenced by name: Grant Mitchell, Director of the International Detention Coalition.
[54] Helen Ingram and Dean Mann (eds), *Why Policies Succeed or Fail* (Sage, 1980) 12.
[55] David Nelken, 'Towards a Sociology of Legal Adaptation' in David Nelken and Johannes Feest (eds), *Adapting Legal Cultures* (Hart, 2001) 7, 35; See also Nelken, 'Comparatists and Transferability', above n 32, 453 (stating that '[t]here is no consensus about how to define success, nor about the way it should be measured').
[56] Roger Cotterrell, 'Is there a Logic of Legal Transplants' in David Nelken and Johannes Feest (eds), *Adapting Legal Cultures* (Hart, 2001) 71, 78–80.
[57] See, also, David Nelken, 'Law as Communication: Setting the Field' in David Nelken (ed), *Law as Communication* (Dartmouth Publishing, 1996) 3–25 (distinguishing between viewing 'law as an instrument' and 'law as a narrative').

culture.[58] For Legrand, successful legal transfers are impossible, as rules are too laden with historical, epistemological and cultural baggage to be transferred between jurisdictions.[59] In essence, the argument here is that law is much more than its enacted rules. Legrand distinguishes between a propositional statement and its invested meaning. While the words that make up the propositional statement can be transported from one culture to another, the invested meaning cannot, as it is culturally specific. The imported form of the words is ascribed a different, local meaning when transported, transforming it to a different rule. In a similar vein, Siedman and Siedman take the view that law is a culturally determined artefact that cannot be transferred,[60] and have gone as far as formulating the 'law of the non-transferability of law'.[61]

At the other extreme, scholars like Alan Watson advocate the ease and feasibility of legal transfers from one jurisdiction to another.[62] Watson argues that legal transfers are socially easy and common in practice, being the most important source of change in the Western legal tradition. Watson's assertion that laws move easily, and are accepted in other legal systems without great difficulty, rests on a view of law as a set of positive rules that operate quite separately from other social systems. As such, he argues that 'successful borrowing could be achieved even when nothing [is] known of the political, social or economic context of the foreign law'.[63]

Occupying the middle ground, Otto Kahn-Freund argues that degrees of transferability are possible, but success depends on a range of variables such as geographical, economic, social and, above all, political factors.[64] Legal phenomena exist along a continuum of transferability.[65] Technical areas of law, such as contract and commercial law, can be viewed as a neutral set of positive rules that easily lend themselves to transfers. Other areas of law, such as rules designed to allocate power, rule-making and decision-making, remain deeply embedded in social institutions and are unlikely to easily transfer. Building on the work of Kahn-Freund, Gunther Teubner supposes that the ease or difficulty of legal transfer depends on the degree of connection between law and various social contexts.[66] Naming his theory the 'Legal Irritants' thesis, Teubner argues that transfers are relatively easy in areas of law that have only loose contact with social processes, but there is greater resistance to change where laws are tightly coupled with other social discourses. However, even where there is loose coupling and transfers are apparently easier, the process is not mechanical:

---

[58] Pierre Legrand, 'The Impossibility of "Legal Transplants"' (1997) 4 *Maastricht Journal of European and Comparative Law* 111.

[59] Ibid.

[60] Ann Seidman and Robert Seidman, *State and Law in the Development Process: Problem Solving and Institutional Change in the Third World* (MacMillan, 1994); Ann Seidman and Robert Seidman, 'Drafting Legislation for Development: Lessons from a Chinese Project' (1996) 44 *American Journal of Comparative Law* 1.

[61] Seidman and Seidman, *State and Law in the Development Process*, ibid 44–6.

[62] Watson, *Legal Transplants: An Approach to Comparative Law*, above n 11; Alan Watson, 'Legal Transplants and Law Reform' (1976) 92 *Law Quarterly Review* 79; Alan Watson 'Comparative Law and Legal Change' (1978) 37 *Cambridge Law Journal* 313.

[63] Watson, 'Legal Transplants and Law Reform', ibid 79.

[64] Otto Kahn-Freund, 'On Uses and Misuses of Comparative Law' (1974) 37 *Modern Law Review* 1.

[65] For a discussion of Kahn-Freund's metaphor, see Twining, 'Diffusion of Law: A Global Perspective', above n 12, 29.

[66] Teubner, 'Legal Irritants: Good Faith in British Law or How Unifying Law Ends Up in New Divergences', above n 32.

'legal transfer is not smooth and simple, but has to be assimilated to the deep structure of the new law, to the social world constructions that are unique to the different legal culture'.[67] Where there is tight coupling, Teubner supposes that not only does the imported rule change, but also the foreign rule may cause 'irritations' which change the social discourses of the new setting.[68]

The debate between proponents of 'law as culture' and those of 'law as positive rules' is centred on the semantics of what we understand as 'success', rather than on any profound disagreement about the underlying processes which are occurring. If, like Legrand, we take the *strong* 'law as culture' approach, and limit our view of success to situations where the imported laws reproduce identical meanings and effects to what they produced in the source jurisdiction, then the prospects of success do indeed look grim. If we take the *weak* 'law as culture' approach, and define transfers as a success where the imported laws reproduce similar meanings and effects to what they produced in their source jurisdictions, then the predictions of Kahn-Freund and Teubner – that transfers of certain types of law are more probable to succeed than others – likely ring true. If we take the 'law as positive rules' approach, and define success as mere introduction or promulgation of a transferred law, then success is easy, if not inevitable.

This debate is becoming increasingly irrelevant as legal scholars adopt a more pragmatic approach to the issue. It is now recognised that legal transfers are occurring in almost every area of law. Scholars acknowledge that the close connection between law and society means transferred laws will never operate in exactly the same way in source and receiving systems.[69] Nor do the agents of transfer generally want such identical recreation. The focus is on more nuanced transfers, where foreign rules are adapted to meet local needs and conditions. This reflects the instrumental view of law, where transfers are judged by whether or not they had their intended effects; or as Michal Gal describes it, 'the ability of the transplanted law to achieve its goals in the transplanting country'.[70]

Public policy scholars have developed a robust approach to examining instrumental success of policies. Bovens, 't Hart and Peters propose a framework that distinguishes between two primary types of instrumental success: *programmatic* and *political*. The *programmatic* mode of assessment focuses 'on the effectiveness, efficiency and resilience of the specific policies being evaluated'.[71] The *political* dimension of assessment 'refers to the way policies and policymakers become evaluated in the political arena'.[72] Marsh and McConnell propose a third dimension to policy success: *process*.[73] They define process as the 'stages of policy-making in which issues emerge and are framed, options are explored, interests are consulted and decisions made'.[74] Relevant factors for determining *process* success include: whether policy was produced through constitutional and quasi-constitutional

---

[67] Ibid 19. [68] Ibid 21–4. [69] See, eg, Siems, above n 10, 195–200.
[70] Michal Gal, 'The "Cut and Paste" of Article 82 of the EC Treaty in Israel: Conditions for a Successful Transplant' (2008) 9 *European Journal of Law Reform* 467, 472.
[71] Mark Bovens, Paul 't Hart and B Guy Peters, 'Analysing Governance Success and Failure in Six European States' in Mark Bovens, Paul 't Hart and B Guy Peters (eds), *Success and Failure in Public Governance: A Comparative Analysis* (Edward Elgar, 2001) 20.
[72] Ibid. [73] Ibid.
[74] David Marsh and Allan McConnell, 'Towards a Framework for Establishing Policy Success' (2010) 88 *Public Administration* 564, 572; See also Allan McConnell, *Understanding Policy Success: Rethinking Public Policy* (Palgrave MacMillan, 2010) 40.

procedures; whether there was a strong coalition of supporters driving the policy; and, most importantly, if the core proposal was successfully implemented as law.[75]

Beyond identifying which dimension of success we wish to measure, there are a number of further impediments to measuring instrumental success identified in both the legal transfer and public policy literature that warrant further exploration. One of the primary hurdles to developing criteria for measuring success is that success inevitably lies in the eye of the beholder. In other words, when we talk about success, it is important to define *success for whom*. As Marsh and McConnell observe, '[t]he nature of politics, especially in liberal democracies, means that "success" will always be contested to some degree'.[76] As a result, we should expect a divergence of views between various stakeholders as to whether or not any aspect of a particular policy is successful. David Nelken makes a similar point in the context of legal transfers:

> In all but the most technical of legal transfers there are likely to be conflicting interests at stake, involving different governments or different economic interests, or amongst members of governmental and non-governmental organisations, parliamentarians, judges, lawyers, other professionals – as well as the various parties likely to be most affected by the law.[77]

Such considerations are very important in the context of transfers of restrictive asylum measures. For example, harsh policies that result in the reduction of boat migration could be viewed as a success by governments, while at the same time widely condemned by human rights groups, academics and other observers. As such, it is essential to be clear about which perspective is being assessed.

Even when we are clear as to the perspective from which we are measuring success, additional impediments remain. The first challenge is to establish the objective of the law or policy. This can be a difficult task given there will often be multiple objectives. Some can be unstated: for example, securing votes, boosting leadership or appeasing stakeholders. Even where a law's objectives are clear, there is the problem of attempting to identify the causal effect, compared to other independent variables. In order to say that successful outcomes are the product of a particular policy initiative or law, it must be possible to ascertain that the law or policy actually produced the outcomes in question. Marsh and McConnell frame this challenge as the

> need to isolate and ascertain the effect of the policy on the outcome, controlling for other potential causal factors such as media coverage, the broader economic climate, external shocks, interest group activity, the role of private sector pressure (particularly if public/private partnerships are involved), the actions of other jurisdictions, whether national or international, and even other linked policy sectors.[78]

The situation is made more difficult by the fact that often the relevant outcome data may not be available. This may be because the data does not exist or is difficult to quantify, or due to the refusal of official sources to release relevant data.

One final issue to note is that there can be varying degrees of success. While it is tempting to conceptualise outcomes in binary terms as either a success or failure, in reality

---

[75] Marsh and McConnell, ibid 572.   [76] Ibid 575.
[77] Nelken, 'Towards a Sociology of Legal Adaptation', above n 55, 48.
[78] Marsh and McConnell, above n 74, 580–1.

such black and white outcomes are extremely rare. Where a policy has multiple objectives, it may be successful in meeting one objective, but fail to meet others. Even in more straightforward scenarios, where a policy has a single objective with clearly measurable outcomes, problems may still persist. Take the example of a policy which has the goal of reducing infant mortality rates from 15 per cent to 5 per cent but only manages to reduce mortality to 10 per cent. While not successful in meeting its target, it cannot be said that the policy was a complete failure. Problems also arise when outcomes are compared across the various dimensions of policy success.[79] Process, programmatic and political success do not always go hand in hand. It is possible for a policy to be successful on one of these levels, but to fail on another.[80] For example, a restrictive asylum policy may be popular with the electorate regardless of the quality of the policy development process or whether it is actually effective in reducing asylum flows.

In this study, I propose an additional dimension to measuring the success of transfers: *legal success*. I define *legal success* as occurring when an imported law or policy survives judicial challenges in domestic courts. *Legal failure* occurs when there is a judicial finding that an imported law or policy is unlawful, or where the judiciary adopts an interpretation of the imported provisions which frustrates the original intention of the drafters of the law or policy.

This measure of success captures elements of both the 'law as an instrument' and 'law as culture' approaches identified by Roger Cotterrell.[81] From a 'law as an instrument' perspective, laws will only be a success if they achieve the purpose for which they were introduced. A finding by a court that a law or policy is unlawful will preclude the law or policy from having such an effect. From a 'law as culture' perspective, the judiciary's response to an imported law sheds light on the degree to which the imported law is successfully integrated into the legal culture of the receiving country. A finding by a court that an imported law or policy is unlawful represents perhaps the most clear and explicit indication of cultural incompatibility.

This approach to measuring success is attractive as it avoids some of the methodological problems identified above. In relation to the *success for whom* question, the focus is clearly on the perspective of the government officials who introduced the law or policy under challenge. This measure also has the advantage of being comparatively easy to quantify. Rather than the complex, and often unavailable, quantitative data required to measure programmatic and political success, *legal success* can generally be easily gleaned from publicly available judicial decisions.

The *legal* dimension has hitherto been neglected in the public policy literature on success. As noted, evaluation of success in public policy scholarship has focused on three main dimensions of success: *programmatic, political* and *process*. None of these dimensions pay sufficient regard to whether a law or policy is fully integrated into the legal system of the receiving state. This is not to deny that legal success has bearing on the three dimensions of

---

[79] Bovens, 't Hart and Peters, and Marsh and McConnell acknowledge that their respective frameworks may produce contradicting results: Bovens, 't Hart and Peters, above n 71, 20; Marsh and McConnell, above n 74, 578.
[80] Marsh and McConnell, above n 74, 569.
[81] See Cotterrell, above n 56 and accompanying text.

success identified in the public policy literature. Legal failure in the form of a law or policy being struck down by the courts will obviously impact on whether a policy can meet its *programmatic* goals. Legal failure may also turn public sentiment against the government, influencing the *political* success of the policy. The quality of the *process* adopted in developing and implementing the law or policy will have a bearing on the likelihood of legal success or failure.

This measure of *legal success* will not be relevant to all instances of legal and policy transfer. Most transfers are relatively uncontroversial and do not result in legal challenges in the receiving state's courts. However, where such challenges occur, the judiciary's response provides a rich source for measuring success or failure. This *legal* dimension of success is particularly relevant to the transfer of restrictive asylum measures. These laws push the boundaries of domestic and international legal protections, and as such have been challenged in the highest courts of both the United States and Australia. The existence of case law challenging the legality of the measures in both the donor and recipient states provides a unique opportunity to explore the factors which influence successful integration or rejection of an imported law or policy. While the legal systems of Australia and the United States share many commonalities, they also exhibit some significant differences. This study will explore the extent, if any, to which these differences may have affected judicial responses to the case-study policies.

Australia and the United States are both democratic, federal settler states with bicameral legislatures that evolved from British colonial rule. They are frequently grouped together by immigration scholars as classic countries of immigration. They have a common history of population growth through large-scale immigration and this forms an important part of their national identities.[82] Both nations relied heavily on British common law when designing their legal systems. Moreover, Australians drew on the *US Constitution* of 1787 when devising their own constitution in 1900. The courts in both nations use similar common law logic today. They have federal systems in which immigration policy is dictated at the level of national (rather than state) government. In the past, the immigration policies of both countries have been used to extend protection to displaced people in need. The United States and Australia have common histories of generous refugee resettlement, particularly in the post-World War II and post-Vietnam eras.

Despite these similar roots, the two countries have adopted different legal, institutional and political structures that may affect judicial determinations on the legality of immigration control measures. A major distinction between the jurisdictions is the existence of a constitutionally entrenched bill of rights in the United States,[83] and the absence of any equivalent protections, constitutional or otherwise, in Australia. Another major variation is the degree of separation between the executive and the legislature. In the United States, the two are strictly separated. This can be viewed as a deliberate rejection of the untrammelled power of the British king, reflecting the Madisonian concept of checks and balances.[84] In contrast,

---

[82] Gary Freeman, 'Modes of Immigration Politics in Liberal Democratic States' (1995) 19 *International Migration Review* 881, 882; Gary Freeman and James Jupp, 'Comparing Immigration Policy in Australia and the United States', in Gary Freeman and James Jupp (eds), *Nations of Immigrants: Australia, the United States and International Migration* (Oxford University Press, 1992) 1, 1.

[83] *US Constitution* amends I–X.

[84] Beryl Radin and Joan Price Boase, 'Federalism, Political Structure, and Public Policy in the United States and Canada' (2000) 2 *Journal of Comparative Policy Analysis: Research and Practice* 65, 66.

Australia has a dominant executive resulting from the fusion of the executive and legislative powers that typifies the Westminster system of government. There is also a difference in the reception of international law into the national legal systems of the two countries. Australia adopts a dualist approach under which international law and national law are viewed as distinct legal orders. Accordingly, treaties, such as the *Refugee Convention* and *Protocol*, have no force in domestic law unless implemented through legislation.[85] In contrast, the United States uses a mixed dualist/monist system under which some international treaties can be deemed automatically to have force in domestic law, without the need for enabling legislation.[86]

Other differences between the United States and Australia are noteworthy. While both countries have land masses of approximately equal size, the fact that Australia is an island nation makes it more geographically isolated. Accordingly, it is able to exercise far greater control over its territorial borders than the United States, which has thousands of kilometres of shared land borders, with Mexico to the south and Canada to the north. These geographies have resulted in a significant divergence in the scale of undocumented migrants seeking entry and/or living in each country. Estimates suggest that there are approximately 11.4 million undocumented migrants living in the United States,[87] compared with 62,000 in Australia.[88]

1.4 Definitions

In this book, the term 'migrant' is used broadly to cover people who move on both a voluntary and involuntary basis. Reference is also made to 'entrants' and 'arrivals' to describe migrants at a specific stage of their journey, namely arrival at their destination country. These terms are used in conjunction with the descriptors 'unauthorised', 'undocumented' and 'irregular' to describe persons who have entered or who seek to enter a country without the required legal authority. I refer to undocumented arrivals that travel by boat as 'boat migrants'. I avoid using the term 'illegal' to describe asylum seekers or migrants. While it may be appropriate to label an *action* as illegal, the term is both inaccurate and dehumanising when used to brand a person. The terms 'alien' and 'non-citizen' are used interchangeably. While acknowledging the negative connotations attached to the former, the term is difficult to avoid given it appears in both the US *Immigration and Nationality Act* ('*INA*')[89] and the *Australian Constitution*.[90] The phrases 'extraterritorial processing'

---

[85] *Dietrich v The Queen* (1992) 177 CLR 292, 305; Senate Legal and Constitutional Reference Committee, Parliament of Australia, *Trick or Treaty? Commonwealth Power to Make and Implement Treaties* (1995) 86.

[86] See Maryellen Fullerton, 'Stealth Emulation: The United States and European Protection Norms' in Hélène Lambert, Jane McAdam and Maryellen Fullerton (eds), *The Global Reach of European Refugee Law* (Cambridge University Press, 2013) 201, 205 (noting that '[a]lthough there are mixed monist and dualist elements in the US legal framework, US law strongly favours domestic legislation to implement international obligations).

[87] Bryan Baker and Nancy Rytina, 'Estimates of the Unauthorized Immigrant Population Residing in the United States: January 2012' (Population Estimates, Office of Immigration Statistics, Department of Homeland Security (US), March 2013) 1.

[88] Department of Immigration and Border Protection, *Australia's Migration Trends 2014–15* (Commonwealth of Australia, 2016) 67.

[89] See, eg, *INA* 8 USC § 1101(a)(3), defining 'alien' as 'any person not a citizen or national of the United States'.

[90] *Australian Constitution* s 51(xix).

and 'offshore processing' are also used interchangeably to refer to any screening or processing of asylum claims carried out beyond a state's traditional geographic borders.

It is also important to articulate the nuances in the terms 'policy' and 'law'. As Richard Rose explains, 'policy'

> can refer to any topic that is a concern of government, such as foreign policy or economic policy; this usage leaves vague what, if anything, government is doing to deal with that concern. Policy can also refer to the end intentions of politicians. An election campaign pledge to introduce a full-employment policy does not specify the means by which this goal is to be achieved. Third, policy can refer to the policy programmes that government uses to realise the policy intention that politicians declare.[91]

When the term 'policy' is used in this book, it is generally used in the third sense identified by Rose, namely a specific policy program. These are prescriptions that direct the major resources of government – such as laws, money, personnel and organisations – towards an identifiable end.[92] Law is one of the strongest means that can be used to implement policy. It creates a set of binding rules that can be implemented by government institutions, including the courts. It includes legislation, regulations and legally binding directives. Binding judicial decisions are also law, in that they provide normative guidance on how policy and legislation must be interpreted and applied. However, case law is qualitatively different from primary enactments, regulations and directives as it emanates from the judiciary, and not the political branches. As such, judicial decisions can modify law in a way that diverges from the intent or will of the country's elected elites.

The term 'legal and policy transfer' is used to describe the processes by which knowledge of laws, policies, administrative arrangements, institutions and ideas in one political system is used in another political system to develop its laws, policies, administrative arrangements, institutions and ideas. This interpretation is based on David Dolowitz and David Marsh's definition of policy transfer,[93] but has been expanded to explicitly include the transfer of law as well as policy. In this context 'law' refers primarily to legal rules created by the political branches, and not judicial decisions. Of course, it is well documented that judges do draw on foreign law in the judicial decision-making process.[94] However, the focus of this study is on the cross-jurisdictional transfers of law and policy carried out by the political arms of government.

Australia's immigration program is administered by the Department of Immigration and Border Protection ('DIBP'), which is overseen by a minister who is a member of the federal parliament. The agency has carried many names over the years, with the title of the minister also changing accordingly. For the sake of consistency, I use the terms 'Department of Immigration' to refer to the agency, and 'Minister for Immigration' to refer to the minister throughout my period of analysis.[95] Until recently, certain immigration

---

[91] Richard Rose, *Learning from Comparative Public Policy: A Practical Guide* (Routledge, 2005) 15–16.
[92] Ibid 16.
[93] Dolowitz and David Marsh, 'Who Learns What from Whom: A Review of the Policy Transfer Literature', above n 39, 344.
[94] See, eg, Christopher McCrudden, 'Common Law of Human Rights? Transnational Judicial Conversations on Constitutional Rights' (2000) 20 *Oxford Journal of Legal Studies* 499.
[95] Where the Department or Minister appears in a citation (whether that be as a party to a case, or as the author of secondary materials), I use the abbreviations set out in the table on pp. xvi–xvii.

enforcement activities were carried out by the Australian Customs and Border Protection Service. In 2015, this merged with the Department of Immigration and the Australian Border Force was established within the Department to carry out compliance, detention and enforcement functions.

Between 1933 and 2003, the US immigration program was administered by the US Immigration and Naturalization Service ('INS'), which was an agency of the Department of Justice. In 2003, the INS was abolished, and its functions transferred to the newly created Department of Homeland Security ('DHS'). The three main entities within DHS which deal with immigration issues are the US Citizenship and Immigration Services ('USCIS'), US Immigration and Customs Enforcement ('ICE') and US Customs and Border Protection ('CBP').

1.5 The Road Ahead

Before examining specific examples of transfers, it is useful to set out the contemporary context in which states develop and implement asylum policy and immigration policy more broadly. This task is taken up in Chapter 2, where I engage in an interdisciplinary endeavour to identify the ways in which policy settings in one state can influence policies in other jurisdictions and interrogate the reasons behind governments' quests for control over their borders. That sets the stage for the examination of the case-study transfers of restrictive asylum measures between the United States and Australia. Chapter 3 examines long-term mandatory detention, Chapter 4 looks at maritime interdiction and push-back operations, and Chapter 5 is devoted to extraterritorial processing. I apply my framework for identifying contemporary legal and policy transfers to identify the ways in which US and Australian policymakers have drawn lessons from each other's jurisdictions. I then undertake a detailed comparative analysis of the relevant case law in each jurisdiction with a view to exploring the factors that may influence legal success or failure of the transferred policies. The case-study policies' compatibility with international law is taken up in Chapter 6. Chapter 7 sets out my conclusions for lawmakers around the world considering adopting harsh border control measures modelled on US and Australian practice.

2

Managing Asylum-Seeker Flows in the Twenty-First Century

> Refugees are in some ways a microcosm of our world. They reveal how we are increasingly interdependent – how the actions taken at home can resonate far beyond the borders of our communities and countries. They confront us with the stark realities and unimaginable choices that so many face in zones of conflict around the world. They force us to ask ourselves the difficult questions about where responsibilities lie for the making and unmaking of crises and the drivers of displacement.
> Volker Türk, Assistant High Commissioner for Protection, UNHCR, March 2017

Lawmakers have always looked abroad for inspiration. More than 2,300 years ago, Aristotle used the different ways in which Greek cities governed themselves as the basis for his theories on politics and social organisation.[1] At a practical level it makes good sense to examine the experiences and policy responses of other jurisdictions. Why reinvent the wheel when there are existing, tried-and-tested models operating elsewhere? The incidence of legal and policy transfer has been made all the more acute by the process of globalisation. In an increasingly interconnected world, the diffusion of law, policy and many other things has become commonplace. Indeed, it is to be expected.[2] In this chapter, I examine the varying (and sometimes conflicting) mechanisms driving this diffusion. I begin by surveying the legal transfer, policy transfer and diffusion scholarship to aggregate three mechanisms that are relevant to all policy fields: *efficiency*, *prestige* and *coercion*. I then draw on the diffusion and regulatory theory scholarship to describe and conceptualise two additional forces that are only relevant to interdependent policy areas – that is, areas such as asylum or immigration control, where policy changes in one jurisdiction can have flow on effects for other jurisdictions. In such contexts, transfers can be fuelled by *cooperation* as states seek to work together in achieving common goals, and by *competition* as states copy and adapt laws and policies in an attempt to gain a competitive advantage over one another. One arena in which this competition has played out is in relation to deterring undocumented asylum seekers and migrants. The chapter concludes with an analysis of the reasons why governments are so vigorously pursuing their quest for control over borders.

---

[1] Charles Donahue, 'Comparative Law before the Code Napoléon' in Mathias Reimann and Reinhard Zimmermann (eds), *The Oxford Handbook of Comparative Law* (Oxford University Press, 2006) 4, 44.
[2] David Westbrook, 'Theorizing the Diffusion of Law in an Age of Globalization: Conceptual Difficulties, Unstable Imaginations, and the Effort to Think Gracefully Nonetheless' (2006) 47 *Harvard International Law Journal* 489, 490.

2.1 Efficiency, Prestige and Coercion

Legal and policy transfer can be driven by a desire for *efficiency*. In terms of the policy development process, transfers provide a way to deal with problems more quickly and at a lower cost than devising innovative indigenous responses. Jonathan Miller provides the example of 'a drafter who when confronted with a new problem pulls a solution from elsewhere off the shelf of the library to save having to think up an original solution'.[3] Transfers can also be a tool for achieving efficient policy outcomes. Lawmakers may look abroad and rationally compare the laws of other countries to choose 'the best one'.[4] As discussed further below, the policy goals of wealthy liberal democracies are converging when it comes to asylum. The main imperative is to maximise control over borders and limit irregular migration. The policy responses available to achieve these goals are limited by the *non-refoulement* obligations contained in the *Refugee Convention* and other regional and international human rights instruments.[5] Examining and learning from how other states have balanced these competing policy considerations makes sense from an efficiency perspective.

The problem is that transfers do not always achieve their intended outcomes. Both the quality of information relied on in the transfer process and differences in institutional and legal structures can result in the 'failure' of an imported law or policy. There can be a complete rejection of the imported rule, institution or program by the receiving legal system – for example through legal challenge in the courts (*legal failure*). Or, there may be a simple failure to achieve the desired outcomes for which the law or policy was introduced (*programmatic failure*).[6] In relation to the quality of the information relied upon, diffusion and policy transfer scholars distinguish between learning that is fully rational and learning that is bounded.[7] Fully rational learning occurs when actors use the experience of others to update their prior beliefs and select appropriate policies.[8] Bounded learning occurs when actors try to gather relevant information from observation of the behaviour of others, but due to a lack of information or the use of 'cognitive shortcuts' they do not reach a strictly rational outcome.[9] Dolowitz and Marsh argue that perfect rationality is very rare and that most learning occurs in the confines of 'bounded rationality': 'As such transfer may be based upon inaccurate assessment of the "real" situation; in particular, it may be based upon incomplete or mistaken information about the nature of the policy and how it operates in the transferring political system or about the difference between the relevant economic, social and political consequences in the transferring and the borrowing systems.'[10]

In other instances, policymakers may not even purport to act in accordance with rational (or even semi-rational) calculations as to which foreign model may best address a domestic

---

[3] Jonathan Miller, 'A Typology of Legal Transplants: Using Sociology, Legal History and Argentine Examples to Explain the Transplant Process' (2003) 51 *American Journal of Comparative Law* 839, 845.
[4] Mathias Siems, *Comparative Law* (Cambridge University Press, 2014) 192.
[5] *Convention Relating to the Status of Refugees*, opened for signature 28 July 1951, 189 UNTS 137 (entered into force 22 April 1954) ('*Refugee Convention*').
[6] See Chapter 1, nn 54–82 and accompanying text.
[7] David Dolowitz and David Marsh, 'Learning from Abroad: The Role of Policy Transfer in Contemporary Policy-Making' (2000) 13 *Governance* 5, 14; Dietmar Braun and Fabrizio Gilardi, 'Taking "Galton's Problem" Seriously: Towards a Theory of Policy Diffusion' (2006) 18 *Journal of Theoretical Politics* 298, 306.
[8] Braun and Gilardi, ibid.   [9] Ibid.   [10] Dolowitz and Marsh, above n 7, 14.

policy problem. Rather, transfers may be motivated by considerations relating to *prestige*.[11] This occurs when the prominent motivation driving a transfer is the reputation of the model or the source jurisdiction more broadly. This reputation or esteem is used to give 'legitimacy'[12] or 'authority'[13] to assist in garnering support for the adoption of the new policy. Diffusion scholars refer to this form of transfer as emulation, which is defined 'as the process whereby policies diffuse because of their normative and socially constructed properties instead of their objective characteristics'.[14]

Transfers can involve varying degrees of *coercion*. An extreme example is where a foreign model is forced on a state through military conquest or expansion. Coercion can also occur through economic pressures, with governments requiring the adoption of a foreign model as a condition for investment, trade concessions or the allocation of aid funding. In this broader sense, coercion is at play whenever the acceptance of a transfer is 'motivated by a desire to please foreign states, individuals or entities – whether in acquiescence of their demands, or to take advantage of opportunities and enticements that they offer'.[15] Diffusion scholars refer to this as *conditionality*.[16] Such transfers are becoming common in the asylum space as wealthy liberal democracies pressure their less economically developed neighbours to implement harsh border control measures as a buffer against irregular migration. For example, the European Union has used the carrot of potential future membership as a means to encourage states in Central and Eastern Europe to establish stricter visa regimes and tighter border control measures.[17] A similar dynamic is also evident in relation to the EU–Turkey deal examined in Chapter 7. In Australia, successive governments have directed considerable sums of aid funding to induce Pacific and Asian nations to participate in extraterritorial processing and third country transfer arrangements.[18] Policy transfer, legal transfer and diffusion scholars all note that the distinction between imposed and voluntary transfers is not binary, but that transfers can be viewed as being spread across a spectrum, with completely voluntary transfers at one end, and completely coercive transfers at the other.[19]

2.2 Cooperation and Competition

Cooperative transfers take place when states coordinate or harmonise their policies in order to secure common goals. *Competitive* transfers occur when states react to changes in policies

---

[11] Gianmaria Ajani, 'By Chance and Prestige: Legal Transplants in Russia and Eastern Europe' (1995) 43 *American Journal of Comparative Law* 93.
[12] Miller, above n 3, 854–67.
[13] Alan Watson, 'Aspects of Reception of Law' (1996) 44 *American Journal of Comparative Law* 335, 346.
[14] Fabrizio Gilardi, 'Transnational Diffusion: Norms, Ideas and Policies' in Walter Carlsnaes, Thomas Risse and Beth Simmons (eds), *Handbook of International Relations* (Sage Publishing, 2012) 453, 475.
[15] Ibid.
[16] Frank Dobbin, Beth Simmons and Geoffrey Garrett, 'The Global Diffusion of Public Policies: Social Construction, Coercion, Competition, or Learning?' (2007) 33 *Annual Review of Sociology* 449, 455–6.
[17] Sandra Lavenex and Emek Uçarer, 'The External Dimension of Europeanization: The Case of Immigration Policies' (2004) 39 *Cooperation and Conflict* 417.
[18] Brian Opeskin and Daniel Ghezelbash, 'Australian Refugee Policy and its Impacts on the Pacific' (2016) 36 *Journal of Pacific Studies* 73.
[19] Dolowitz and Marsh, above n 7, 13–17; Margit Cohn, 'Legal Transplant Chronicles: The Evolution of Unreasonableness and Proportionality Review of the Administration in the United Kingdom' (2010) 58 *American Journal of Comparative Law* 583, 591; Dobbin, Simmons and Garrett, above n 16, 454–7.

in other jurisdictions in a bid to obtain a competitive advantage. Both mechanisms fall under the broader concept of *strategic adjustment*, which occurs when 'actual or anticipated changes in the policies of other countries push a government to adapt accordingly'.[20] The way that these processes play out in the context of asylum policy can be understood with an analogy to the cooperative and competitive regulatory interdependence that occurs in the area of economic regulation. Cooperative regulatory interdependence refers to situations where governments benefit from having compatible policies.[21] In economic regulation, cooperation delivers increased market access and economies of scale in relation to production costs.[22] In the context of asylum policy, cooperation can minimise deflection of asylum applicants from one destination to another and reduce costs related to border enforcement. It can also enhance protection outcomes for asylum seekers by facilitating burden sharing.

Competitive regulatory interdependence occurs as governments implement measures to attract economic activity to their jurisdiction.[23] In this context, 'policy choices create externalities for those in the same competition space'.[24] In the same way that one government's decision to reduce corporate taxes to attract investment may place pressure on other governments to do the same, the introduction of certain asylum policies by one government can create externalities for other governments. For example, the adoption of harsh deterrent measures targeting asylum seekers will create pressure on comparator jurisdictions to follow suit, or face a possible increase in the number of asylum seekers attempting to enter their territory. In the context of economic regulation, Simmons and Elkins argue that competitive interdependence means that '[g]overnments' liberalisation policies will be influenced by the policies of their most important foreign economic competitors'.[25] I argue that a similar competitive interdependence in the area of asylum regulation leads to the prediction that governments' asylum policies will be influenced by the policies of their most important competitors for asylum flows.

Governments are increasingly aware of the fact that effective management of borders requires the coordination of policy responses across multiple states. Recent years have seen an increase in regional and international activities and structures dedicated to international migration policy and practice.[26] These initiatives provide forums in which state representatives meet to discuss, share and coordinate immigration and asylum policies. Attempts to coordinate or harmonise inherently involve legal transfers. Policies sourced in international law, regional instruments, informal bilateral or regional discussions or the domestic law of one state are imported into the domestic legal systems of other states.

The 1951 *Refugee Convention* and 1967 *Protocol* are the main instruments underpinning the international refugee protection regime.[27] Their development and subsequent

---

[20] David FitzGerald and David Cook-Martin, *Culling the Masses: The Democratic Origins of Racist Immigration Policy in the Americas* (Harvard University Press, 2014) 26–7.
[21] David Lazer, 'Regulatory Interdependence and International Governance' (2001) 8 *Journal of European Public Policy* 474, 476.
[22] Ibid.
[23] Beth Simmons and Zachary Elkins, 'The Globalization of Liberalization: Policy Diffusion in the International Political Economy' (2004) 98 *American Political Science Review* 171, 172.
[24] Braun and Gilardi, above n 7, 308.   [25] Simmons and Elkins, above n 23, 173.
[26] Colleen Thouez and Frédérique Channac, 'Shaping International Migration Policy: The Role of Regional Consultative Processes' (2006) 29 *West European Politics* 370, 372.
[27] *Protocol Relating to the Status of Refugees*, opened for signature 31 January 1967, 606 UNTS 267 (entered into force 4 October 1967) ('*Protocol*').

implementation into the domestic law of state parties is one of the most prominent examples of a cooperative transfer of asylum law. The *Refugee Convention* was drafted to deal with problems caused by the mass displacement of persons in Europe at the end of the Second World War.[28] European nations faced the problem of how best to deal with large numbers of persons who were outside their countries of origin and for whom repatriation was not a reasonable solution. The Convention represented a global coordinated response to this problem.

The preamble of the *Refugee Convention* acknowledges that cooperation is essential to dealing with refugee flows: 'the grant of asylum may place an unduly heavy burden on certain countries ... a satisfactory solution of a problem of which the United Nations has recognised the international scope and nature cannot therefore be achieved without international cooperation'.

The need for a coordinated response to refugee crises was also underscored by the recommendation of a 1949 background study undertaken by the UN Department of Social Affairs in the lead-up to the development of the Convention. The report notes that no government would be willing to act unilaterally in providing protection because of fears that such a move would cause an influx of asylum seekers into their territory.[29]

In all, 148 states have ratified the *Refugee Convention* and/or *Protocol*.[30] Like any other international treaty, the means of implementing these obligations into domestic law depends on the structure of each national legal system. In monist jurisdictions, international and national law are viewed as being part of a single legal order. Treaties are immediately effective in domestic law without the need for any implementing legislation. States such as France, the Netherlands, Switzerland, many Latin American countries and Francophone African countries adopt a monist approach. In dualist jurisdictions, international and national law are viewed as distinct legal orders. Accordingly, treaties do not have force in domestic law unless executed or implemented by the legislature. This is the approach followed in most Commonwealth and Scandinavian jurisdictions. For example, in Australia the *Refugee Convention* and *Protocol* are partially incorporated into domestic law through the *Migration Act 1958* (Cth) ('*Migration Act*'). The United States adopts a mixed monist/dualist approach where some ratified treaties automatically have force domestically, while others do not.[31] Obligations under the *Refugee Convention* (as acquired through the US government's ratification of the *Protocol*) have generally been held not to apply domestically. The Convention's provisions are instead enacted through the *Refugee Act of 1980*.[32] It is important to note, though, that as in Australia, the protections are not implemented in their entirety.

The machinery created around the *Refugee Convention* provides mechanisms for continued dialogue and cooperation on asylum issues. The Executive Committee (ExCom) meetings of UNHCR provide an opportunity for state parties to discuss recent

---

[28] Gil Loescher, *Beyond Charity: International Cooperation and the Global Refugee Crisis* (Oxford University Press, 1993) 51–8.

[29] United Nations Ad Hoc Committee on Refugees and Stateless Persons, *A Study of Statelessness*, UN Doc E/1112; E/1112/Add.1 (August 1949). Note that in discussion leading up to the 1951 *Refugee Convention*, the term 'stateless' was used interchangeably with 'refugee'.

[30] A total of 145 countries have ratified the 1951 *Refugee Convention*, while 146 have ratified the 1967 *Protocol*. Madagascar, Saint Kitts and Nevis have only ratified the 1951 *Refugee Convention*, while Cape Verde, United States, and Venezuelan have only ratified the 1967 *Protocol*.

[31] See Chapter 1, n 86 and accompanying text.   [32] Pub L No 96–212, 94 Stat 102.

developments and issues relating to the interpretation and implementation of the *Refugee Convention*. The Committee issues 'Conclusions on International Protection' which embody the consensus opinion of Committee members on a particular issue. While not formally binding, these conclusions can play a persuasive role in influencing and harmonising the interpretation of the *Refugee Convention* in the domestic law of state parties.

There are also examples of regional efforts to develop formal binding cooperative mechanisms for dealing with asylum. Perhaps the most prominent example is the EU's Common European Asylum System ('CEAS'). This consists of a series of directives and regulations which set out minimum standards regarding the processing and assessment of asylum claims and reception conditions. It also includes the Dublin System for the allocation of state responsibility for the processing of asylum claims. The purpose of the Dublin System is to prevent multiple asylum claims by persons who have their claim rejected in one member state and then subsequently apply again in a second member state. It also aims to prevent *forum shopping*, where asylum seekers travel through a number of EU countries without applying for asylum as they attempt to reach a destination where they believe they have a better prospect of having their asylum claim accepted or will receive more generous reception services. While technically binding, to date the implementation of the regulations and directives which form the CEAS has been patchy at best. The system is also facing mounting pressure as a result of the surge in asylum seekers and migrants making their way to Europe in recent years.

The reluctance of states to cede any sovereignty in relation to their ability to control their borders means that formal cooperative initiatives such as the CEAS are very rare. There is however an increasing willingness to meet and cooperate in more informal, non-binding ways. Recent years have seen the proliferation of Regional Consultative Processes ('RCPs'). These are regular, informal, closed-door meetings in which states with similar backgrounds and interests meet to discuss migration and asylum policy for the purpose of exchanging ideas, fostering cooperation, and developing 'best practice' models. The term 'region' is used loosely here. For example, Australian migration officials meet regularly with their counterparts at the Five Country Conferences. This forum includes the geographically remote but culturally and experientially close countries of Australia, Canada, the United States, the United Kingdom and New Zealand. RCPs vary greatly in composition, history, purpose and organisational frameworks. However, they share the principal goal of facilitating regular meetings for the specific purpose of discussing migration issues and generating informal, non-binding agreements.

By design, RCPs are mechanisms that foster the transfer of migration policy and practice. Their role as facilitators of policy learning and transfer is well documented,[33] and is evident by one of the oft-cited goals of these institutions: to build capacity to manage migration. Capacity building involves the transfer of knowledge, skills and best-practice policies.

---

[33] Randall Hansen, 'Interstate Cooperation: Europe and Central Asia' in Gervais Appave and Frank Laczko (eds), *Interstate Cooperation and Migration* (International Organization for Migration, 2005) 17; Colleen Thouez and Frederique Channac, 'Shaping International Migration Policy', above n 26; Bimal Ghosh, 'New International Regime for Orderly Movements of People: What Would It Look Like?' in Bimal Ghosh (ed), *Managing Migration: Time for a New International Regime?* (Oxford University Press, 2000) 220; Jobst Koehler, 'What Government Networks Do in the Field of Migration: An Analysis of Selected Regional Consultative Processes' in Randall Hansen, Jobst Koehler and Jeannette Money (eds), *Migration, Nation States, and International Cooperation* (Routledge, 2011) 101.

It occurs at a general level through the sharing of migration information and lessons learned in migration management, and through specific capacity-building workshops.

RCPs have been established in most regions of the world. Examples include: between Europe, North America and Australia through the Intergovernmental Consultations on Migration, Asylum and Refugees ('IGC'); in Northern and Central America through the Puebla Process; in Asia through the Manila Process; within Europe with the Budapest Process and the Mediterranean 5 + 5 Dialogue; and in Africa with the International Dialogue on Migration in West Africa and International Dialogue on Migration in Southern Africa. Their success at the cost of formal binding international regimes has been explained in terms of states' reluctance to lose any control over their migration policies. States find the informal, non-binding nature of RCPs preferable as they require no loss of sovereignty or upfront commitments and allow for easy exit.[34]

The International Organisation of Migration ('IOM') has also played an important role in fostering cooperation and facilitating the transfer of asylum laws and policies. The IOM is the principal intergovernmental organisation in the migration area. Its primary focus is on the promotion of humane and orderly migration, acting as a service provider to individual states that pay for its assistance. Since 2001, the IOM has facilitated informal and non-binding consultative processes through its International Dialogue on Migration. The annual sessions bring together migration policymakers from states around the world and are generally structured around a specific theme. These often deal with asylum-related issues. For example, the 2012 Council session was devoted to the topic 'Managing Migration in Crisis Situations'. In addition, IOM holds two intersessional workshops a year, which 'present an opportunity for governmental migration policymakers and practitioners from around the world to have focused technical and policy exchanges on migration issues in a non-binding context'.[35]

The transfer of asylum law and policy is also being driven by competition, as nations vie to deter unwanted asylum seekers and irregular migration more generally. Asylum flows are becoming globalised, with more people willing to travel beyond their region in search of safety. The success of carrier sanctions has limited undocumented migrants' access to air travel. The globalisation of flows is being driven by increasingly sophisticated and expansive people-smuggling networks, as well as a willingness on the part of asylum seekers to undertake longer and more perilous journeys. For example, a Syrian family wishing to flee their home country can choose between a multitude of smuggling routes that could lead them to various destinations around the globe. To reach the European Union, they can select from at least three common routes. They could travel overland or by air to Libya or Tunisia, from where they could board a boat and travel across the Central Mediterranean route to Lampedusa or Malta. Alternatively, they could use the Eastern Mediterranean route by taking a boat trip from the Turkish coast to Greece, or the Western Balkan overland route through Serbia, Bosnia and Herzegovina, Montenegro, Kosovo, Macedonia or Albania. As tighter border security policies in transit countries have made these more common

---

[34] Randall Hansen, 'Making Cooperation Work: Interests, Incentives, and Action' in Randall Hansen, Jobst Koehler and Jeannette Money (eds), *Migration, Nation States, and International Cooperation* (Routledge, 2011) 14, 21.

[35] Michele Klein Solomon, 'International Migration Management through Inter-State Consultation Mechanisms', report prepared for UN Expert Group Meeting on International Migration and Development, International Organization for Migration, July 2005, UN/POP/MIG/2005/13, 5.

routes less accessible, some migrants have been opting for more creative journeys. For example, there are reports that some Syrians have been flying to Russia and entering Norway via an Arctic border crossing.

Until recently, another popular route took Syrian asylum seekers to Australia. This involved a flight to Malaysia or Indonesia, then a boat trip from one of Indonesia's southern islands. The Australian government's use of interdiction and push-back operations at sea has dramatically reduced the numbers of asylum seekers making this journey.[36] As one route is cut off, a new one often opens in its place, providing access to new destinations. Recent reports document an increase in Syrian asylum seekers attempting to reach the United States. Their journey involves a flight to a destination in Central or South America with relatively lax border controls. Ecuador is popular in this regard as it is one of the few countries that does not require visas for Syrian visitors. Once there, the asylum seekers utilise local smugglers who guide them through the well-trodden routes through Central America and into the United States.

The shifting people-smuggling routes illustrate that changes in government asylum and border security policies can divert asylum flows. The assumption is that asylum seekers consider the stringency of border control measures and the generosity of reception services in destination and transit countries when choosing where to travel. That is not to say that these are the only factors considered by would-be asylum seekers. Selecting a destination is a complex process involving economic, social and political issues.[37] Other considerations that can influence this decision include the presence of family and friends, shared language and cultural affinity. Mapping the specific motivations of asylum seekers and the relative weight given to these various factors is an area in which more research is needed. The few studies that do exist all emphasise the importance of asylum seekers' agency in the decision-making process of selecting a destination for refuge.[38] This has fostered a view, in certain nations, that unless they match or outdo deterrence measures in other comparable jurisdictions, they will be viewed as a 'soft touch' and experience an increase in asylum flows and irregular migration more broadly.

To illustrate this point, it may be useful to refer again to an example relating to the interdependence of economic regulatory policies:

> The key assumption in the competitive mode of regulatory interdependence is that states care about the competitiveness of their industry and their ability to attract investment on the one hand, and on the other, value reducing the 'bad' at which potential regulations are aimed. It is often asserted that this competitive dynamic will result in a 'race to the bottom' where states set suboptimal levels of social regulation to attract capital.[39]

---

[36] See Appendix, Table A.2 and Table A.3.
[37] Hein De Haas, 'The Determinants of International Migration: Conceptualizing Policy, Origin and Destination Effects (International Migration Institute, Working Paper 32, 2011); Khalid Koser and Marie McAuliffe, 'Establishing an Evidence-Base for Future Policy Development on Irregular Migration to Australia' (Department of Immigration and Citizenship, Irregular Migration Research Programme Occasional Paper Series, 2013).
[38] Vaughan Robinson and Jeremy Segrott, 'Understanding the Decision Making of Asylum Seekers' (Home Office Research Study 243, 2002); Jean-Paul Brekke and Monic Five Aarset, 'Why Norway? Understanding Asylum Destinations' (Institute for Social Research, 2009).
[39] Lazer, above n 21, 475.

In the case of deterrent measures, we have the inverse scenario. Here, states weigh their competitiveness in *deterring* unwanted immigration against the value of being good global citizens and abiding by their obligations under the *Refugee Convention*. The result is a 'race to the bottom' where states introduce increasingly punitive deterrent measures at the cost of protection outcomes for asylum seekers.[40]

What is important here is not the objective existence of interdependence between asylum flows, but the *perception* that such a link exists. A belief among politicians and policymakers that they are receiving more migrants because of their comparatively laxer policies will fuel the adoption of restrictive measures. We see such a view taking root in Europe, with some politicians going as far as linking recent increases in undocumented migrant arrivals to the introduction of harsh border control measures in Australia.[41] The competition to appear tough on irregular arrivals can be pitched as much to a domestic audience as it is to potential undocumented migrants. The arrival (or threat of arrival) of irregular migrants can be damaging to the re-election prospects of governments. The introduction of many so-called 'deterrent' measures has as much to do with reassuring the public that the government is doing something as it does with actually reducing the number of arrivals. When one state introduces a new deterrent measure, pressure mounts for other governments to do the same or risk being viewed as soft by their constituents. The result of this competition is a situation in which deterrence has become the 'dominant paradigm' for international refugee policy.[42]

2.3 The Quest for Control

But why this obsession with deterrence? The answer lies in sovereignty and the related desire to maximise control over who can enter a country's territorial boundaries. Restrictions on immigration are a relatively recent invention. For most of human history, freedom of movement has been the norm. Immigration was not only permitted, but encouraged. It was viewed as a vehicle for strengthening the power of the host society, by increasing the population and growing the economy.[43] It was not until the late nineteenth century that this view began to change. In their bid to justify laws excluding Chinese immigration, certain governments began claiming a complete and unfettered sovereign right to control their borders.[44] This right was legitimised by sympathetic judges. The prerogative power to exclude non-citizens from entry was affirmed by the Privy Council in 1881 in *Musgrove v Chun Teeong Toy*.[45] In the 1889 US Supreme Court case of *Chae Chan Ping*,

---

[40] This is explored further in Chapter 7, nn 114–19.
[41] Latika Bourke, 'Europe Needs a Tony Abbott–Style Approach to Stopping the Boats, Says Tory MEP', *Sydney Morning Herald* (online) (3 June 2016) www.smh.com.au/world/europe-needs-a-tony-abbott-style-approach-to-stopping-the-boats-says-tory-mep-20160602-gpaggq.html.
[42] Thomas Gammeltoft-Hansen and Nikolas Tan, 'The End of the Deterrence Paradigm? Future Directions for Global Refugee Policy' (2017) 5 *Journal of Migration and Human Security* 28, 31.
[43] Vincent Chetail, 'The Transnational Movement of Persons under General International Law – Mapping the Customary Law Foundations of International Migration Law' in Vincent Chetail and Céline Bauloz (eds) *Research Handbook on International Law and Migration* (Edward Elgar, 2014) 29.
[44] See, generally, Daniel Ghezelbash, 'Legal Transfers of Restrictive Immigration Laws: A Historic Perspective' (2017) 66 *International and Comparative Law Quarterly* 235–55.
[45] *Musgrove v Chun Teeong Toy* [1891] AC 272.

Field J reasoned that the power to exclude aliens 'is an incident of every independent nation ... If it could not exclude aliens it would be to that extent subject to the control of another power'.[46] The principle was reiterated three years later in *Nishimura Ekiu v United States*, where the Court stated: 'It is an accepted maxim of international law that every sovereign nation has the power, as inherent in sovereignty, and essential to self-preservation, to forbid the entrance of foreigners within its dominions, or to admit them only in such cases and upon such conditions as it may see fit to prescribe.'[47]

The legal foundations of this claimed unfettered right to exclude aliens have been the subject of much controversy.[48] Nevertheless, it has become deeply entrenched in the contemporary discourse on immigration control. The commitment to the sovereign right to exclude underpinned the much publicised 2001 statement of Australia's then Prime Minister, John Howard, that '[w]e will decide who comes to this country and the circumstances in which they come'.[49]

Public opinion no doubt plays a role in shaping this issue. Governments perceive border control as being a vote winner.[50] There also appears to be a view among politicians that public acceptance of regular migration is contingent on a public perception that the government is exercising its sovereignty effectively by securing the nation's borders. Former Australian Minister for Immigration, Phillip Ruddock summed up this view with his argument that 'to maintain public confidence in immigration programs, you need to be able to demonstrate that the people who get here are those who come essentially through the front door and not through the window'.[51] Former Australian Prime Minister John Howard expressed a similar view when he claimed that his tough border control policies led to 'a sharp increase in support in the community for orthodox immigration'.[52] This is supported by polling data, with a 2011 study finding a direct correlation between an increase in the number of asylum-seeker arrivals and a decrease in public support for immigration.[53] A similar assumption was evident in the debate surrounding immigration reform in the United States during President Obama's second term. The proposal for comprehensive immigration reform put forward by a bipartisan group of US senators in 2013 conditioned the path to regularisation for undocumented migrants living in the United States upon securing the US–Mexico border.[54]

---

[46] *Chae Chan Ping v United States*, 130 US 581, 603–4 (1889).
[47] *Nishimura Ekiu v United States*, 142 US 651, 659 (1892).
[48] See Chetail, above n 43; James Nafziger, 'The General Admission of Aliens under International Law' (1983) 77 *American Journal of International Law* 804.
[49] John Howard, Prime Minister of Australia (Speech delivered at the Federal Liberal Party Campaign Launch, Sydney, 28 October 2001).
[50] See Chapter 7, nn 110–13 and accompanying text.
[51] ABC Radio National, *Australia Talks Back with Sandy McCutcheon*, 5 December 2002 (Hon Phillip Ruddock), cited in Murray Goot and Ian Watson, 'Population, Immigration and Asylum Seekers: Patterns in Australian Public Opinion' (Parliamentary Library Pre-Election Policy Unit Report, Parliamentary Library, May 2011) 28.
[52] Quoted in George Megalogenis, 'Trivial Pursuit: Leadership and the End of the Reform Era' (2010) 40 *Quarterly Essay* 1, 22.
[53] Goot and Watson, above n 51, 28.
[54] Senators Charles Schumer, John McCain, Richard Durbin, Lindsey Graham, Robert Menendez, Marco Rubio, Michael Bennet and Jeff Flake, 'Bipartisan Framework for Comprehensive Immigration Reform' (28 January 2013).

Different explanations have been advanced to explain this fixation on border control. For some, sovereign control of state boundaries is equated with the very idea of nationhood. Such a view is apparent in President Ronald Reagan's reputed statement that 'a nation that cannot control its borders is not a nation'.[55] President Donald Trump has repeated this statement almost verbatim.[56] This quest for control over borders has also been justified in terms of national security. For example, in *Chae Chan Ping*, Grey J argued that without the power to exclude aliens, the United States would be unable to defend itself against 'vast hordes of [a foreign] people crowding in upon us'.[57] Aleinikoff et al put it this way:

> Foreign powers could send *agents provocateurs* or suicide bombers to disrupt American institutions; developing nations could send workers to take advantage of American jobs; other countries could seek to solve their problems of overpopulation by exporting people to the United States. Perhaps to lose control over one's borders is to 'defeat the venture at hand' by losing our ability to achieve the objects for which the Constitution was established: 'to ensure domestic Tranquillity, provide for the common defense, promote the general Welfare.'[58]

A related explanation views the preoccupation with border control as stemming from xenophobia or racism.[59] The majority of irregular arrivals in Australia and the United States are from particular ethnic backgrounds. In the United States, most come from Latin America or Caribbean nations. In Australia, the mix has changed over the years, but the majority have come from East Asia, the Middle East, South Asia and Africa.[60] These arrivals have been viewed by some elements of the public as a threat to the white Anglo-Saxon identities of the United States and Australia.[61] As Myron Weiner notes:

> In many countries, citizens have become fearful that they are now being invaded not by armies and tanks but by migrants who speak other languages, worship other gods,

---

[55] President Ronald Reagan is often credited for having said words to this effect at some time in the 1980s: see Robert Owens, *The Constitution Failed: Dispatches from the History of the Future* (Xulu Press, 2010) 159; cf Patrick J Buchanan, *A Republic, Not an Empire: Reclaiming America's Destiny* (Regnery Publishing, 1999) 373 (quoting Reagan as having said 'a country that cannot control its borders isn't really a country anymore').

[56] Trump stated 'a nation without borders is not a nation' and 'a country that can't control its borders sooner or later loses control of its future': 'Trump Signs Order for Mexico Border Wall', *Aljazeera* (online), 26 January 2017 www.aljazeera.com/news/2017/01/trump-signs-order-border-wall-mexico-170125185244055.html.

[57] *Chae Chan Ping v United States*, 130 US 581, 606 (1889).

[58] Alexander Aleinikoff et al, *Immigration and Citizenship: Process and Policy* (Thomson Reuters, 7th ed, 2012) 193 (citations omitted).

[59] See, eg, Stuart Rintoul, 'Emerging from the Shadows to Face New "Crisis of Whiteness"', *The Australian*, 6 May 2002, 8 (questioning: 'was it border protection or … a deeper racism that underpinned the [recent] closing of Australia's doors?').

[60] On the ethnic composition of the most recent arrivals of maritime asylum seekers in Australia see Elibritt Karlsen, 'Australia's Offshore Processing of Asylum Seekers in Nauru and PNG: A Quick Guide to the Statistics and Resources' (Parliamentary Library Research Paper, Parliamentary Library, December 2016).

[61] Michael Welch, *Detained: Immigration Laws and the Expanding INS Jail Complex* (Temple University Press, 2002) 13 (citing concerns of certain nativists that US immigration policy is diluting the whiteness of American society and culture); for an Australian perspective, see Danielle Every and Martha Augoustinos, 'Constructions of Racism in the Australian Parliamentary Debates on Asylum Seekers' (2007) 18 *Discourse and Society* 411.

belong to other cultures, and who, they fear, will take their jobs, occupy their land, live off the welfare system, and threaten their way of life, their environment and even their polity.[62]

Both the US and Australian governments have at times sought to justify deterrence as being in the best interest of the asylum seekers themselves. This is particularly the case with respect to measures aimed at stopping asylum-seeker boats and preventing deaths at sea.[63] The argument is that returning one group of asylum seekers back to persecution is justified as it may prevent other groups from making the dangerous journey. This spurious argument ignores the fact that there may be other ways to prevent deaths, such as increasing search and rescue capacity or providing safe pathways for migration.

2.4 Impediments to Control

Putting aside the factors driving public desire for effective migration control measures, the policy imperative from the perspective of politicians remains the same – to control the flow of unauthorised arrivals, or risk electoral backlash. In both the United States and Australia, the political branches have come up against two primary constraints. First are the obligations created by the *Refugee Convention* and *Protocol*, and other human rights instruments. Second is each country's judiciary, which at times has been viewed as overly sympathetic to irregular migrants and asylum seekers.

The *non-refoulement* obligations in the *Refugee Convention* and *Protocol*, and other human rights instruments, operate to qualify the otherwise absolute nature of the sovereign power to control immigration. Article 33 of the *Refugee Convention* requires that state parties refrain from returning a refugee to a country where she or he may face certain forms of persecution.[64] Similar *non-refoulement* provisions in other human rights instruments prohibit the return of asylum seekers to places where they would be subject to certain harms.[65]

---

[62] Myron Weiner, *The Global Migration Crisis: Challenge to States and to Human Rights* (Harper Collins, 1995) 2.

[63] Carl Anderson, 'Justice Blackmun's Query Said It All: Reflections on Haiti, Refugees, and the US Supreme Court' (1993) 1 *Hybrid: A Journal of Social Change* 73, 73; Tony Abbott, 'Second Annual Margaret Thatcher Lecture' (Speech delivered at the Margaret Thatcher Centre, London, 27 October 2015).

[64] The *Refugee Convention* and *Protocol* combine to define a refugee as any person who, 'owing to a well-founded fear of being persecuted for reasons of race, religion, nationality or membership of a particular social group or political opinion, is outside the country of his nationality and is unable or, owing to such fear, is unwilling to avail himself of the protection of that country': *Refugee Convention* art 1A(2); *Protocol* art 1(A)(2).

[65] See, eg, *Convention against Torture and other Cruel, Inhuman or Degrading Treatment or Punishment*, opened for signature 10 December 1984, 1465 UNTS 85 (entered into force 26 June 1987) art 3 (express prohibition against the expulsion, return or extradition of a person to a place where he or she would be in danger of being subjected to torture); *International Covenant on Civil and Political Rights*, opened for signature 16 December 1966, 999 UNTS 171 (entered into force 23 March 1976) arts 6 and 7 (implied prohibition against the expulsion or return of a person to a territory where they face a real risk of irreparable harm, such as a threat to the right to life or torture or other cruel, inhuman or degrading treatment or punishment); *Convention on the Rights of the Child*, opened for signature 20 November 1989, 1577 UNTS 3 (entered into force 2 September 1990) arts 6 and 37 (implied prohibition against the expulsion or return of a child where there are substantial grounds for believing that there is a real risk of irreparable harm).

While irregular migrants can be expelled or returned upon detection, the obligations contained in these international instruments mean that asylum seekers cannot be removed until their refugee claims have been considered. In both Australia and the United States, it is no coincidence that public paranoia about loss of border control has been highest at times when these countries have experienced significant flows of asylum seekers. The introduction of the policies of mandatory detention, maritime interdiction and extraterritorial processing examined in the forthcoming chapters can be directly linked to specific cohorts of asylum-seeker arrivals. These policies are specifically designed to circumvent or mitigate the protections owed to asylum seekers under international law and hence reassert control over borders. The result is what Thomas Gammeltoft-Hansen and James Hathaway refer to as a 'schizophrenic' attitude to international refugee law.[66] Wealthy states such as Australia and the United States continue to be engaged with and pay lip service to their protection obligations, while at the same time adopting policies aimed at keeping refugees away from their territories.

The second important impediment to the quest for control over borders in the United States and Australia has been the independent judiciary. The political branches in both the United States and Australia have come to view the courts as undermining their migration control efforts. The independence and power of the judiciary in the two countries is cemented in the principles of the rule of law and judicial review. As constitutional democracies, the courts in Australia and the United States can declare statutes passed by federal and state legislatures unconstitutional.[67] In both countries, the courts are also empowered to review administrative action by the executive branch of government. In carrying out this function, US and Australian courts do not remake decisions on their merits. Rather, they check for administrative error, such as whether the administrative decision-maker has interpreted the relevant legal provisions in the correct way. If there has been an error, the courts can quash the decision and refer the matter to the original decision-maker for reconsideration according to the proper principles.

In the United States, somewhat conflicting trends can be identified in the judiciary's approach to reviewing immigration-related matters.[68] By consistently maintaining that Congress has 'plenary power' over immigration, the courts have generally showed deference to Congress when assessing the constitutional validity of immigration laws. The plenary power doctrine is explored in depth in Chapter 3. For our current purposes, it suffices to say that it has been applied to generally exclude unauthorised arrivals from claiming constitutional protections. The approach of the judiciary is starkly different when interpreting the application of immigration laws (as opposed to their validity). Here, the courts have frequently adopted a more critical approach in the interpretation and application of statutes, and often do so for 'policy reasons'.[69] This 'alien-friendly' approach to interpreting

---

[66] Thomas Gammeltoft-Hansen and James Hathaway, 'Non-Refoulement in a World of Cooperative Deterrence' (2015) 53 *Columbia Journal of Transnational Law* 235.

[67] This principle was first established in the US context in *Marbury v Madison*, 5 US 137 (1803). The Australian High Court often refers to *Marbury* when discussing the basis of Australian judicial review. For example, in 1951 Justice Fullager stated that 'in [Australia's] system the principle of *Malbury v Madison* is accepted as axiomatic': *Australian Communist Party v The Commonwealth* (1951) 83 CLR 1, 262.

[68] See Brian Slocum, 'Canons, the Plenary Power Doctrine, and Immigration Law' (2007) 34 *Florida State University Law Review* 363, 363 (describing the conflicting trends as a 'fundamental dichotomy').

[69] Ibid 365; Hiroshi Motomura, 'Immigration Law after a Century of Plenary Power: Phantom Constitutional Norms and Statutory Interpretation' (1990) 100 *Yale Law Journal* 545.

immigration law has fostered a view in government that judicial review constrains efficient immigration enforcement. This tension between the judiciary and the political branches can be traced as far back as to the approach of the courts in interpreting the Chinese Exclusion Acts of the late nineteenth century.[70] While the US Supreme Court relied on the plenary power doctrine to uphold the validity of what can only be described as racist laws,[71] in many cases federal courts rejected the executive's interpretations of various provisions of the Exclusion Acts, overruling the admission officers.[72] Each time the litigation strategy of a Chinese applicant succeeded, Congress amended the Exclusion Acts to plug the holes.[73] This pattern of 'tit for tat' lawmaking has persisted in the United States to this day.[74]

A similar pattern is evident in the judicial review of immigration laws in Australia. Given that the *Australian Constitution* provides little in the way of individual rights protection, immigration legislation is rarely struck down on constitutional grounds. Yet, attempts by the political branches to curtail judicial review of immigration decisions appear to be based on a view that the judiciary is overly sympathetic to immigration applicants when reviewing immigration decisions. Attempts to limit judicial review have seen a 'battle royal' develop over the role the courts should play in the review of migration decisions.[75] Unlike in the United States, this friction is relatively new in Australia. Historically, migrants in Australia fared badly because of limitations of the prerogative writs – and the deference shown by the courts to Ministers of the Crown. The situation changed with the creation of the Federal Court of Australia,[76] and with the passage of the *Administrative Decision (Judicial Review) Act* in 1977.[77] The new legislation cut through the technicalities of the writ system and provided a neat list of the circumstances in which either decisions,[78] or conduct engaged in for the purpose of making a decision,[79] could be rendered unlawful. The newly appointed Federal Court judges made rulings that had far-reaching effects on administrative decision-making, preventing deportations and in one case ordering officials to return an individual whom it was claimed had been removed from the country illegally.[80] Parliament reacted by passing a series of bills aimed at limiting or completely ousting judicial review. The High Court responded by striking out or reading down these provisions. Crock and Berg argue that successive governments 'have come to see the courts as political subversives which preference the human rights of individuals over the policy objectives of those elected to govern'.[81]

---

[70] The *Chinese Exclusion Act of 1882*, ch 126, 22 Stat 58, suspended the admission of new Chinese labourers for ten years but preserved the right of Chinese person previously residing in the United States to return by presenting a certificate of identity which documented their prior residence; the *Scott Act of 1888* expanded on the *Chinese Exclusion Act* by restricting re-entry.

[71] See *Chae Chan Ping v United States*, 130 US 581 (1889); *Fong Yue Ting v United States*, 149 US 698 (1893).

[72] Lenni Benson, 'Back to the Future: Congress Attacks the Right to Judicial Review of Immigration Proceedings' (1997) 29 *Connecticut Law Review* 1411, 1420–5.

[73] Ibid 1421–4.

[74] Lenni Benson, 'Making Paper Dolls: How Restrictions on Judicial Review and the Administrative Process Increase Immigration Cases in the Federal Courts' (2007) 51 *New York Law School Law Review* 37.

[75] Mary Crock, 'Judging Refugees: The Clash of Power and Institutions in the Development of Australian Refugee Law' (2004) 26 *Sydney Law Review* 51, 58–61, 72.

[76] *Federal Court of Australia Act 1976* (Cth).

[77] *Administrative Decision (Judicial Review) Act 1977* (Cth).   [78] Ibid s 5.   [79] Ibid s 6.

[80] *Azemoudeh v MIEA* (1985) 8 ALD 281.

[81] Mary Crock and Laurie Berg, *Immigration, Refugees and Forced Migration: Law, Policy and Practice in Australia* (Federation Press, 2012) 342.

This has been most apparent in the review of asylum determinations, where there has been a perception that some judges are searching for loopholes to deliberately undermine the government's refugee policies. The politicians' desire to 'regain' control over immigration was summed up by then Immigration Minister Phillip Ruddock:

> It is the government, not some sectional interests, or loud intolerant individual voices, or ill-defined international interests, or, might I say, the courts that determines who shall and shall not enter this country, and on what terms ... [T]he courts have reinterpreted and rewritten Australian law – ignoring the sovereignty of Parliament and will of the Australian peoples.[82]

The implementation of mandatory detention, maritime interdiction and extraterritorial processing policies in the United States and Australia examined in the forthcoming chapters are part of wider efforts by governments in both countries to maximise control over the flow and processing of asylum seekers and irregular migrants. They are designed specifically to sidestep the main impediments to this control: court rulings generated in the judicial review of government action and international legal obligations towards asylum seekers arising out of the *Refugee Convention* and *Protocol*.

---

[82] Phillip Ruddock, Minister for Immigration (Speech to the National Press Club, Canberra, 18 March 1998).

3

Long-Term Mandatory Immigration Detention

> Under my Administration, anyone who illegally crosses the border will be detained until they are removed out of our country.
>
> Donald Trump, September 2016

This chapter examines the long-term detention of persons seeking admission pending a determination of their claim to enter. Since the advent of the universal visa system, most non-citizens' admissibility can be assessed on the spot. If they have a valid visa they are generally granted entry. If not, they are placed in removal proceedings. The period of pre-admission detention is thus generally short. Asylum seekers are the exception to this rule. In order to assess their right to enter, they must go through a lengthy status determination process during which their protection claims are assessed. This can often take many years. In most countries, asylum seekers are released into the community while their claims are assessed. Where detention does occur, it is usually limited to the time it takes to establish identity and run health and security checks.[1] My focus in this chapter is on the policy of longer-term mandatory detention of asylum seekers. By mandatory, I refer to detention which is *automatic*, without any individualised assessment as to whether it is required or appropriate in the circumstances. Such detention is a tool which is used to maximise government control over asylum seekers while their protection claims are assessed. While the asylum seekers may physically be present in the state, they are precluded from entering the community. Control is also achieved with reference to legal fictions which limit the rights of detainees. Detained persons have been designated, either by geographic location of detention or by mode of entry, to have fewer substantive and procedural rights than immigrants who enter the country with authorisation. Judicial review is further restricted by the mandatory nature of detention, which precludes challenges as to whether detention is appropriate in a given circumstance.

Immigration detention is typically of an 'administrative' or 'civil' character, carried out pursuant to administrative orders. This stands in contrast to criminal incarceration, which can generally only be imposed by a judicial order.[2] There are two other relevant categories of immigration detention in addition to detention pending admissibility. The first is the detention of persons who have been granted admission, but later face deportation. This

---

[1] Guy Goodwin-Gill, 'Article 31 of the 1951 Convention Relating to the Status of Refugees: Non-Penalisation, Detention, and Protection' in Erika Feller, Volker Türk and Frances Nicholson (eds), *Refugee Protection in International Law: UNHCR's Global Consultations on International Protection* (Cambridge University Press, 2003) 185, 187.

[2] Note that in some jurisdictions, irregular migration is a criminal offence and thus detention in such a context can be criminal in nature.

could be due to a violation of the condition of their visa or the result of criminal or morally questionable conduct. The second category of detention is that which occurs after the final determination that a person is to be deported. While the focus of this chapter is on detention pending admissibility, particularly of asylum seekers, the development of this form of detention in the United States and Australia is inextricably linked to the development of the other categories of detention.

3.1 United States

The United States has a long history of detaining arriving aliens. The *Immigration Act of 1891* empowered officers to 'inspect all such aliens' or 'to order a temporary removal of such aliens for examination at a designated time and place, and then and there detain them until a thorough inspection is made'.[3] These provisions led to the creation of the 'entry fiction', stating that transfer of an alien from a vessel to shore for examination 'shall not be considered a landing during the pendency of such examination'.[4] Daniel Wilsher comments:

> This was a critical legal (and constitutional) innovation because it meant that those incarcerated must be treated as if they were not there. This was both an attempt to treat the place of detention as if it were simply an extension of being held onboard ship, but also something more serious. The concept of being physically detained within the territorial land-mass of the United States but not being considered legally present was radical. It suggested a type of limbo – with the detention centre constituting perhaps an extra-legal space – putting immigrants beyond the reach of constitutional norms, pending a final executive decision to land or deport them.[5]

In the face of concerns around lax enforcement resulting from apparent corruption and a softness on the part of federal immigrant inspectors, the government introduced a stricter detention regime in the *Immigration Act of 1893*. These provisions confirmed that 'it shall be the *duty* of every inspector of arriving alien immigrants to detain for special inquiry ... *every* person who may not appear to him to be clearly and beyond doubt entitled to admission'.[6] The effect was to make detention mandatory and 'remove even the discretion to determine the *necessity* and *suitability* of detention'.[7] The 'entry fiction' of the 1891 Act and the 'mandatory' (or automatic) nature of detention of the 1893 Act were innovations that would go on to play a defining role in the US and Australian detention regimes.

For the next six decades, arriving immigrants in the United States were met with presumptive detention. All arrivals were detained while medical checks were carried out and their admissibility determined.[8] This changed shortly after the passage of the *Immigration and Nationality Act of 1952* ('*INA*') and the establishment of the universal visa system.[9] Screening would henceforth be carried out by consuls stationed abroad prior to the grant of

---

[3] *Immigration Act of 1891*, § 8, ch 551, 26 Stat 1084, 1085–6. [4] Ibid.
[5] Daniel Wilsher, *Immigration Detention: Law, History, Politics* (Cambridge University Press, 2012) 13.
[6] *Immigration Act of 1893* § 5, ch 206, 27 Stat 569, 570 (emphasis added).
[7] Wilsher, above n 5, 15 (emphasis original).
[8] Arthur Helton, 'The Legality of Detaining Refugees in the United States' (1986) 14 *New York Review of Law and Social Change* 353, 354.
[9] Pub L No 82-414, 66 Stat 163.

a visa. This made blanket detention of all arrivals unnecessary. The mandatory detention of those suspected of lacking authorisation to enter was to continue. Section 235(b) of the new *INA* stated that an applicant for admission who 'is not clearly and beyond a doubt entitled to be admitted shall be detained'.[10] However, the Act created parole provisions to permit aliens conditional entry while their ultimate legal status was determined. Section 212(d)(5) granted the Attorney General discretion to parole rather than detain any applicant for admission 'for emergent reasons or reasons deemed strictly in the public interest'. From 1954 onwards, the US Immigration and Naturalization Service ('INS') adopted a policy of using these parole provisions to release all arrivals, except those deemed to pose a risk to the community.[11] The liberal release policy was explained by the Supreme Court in *Leng May Ma v Barber*:

> The parole of aliens seeking admission is simply a device through which needless confinement is avoided while administrative proceedings are conducted ... Physical detention of aliens is now the exception, not the rule, and is generally employed only as to security risks and those likely to abscond ... Certainly this policy reflects the humane qualities of an enlightened civilisation.[12]

The arrival of a large number of Haitian and Cuban unauthorised boat arrivals in the early 1980s led to a reconsideration of the liberal parole policy. An announcement by Cuban President Fidel Castro that those who wished to leave Cuba were free to do so led to more than 125,000 Cubans making their way to the United States as part of what became known as the Mariel Boatlift. While Cuban asylum seekers were automatically recognised as political refugees under US law,[13] the large number of arrivals prompted a reversion to presumptive detention upon arrival. Existing detention laws were used to detain Cuban arrivals for preliminary screening and assessment as to whether they posed a risk to the community. While the majority were quickly released, a small minority who were deemed inadmissible were held in long-term detention.[14]

The arrival of a comparatively smaller group of Haitian asylum seekers prompted the government to formally amend the rules relating to parole. The number of Haitian asylum seekers travelling by boat to Florida had been gradually increasing throughout the 1970s.[15] The number of arrivals peaked in 1980, with 15,093 Haitians interdicted at sea en route to the United States in that year.[16] In May 1981, the administration of President Reagan implemented an informal rule that prohibited Haitians arriving by boat without documentation from being released on parole. The new policy was based on a recommendation

---

[10] This was renumbered in 1996 to 235(b)(2)(A) and remains in force to date.
[11] Helton, above n 8, 355.   [12] 357 US 185, 190 (1958).
[13] *The Cuban Adjustment Act of 1966*, Pub L No 89-732, 80 Stat 1161 as amended and codified at 8 USC 1255, recognises Cuban nationals as political refugees and allows them to apply for permanent residence one year after entry.
[14] See Roger Daniels, *Guarding the Golden Door: American Immigration Policy since 1882* (Hill and Wang, 2004) 205 (stating that four-fifths of the detainees were quickly released; another 22,000 were held for a longer time and then paroled, leaving 1,800 suspected of crime or mental illness. Most of these were later paroled).
[15] Adam Cox and Cristina Rodriguez, 'The President and Immigration Law' (2009) 119 *Yale Law Journal* 458, 492.
[16] US General Accounting Office, 'Detention Policies Affecting Haitian Nationals' (Report No GOA/GGD-8368, 16 June 1983) i.

by the Select Commission on Immigration and Refugee Policy for the establishment of closed asylum-processing centres.[17] The need for such centres was justified on the following grounds:

- Ineligible asylum applicants would not be released into communities where they might later evade US efforts to deport them or create costs for local governments;
- A deterrent would be provided for those who might see an asylum claim as a means of circumventing US immigration law. Applicants would not be able to join their families or obtain work while at the processing centre.[18]

The new parole regulations were struck down by the courts on a technical point. The government authorities had not followed the required administrative rule-making procedures when introducing the rule.[19] In response, a fresh regulation was introduced (this time following the correct procedures) that expanded mandatory detention, with no parole, to apply to *all* aliens arriving without proper documentation.[20] The regulations stated that '[a]ny alien who appears to the inspecting officer to be inadmissible, and who arrives without documents or who arrives with documentation which appears to be false, altered, or otherwise invalid ... shall be detained'.[21] While parole was still available for 'emergent reasons' or on 'public interest' grounds, such conditional release was restricted to limited enumerated circumstance. 'Emergent reasons' were defined to exist when the immigrant had a serious medical condition and continued detention would not be appropriate.[22] Parole was only considered to be 'strictly in the public interest' if a person posed 'neither a security risk nor a risk of absconding', and was pregnant, a juvenile, an infant, a beneficiary of an immigrant visa petition filed by a close relative, or a witness to a judicial, administrative or legislative proceeding.[23] Despite the apparent restrictiveness of the regulations dealing with parole, there was significant variation in the way release decisions were made.[24] This was in part the result of a shortage of detention facilities. There was simply not enough space to hold all persons who were liable to incarceration under the new regulations.[25]

The *Illegal Immigration Reform and Immigrant Responsibility Act of 1996* ('*IIRIRA*') broadened the classes of arriving aliens subject to mandatory detention without access to parole.[26] It introduced new expedited removal procedures which remain in force today.

---

[17] US Select Commission on Immigration and Refugee Policy, *US Immigration Policy and the National Interest* (1981).

[18] Ibid 168.

[19] See *Louis v Nelson*, 544 F Supp 973, 1003 (SD Fla, 1982) holding that the INS had violated the *Administrative Procedure Act*, 5 USC § 553 (1982) by instituting a new rule without first publishing notice of the proposed change in the Federal Registrar and giving opportunity for interested parties to comment.

[20] 47 Fed Reg 30 044, 30 044-6 (9 July 1982) (codified at 8 CFR § 212.5 (1982), additional regulations codified at § 235.3 (1997)).

[21] 8 CFR § 235.3(b) (1982).   [22] 8 CFR § 212.5(a)(1) (1982).   [23] 8 CFR § 212.5(a)(2) (1982).

[24] Michele Pistone, 'Justice Delayed Is Justice Denied: A Proposal for Ending the Unnecessary Detention of Asylum Seekers' (1999) 12 *Harvard Human Rights Journal* 197, 203 (noting the tendency of local districts not to follow policy directives from headquarters); see also Arthur Helton, 'A Rational Release Policy for Refugees: Reinvigorating the APSO Program', *Interpreter Releases*, 18 May 1998 (stating 'INS detention and release practices have been inconsistent to the point of whimsy').

[25] See US General Accounting Office, 'Immigration Control: Immigration Policies Affect INS Detention Efforts' (Report No GOA/GGD-92-85, June 1992) 3-4.

[26] Pub L No 104–208, 110 Stat 3009.

These allow aliens who arrive in the United States without valid documentation or with false documentation to be ordered removed without further hearings, reviews or appeals.[27] Even valid visas may be rejected if the Border Inspector does not agree that the category matches the individual's purpose for entering the United States or if the inspector believes a misrepresentation or fraudulent statement was used to secure the visa. Judicial review of expedited removal decisions is expressly barred. However, a limited form of habeas review is available for a narrow class of persons with special status.[28]

All persons subject to expedited removal procedures are to be mandatorily detained.[29] Aliens who indicate an intention to apply for asylum are referred to an asylum officer for a 'credible fear' interview.[30] Those found to have credible claims, either by the asylum officer or upon review by an immigration judge, are no longer subject to expedited removal and are able to pursue their asylum application through regular removal procedures.[31] As such, they may be eligible for parole under the normal parole criteria.[32] Those awaiting their 'credible fear' determination and those found not to hold such a fear have no access to parole.[33] INS policy issued shortly after the new laws were introduced stated that asylum seekers who established a 'credible fear' of persecution should normally be released.[34] However, given the wide discretion provided to individual INS district directors, this policy was not uniformly enforced across the nation, with many asylum seekers continuing to be detained for prolonged periods.[35] Under the original regulations, expedited removal only applied to arriving aliens at ports of entry.[36] In November 2002, it was expanded to aliens arriving by sea who are not admitted or paroled.[37] In August 2004, it was

---

[27] INA § 235(b)(1)(A)(i); see also Alison Siskin and Ruth Ellen Wasem, 'Immigration Policy on Expedited Removal of Aliens' (Congressional Research Service, Library of Congress, September 2006).

[28] INA § 235(b)(1)(a)(1). Returning lawful permanent residents, asylees or refugees with a prior grant of protection or putative US citizens are entitled to a habeas review of an inspector's rejection of their application for admission: INA § 242(e).

[29] INA § 235(b)(1)(B)(iii)(IV); 8 CFR § 235.3(b)(2)(iii) clarifies that the Attorney General may exercise discretion to allow parole of an otherwise detainable individual only when required to meet a medical emergency or a necessary law enforcement objective.

[30] INA § 235(b)(1)(B)(v) defines 'credible fear of persecution' as a significant possibility, taking into account the credibility of the statements made by the alien in support of the alien's claim and such other facts as are known to the officer, that the alien could establish eligibility for asylum as defined in INA § 208.

[31] INA § 240.   [32] INA § 212(5)(A).   [33] Ibid.

[34] Memorandum from INS Deputy Commissioner, 'Implementation of Expedited Removal' (31 March 1997) (stating that once an alien has established a 'credible fear' of persecution, release may be considered under normal parole criteria); Memorandum from INS Executive Associate Commissioner for Field Operations, 'Expedited Removal: Additional Policy Guidance' (30 December 1997) (stating that parole is a viable option for aliens who have met the 'credible fear' standard); Memorandum from INS Executive Associate Commissioner for Field Operations, 'Detention Guidelines' (9 October 1998) (stating that it is INS policy to favour release of aliens who have been found to have a 'credible fear' of persecution).

[35] See statement of Wendy Young, Director of Government Relations and US Programs, Women's Commission for Refugee Women and Children, in Subcommittee on Immigration of the Committee on the Judiciary, 'An Overview of Asylum Policy' (US Senate, 107th Congress, 2001) 36. In her testimony before the committee, Ms Young explains that there were thirty-three different detention policies across the United States, with some INS districts being more generous than others: at 65.

[36] Department of Justice, 'Inspection and Expedited Removal of Aliens; Detention and Removal of Aliens; Conduct of Removal Proceedings; Asylum Procedures; Final Rule', 62 Fed Reg 10,312 (6 March 1997).

[37] Department of Justice, 'Notice Designating Aliens Subject to Expedited Removal Under §235(b)(1)(A)(iii) of the Immigration and Nationality Act', 67 Fed Reg 68,924 (13 November 2002).

further expanded to apply to certain unadmitted aliens found within 100 air miles of the US southwest land border.[38]

A number of policy initiatives have since been implemented which removed access to parole for asylum seekers who had met the 'credible fear' threshold. The impact on those asylum seekers targeted by these policies was mandatory detention without parole for the entire duration of the status determination procedures. In 2001, the INS Deputy Commissioner implemented a new parole policy targeting Haitian boat arrivals. The policy stated that no Haitian should be paroled from detention except in the most demanding circumstances, and even then only with approval from Washington.[39] The Justice Department confirmed that the change of detention was needed to 'prevent against a potential mass migration to the United States'.[40] This policy of detaining Haitian asylum seekers for the entire duration of their status determination was reinforced by then Attorney General Ashcroft in April 2003. In the decision issued in *Re D-J-*, the Attorney General determined that release on bond pending the determination of the asylum claim of a Haitian man, or 'similarly situated undocumented seagoing migrants', was unwarranted due to 'adverse consequences for national security and sound immigration policy' that would result from such a release.[41] This position was expressly justified with reference to the deterrence effect it would have on future arrivals.[42] A similar policy was introduced as part of 'Operation Liberty Shield' in March 2003, targeting asylum seekers from thirty-three Arab-Muslim countries.[43] The directive stipulated that asylum seekers from the listed countries were to be mandatorily detained, without parole, for the entire duration of their status determination. It was introduced as part of a series of post-9/11 security measures and targeted countries where al Qaeda or related terrorist groups were thought to operate. In the face of widespread public criticism, the policy was abandoned after only one month.[44]

In response to reports of endemic problems in the detention system, including repeated incidents of human rights violations and denial of basic medical care, the administration of President Obama embarked on a program of detention reform.[45] A series of changes were announced in 2009 with the purpose of addressing human rights concerns regarding detainees in the immigration detention system.[46] Notable initiatives included the reduction

---

[38] Department of Homeland Security, 'Designated Aliens for Expedited Removal', 69 Fed Reg 48,877 (11 August 2004).

[39] Subcommittee on Immigration of the Committee on the Judiciary, 'The Detention and Treatment of Haitian Asylum Seekers' (United States Senate, 107th Congress, 2002) 1.

[40] Ibid 2, 30.

[41] *Re D-J-*, 23 I&N Dec 572, 579 (AG 2003). For an analysis of this decision see Judy Amorosa, 'Dissecting *In Re D-J-*: The Attorney General, Unchecked Power, and the New National Security Threat Posed by Haitian Asylum Seekers' (2005) 38 *Cornell International Law Journal* 263.

[42] *Re D-J-*, 23 I&N Dec 572, 580 (AG 2003).

[43] Elizabeth Shaffer-Wishner, Implications of Post-9/11 Immigration Policy for Muslim Americans: National Security and Human Rights Considerations (Master of Public Policy Thesis, University of Minnesota, 2011), Appendix C.

[44] See Human Rights First, *Operation Liberty Shield Quietly Terminated* (15 May 2003) www.humanrightsfirst.org/2003/05/15/asylum-news-15.

[45] For analysis of these reforms see Anil Kalhan, 'Rethinking Immigration Detention' (2010) 110 *Columbia Law Review* 42; Geoffrey Heeren, 'Pulling Teeth: The State of Mandatory Immigration Detention' (2010) 45 *Harvard Civil Rights-Civil Liberties Law Review* 601, 626–9; Sarah Gryll, 'Immigration Detention Reform: No Band-Aid Desired' (2011) 60 *Emory Law Journal* 1211.

[46] See US Immigration and Customs Enforcement, *Fact Sheet: 2009 Immigration Detention Reforms* (6 August 2009) www.ice.gov/news/library/factsheets/reform-2009reform.htm; US Department of

of the use of penal facilities for immigration detention purposes, the creation of the independent office of detention oversight to inspect facilities and review complaints and the expansion of community-based alternatives to detention. While most reforms focused on the conditions of detention, changes were also made to parole policies. An Immigration and Customs Enforcement ('ICE') policy directive issued in December 2009 instructed agents to individually assess the suitability of all detained asylum seekers for release. All those found to hold a credible fear of persecution were to be released, provided they could verify their identity and did not pose a security or flight risk.[47]

This liberalisation of the parole practices for asylum seekers was short-lived. In 2014, there was a significant increase in the number of asylum seekers travelling irregularly to the United States from Honduras, Guatemala, and El Salvador. This surge included a significant number of mothers and their minor children. A reported 61,000 family units, as well as 51,000 unaccompanied minors, crossed into the United States in 2014.[48] While the 2009 ICE directive to release asylum seekers who had established a 'credible fear' remained in force, from June 2014 onwards the Department of Homeland Security ('DHS') appears to have adopted a policy of limiting access to parole, particularly for Central American mothers and children, with the aim of deterring potential future migrants.[49] This was justified in reference to Attorney General Ashcroft's determination in *Re D-J-*.[50] The 'no parole' policy has been the subject of a number of judicial challenges.[51] However, for now, children and their families continue to be routinely detained.

The use of mandatory detention is set to be further expanded under the Trump Administration. Public and judicial attention has been focused on the temporary travel ban imposed on persons from certain Muslim-majority countries and the temporary suspension of the refugee resettlement program.[52] However, President Trump has also

---

Homeland Security, *ICE Detention Reform: Principles and Next Steps* (6 October 2009) www.dhs.gov/xlibrary/assets/press_ice_detention_reform_fact_sheet.pdf; see also Dora Schriro, 'Immigration Detention Overview and Recommendations' (US Department of Homeland Security: Immigration and Customs Enforcement, October 2009).

[47] US Immigration and Customs Enforcement, 'Parole of Arriving Aliens Found to Have a Credible Fear of Persecution or Torture' (Directive No 11002.1, 8 December 2009).

[48] Wil Hylton, 'The Shame of America's Family Detention Camps', *New York Times Magazine* (online), 4 February 2015 www.nytimes.com/2015/02/08/magazine/the-shame-of-americas-family-detention-camps.html?_r=0.

[49] A 2015 decision in the District Court for the District of Columbia found DHS and ICE have been taking deterrence of mass migration into account in making custody determinations, and that such considerations have played a significant role in the large number of Central American families detained since June 2014: *RIL-R v Jeh Charles Johnson* (DC, Civ No 15-11-JEB, 20 February 2015).

[50] *Re D-J-*, 23 I&L Dec 572 (AG 2003); The use of blanket mandatory detention for the purpose of deterrence was found to be unlawful in *RIL-R v Jeh Charles Johnson* (DC, Civ No 15-11-JEB, 20 February 2015).

[51] *RIL-R v Jeh Charles Johnson* (DDC, Civ No 15-11-JEB, 20 February 2015) (examined further below at nn 187–9); *Flores v Jeh Johnson* (CD Cal, Civ No 85-4544-DMG, 24 July 2015) (finding that the 'no parole' policy towards women and children violated provisions of the 1997 *Flores* agreement which required children to be detained in the least restrictive setting possible: see *Flores v Reno* (CD Cal, Civ No 85-4544-RJK, Stipulated Settlement Agreement, 17 January 1997)); *Flores v Lynch* (9th Cir, Civ No 15-56434, 6 July 2016) (affirming in part and reversing in part the district court decision and remanding the case).

[52] These were originally set out in Exec Order No 13769, 82 Fed Reg 8977 (1 February 2017). Major elements of this order were the subject of a nationwide Temporary Restraining Order (TRO) issued by the United States District Court for the Western District of Washington and upheld by the Court of

issued a number of other executive orders in relation to immigration enforcement.[53] The most significant for current purposes is titled 'Border Security and Immigration Enforcement Improvements'.[54] It calls for the detention of aliens who have violated immigration law 'pending the outcome of their removal proceedings ... to the extent permitted by law'.[55] As the National Immigrant Justice Center has noted, this essentially amounts to the President mandating 'that non-citizens not be considered for release from detention except as required by statute'.[56] Given the discretionary nature of parole provisions, a strict literal reading of this provision would result in no one being released.[57] The order goes on to explicitly mandate that the statutory authority to grant parole for humanitarian reasons or public benefit be used more sparingly, and only on a case-by-case basis.[58] While the 2009 ICE policy directive authorising the grant of parole for asylum seekers found to have a credible fear of persecution remains in force,[59] there is now greater emphasis on placing the onus on the asylum seeker to demonstrate that they would not pose a danger to the community, nor a flight risk.[60] The procedures and standards for establishing a credible fear are also set to be made more restrictive.[61] The Executive Order and implementing memorandum also significantly expand the application of expedited removal procedures.[62] The procedures are to be broadened to apply to aliens arrested anywhere in the United States who cannot show, to the satisfaction of an immigration officer, that they have been continuously present in the United States for two years.[63] The discretion this gives to immigration officers is concerning, with a risk that people who have been in the United States for longer than two years, but cannot readily produce paperwork to attest to this, may be subject to the procedures. These changes will all contribute to more asylum seekers being detained for the entire duration of their refugee status determination procedures. This continues the trend established under President Obama, with the percentage of asylum seekers found to have a credible fear and granted parole dropping from 80 per cent in 2012 to 47 per cent in 2015.[64] Given the significant expansion of

---

Appeals for the Ninth Circuit: see *State of Washington v Trump* 847 F 3d 1151 (9th Cir, 2017). President Trump responded by revoking the order and replacing it with Exec Order No 13780, 82 Fed Reg 13209 (9 March 2017). This was in turn prevented from going into effect by a TRO issued in *State of Hawai'i v Trump* (D Haw, Civ No 17-00050 DKW-KSC, 15 March 2017).

[53] Exec Order No 13767, 82 Fed Reg 8793 (30 January 2017) ('Border Enforcement Order'); Exec Order No 13768, 82 Fed Reg 8799 (30 January 2017).

[54] Border Enforcement Order, ibid, operationalised through DHS Secretary John Kelly, 'Memorandum Implementing the President's Border Security and Immigration Enforcement Policies' (17 February 2017) ('Border Enforcement Memorandum').

[55] Border Enforcement Order, above n 53, s 6.

[56] National Immigrant Justice Centre, 'Executive Order: Border Security and Immigration Enforcement Improvements: Annotated by the National Immigrant Justice Centre' (25 January 2017) www.immigrantjustice.org/sites/default/files/content-type/research-item/documents/2017-01/EOBorderSecurityAnnotatedFINAL.pdf.

[57] Ibid. [58] Border Enforcement Order, above n 53, 11(d).

[59] US Immigration and Customs Enforcement, 'Parole of Arriving Aliens Found to Have a Credible Fear of Persecution or Torture', above n 47, and accompanying text.

[60] Border Enforcement Memorandum, above n 54, section H.

[61] Border Enforcement Order, above n 53, s 11(b); Border Enforcement Memorandum, above n 54, s I.

[62] Border Enforcement Order, above n 53, s 11(b); Border Enforcement Memorandum, above n 54, s G.

[63] Border Enforcement Memorandum, above n 54, s G.

[64] Olga Byrne, Eleanor Acer and Robyn Barnard, *Lifeline on Lockdown: Increased U.S. Detention of Asylum Seekers* (Human Rights First, 2016) 3.

detention practices, the order also calls for immediate action to construct, operate or control new detention facilities.[65]

3.2 Australia

Australian law has provided for the detention of unauthorised non-citizens since shortly after federation. Originally, this was in the form of a criminal sanction. Section 7 of the *Immigration Restriction Act 1901* (Cth) provided for the summary conviction and imprisonment, for up to six months, of anyone deemed to be a 'prohibited immigrant'.[66] The first administrative immigration detention provisions were introduced in 1925. A new s 8C was inserted into the *Immigration Restriction Act 1901* (Cth) authorising the incarceration of any person ordered by the Minister to be removed, 'pending deportation and until he is placed on board a vessel for deportation from Australia'.[67] The *Migration Act 1958* (Cth) created a new class of persons who could be subject to administrative detention: those arriving in Australia without authorisation. Section 36 introduced the 'entry fiction' similar to that which operated in the United States, deeming persons arriving in Australia without authorisation as not having 'entered' Australia. Such persons could be detained pending their removal on the vessel on which they arrived.[68] While detention provisions existed in law, they were used sparingly until relatively recently.

The arrival of vessels carrying asylum seekers was the catalyst for change. The first asylum-seeker boat to arrive in Australia landed at Darwin Harbour in April 1976, carrying five Vietnamese men.[69] Over the next five years, a little more than 2,000 Vietnamese nationals fled the war in their homeland, making the journey to Australia by boat.[70] Although the *Migration Act* contained provisions that would have authorised detention and refusal of entry,[71] these measures were not invoked at first. As the arrivals continued, however, the initial good will faded and both sides of Australian politics began considering harsher measures. It is at this point that we see the first discussion of establishing 'processing camps' in Australia. Such a proposal was raised in 1979 in the Cabinet discussions of the governing Australian Liberal Party, as a possible solution should

---

[65] Border Enforcement Order, above n 53, s 5(b).
[66] The term 'prohibited migrant' was defined at s 3 of the *Immigration Restriction Act 1901* (Cth). Similar offence provisions remained in force until 1994: see *Migration Act 1958* (Cth) s 27 (later renumbered to s 77), repealed by s 17 of the *Migration Reform Act 1992* (Cth).
[67] Inserted by the *Immigration Act 1925* (Cth) s 8.
[68] *Migration Act 1958* (Cth) ('*Migration Act*') s 36(1).
[69] Janet Phillips and Harriet Spinks, 'Boat Arrivals in Australia since 1976' (Research Paper, Parliamentary Library, 23 July 2013). Note that Australia had received asylum flows prior to this date, the most notable of which was the arrival of a large number of West Papuan asylum seekers in Papua New Guinea ('PNG') between 1963 and 1973, a time when PNG was an Australian territory: see David Palmer, 'Between a Rock and Hard Place: The Case of Papuan Asylum-Seekers' (2006) 52 *Australian Journal of Politics and History* 576.
[70] Phillips and Spinks, ibid 1; see also Frank Brennan, *Tampering with Asylum: A Universal Humanitarian Problem* (University of Queensland Press, 2003) 29 (putting the figure at 2,077 arrivals on fifty-four boats between 1976 and 1981).
[71] See former ss 35(1), 36, 37 and 38. Writing in 1977, Schaffer warned that these provisions could be used to detain Vietnamese boat people: RP Schaffer, 'South-East Asian Refugees – The Australian Experience' (1977) 7 *Australian Year Book of International Law* 200, 226.

the unauthorised arrival of boats continue.[72] The proposal called for the construction of a holding centre for persons arriving unauthorised in Australia.[73] Foreshadowing the future development of remote processing centres, it stipulated that '[a]n essential feature of any such centre would be its capacity for secure containment. This would necessitate the choice of remote location with some form of natural protection eg. a remote island or inland centre'.[74]

The Labor Party adopted a similar proposal as their policy platform at their 1979 national conference, which called for the establishment of camps where 'uninvited refugees' would be held until another resettlement country could accept them.[75] However, it took more than a decade until a policy of systematic mandatory detention of unauthorised asylum seekers was introduced.

Starting in 1989, groups of Cambodian nationals, then Sino-Vietnamese and Chinese nationals, began arriving in Australia by boat in search of asylum.[76] Despite their modest numbers, these arrivals provoked a strong reaction from the government and community. Prime Minister Bob Hawke's Labor government began detaining all unauthorised boat arrivals. Existing 'turn-around' laws were invoked under which persons arriving by boat who were suspected of not holding an entry permit could be detained while arrangements were made to return them to their point of departure.[77] The decision not to release the Cambodians enjoyed bipartisan support, but ultimately the policy did not sit easily with the *Migration Act* as it stood at that time. The 'turn-around' provisions were supposed to operate within a timeframe of seventy-two hours. A legal challenge brought on behalf of fifteen of the detained Cambodians who had been held for more than two years prompted amendments to the legislation in 1992.[78] The changes reinforced and formalised the policy of mandatory detention, albeit with a nominal limit of 273 days on the period for which a person could be incarcerated.[79] Newly declassified Cabinet papers provide an insight into the motivations behind these measures. Then Immigration Minister, Gerry Hand made it clear that the change in policy was required in order to deter boat arrivals.[80] To achieve this, he stressed the need to restrict the scope for judicial review: 'To be effective, the legislation needs to be made as far as possible inviolable from interference by the Courts [other than the High Court] so that it is not possible to release persons so detained under those provisions into the community.'[81]

The *Migration Reform Act 1992* (Cth), which came into force on 1 September 1994, created a scheme that provided simply that all 'unlawful non-citizens' must be detained

---

[72] Commonwealth, *Review of the Indo-Chinese Refugee Situation*, Cabinet Minute Decision No 7510 (1979) Attachment C, 25.
[73] Ibid.   [74] Ibid.
[75] Laurie Oakes, *Labor's 1979 Conference, Adelaide* (Objective Publications, 1979) 40–1, 154; Australian Labor Party, *Platform, Constitution and Rules as Approved by the 33rd National Conference, Adelaide, 1979* (David Combe, National Secretary, 1979).
[76] Between November 1989 and January 1994, eighteen boats carrying a total of 735 asylum seekers (predominantly from Cambodia) arrived in Australia: Joint Standing Committee on Migration, *Asylum, Border Control and Detention* (Australian Government Publishing Service, 1994).
[77] See *Migration Act* s 88, inserted by *Migration Legislation Amendment Act 1989* (Cth). Note that these provisions existed as s 36 prior to this amendment: see above n 68 and accompanying text.
[78] *Chu Kheng Lim v MILGEA* (1992) 176 CLR 1: see discussion below at nn 195–209 and accompanying text.
[79] *Migration Amendment Act 1992* (Cth), inserting the new pt 2 div 4B into the *Migration Act*. The time limit appeared in s 54Q.
[80] Commonwealth, *Custody of Boat People*, Cabinet Minute No 326 (1992) 11.   [81] Ibid.

until they were either granted a visa or removed from Australia.[82] This change broadened mandatory detention, initially introduced as a temporary and 'exceptional' measure to deal with a particular cohort of boat arrivals, to apply to all persons who either arrived without a visa or who were in Australia on an expired or cancelled visa. Significantly, the 273-day time limit which had applied under the earlier law was omitted.

Unlike the US system, no provisions were made in the Australian laws for release on parole. Instead, a system of bridging visas was introduced which would allow the release of certain 'unlawful non-citizens' pending the determination of their claim for a substantive visa. Reflecting the 'entry fiction' in the United States, which distinguishes between admitted and non-admitted aliens, eligibility for a bridging visa was made dependent upon 'immigration clearance'.[83] Only persons who had been cleared through immigration control and admitted into Australia were eligible for bridging visas.[84] Unauthorised arrivals, who by definition were not and could not be immigration-cleared, could only be released if they belonged to certain 'prescribed classes' defined at the Minister for Immigration's discretion. Hence asylum seekers who arrived irregularly were routinely detained for the entire duration of their status determination procedures. While there have been a number of minor recent reforms, the overall architecture of mandatory detention remains in force.

Under pressure from mounting criticism surrounding the wrongful detention of lawful residents and Australian citizens,[85] and concerns about the cost of detention on the mental health of children and detainees, the Liberal/National Coalition government announced a series of immigration detention reforms in June 2005.[86] These included: a new community detention program for women and children;[87] the introduction of visas that provided an alternative to indefinite detention for persons who could not be removed from the country;[88] and giving the Commonwealth Ombudsman oversight of persons held in long-term immigration detention.[89] These reforms were extended by the Labor government when it took office in 2007. The new Immigration Minister, Chris Evans, announced a commitment to using detention as a last resort and for the shortest period of time, and avoiding indefinite detention and the detention of children.[90] In October 2010, the government announced the expansion of the community detention program for women and children. This program was further extended to apply to all vulnerable individuals in November 2011. In the same month, the Labor government announced that eligibility criteria for bridging visas were to

---

[82] *Migration Act* ss 54W, 54ZD, inserted by the *Migration Reform Act 1992* (Cth).
[83] *Migration Act* s 72(1) (definition of 'eligible non-citizen') inserted by the *Migration Reform Act 1992* (Cth).
[84] *Migration Act* s 54HS, inserted by the *Migration Reform Act 1992* (Cth) and renumbered to s 172 by the *Migration Amendment Act 1994* (Cth).
[85] See Mike Grewcock, 'Slipping through the Net? Some Thoughts on the Cornelia Rau and Vivian Alvarez Inquiry' (2005) 17 *Current Issues in Criminal Justice* 284.
[86] For a detailed examination of these reforms, see Savitri Taylor, 'Immigration Detention Reforms: A Small Gain in Human Rights' (2006) 13 *Agenda* 49.
[87] See *Migration Act* pt 2 div 7 sub-div B ('Residence Determinations') inserted by *Migration Amendment (Detention Arrangements) Act 2005* (Cth).
[88] See *Migration Regulations 1994* (Cth) sch 2 subclass 070 ('Bridging (Removal Pending)').
[89] See *Migration Act* Part 8C ss 486L–486Q inserted by the *Migration Amendment (Detention Arrangements) Act 2005* (Cth).
[90] See Chris Evans, Minister for Immigration, 'New Directions in Detention: Restoring Integrity to Australia's Immigration System' (Speech delivered at Australian National University, Canberra, 29 July 2008).

be significantly expanded. Asylum seekers entering Australia without authorisation became eligible for release, provided they had undergone health, security and identity checks.[91] Reflecting the practice of parole in the United States, reporting conditions could be imposed on those released. It is important to note, however, that a detainee's access to both bridging visas and community detention remains reliant on the discretion of the Minister. The Minister does not have a duty to consider exercising these powers, even if requested by a person in immigration detention.

A number of recent restrictive policy changes have had ramifications for the country's immigration detention program. In November 2012, the government introduced a new 'no advantage' principle, which stipulated that sea-borne asylum seekers should not receive an 'advantage' over refugees from overseas who are waiting to be resettled.[92] The result was the temporary suspension of processing of asylum claims. While the majority of asylum seekers affected by this policy were released into the community pending the resumption of processing, others were subject to prolonged detention. With the reintroduction of offshore processing, asylum seekers who travel by boat are liable to be transferred to detention facilities in Nauru and Papua New Guinea ('PNG').[93] The onshore detention program continues to apply to asylum seekers who arrive in Australia by plane, and to sea-borne asylum seekers who arrived in Australia before 19 July 2013.

3.3 Identifying Transfers

There are clear parallels in the development of policies relating to the detention of unauthorised arrivals in the United States and Australia. The similarities point to three distinct phases of legal and policy transfer. *Phase one* involved Australian lawmakers drawing on US practice when implementing and formalising the Australian system of mandatory detention between 1989 and 1994. Since then, the United States and Australia have operated similar detention regimes. Both have a system of mandatory detention for persons that arrive without authorisation, pending determination of their claims to a substantive visa. Both have provided grounds of release pending determination for certain classes of persons. In the United States, this is achieved primarily through parole or release on bond, although recent years have also seen the implementation of community-based models of detention. In Australia, release is achieved through temporary bridging visas and community detention arrangements. *Phase two* of the transfers dealt with the stringency of these conditional release programs. From 1996 to 2003, US policymakers appear to have drawn on Australia's restrictive rules limiting the classes of people eligible for release. *Phase three*, which occurred from 2004 to 2016, involved a two-way transfer process with policymakers from both jurisdictions drawing lessons from each other regarding attempts at reforming and mitigating some of the excesses of detention practices. While the United States did revert to more stringent parole policies in 2014, they were simultaneously developing alternatives to detention programs based on the Australian model. With the election of President Donald Trump, we may be entering a fourth phase, with the United States

---

[91] Chris Bowen, Minister for Immigration, 'Bridging Visas to be Issued for Boat Arrivals' (Media Release, 25 November 2011).

[92] Chris Bowen, Minister for Immigration, 'No Advantage Onshore for Boat Arrivals (Media Release, 21 November 2012).

[93] Australia's offshore processing policy is examined in detail in Chapter 5.

attempting to recreate Australia's former policy of blanket mandatory detention without parole. However, this development falls outside the period of analysis covered by my interviews.

These phases of transfer were facilitated by ongoing dialogue between US and Australian immigration policymakers, who regularly meet in numerous formal and informal forums. The existence of these *opportunities* for exchange provides strong circumstantial evidence of the occurrence of transfers. In Chapter 2, I discussed the proliferation of regional and international forums dedicated to the discussion of migration policy and practice. Here, I focus on the forums identified by my interview subjects as being the most important in terms of facilitating the transfer of immigration detention policies between the United States and Australia.

US and Australian policymakers regularly meet and discuss policy developments in intergovernmental meetings facilitated by formal international institutions. These forums include the yearly UNHCR Executive Committee meetings and the yearly International Organization for Migration ('IOM') International Dialogue on Migration. US and Australian policymakers also gather at ad hoc meetings facilitated by international forums. Prominent examples include the UNHCR Global Consultations on International Protection, held in 2001 and 2002; the first UN High-Level Dialogue on International Migration and Development ('HLD'), held in 2006; the Informal Thematic Debate on International Migration and Development, convened by the General Assembly in 2011; the second HLD, held in October 2013; and the UN General Assembly's Summit for Refugees and Migrants and the accompanying Leaders' Summit on Refugees hosted by President Obama in 2016.

Feedback from my interview subjects suggested that informal bilateral talks that take place alongside these formal meetings were important forums for the transfer of policy ideas between US and Australian policymakers.[94] As one former senior Australian bureaucrat put it, the most significant form of dialogue was the 'conversations on the margins in Geneva with the American delegation ... We took the opportunities when we were all together at those sorts of meetings to have our own bilaterals [sic] around particular issues'.[95] Another official reported that 'the Australians, the Americans and the Canadians would always caucus before a major Geneva meeting and would always discuss what came out of it. There were semi-formalised groups who would meet in Geneva around UNHCR and the Australians, the Canadians and Americans were always at the forefront of that'.[96]

Regional Consultative Processes ('RCPs')[97] were identified by a number of my interview subjects as the key forums for the diffusion of migration policy ideas.[98] They reported that the two most important RCPs for the transfer of migration policy ideas between the United States and Australia are the Five Country Conferences and the Intergovernmental Consultations on Migration, Asylum and Refugees ('IGC').[99] The Five Country Conferences evolved from the 'Group of Four' conferences held between Australia, the United States, the United Kingdom and Canada since the 1980s. It was renamed the Five Country Conference after the addition of New Zealand in 2009. The forum allows senior officials to exchange ideas in an off-the-record manner. Interview respondents cited the small number of countries involved, the similar legal systems of participant countries, the similar immigration issues faced by the countries and the informal nature of the discussions as

---

[94] AUB01, AUB19, AUB41.   [95] AUB41.   [96] AUB19.
[97] See Chapter 2, nn 33–4 and accompanying text.   [98] AUB01, AUB77, AUB19.
[99] AUB77, AUB01.

contributing to making the dialogue one of the most important forums for frank discussion and diffusion of policy ideas.[100]

The IGC was founded within UNHCR in 1985 to examine asylum issues in Europe.[101] It became an independent state-run consultative process in 1991 and its membership has gradually expanded to include thirteen European states, as well as the United States, Australia, Canada and New Zealand.[102] The stated purpose of the consultations includes 'discussion and information exchange on migration policies and their implementation'.[103] While made up of a somewhat larger cohort of participant countries than the Five Country Conference, the confidential and informal nature of discussions facilitates a full and frank exchange of policy ideas. As one senior Australian bureaucrat whom I interviewed put it:

> [The IGC] was a place where there was opportunity to meet senior officials face to face at a multilateral basis and scan world developments in all fields of migration. In those circumstances, if you feel you have some burning problem and need some inspiration and someone seems to have a good model, then you talk to them about it. [You can then consider] will any of this work for us? Or will it not work for us?[104]

Australian and US immigration policymakers also exchange ideas through bilateral channels. Of the Australian policymakers interviewed, five (two former ministers and three bureaucrats) indicated they had travelled to the United States on fact-finding missions.[105] One Australian politician indicated they had undertaken a period of 'study leave' in the United States where they had met with both senior bureaucrats and politicians to learn about US immigration policy.[106] All interview subjects who went on such trips also noted that they used the opportunity to furnish US officials with information about Australian policy developments.

Another prominent channel for communication cited by interview subjects involves the immigration representatives (or Immigration Consulers) based at the Australian Embassy in Washington and the US Embassy in Canberra.[107] These officials provide a permanent channel through which policymakers from each country can request information regarding the operation or implementation of migration policies. As one former senior Australian bureaucrat puts it, immigration representatives 'are your person on the ground. They are the one[s] who can move around an agency and deal with people on a day-to-day basis ... Your interest in policy development elsewhere is continuing and is not limited to say, one meeting a year'.[108]

In addition to this circumstantial evidence relating to *opportunity* for dialogue, there is the following *direct* evidence of transfers for each phase.

3.3.1 Phase One: United States → Australia (1989–1994)

There is evidence on the public record that demonstrates that Australian policymakers were well acquainted with the US mandatory detention regime when developing Australia's

---

[100] AUB01, AUB77, AUB19.
[101] Charles Harns, 'Regional Inter-State Consultation Mechanisms on Migration: Approaches, Recent Activities and Implications for Global Governance of Migration' (IOM Migration Research Series Report No 45, 2013) 65.
[102] Ibid. [103] Ibid. [104] AUB77. [105] AUB01, AUP11, AUB19, AUP35, AUB77, AUB15.
[106] AUP11. [107] AUB01. [108] AUB01.

original mandatory detention laws. This fact is evident when one reads the Joint Standing Committee on Migration's 1994 report, *Asylum, Border Control and Detention*, which immediately preceded the legislative moves to formalise mandatory detention.[109] In that report the committee considers examples of detention practices in comparable countries, including the United States, noting that 'the issues and problems which Australia is addressing are as relevant to and of crisis proportions amongst developed and developing countries in Europe, North America and Asia'.[110] During the inquiry, the Committee received evidence from US refugee expert, Arthur Helton in relation to the parole program used in the United States.[111]

The fact that Australian policymakers were aware of US practice was also evident in interviews undertaken by the author with six key policymakers involved in developing and implementing the policy of mandatory detention in Australia during this period.[112] All agreed that they and others involved in the development of the policy had detailed knowledge of US detention practices. When pressed, all denied that the US policy had been used as a model, claiming instead that the policy was a unique response to Australia's domestic problems. Of the six, three cited the different approaches to parole in the Australian and US systems as proof of the originality of the Australian policy.[113] However, their acknowledgement that they were aware of and had considered the policies in the United States demonstrates that some degree of transfer had in fact taken place. One interview subject put it in the following way: 'Direct influence? Did we go looking? I don't think so. Were we influenced? Definitely.'[114]

As discussed in Chapter 1, legal and policy transfer rarely involves verbatim copying of laws. More often foreign practices are drawn upon and adapted to fit local conditions. In this instance the basic model of mandatory detention was adopted. However, the parole system utilised in the United States was deemed to be undesirable. As one interview subject put it, 'we had reasonable knowledge of parole and it was basically viewed as a broken system. The [US] parole system was basically an entry system, and you might as well issue entry permits, rather than use a parole system'.[115] The comparatively smaller number of unauthorised arrivals in Australia made it possible to discard the parole system and simply detain all irregular arrivals for the entire duration of their status determination procedures.

3.3.2 Phase Two: Australia → United States (1996–2003)

The second phase of transfer involved policymakers in the United States learning from Australian immigration detention policies. Up until 1996, US parole provisions allowed for the release of certain asylum seekers at any stage of the determination of their claim. A trend towards an Australian approach of limiting release from detention pending final adjudication began with changes implemented by the *IIRIRA* in 1996. The new expedited removal process removed access to parole for asylum seekers awaiting 'credible fear'

---

[109] Joint Standing Committee on Migration, Parliament of Australia, *First Report of the Inquiry into Immigration Detention: Asylum, Border Control and Detention* (1994).
[110] Ibid 49.
[111] Ibid 150 (note that this the relevance of this program for Australia was considered and explicitly rejected).
[112] AUB01, AUB19, AUB15 and AUP11, AUB77, AUB41. [113] AUB19, AUB15, AUB41.
[114] AUB15. [115] AUB41.

determinations. Then certain asylum seekers were barred from accessing parole for the entire duration of their status determination procedures. Such a policy was implemented in 2001 with respect to Haitian asylum seekers arriving by boat. In March 2003, a similar, albeit short-lived, directive was issued in relation to asylum seekers from certain Arab Muslim countries.

Documentary evidence supporting this phase of transfer is scarce. An examination of debates and congressional and departmental reports produced in the United States during this period did not turn up any direct references to Australian detention practices. In relation to Australian sources, the Department of Immigration was on the record during this period as stating that 'Australia's border management strategies are increasingly being looked at by other countries as a model on which to base the development of their own programs'.[116] A number of my Australian interview subjects confirmed the United States was examining Australian detention practices during this period.[117] One senior Australian bureaucrat stated that US officials had expressed great interest in the fact that, under Australia's policy of mandatory detention without parole, detention was automatic and not pursuant to any reviewable decision.[118] The same policymaker revealed he had furnished information regarding the operation and implementation of this policy to US officials in the context of the Five Country Conference meetings during the 1990s.[119] A second senior Australian bureaucrat working in the Department from 1993 to 1996 confirmed that he was in regular contact with US policymakers during this period and had discussed immigration detention policy with them: 'I'm sure it would have been explored. I'm sure they would have known about it and I'm sure we would have swapped perspectives on what each of us were doing.'[120] Regrettably, none of the US policymakers identified as being directly involved in the development of immigration detention policy during the relevant period agreed to be interviewed. However, a senior US policy official who was working for the INS during this period, but not directly involved in immigration detention policy development, confirmed his department would have been well acquainted with Australian policies:

> When you are in a policy job, when you are faced with large policy issues, unless you are totally oblivious to the rest of the world, you are going to look at how other countries deal with these similar issues. You are going to gather as much information as you can, and you attempt to take, from your perspective, the best policies that exist out there.[121]

3.3.3 Phase Three: Australia ↔ United States (2004–2016)

Clear parallels can also be seen in recent reforms to the detention policy in both Australia and the United States. The excesses of the mandatory detention policy gave rise to a similar backlash in both countries. Reports about systematic failings in the detention system and the serious mental health consequences for long-term detainees led to the introduction of a series of reforms. Similar provisions were introduced in both countries to provide more independent oversight over detention operations, the rules governing the release of certain

---

[116] DIMIA, 'Australia Not Alone in Detention Stance' in United Nations High Commissioner for Refugees, 'Temporary Protection' (Discussion Paper No 2, Regional Office for Australia, New Zealand, Papua New Guinea and the South Pacific, 2002) 7.
[117] AUB41, AUB19, AUB77, AUB15. [118] AUB19. [119] Ibid. [120] AUB01. [121] USB33.

asylum seekers pending a determination of their claims were relaxed and community-based alternatives to detention ('ATD') were expanded.

The similarities in the ATD models introduced in both jurisdictions are particularly striking. Community-based ATD programs were first trialled in the United States in the late 1990s.[122] Despite studies demonstrating high rates of compliance and the significantly lower costs when compared to conventional detention, these programs were not rolled out on a large scale.[123] However, the idea gained traction in Australia. A community-based ATD program for women and children was introduced in 2005.[124] Section 197AB of the *Migration Act* gave the Minister a discretionary power to make 'Residence Determinations' to define what constituted a place of detention. Persons held in community detention are not under guard and are free to move around the community, provided they spend their nights at the designated address. A crucial element of the Australian ATD program has been the provision of case management and support services provided by NGOs. The key elements of this model are the following:

> Firstly, there is an initial assessment phase where the client's needs are determined in conjunction with those of the case manager and a detailed plan is developed. The second stage centres on the establishment of a plan to meet those needs, and ensuring communication, education, advocacy and facilitation of appropriate service involvement. Finally, the case manager will continuously monitor the situation so any change in need can be identified and responded to accordingly.[125]

The use of community-based ATD has been progressively expanded over the years. The policy was instrumental in achieving a dramatic reduction in the number of children held in immigration detention.[126] The ATD program has now been expanded and is used for not only women and children, but also other categories of detainees.

Australia's case-management model of ATD appears to have been influential in shaping recent US ATD programs. The first large-scale ATD program was implemented in the United States in 2004. Known as the Intensive Supervision Appearance Program ('ISAP'), the focus was on ensuring compliance through intrusive reporting and electronic tagging.[127] The program did not use individual case-management services as in Australia.[128] This changed in 2009 with the introduction of the Intensive Supervision Appearance Program II (ISAP II), which included a 'needs-based case management component'.[129] These services were criticised as being rudimentary, and the over-arching enforcement focus appears to have impeded the ability of the program to foster trust with immigration

---

[122] See, eg, Lutheran Immigration and Refugee Service, *Unlocking Liberty: A Way Forward for US Immigration Detention Policy* (2011); Sue Weishar, 'A More Human System: Community-Based Alternatives to Immigration Detention (Part 2)' [2011] (Spring) *Just South Quarterly* 4; Megan Golden, Oren Root and David Mizner, *The Appearance Assistance Program: Attaining Compliance with Immigration Laws through Community Supervision* (Vera Institute of Justice, 1998).

[123] Ibid.   [124] See *Migration Act* pt 2 div 7 sub-div B.

[125] International Detention Coalition (IDC), Case Management as an Alternative to Immigration Detention: The Australian Experience (2009) 5.

[126] See Interview with Peter Dutton (Doorstop Interview, Brisbane, 3 April 2016) (claiming that there were no longer any children in onshore immigration detention). Note that this point has been disputed: Ben Doherty, 'Asylum Seeker Children Still in Detention Despite Claims All Have Been Released', *Guardian* (online), 3 April 2016 www.theguardian.com/australia-news/2016/apr/03/asylum-seeker-children-still-in-detention-despite-claims-all-have-been-released.

[127] Lutheran Immigration and Refugee Service, above n 122, 30.   [128] Ibid.   [129] Ibid 31.

participants.[130] The program was operated by for-profit company GEO Group, which also runs an extensive network of private prisons. A more robust case-management model of ATD was announced in September 2015, which was targeted specifically at accompanied children and their families. The Family Case Management program draws heavily on the Australian model, providing individualised needs assessments and service plans, information sessions on legal rights and immigration procedures and help accessing legal assistance and housing, education and health services.[131] However, the Obama Administration was criticised for awarding the contract for the program to the GEO Group, rather than NGO groups working in the sector.[132] In June 2017, the Trump Administration announced that the case-management program would be discontinued.[133] With the privatisation of detention facilities in both Australia and the United States, private detention companies are emerging as agents of transfer. In June 2015, a leaked document revealed that Serco (which runs the onshore detention network in Australia) was lobbying to secure the contracts to run family detention centres in the United States.[134] In the document, the company proposes that the United States adopt Serco's Family Residential Framework, which they claim has been 'proven for nearly a decade in the UK and Australia'.[135]

Australia and the United States both moved towards a risk-based model of determining the need and type of detention during this period. In July 2008, Chris Evans, Minister for Immigration, announced a new 'modern risk management approach' where the 'key determinant of the need to detain a person in an immigration detention centre will be risk to the community'.[136] The need for risk analysis in decision-making about the appropriateness of immigration detention was first flagged in the United States in 2009.[137] ICE then worked with a number of NGOs to develop a 'risk assessment tool', which was rolled out nationally between July 2012 and January 2013.[138] The tool is used to determine whether an alien should be released or detained and the conditions which are to be imposed. While details of the precise factors considered are not publicly available, they reportedly include 'mathematically weighted factors that should signal the likelihood of threat to the community based on past behaviour as well as of absconding for each and every individual ICE apprehends'.[139]

---

[130] Ibid.
[131] Mary Loiselle, 'GEO Care's Family Case Management Program' [2016] (2nd Quarter) *GEO World* 2.
[132] See, eg, American Immigration Council, 'Obama Administration Again Hands Families Over to Private Prison Company' (Press Release, 18 September 2015); Grassroots Leadership, 'Obama Administration Should Rescind Award for Family Case Management from Private Prisons' (Press Release, 18 September 2015); Katharina Obser, *Missing the Point: Alternatives to Detention to Be Run by Private Prison Contractors*, New America Media, 25 September 2015 http://newamericamedia.org.
[133] Aria Bendix, 'ICE Shuts Down Program for Asylum-Seekers', *The Atlantic* (online), 9 June 2017 www.theatlantic.com/news/archive/2017/06/ice-shuts-down-program-for-asylum-seekers/529887/
[134] Oliver Laughland, 'Controversial Security Firm Serco Lobbies for US Migrant Detention Contracts', *The Guardian* (online), 20 June 2015 www.theguardian.com/us-news/2015/jun/19/serco-immigration-detention-centers-united-states.
[135] Ibid.   [136] See Evans, above n 90.
[137] Schriro, above n 46, 20–1 (identifying the need for a 'validated risk assessment instrument specifically calibrated for the US alien population' to be used to assess suitability for ADT programs).
[138] US Immigration and Customs Enforcement, *Detention Reform Accomplishments* http://www.ice.gov/detention-reform.
[139] Lutheran Immigration and Refugee Service, above n 122, 20.

My interviews confirmed that Australian and US officials exchanged ideas on the issue of detention reform.[140] The NGO working group set up by the Obama Administration in 2008 to facilitate detention reform included an Australian representative: the Director of the International Detention Coalition, Grant Mitchell.[141] Mr Mitchell confirmed that he provided information to the Obama Administration about Australian detention reform measures.[142] The Obama Administration was very interested in Australia's use of alternatives to detention and its use of individualised risk assessments, and Mr Mitchell reported furnishing detailed policy advice in relation to the operation of these policies in Australia.[143] Additionally, a number of NGOs directly lobbied the US government to follow the 'Australian model' of case-managed community detention.[144]

3.4 Comparing the US and Australian Jurisprudence

Legal challenges to immigration detention policies in the United States and Australia have primarily focused on two issues. The first relates to the *mandatory* nature of detention and whether non-citizens can be detained without individualised assessments of the need for incarceration. The second relates to the *duration* of detention and whether legislation can authorise the potentially indefinite detention of non-citizens at the discretion of the executive branch of government. The US Supreme Court and the Australian High Court have adopted similar forms of proportionality analysis to uphold the legality of mandatory immigration detention imposed without individualised findings as to the necessity of detention. In terms of provisions purporting to provide for indefinite, administrative, post-deportation order detention, courts in the two countries have diverged in their approach. Before examining the case law, it is first necessary to introduce and compare relevant aspects of the US and Australian legal systems.

The *US Constitution* contains positive and negative constraints on Congress's power. As a consequence, 'federal action will ordinarily be constitutional only if it is authorised in the Constitution and then only if nothing in the Constitution prohibits it'.[145] In terms of positive constraints, the federal government's power is generally restricted to those grounds expressly enumerated in the Constitution and actions 'necessary and proper' to the execution of those delegated powers. However, immigration is an exception to this rule as there are no provisions in the Constitution which grant the government power in this area. Rather, Congress's authority to control immigration is said to derive from powers inherent in sovereignty. In *Chae Chan Ping v United States* ('*Chae Chan Ping*'), the Supreme Court held unanimously:

---

[140] Interview with Grant Mitchell, Director of the International Detention Coalition (Telephone Interview, 7 August 2012).
[141] Ibid. [142] Ibid. [143] Ibid.
[144] See, eg, National Immigrant Justice Center, 'Creating "Truly Civil" Immigration Detention in the United States: Lessons from Australia' (Report, May 2010); National Immigrant Justice Center et al, 'Year One Report Card: Human Rights and the Obama Administration's Immigration Detention Reforms' (Report, 6 October 2010) 9, 18; Detention Watch Network, 'Community-Based Alternatives to Immigration Detention' (Policy Brief, August 2010).
[145] Stephen Legomsky, *Immigration and the Judiciary: Law and Politics in Britain and America* (Clarendon Press, 1987) 177, citing *Monongahela Navigation Co v United States*, 148 US 312, 336 (1893).

> That the government of the United States ... can exclude aliens from its territories is a proposition which we do not think open to controversy. Jurisdiction over its own territory to that extent is an incident of every independent nation. It is part of its independence. If it could not exclude aliens, it would to that extent be subject to the control of another power.[146]

This sovereign power vested in Congress and the executive to control immigration has been understood to extend not only to the removal of non-citizens, but also to the detention of such persons pending their removal. In *Wong Wing v United States*, Shiras J stated: 'Proceedings to exclude or expel would be in vain if those accused could not be held in custody pending the inquiry into their true character and while arrangements were being made for their deportation.'[147]

In terms of negative constraints, the *US Constitution* imposes explicit limitations which describe things that the federal government may not do. The most important of these provisions for present purposes are those aimed at protecting individual rights. Known collectively as the Bill of Rights, these appear as the first ten amendments to the *US Constitution*.

The Fifth Amendment Due Process Clause is particularly relevant to immigration detention. It provides that '[n]o person shall ... be deprived of life, liberty, or property, without due process of the law'.[148] This clause creates a *procedural* due process right pursuant to which individuals are to be afforded certain hearing rights before they are deprived of life, liberty or property. The clause also provides a *substantive* due process right pursuant to which a law or regulation can be challenged for being inherently unfair or arbitrary because it infringes a fundamental right.

The operation of the Due Process Clause and other constitutional protections in immigration decision-making is restricted by the plenary power doctrine. The contours of the doctrine have evolved over the years, but in general it declares that the political branches have a broad and largely exclusive authority over immigration. Accordingly, courts have generally declined to review federal immigration statutes and decisions made under those statutes for compliance with constitutional restraints. The result has been a line of cases in which the judiciary has upheld immigration provisions that explicitly discriminate against entrants based on factors which have included race, gender and legitimacy.[149] This has made US immigration law 'a constitutional oddity', which has developed in isolation from mainstream American public law.[150] The plenary power doctrine has attracted a great deal of criticism, and numerous observers have predicted its demise.[151]

---

[146] 130 US 581, 603–4 (1889).   [147] 163 US 228, 235 (1896).
[148] *US Constitution* amend V ('Due Process Clause').
[149] See *Chae Chan Ping v United States*, 130 US 581 (1889) (race); *Fong Yue Ting v United States*, 149 US 698 (1893) (race); *Fiallo v Bell*, 430 US 787 (1977) (gender and legitimacy). For a critical analysis of origins and continued application of the plenary power doctrine see Stephen Legomsky, 'Immigration Law and the Principle of Plenary Congressional Power' (1984) *Supreme Court Review* 255.
[150] Legomsky, ibid 255.
[151] See Ibid; Peter Schuck, 'The Transformation of Immigration Law' (1984) 84 *Columbia Law Review* 1; Charles Weissberg, 'The Exclusion and Detention of Aliens: Lessons from the lives of Ellen Knauff and Ignatz Mezei' (1995) 143 *University of Pennsylvania Law Review* 933; Alexander Aleinikoff, 'Detaining Plenary Power: The Meaning and Impact of *Zadvydas v Davis*' (2002) 16 *Georgetown Immigration Law Journal* 365; Peter Spiro, 'Explaining the End of the Plenary Power' (2002) 16 *Georgetown Immigration Law Journal* 339.

However, for now, the doctrine continues to play a significant role in US judicial decision-making.

The plenary power doctrine was developed in a line of Supreme Court decisions dealing with challenges to laws designed to exclude and deport Chinese nationals in the latter part of the nineteenth century. In *Chae Chan Ping*, the US Supreme Court held that the US federal government has the power to pass laws regulating migration and that the plenary power doctrine means that these laws cannot be challenged on substantive due process grounds.[152] In *Nishimura Eiku v United States*, three years later, the Court made it clear that the plenary power doctrine extended to bar review on procedural due process grounds as well.[153] However, by explicitly contrasting the position of excludable aliens seeking entry at the border (who had no constitutional rights in the immigration context) to that of aliens who had 'entered' the United States and had subsequently been placed in deportation proceedings, the Court left open the possibility that the latter category may be entitled to at least some degree of constitutional protection. This issue was resolved in the case of *Yamataya v Fisher*, which affirmed the distinction between excludable and deportable aliens.[154] The majority in that case ruled that deportable aliens could challenge their deportation on procedural due process grounds.[155]

The main contours of the plenary power doctrine were set. Subject to minor exceptions, the doctrine remains relatively unchanged to this day. The fault line continues to be based on notions of entry and non-entry. Aliens that have entered the United States by crossing US borders, either legally or illegally, can raise limited procedural due process challenges in deportation cases. However, the extent of the due process which must be afforded remains unclear. A long line of cases recite the procedural due process requirement, but do not apply it for the alien's benefit.[156] Recent decisions have also signalled a willingness on the part of the Court to entertain substantive due process challenges brought by deportable aliens.[157] In contrast, aliens seeking entry at the border have not been extended procedural or substantive due process rights during their removal process.[158] The one notable caveat to this rule relates to returning former long-term residents who may in certain circumstances be entitled to limited due process rights.[159]

The US Supreme Court has maintained the distinction between aliens who have 'entered' the United States and those who have not, despite Congress abolishing the division between exclusion and deportation proceedings. In 1996, Congress replaced exclusion and deportation proceedings with a single removal procedure. Following the 1996 reforms, the concept of 'admission' was adopted as the fundamental distinction in immigration proceedings.[160]

---

[152] 130 US 581 (1889).   [153] 142 US 651(1892).   [154] 189 US 86 (1903).

[155] Ibid 101. It is important to note, however, that although recognising the competency of the court to hear constitutional challenges based on due process in deportation proceedings, no procedural due process violation was found to have occurred in this case. This was despite the fact that Ms Yamataya could not speak English, had not received notice of the charges against her, and had not been allowed to consult with a lawyer: 101–2.

[156] See, eg, *Carlson v Landon*, 342 US 524 (1952).

[157] See analysis of *Zadvydas v Davis*, 533 US 678 (2001) in section 3.4.2.

[158] See discussion of *Shaughnessy v United States ex rel Mezei*, 345 US 206 (1953). This position was affirmed by the Court of Appeals of the Third Circuit in *Castro v DHS*, 835 F 3d 157 (3rd Cir, 2016).

[159] *Landon v Plasencia*, 459 US 21 (1982).

[160] Admission refers to inspection by an officer and authorisation to establish presence in the United States: Alexander Aleinikoff et al, *Immigration and Citizenship: Process and Policy* (West, 7th ed, 2012) 554.

Non-citizens placed in removal proceedings who have not been admitted now have to establish an entitlement to admission, regardless of whether they are picked up at the border or inside US territory. Where a person has been admitted, the onus falls on the government to prove deportability. Alexander Aleinikoff explains that '[t]he change in law ended the anomaly that a non-citizen seeking initial entry on an immigrant visa received fewer procedural protections than a non-citizen inside the United States who had entered without inspection'.[161] However, the Supreme Court has to date declined to shift the application of the plenary power doctrine in the direction identified by Congress. As the cases examined in this chapter demonstrate, it has chosen instead to affirm the border/interior distinction.

Australia's interest in learning from the United States long predates the introduction of mandatory detention provisions discussed above. The *US Constitution* was discussed at length during the Australasian Federal Conventions of the 1890s, the forums in which the *Australian Constitution* was drafted.[162] As in the United States, the legislative power of Australia's federal government is restricted to those heads of power mentioned in the *Australian Constitution*. Australia's Constitution is more explicit than its US counterpart in granting the federal government power to legislate with respect to immigration. In this regard, it appears that Australia learnt from the US experience. Speaking shortly after the adoption of the *Australian Constitution*, in 1901, the Attorney-General, Alfred Deakin, stated that it 'marks a distinct advance upon and difference from that of the United States, in that it contains within itself the amplest of powers to deal with [the race] difficulty in all its aspects'.[163]

The two most important powers that have been considered in the context of immigration detention are those relating to naturalisation and aliens,[164] and immigration and emigration.[165] These will be referred to as the aliens and immigration powers respectively. One of the constitutional arguments put forward against both *mandatory* and potentially *indefinite* immigration detention is that such detention is beyond the scope of these (and any other) heads of power.

As in the United States, legislation can also be struck down as invalid for inconsistency with the Constitution. However, the grounds for such challenges are more limited, as Australia does not have a bill of rights, constitutional or otherwise. While the *Australian Constitution* includes limited explicit textual provisions for constitutional rights,[166] none are relevant to immigration detention. The document's main focus is on setting out the relative powers of the different arms of government. The structure of the *Australian*

---

[161] Aleinikoff, 'Detaining Plenary Power', above n 151, 375.

[162] The Australasian Federal Convention met for three sessions in Adelaide, Sydney and Melbourne in 1897 and 1898. For a detailed analysis of the influence of the *US Constitution* on Australian constitutional design, see Erling Hunt, *American Precedents in Australian Federation* (Columbia University Press, 1930).

[163] Commonwealth, *Parliamentary Debates*, House of Representatives, 12 September 1901, 4804 (Alfred Deakin, Attorney General): The relevant powers referred to here are those authorising the government to make laws with respect to (xxvi) the people of any race for whom it is deemed necessary to make special laws; (xxvii) immigration and emigration; (xxviii) the influx of criminals; (xxix) external affairs; (xxx) the relations of the Commonwealth with the islands of the Pacific.

[164] *Australian Constitution* s 51(xix).   [165] Ibid s 51(xxvii).

[166] These are: the right to vote (s 41); trial by jury (s 80); freedom of religion (s 116); the rights of out-of-state residents (s 117); freedom of interstate trade and commerce (s 92); and acquisition of property on just terms (s 51(xxxi)).

Constitution divides the power of the federal government between the parliament (Chapter I), the executive (Chapter II) and the judiciary (Chapter III). The strictest separation is that between executive and judicial power. As Chapter III vests the judicial power of the Commonwealth exclusively with designated Commonwealth Courts, Parliament has no power to make laws which confer judicial power on the executive. This is sometimes referred to as the separation of powers doctrine. One of the implications of this doctrine is that the deprivation of liberty is a judicial power and accordingly, as a general rule, a person can only be detained by an order of a court. However, the administrative detention of non-citizens has emerged as an exception to this rule. The central question explored in relation to this issue in the case law is the scope of this exception.

Legislation may be struck down directly as unconstitutional, for being either beyond the enumerated powers or contrary to other provisions (such as the separation of powers doctrine). As in the United States, constitutional reasoning also has bearing on statutory interpretation: so far as it is possible, statutes must be interpreted consistently with the Constitution. Common law principles of statutory interpretation have also played an important role in the case law challenging immigration detention in Australia. Of most relevance is the 'principle of legality', pursuant to which 'statutory provisions are not to be construed as abrogating important common law rights, privileges and immunities in the absence of clear words or a necessary implication to that effect'.[167]

The early case law examining the legality of the administrative detention of non-citizens in Australia closely mirrored the early US case law. The aliens and immigration powers were interpreted as creating a plenary power to decide who could enter the Australian community. In the 1906 case of *Robtelmes v Brenan*, Griffith CJ stated that the aliens power

> must surely, if it includes anything, include power to determine the conditions under which aliens may be admitted to the country, the conditions under which they may be permitted to remain in the country, and the conditions under which they may be deported from it ... [T]he Commonwealth Parliament has under the delegation of power authority to make any laws that it may think fit for that purpose; and it is not for the judicial branch of the Government to review their actions, or to consider whether the means that they have adopted are wise or unwise.[168]

In a similar vein, in referring, inter alia, to the aliens power and the immigration power, Barton J stated: 'The powers given are plenary within their ambit, it is within these powers to pass legislation, however harsh and restrictive it may seem, and as to that it is not the province of a Court of Justice to inquire, where the law is clear.'[169]

It is interesting to note that the judges in *Robtelmes* explicitly referred to and affirmed the positions taken in the Chinese exclusion cases as applying in Australia.[170] Griffith CJ held

---

[167] *Daniels Corporation International Pty Ltd v Australian Competition & Consumer Commission* (2002) 213 CLR 543, 553 [11] (Gleeson CJ; Gaudron, Gummow and Hayne JJ). The principle was affirmed by the majority in *Al-Kateb v Godwin* (2004) 219 CLR 562, 643 [241] (Hayne J; McHugh and Heydon JJ agreeing).

[168] (1906) 4 CLR 395, 404. Note that part of this passage was cited with approval by Hayne J in *Al-Kateb* (2004) 219 CLR 562, 632–3.

[169] *Robtelmes v Brenan* (1906) 4 CLR 395, 415.

[170] Ibid 401–3, 413 (Griffith CJ and Barton J referring to *Fong Yue Ting v United States*, 149 US 698 (1893); *Chae Chan Ping v United States*, 130 US 581 (1889); *Nishimura Ekiu v United States*, 142 US 651 (1892)).

that the doctrines stated in those cases 'may be taken to be the settled law of the British Empire as well as of the United States'.[171]

3.4.1 Mandatory Detention

On the issue of mandatory detention, contemporary Australian and US jurisprudence is largely in agreement. The US Supreme Court and Australian High Court have both adopted similar forms of proportionality analysis when assessing the constitutional validity of the relevant detention provisions. Both courts have upheld the constitutional validity of mandatory detention, without individualised assessment, of certain classes of non-citizens. The leading US case on this issue is *Demore v Kim*, which dealt with the detention of a long-term resident alien with a criminal conviction.[172] As already noted, aliens who have entered the United States and are subsequently placed in removal proceedings have generally been afforded substantially more constitutional rights than aliens seeking entry at the border.[173] As such, test cases challenging mandatory detention laws in the US tend to be first brought on behalf of deportable former long-term resident aliens. If successful, challenges are then brought by similarly situated inadmissible aliens.[174] The current regime governing the detention of deportable aliens was enacted as part of the *Illegal Immigration Reform and Immigrant Responsibility Act of 1996* ('IIRIRA').[175] In addition to expanding mandatory detention provisions for aliens seeking admission,[176] the IIRIRA introduced INA § 236(c), which required that the Attorney General detain, without bail, a subset of deportable aliens with criminal convictions pending a determination of their removability.[177]

Demore v Kim dealt with a challenge to this detention provision brought on behalf of Hyunk Joon Kim, a South Korean national and US permanent resident.[178] Mr Kim was facing removal proceedings as the result of burglary and theft offences and was being detained under *INA* § 236(c) pending a determination as to his removability. He had argued that § 236(c) violated his Fifth Amendment substantive due process rights because the INS had not made an individualised determination that he posed a danger to society or that he was a flight risk.[179]

Mr Kim had sought to rely on earlier Supreme Court decisions that had found detention violates substantive due process requirements 'unless the detention is ordered in a *criminal* proceeding with adequate procedural protections, or in certain special and "narrow" non-punitive "circumstances," where a special justification, such as harm-threatening mental illness, outweighs the individual's constitutionally protected interest in avoiding physical

---

[171] Ibid 403. [172] 538 US 510 (2003). [173] See above nn 152–9 and accompanying text.
[174] See, eg, *Zadvydas v Davis*, 533 US 678 (2001); *Clark v Martinez*, 543 US 371 (2005) both discussed further in this section.
[175] Pub L No 104–208, 100 Stat 3009. [176] See above nn 26–33 and accompanying text.
[177] This subset includes aliens removable on terrorist grounds, as well as those convicted of crimes of moral turpitude, aggravated felonies, drug-related offenses, firearm offenses, and the catch-all category of 'miscellaneous crimes'. Parole is only available for a very limited subset of detainees: aliens enrolled in witness protection programs who can demonstrate that they do not pose a security or flight risk – see *INA* § 236(c)(2). There is limited scope to challenge such detention through what is known as a *Joseph* hearing, if it can be demonstrated that the government is 'substantially unlikely to prevail' on the grounds for which the immigrant is being held for mandatory detention: Matter of Joseph, 22 I&N Dec. 799 (BIA 1999).
[178] *Demore v Kim*, 538 US 510 (2003). [179] Ibid 514.

restraint'.[180] It was argued that the automatic detention of such a large subset of detainees, without any consideration as to the need for detention in a given circumstance, did not meet the 'narrowness' prerequisite. This Supreme Court disagreed. Rehnquist CJ, who delivered a 5:4 majority opinion on this issue, found that the detention served a legitimate immigration purpose: '[s]uch detention necessarily serves the purpose of preventing deportable criminal aliens from fleeing prior to or during their removal proceedings, thus increasing the chance that, if ordered removed, the aliens will be successfully removed.'[181]

Rehnquist CJ relied on the fact that Congress had looked at evidence on absconding rates for those granted bail and concluded that they were sufficiently high to justify mandatory detention.[182] His Honour also cited evidence showing that in most cases, removal proceedings were completed relatively quickly.[183] Although not explicitly referencing the principle, the Court essentially applied the balancing test from *Mathews v Eldridge*, which states that due process generally requires that administrative procedures balance the governmental and private interests at stake.[184] In *Demore v Kim*, the Court determined that the government purpose of preventing flight and the resulting danger to the community caused by the release of a convicted criminal justified mandatory temporary deprivation of liberty in that case.

Demore v Kim dealt with mandatorily detained resident aliens. The constitutionality of provisions mandating the detention of certain classes of inadmissible aliens pending the assessment of their claim to enter has not yet been determined by the US Supreme Court.[185] The issue was examined in the US District Court for the District of Columbia in February 2015 in the context of the Obama Administration's 'no parole' policy for asylum-seeker families from Central America.[186] The case dealt with detention of families apprehended shortly *after* they had entered the United States irregularly. Judge Bosberg ordered a preliminary injunction to halt the continued application of the 'no parole' policy, noting the fact that it raised serious constitutional due process issues.[187] His Honour reasoned:

> [p]laintiffs in this case were apprehended in the territory of the United States. What is more, they may have legitimate claims to asylum, such that their presence here may become permanent. It is clear, then, that they are entitled to the protection of the Due Process Clause, especially when it comes to deprivations of liberty.[188]

In terms of the justification for detention, the government stated that continued detention was required for the 'deterrence of mass migration'. Boasberg J found that this was unlikely to constitute a valid government interest that could justify detention of asylum seekers.[189]

---

[180] *Zadvydas*, 690 (Breyer J, joined by Stevens, O'Connor, Souter and Ginsburg JJ, citing *Kansas v Hendricks*, 521 US 346, 356 (1997); *United States v Salerno*, 481 US 739, 746 (1987)).

[181] *Demore v Kim*, 538 US 510, 528 (2003).

[182] Ibid. The absconding rates in the studies cited by the Court and considered by Congress were around 20–25 per cent.

[183] Ibid 529. The figures cited indicated that 85 per cent of cases resulted in a final decision within forty-seven days and the remaining 15 per cent, when appeals were conducted, took four months. It was later revealed that these figures were inaccurate and that the average time spent in detention was substantially longer: see n 194 below.

[184] 424 US 319 (1976).

[185] *INA* §235(b)(1)(B)(iii)(IV) (providing for the mandatory detention of asylum seekers pending their credible-fear determination).

[186] This policy is discussed above in nn 48–51 and accompanying text.

[187] *RIL-R v Johnson* (DDC, Civ No 15-11-JEB, 20 February 2015).   [188] Ibid 33.   [189] Ibid.

However, in *Castro v DHS*, handed down a few months later, the Court of Appeals for the Third Circuit adopted a different approach.[190] Even though the asylum seekers in that case had also been apprehended after crossing the border into the United States, the Court determined that the plenary power doctrine precluded their access to not only the Constitution's Due Process Clause, but also the Habeas Suspension Clause. As the petitioners had been intercepted within hours of crossing the border, the Court determined that they could be treated as 'aliens seeking initial admission to the United States'.[191]

The Supreme Court will have an opportunity to examine some of these issues in the upcoming case of *Jennings v Rodriguez*.[192] The class action deals with the detention of both aliens with criminal convictions subject to removal procedures and arriving aliens seeking entry into the United States. More specifically, it addresses the question of whether such aliens are entitled to bond hearings every six months throughout their detention and whether they are entitled to release unless the government can demonstrate that they are a flight risk or danger to the community. The argument is essentially one of statutory interpretation based on constitutional avoidance: a time limit must be imposed on the detention provisions through a process of statutory interpretation, as to do otherwise would raise serious issues under the Constitution's Due Process Clause.[193] The case may provide an opportunity for the Supreme Court to reconsider the scope of the plenary power doctrine and the constitutional rights of arriving inadmissible aliens at the border. Specifically, the Court is being asked to overturn Cold War-era cases such as *Mezei* that had found such persons are not entitled to any due process protections. In relation to aliens who are in removal proceedings as the result of criminal convictions, the Court is being called upon to revisit *Demore v Kim* and the Court's finding that brief detention did not require individualised assessments as to dangerousness or flight risk. In this regard, the recent revelation by the US Justice Department that it underestimated the time immigrants spend in detention in the information it provided to the Court in *Demore v Kim* may prove critical.[194] It was revealed that the average time in detention was more than a year, rather than the five months claimed. This is significant as the briefness of the detention period was one of the factors the Supreme Court relied upon when finding the detention provisions did not raise any constitutional issues.

In Australia, the High Court upheld the legality of mandatory immigration detention in *Chu Kheng Lim v MILGEA* ('*Lim*').[195] The case concerned the long-term mandatory detention of a group of mostly Cambodian asylum seekers between 1989 and 1994. Arriving by boat and without authorisation, the detainees were initially held under 'deemed

---

[190] *Castro v DHS*, 835 F 3d 157 (3rd Cir, 2016).   [191] Ibid 445 (footnotes omitted).

[192] (US No 15-1204, 30 November 2016). Oral arguments were presented in December 2016. In a sign that the Supreme Court was split 4-4 and could not reach a decision, re-argument was ordered in June 2017 to allow newly appointed Justice Gorsuch to take part in deliberations.

[193] This is a similar argument to what was accepted by the Supreme Court in *Zadvydas v Davis* 533 US 678 (2001) in regards to post-deportation order detention provisions: see below nn 216–17 and accompanying text.

[194] Debra Cassens Weiss, 'Justice Department Discloses "Several Significant Errors" in Information Provided for SCOTUS Case', *ABA Journal* (online), 31 August 2016 www.abajournal.com/news/article/justice_department_discloses_several_significant_errors_in_information_prov/.

[195] (1992) 176 CLR 1. For a detailed description of the factual background and judicial history of this case, see Mary Crock, 'A Legal Perspective on the Evolution of Mandatory Detention' in Mary Crock (ed), *Protection or Punishment: The Detention of Asylum Seekers in Australia* (Federation Press, 1993) 25.

non-entry' or 'turn-around' provisions.[196] An appeal against their continued detention was lodged in the Federal Court, on the basis that those provisions did not authorise extended detention.[197] Two days before the case was due to be heard by the Federal Court, the government passed amendments to the *Migration Act* creating new targeted detention provisions.[198] The detainees were given the title of 'designated persons'.[199] A 'designated person' was to be kept in custody until he or she was removed from Australia or issued an entry permit,[200] although a 273-day time limit was placed on such detention.[201] Provisions also stipulated that no court may order their release.[202]

The main argument advanced by the plaintiffs was that the detention provisions breached the separation of powers doctrine by authorising administrative detention of 'designated persons' without giving the judiciary a role in the process. The High Court unanimously rejected this argument, determining that detention of non-citizens for immigration purposes does not necessarily involve an exercise of the judicial power. The majority's reasoning took as its starting point the notion that detention of a citizen by the state is penal or punitive in character. As such, it can only follow from an adjudication of guilt validly carried out by the judicial arm of government.[203] It noted, however, that immigration detention was an accepted exception to this rule, as it serves a protective rather than punitive function. The authority to legislate for such detention stems from the aliens power and is limited to what can be properly construed as falling under that legislative head of power. In what I will refer to as the '*Lim* test', Brennan, Deane and Dawson JJ stated that provisions authorising the detention of unlawful non-citizens pending deportation:

> will be valid laws if the detention which they require and authorise is limited to what is reasonably capable of being seen as necessary for the purposes of deportation or necessary to enable an application for an entry permit to be made and considered ... [I]f this detention which [the impugned laws] require and authorise is not so limited ... they will be of a punitive nature and contravene Ch. III's insistence that the judicial power of the Commonwealth be vested exclusively in the courts which it designates.[204]

The majority in *Lim* determined that the mandatory detention provisions at issue were constitutionally valid as they met this test. Central to this finding were two statutory restrictions placed on detention. First, there were clear restrictions on the duration of detention, which was to be limited to 273 days.[205] Second, and more importantly, the majority placed great weight on the fact that a detainee was to be removed from Australia as soon as was practically possible if the person requested such removal in writing from

---

[196] Section 88 of the *Migration Act 1958* (Cth) ('*Migration Act*') as it stood at that time provided that a person could be held in detention until the vessel on which they arrived left its last Australian port.
[197] The turn-around provisions in question were only supposed to operate within a timeframe of seventy-two hours.
[198] *Migration Amendment Act 1992* (Cth), introducing pt 2 div 4B into the *Migration Act*; renumbered to div 6 by *Migration Amendment Act 1994* (Cth).
[199] *Migration Act* s 54K; renumbered to s 177 by *Migration Legislation Amendment Act 1994* (Cth).
[200] Ibid s 54L, renumbered to s 178 by *Migration Legislation Amendment Act 1994* (Cth).
[201] Ibid s 54Q, renumbered to s 182 by *Migration Legislation Amendment Act 1994* (Cth).
[202] Ibid s 54R, renumbered to s 183 by *Migration Legislation Amendment Act 1994* (Cth).
[203] *Lim* (1992) 176 CLR 1, 27 (Brennan, Deane and Dawson JJ).   [204] Ibid 33.
[205] See former s 54Q of the *Migration Act* (renumbered to s 182: see above n 201).

the Minister.[206] By conferring the power on a detainee to bring their detention to an end, detention was construed as ultimately voluntary and hence non-punitive: 'It is only if an alien who is a designated person elects, by failing to make a request under s 54P(1), to remain in the country as an applicant for an entry permit that detention ... can continue.'[207] The reliance of the majority on the 'voluntary' nature of the detention to demonstrate the non-punitive nature of the detention provisions is highly questionable as it misses the reality of the situation faced by asylum seekers. Mary Crock argues that the Court's position

> ignores the central characteristic of most, if not all, people caught by [the detention provisions] of the Act – namely, that they are applicants for refugee status. By definition, genuine refugees cannot go home without placing themselves in some form of jeopardy ... Given that the plaintiffs have all applied for recognition as refugees, it is perverse to say that they are free to bring their custody to an end by requesting repatriation.[208]

The majority – Brennan, Dawson, Deane and Gaudron JJ – did find one aspect of the detention provisions unconstitutional: the direction that no court could order 'designated persons' to be released.[209] This was held to be a clear breach of the separation of powers doctrine and struck down.

In both *Lim* and *Demore v Kim*, the Court used a form of proportionality analysis to uphold the legality of the detention. In *Lim*, the mandatory temporary deprivation of liberty faced by the plaintiff was determined to be valid as it was reasonably capable of being seen as necessary for the legitimate purpose of carrying out the assessment of admission or removal. In *Demore v Kim*, detention was justified as necessarily serving the legitimate governmental purpose of preventing deportable aliens with criminal convictions from fleeing prior to or during their removal proceedings. While the substance of the tests may be similar, their source is different. In the United States, the balancing act between the interests of the government and the individual's right to liberty is grounded in the Due Process Clause of the *US Constitution*. The *Australian Constitution* does not contain an equivalent right. Instead, the test of proportionality expounded in *Lim* is sourced in the Chapter III requirement of the separation of judicial and legislative power, and a construction of the scope of the Constitution's aliens power.

3.4.2 Indefinite Detention

The US Supreme Court and Australian High Court have adopted divergent approaches when examining statutory provisions that appear to authorise the indefinite post-deportation order detention of non-citizens. In *Zadvydas v Davis* ('*Zadvydas*'), the US Supreme Court was hesitant to adopt an interpretation of the statutory provisions in question that would authorise indefinite detention. In *Al-Kateb v Godwin*, the Australian

---

[206] *Migration Act* s 54P(1), repealed and substituted with s 181(1) by the *Migration Reform Act 1992* (Cth).
[207] *Lim* (1992) 176 CLR 1, 34 (Brennan, Deane and Dawson JJ).
[208] Mary Crock, 'Climbing Jacob's Ladder: The High Court and the Administrative Detention of Asylum Seekers in Australia' (1993) 15 *Sydney Law Review* 338, 347.
[209] *Migration Act* s 54R.

High Court accepted such an interpretation and found that it did not raise any constitutional concerns.

Zadvydas dealt with the post-deportation detention of a removable former resident alien. Legislative reforms introduced in 1996 streamlined deportation and exclusion proceedings into a single removal procedure. The provision stipulates that when an alien is ordered removed, the Attorney General has ninety days to remove them from the United States.[210] Certain classes of inadmissible aliens with criminal convictions *must* be detained during this period.[211] The Act specifies that if, for whatever reason, an alien cannot be removed, they '*may* be detained beyond the [ninety-day] period'.[212] In *Zadvydas*, the Court addressed the question of how long a person could be detained under these discretionary provisions.[213] The case concerned the detention of two resident aliens with criminal histories: Kestutis Zadvydas and Kim Ho Ma. Both had been issued with removal orders that could not be carried out, as no country would accept them. As a result, both remained in custody past the expiration of the statutory ninety-day period and faced possible indefinite detention.[214] In a 5:4 decision, the Supreme Court avoided ruling directly on the issue of whether the detention provisions violated procedural or substantive constitutional due process rights. Instead, the majority relied on a textual analysis of the relevant provisions. The issue was framed as whether the legislative provisions authorised the Attorney General to detain a removable alien '*indefinitely* beyond the removal period or only for a period *reasonably necessary* to secure the alien's removal'.[215] Breyer J, who wrote the majority opinion, adopted the latter interpretation on the grounds that the alternative would raise 'serious constitutional concerns'.[216]

The presumptively reasonable period in which to effect removal was six months. After this period, if an alien shows that there is good reason to believe that 'there is no significant likelihood of removal in the reasonably foreseeable future', the onus shifts to the government to produce evidence to rebut that presumption. The Court was careful to note, however, there may be constitutionally permissive grounds to detain aliens beyond this period, stating that the limit may not apply to 'especially dangerous' aliens.[217]

The key determining factor was an analysis of the express terms of the statute. Breyer J found no 'clear indication of congressional intent to grant the Attorney General the power to hold indefinitely in confinement an alien ordered removed'.[218] In the absence of clear congressional intent, the Court was able to avoid any constitutional issues that indefinite detention may pose. In relation to identifying the constitutional issues which the decision sought to avoid, Breyer J noted that detention had generally only been found to be constitutional only where 'a special justification, such as harm-threatening mental illness, outweighs the individual's constitutionally protected interest in avoiding physical restraint'.[219] There was no sufficiently strong justification for indefinite civil detention in this case. His

---

[210] INA § 241(a)(1)(A).   [211] INA § 241(a)(2).   [212] INA § 241(a)(6) (emphasis added).
[213] 533 US 678 (2001).
[214] At the time of the hearing, Zadvydas had been detained for seven years and Ho Ma for two years: ibid 684–5.
[215] Ibid 682 (emphasis in original).
[216] Ibid 689 (Breyer J, joined by Stevens, O'Conner, Souter and Ginsburg JJ).
[217] Breyer J said that the facts did not require the Court to 'consider terrorism or other special circumstances where special arguments might be made for forms of preventive detention and for heightened deference to the judgments of the political branches with respect to national security': ibid 696.
[218] Ibid 697.   [219] Ibid 667 citing *Kansas v Hendricks*, 521 US 346, 356 (1997).

Honour expressly rejected the two justifications put forward by the government. The first had been that continued detention of deportable aliens was necessary to ensure that aliens do not abscond from immigration proceedings.[220] The Court found this a weak ground for continued detention when the alien's removal was nothing more than a 'remote possibility at best'.[221] Breyer J reasoned that when the goal of removal is no longer practically attainable, detention no longer 'bear[s] [a] reasonable relation to the purpose for which the individual [was] committed'.[222] Second, the government had argued that continued detention was necessary to protect the community from danger.[223] Breyer J responded that preventative detention based on threat has only been upheld when limited to 'specially dangerous individuals and subject to strong procedural safeguards'.[224] In contrast, the detention provisions at issue applied to a broad class of persons, including petty criminals. Further, the purely executive review was determined to be an inadequate safeguard.[225]

The Court avoided procedural due process issues by side-stepping questions as to the constitutionality of the procedural scheme used to decide on detention. Rather, the Court relied on substantive due process grounds: 'We believe that an alien's liberty interest is, at the very least, strong enough to raise a serious question as to whether, irrespective of the procedures used, the Constitution permits detention that is indefinite and potentially permanent.'[226]

As already discussed, US courts have long distinguished between the constitutional rights of aliens seeking entry and those which have not effectuated such entry. In the 1953 case of *Shaughnessy v United States ex rel Mezei* ('*Mezei*'),[227] a majority of the US Supreme Court rejected the constitutional claims of an alien who had left the United States and was seeking readmission at Ellis Island. In doing so, the Court upheld the constitutional validity of his continued and potentially indefinite detention. Clark J's lead judgment stands as one of the Court's strongest statements of the application of the plenary power doctrine.[228] He reasoned that because of Mr Mezei's status as an excludable alien, no statutory or constitutional basis existed for his release. Clark J recognised that 'aliens who have once passed through our gates even illegally, may be expelled only after proceedings conforming to traditional standards of fairness encompassed in due process of law'.[229] But excludable aliens may not assert procedural rights under the Due Process Clause because constitutional protection only extends to persons within US territory.[230] To the dismay of immigrant advocates and academic commentators, the majority decision in *Zadvydas* reaffirmed this distinction. As such, it was unclear if the Supreme Court would extend its reasoning in *Zadvydas* to place a limit on the duration of the post-removal-order detention of aliens who had not been admitted into the United States. When the Federal Courts of Appeal were called upon to examine this question, they adopted divergent approaches,

---

[220] Ibid 690.
[221] Ibid. The Court noted that the INS had made various attempts with respect to both aliens to find a country willing to accept them but was unsuccessful: see 684, 686.
[222] Ibid 690 citing *Jackson v Indiana*, 406 US 715, 738 (1972).   [223] Ibid.
[224] Ibid 691 citing *United States v Salerno*, 481 US 739, 740, 750–2 (1987) (allowing pre-trial detention only for the most serious crimes and subject to stringent time limits) and *Foucha v Louisiana*, 504 US 71, 81–3 (1992) (striking down insanity-related detention that placed the burden on the detainee to prove non-dangerousness).
[225] Ibid 691.   [226] Ibid 696.   [227] 345 US 206 (1953).   [228] See Weisselberg, above n 151, 967.
[229] *Mezei*, 345 US 206, 212 (1953).   [230] Ibid.

with some extending the protections laid down in *Zadvydas* to inadmissible aliens and others declining to do so.[231]

In 2005, the Supreme Court resolved the issue in *Clark v Martinez*.[232] The case involved two Cuban men who had arrived in the United States as part of the Mariel Boatlift in 1980. Both were initially paroled into the United States but had their parole revoked after being convicted of criminal offences. As parole is not regarded as admission, the men retained their status as aliens seeking entry and as such could be removed on the grounds of inadmissibility.[233] Both men were placed in removal proceedings and issued with removal orders. However, these orders could not be carried out, as Cuba would not accept their return. The men remained in detention beyond the ninety-day removal period with no reasonable prospect of removal.

Writing for a 7:2 majority, Scalia J found that the detention provisions should be interpreted as being constrained by the same time limit that applies to the detention of admitted aliens.[234] Inadmissible aliens could be detained 'only for a period consistent with the purpose of effectuating removal'.[235] As in *Zadvydas*, this was held to be a presumptive period of six months, after which a detainee must be released if there is 'no significant likelihood of removal in the reasonable future'.[236] The majority reached this decision by construing the relevant statutory provision as not distinguishing between admitted and inadmissible aliens.[237] As such, the Court felt bound to follow the earlier statutory interpretation adopted in *Zadvydas* rather than 'establish within [their] jurisprudence, beyond the power of Congress to remedy, the dangerous principle that judges can give the same statutory text different meanings in different cases'.[238] The conclusion was reached despite the fact, explicitly noted by the majority, that indefinite detention of inadmissible aliens may not raise any of the constitutional concerns arising in the context of the indefinite detention of admitted aliens. In this regard, the case appears to have affirmed a long line of decisions in which US courts had held that Cubans who came to the United States as part of the Mariel Boatlift could not claim constitutional due process rights.[239] However, relying on the approach to statutory construction outlined previously, the Court deemed the continued indefinite detention of the plaintiffs unlawful, as it was not authorised by the relevant legislative provisions.

As the ruling was based purely on statutory construction, it did not prevent a legislative amendment providing for the indefinite detention of inadmissible aliens. As Scalia J wrote, '[t]he Government fears that the security of our borders will be compromised if

---

[231] The Third, Fifth, Seventh, Eighth and Eleventh Circuits did not extend *Zadvydas*'s prohibition on indefinite detention to inadmissible aliens: see *Sierra v Romaine*, 347 F3d 559 (3rd Cir, 2003); *Benitez v Wallis*, 337 F3d 1289 (11th Cir, 2003); *Borrero v Aljets*, 325 F3d 1003 (8th Cir, 2003); *Rios v INS*, 324 F3d 296 (5th Cir, 2003); *Hoyte-Mesa v Ashcroft*, 272 F3d 989 (7th Cir, 2001). In contrast, the Ninth and Sixth Circuits did extend *Zadvydas*'s prohibition on indefinite detention to inadmissible aliens: see *Rosales-Garcia v Holland*, 322 F3d 386 (6th Cir, 2003); *Xi v INS*, 298 F3d 832 (9th Cir, 2002).
[232] 543 US 371 (2005).   [233] See 8 USC § 1182(d)(5)(A) (Supp IV 1992).
[234] *Clark v Martinez*, 543 US 371 (2005). Stevens, O'Connor, Kennedy, Souter, Ginsburg and Breyer JJ joined Scalia J's opinion, while O'Connor J filed a concurring opinion. Thomas J filed a dissenting opinion in which Rehnquist CJ joined.
[235] Ibid 384.   [236] Ibid 378.   [237] § 241(a)(6); Ibid 378.   [238] Ibid 391.
[239] See, eg, *Barrera-Echavarria v Rison*, 44 F3d 1441 (9th Cir, 1995); *Gisbert v US Attorney General*, 988 F 2d 1437 (5th Cir, 1993); and Margaret Taylor, 'Detained Aliens Challenging Conditions of Confinement and the Porous Border of the Plenary Power Doctrine' (1995) 22 *Hastings Constitutional Law Quarterly* 1087, 1142–3.

it must release into the country inadmissible aliens who cannot be removed. If that is so, Congress can attend to it'.[240] The Court noted that following *Zadvydas*, Congress had indeed enacted powers to authorise indefinite detention beyond six months where removable aliens presented national security risks or had been involved in terrorist activities.[241] Accordingly, they could pass similar amendments relating to the detention of dangerous inadmissible aliens.

The Australian jurisprudence has been more accepting of potentially indefinite mandatory immigration detention. In *Al-Kateb v Godwin* ('*Al-Kateb*'), the High Court examined the legality of the detention of a stateless Palestinian asylum seeker, Ahmad Ali Al-Kateb.[242] Mr Al-Kateb arrived in Australia without a visa in search of asylum and was placed in immigration detention. His claim for asylum was denied, and after legal appeals failed, he asked to be returned to Kuwait (where he was born) or Gaza. Kuwait refused to accept Mr Al-Kateb as he was not a citizen of that country. Removal to Gaza required cooperation from Israel, which was not forthcoming. As such, the government was unable to effect his removal. Mr Al-Kateb then sought a declaration in the Federal Court that his continued detention was unlawful. Von Doussa J found that there was 'no real likelihood or prospect of removal in the reasonably foreseeable future', but nevertheless dismissed the application.[243] Mr Al-Kateb appealed to the Full Court of the Federal Court, but the matter was removed to the High Court for determination.[244]

The relevant provisions of the *Migration Act* stated that 'unlawful non-citizens' were to be held in detention until removal from Australia at their own request, deportation or grant of a visa.[245] The Act also stipulated that a person such as Mr Al-Kateb, who had requested removal, was to be removed 'as soon as reasonably practicable'.[246] The appeal focused on two questions. Did the detention provisions, when properly construed, purport to authorise the potential indefinite detention of non-citizens in circumstances where there were no real prospects of removal? If so, were the provisions constitutionally valid?

The majority of the High Court in *Al-Kateb* answered both these questions in the affirmative. On the issue of statutory construction, McHugh, Hayne, Callinan and Heydon JJ found that the relevant legislative provisions authorised detention until a detainee was removed, deported or given a visa, no matter how long that may take.[247] As the words of the relevant sections were clear,[248] there was no place to consider interpretive principles such as the principle of legality, or compatibility with international law.[249]

---

[240] *Clark v Martinez*, 543 US 371, 386 (2005).

[241] See Uniting and Strengthening America by Providing Appropriate Tools Required to Intercept and Obstruct Terrorism Act of 2001 ('USA PATRIOT Act'), Pub L No 107–56, § 412(a), 115 Stat 272, 351 (2001), inserting a new § 236A into the *INA*.

[242] (2004) 219 CLR 562.   [243] *SHDB v Goodwin* [2003] FCA 300, [9] (von Doussa J).

[244] Pursuant to s 40 of the *Judiciary Act 1903* (Cth).

[245] Section 189 (providing for the mandatory detention of unlawful non-citizens). Under s 196(1) of the *Migration Act* as it stood at the time, a person who had qualified for immigration detention had to be kept there until the person was (a) removed from Australia under section 198 or 199; or (b) deported under section 200; or (c) granted a visa.

[246] *Migration Act* s 198.

[247] *Al-Kateb* (2004) 219 CLR 562, 581 [35] (McHugh J), 640 [231] (Hayne J), 661–2 [298] (Callinan J). Note that McHugh, Hayne and Callinan JJ each delivered separate judgments, with Hayden J substantially concurring with Hayne J.

[248] Ibid 643 [241] (Hayne J) (words were 'intractable' in providing for indefinite detention).

[249] See, eg, ibid 661–2 [298] (Callinan J).

Having determined that the detention provisions purported to authorise the indefinite detention of non-citizens, the majority considered the issue of whether this raised any constitutional concerns. The Justices examined two related questions which together determined the nature and scope of the implied constitutional immunity from administrative detention. The first was whether the scope of the federal legislative power with respect to aliens was broad enough to authorise such detention. The second was whether such detention breached the separation of powers doctrine.

In relation to the scope of the aliens power, the majority took an expansive approach. For Hayne J, the aliens power created an authority to subject unlawful non-citizens to administrative detention not only for the purpose of processing and removal, but also for the purpose of 'excluding' or 'segregating' such persons from the Australian community.[250] Callinan J suggested that detention for the purpose of deterrence may also be permissible.[251] McHugh J took an even broader view, stating that 'any law that has aliens as its subject is a law with respect to aliens'.[252] This represented a significant shift from the majority position in *Lim*. In relation to the separation of powers issue, the majority was of the view that even if there was a constitutional immunity from administrative detention, their broad reading of the aliens power created a general exception for immigration detention.[253]

The dissenting judges held that the relevant legislation was ambiguous in that it did not explicitly address the possibility before them: namely, what should happen when removal is not practically possible.[254] Adopting differing approaches, all three minority Justices concluded that the provisions, properly construed, did not authorise indefinite detention. Gleeson CJ (with Gummow J agreeing) resolved the ambiguity in the statute by reference to the principle of legality.[255] As the legislature had not expressly addressed the issue of indefinite detention in the Act, Gleeson CJ read down the provisions as authorising detention for only as long as removal is a practical possibility. Gummow and Kirby JJ both agreed that post-deportation order detention would breach the separation of powers doctrine if removal was no longer a reasonable possibility. To avoid this constitutional issue, the relevant provisions were construed as not providing for such detention. For Kirby J, 'indefinite detention at the will of the Executive ... is alien to Australia's constitutional arrangements'.[256]

It is tempting to attribute the divergent judicial approaches to indefinite post-deportation order detention in the United States and Australia to the different legal structures operating in each jurisdiction – in particular, the existence of a constitutional right to due process in the United States and the absence of a comparable right in Australia. Such a view appears to be supported by statements made by a number of the majority Justices in *Al-Kateb*. Callinan J refers to the decision in *Zadvydas* but dismisses its applicability in the Australian case by reasoning that Australia does not have the constitutional 'complication' of the US Fifth Amendment.[257] McHugh J also distinguished *Zadvydas* on the basis that it dealt with constitutional due process considerations that do not exist in Australia.[258] His Honour expanded on this in extrajudicial comments, confirming that the outcome of the case would likely have been different if Australia had a bill

---

[250] Ibid 648 [255] (Hayne J). [251] Ibid 659 [291] (Callinan J). [252] Ibid 583 [41] (McHugh J).
[253] Ibid 648-9 [257]-[261] (Hayne J), 584-5 [44]-[46] (McHugh J).
[254] Ibid 575 [13]-[14], 577 [20]-[21] (Gleeson CJ). [255] Ibid 577 [19] (Gleeson CJ).
[256] Ibid 615 [146]. [257] Ibid 654 [284]. [258] Ibid 587 [52].

of rights.[259] Such a view was echoed by academics, politicians and other commentators.[260] For current purposes, it is not necessary to assess the validity of this claim. Any analysis of the impact of a bill of rights on the decision in *Al-Kateb* would need to consider the nature and exact wording of the instrument's provisions. My contention is that the absence of a bill of rights in Australia did not necessarily preclude the High Court from imposing an implied limit to the duration of detention. Nor did the existence of the constitutional Due Process Clause in the United States necessarily require that it read in such a limitation. In both *Zadvydas* and *Al-Kateb*, there was sufficient ambiguity in the relevant statutory provisions, the principles of statutory construction and the relevant constitutional considerations, to give the Court in each of those cases enough leeway to adopt either approach.

In the United States, the relevant provision stipulates that certain removable aliens may be detained beyond the ninety-day statutory time limit.[261] In Australia, the provision in question provides that detention is to continue until certain specified events occur.[262] A strict literal reading would likely conclude that even though these provisions do not address directly the issue of whether continued detention is permitted, once it becomes clear that removal is not practicable, such detention is authorised. However, the established principles of statutory interpretation in both Australia and the United States dictate that the literal meaning of a legislative provision is not always the correct construction. In the United States, the relevant principle is the presumption that Congress intends statutes to be read in a way that avoids constitutional concerns.[263] Given that indefinite detention may contravene the Due Process Clause, the majority in *Zadvydas* read an implicit limit into the post-removal-order detention provisions at issue. Detention was limited to the period that is reasonably necessary to effectuate the alien's removal from the United States. The majority settled on a presumptive time limit of six months, which had no basis in the statutory text. This outcome was far from obvious, based on a reading of the statutory provisions and relevant constitutional protections.

The decision of the majority of the US Supreme Court to rely on the principle of constitutional avoidance was based on two assumptions that may be open to challenge. The first was that the relevant statutory provisions were sufficiently ambiguous to warrant the application of the principle in the first place. The four dissenting Justices strongly disagreed with such an assertion. Kennedy J, with whom Rehnquist CJ and Thomas and Scalia JJ joined,[264] argued that the statute is 'straightforward', and not susceptible to two meanings.[265] The second questionable assertion related to whether an interpretation of the statute authorising indefinite detention would raise any constitutional concerns.

---

[259] Michael McHugh AC, 'The Need for Agitators – the Risk of Stagnation' (Speech delivered at the Sydney University Law Society Public Forum, The University of Sydney, 12 October 2005) www.hcourt.gov.au/publications/speeches/former/speeches-by-the-hon-michael-mchugh

[260] See, eg, Alice Rolls, 'Avoiding Tragedy: Would the Decision of the High Court in Al-Kateb Have Been Any Different if Australia Had a Bill of Rights Like Victoria?' (2007) 18 *Public Law Review* 119; Hon Justice John Basten, 'Book Review: *The Ultimate Rule of Law* by David M Beatty' (2005) 29 *Melbourne University Law Review* 930, 938; See Rayner Thwaites, *The Liberty of Non-Citizens: Indefinite Detention in Commonwealth Countries* (Hart, 2014) 38–9, citing Meaghan Shaw, 'Ban Indefinite Detention: Lawrence', *The Age*, 12 August 2004, 4; Australian Greens, 'Bill of Rights: One Way to Defeat Indefinite Detention' (Media Release, 6 August 2004).

[261] INA § 241(a)(6)   [262] *Migration Act* s 196(1).

[263] For a critique of this principle, see Aleinikoff, 'Detaining Plenary Power', above n 151, 367.

[264] Thomas and Scalia JJ only joined in Part I of Kennedy's dissent.   [265] 533 US 678, 706 (2001).

The majority was of the opinion that such a construction would breach Zadvydas's substantive due process rights. However, Zadvydas's entitlement to constitutional due process was by no means obvious. As discussed, the plenary power doctrine means that in many circumstances, non-citizens in immigration-related proceedings are precluded from constitutional protections. While it was generally accepted that aliens who had entered the United States were entitled to limited constitutional rights, prior to *Zadvydas* there was a question as to whether those rights were extinguished once an alien was deemed to be removable. US Federal Circuit Courts had split on the issue. The US Court of Appeals for the Fifth Circuit decision adopted a restrictive interpretation that precluded Zadvydas from relying on constitutional due process protection. There, the Court reasoned that aliens finally ordered removed were in the same position, for constitutional purposes, as aliens seeking initial entry. Both had no right to claim that they should be allowed into the United States, and therefore, the Fifth Circuit reasoned, no constitutional rights.[266] The Ninth Circuit disagreed, ruling that serious constitutional concerns would be raised by interpreting the immigration law to permit indefinite detention.[267]

While the majority of the Supreme Court in *Zadvydas* adopted the approach taken by the Ninth Circuit, at least two of the four dissenting judges favoured the Fifth Circuit approach. Scalia J, with whom Thomas J concurred, accepted the government's arguments that as deportable aliens have no right of entry into the United States, they stand on equal footing with inadmissible aliens and as such are not protected by the Due Process Clause.[268] Academic commentary in the aftermath of the Supreme Court decision supports the proposition that the *Zadvydas* decision had at least in part eroded the plenary power doctrine.[269] This suggests that if the Court had applied the plenary power doctrine in the same manner as it had been applied up until then, the outcome may have been different. In particular, the statutory interpretation adopted by the majority was based on an understanding that an alternative construction authorising indefinite detention may breach constitutional substantive due process rights. However, before *Zadvydas*, the Supreme Court had generally only extended procedural, rather than substantive, due process rights to deportable long-term residents.[270] The contingency of the outcome in *Zadvydas* is further evidenced by subsequent divisions in the Supreme Court as to the validity of the majority's reasoning. In *Clark v Martinez*, decided almost four years later, Thomas J maintained that *Zadvydas* had been wrongly decided, stating that the majority 'was wrong in both its statutory and its constitutional analysis for the reasons expressed well by the dissents in that case. I continue to adhere to those views'.[271]

It is also important to again stress the fact that *Zadvydas* concerned the indefinite detention of a US resident. In *Zadvydas* and *Clark v Martinez*, the Court expressed doubt that the detention of inadmissible aliens seeking entry into the United States would give rise to any comparable constitutional concerns. However, the Court did not find it necessary to

---

[266] *Zadvydas v Underdown*, 185 F3d 279, 289 (5th Cir, 1999).
[267] *Ma v Reno*, 208 F3d 815, 830–1 (9th Cir, 2000).   [268] *Zadvydas v Davis*, 533 US 678, 704.
[269] See Aleinikoff, 'Detaining Plenary Power', above n 151, 366, 368, 386; Joshua Gardner, 'Halfway There: *Zadvydas v. Davis* Reins in Indefinite Detentions, but Leaves Much Unanswered' (2003) 36 *Cornell International Law Journal* 177, 190, 196; cf Michele Pistone, 'A Times Sensitive Response to Professor Aleinikoff's Detaining Plenary Power' (2002) 16 *Georgetown Immigration Law Journal* 391, 392 (arguing 'that ultimately *Zadvydas* will leave no constitutional legacy').
[270] See, eg, *Yamataya v Fisher*, 189 US 86 (1903).   [271] 543 US 371, 401 (2005) (references omitted).

determine this question definitively. The presumptive time limit was extended to the detention of inadmissible aliens because they were being detained under the same statutory provision that applied to resident aliens. While the issue is still a matter of contention, a person in the analogous position of Mr Al-Kateb in the United States, that is, an inadmissible alien seeking entry, may fall outside the protections of the Constitution, including the Due Process Clause.

Similarly, the High Court decision in *Al-Kateb* could easily have been decided differently.[272] The decision was by the narrowest of majorities, with a 4:3 split. Only three of the majority judges provided substantive reasons, and there were strong minority judgments, including from the Chief Justice. Arguably, the adoption of an interpretation of the provisions as not authorising detention when removal was no longer reasonably practicable would have been more in line with constitutional precedent and established principles of statutory interpretation. As explored above, the Australian High Court had a number of principles of statutory interpretation upon which it could have relied to reach such an outcome. These included the common law principle of legality and the rule that legislation should be read so as to avoid constitutional issues. Kirby and Gummow JJ, in dissent, found the approach of the majority to the constitutional issue particularly problematic. In a reference to *Zadvydas*, Kirby J argued that the High Court 'should be no less vigilant in defending those arrangements ... than the United States Supreme Court has lately been in responding to similar Executive assertions in that country'.[273] The *Australian Constitution* does not have an equivalent of the Fifth Amendment Due Process Clause. However, His Honour reasoned that the constitutional principle that only courts can impose punishment (in exercise of the judicial power) has similar effect.[274] There is a strong argument to be made that this approach to the separation of powers issue was more in line with the High Court's decision in *Lim*.[275] In *Lim*, the constitutional validity of immigration detention provisions was dependent on whether they were reasonably capable of being seen as necessary for the legitimate purpose of carrying out the assessment of *admission* or *removal*. Post-deportation detention in circumstances where there is no reasonable likelihood of removal being carried out in the near future cannot be connected to either of those legitimate purposes. Assessment of admission has already been finally determined and detention cannot be said to be for the purpose of removal where it is clear removal is not possible.

The High Court had the opportunity to revisit its decision in *Al-Kateb* in two subsequent cases: *Plaintiff M47/2012 v Director-General Security* ('*Plaintiff M47*')[276] and *Plaintiff M76/2013 v MIMAC* ('*Plaintiff M76*').[277] Both cases dealt with the detention of asylum seekers who had been recognised as refugees, but were detained on the grounds that they posed a risk to the Australian community. They could neither be returned home nor released into the Australian community. As such, they faced potentially indefinite detention. However, in both cases, the majority of the Court avoided directly reopening *Al-Kateb* by deciding for the plaintiff on other grounds.[278] A number of Justices did directly address *Al-Kateb*.

---

[272] See Thwaites, above n 260, chs 3 and 4; Matthew Zagor, 'Uncertainty and Exclusion: Detention of Aliens and the High Court' (2006) 34 *Federal Law Review* 127.
[273] *Al-Kateb* (2004) 219 CLR 562, 615 [147].   [274] Ibid 617 [153] (citing *Lim* (1992) 176 CLR 1, 33).
[275] See above nn 203–7 and accompanying text; Zagor, above n 272, 138; Thwaites, above n 260, 72.
[276] (2012) 251 CLR 1.   [277] (2013) 251 CLR 322.
[278] In both cases, the regulations pursuant to which the plaintiffs were deemed a security risk were found to be invalid.

In *Plaintiff M47*, Gummow and Bell JJ, in dissent, argued that the construction of ss 189, 196 and 198 adopted by the majority in *Al-Kateb* should not be regarded as binding precedent. Their Honours affirmed the approach of Gleeson CJ in *Al-Kateb*, who read down the relevant detention provisions as only authorising detention as long as removal remains a practical possibility.[279] In contrast, Heydon J found that despite the fact that 'the dissentients' arguments had obvious force', the majority's approach in *Al-Kateb* was to be preferred.[280] In *Plaintiff M76*, Hayne, Kiefel and Keane JJ expressly affirmed the majority approach in *Al-Kateb*. This ongoing disagreement further illustrates the contingent nature of the *Al-Kateb* decision. It will be interesting to see how the Court will respond to this issue in the future. As of June 2017, Bell J is the only sitting member of the Court who has displayed a willingness to overrule *Al-Kateb*. Kiefel CJ and Keane J have indicated that they will not reopen *Al-Kateb*. Gageler, Nettle, Gordon and Edelman JJ are yet to express a view on the issue.

The High Court's response to any future case in which they are called upon directly to reconsider *Al-Kateb* will be influenced by the opinion of the Court on the continued relevance of the *Lim* test. In *Al-Kateb*, Hayne and McHugh JJ appeared to retreat from the position taken in *Lim* that detention will ordinarily be punitive and therefore an incident of judicial power.[281] Even if the separation of powers doctrine did supply constitutional immunity from administrative detention, they reasoned that their broad reading of the aliens power created a general exception for immigration detention. By making such a determination, they arguably expanded the non-punitive purposes identified in *Lim* that would sustain administrative detention of non-citizens. In *Lim*, the majority held that immigration detention of unlawful non-citizens was only constitutionally valid if it was reasonably capable of being seen as necessary for the purpose of facilitating *admission* and *removal*.[282] Hayne and McHugh JJ expand this test to include all detention that has the purpose of *excluding persons from the Australian community*.[283] Hayne J expressly acknowledged that this was a broader expression of the power of detention articulated in *Lim*.[284] McHugh J made comments to a similar effect in his judgment in *Re Woolley; Ex parte M276/2003* ('*Woolley*'),[285] handed down a few months after *Al-Kateb*. There, McHugh J noted that the majority in *Al-Kateb* overturned two principles set out in *Lim*, by rejecting the claim that there is a general constitutional immunity from administrative detention,[286] and declining to use the *Lim* test for determining whether the purpose of detention is non-punitive.[287] However, McHugh J may have been premature in declaring the demise of the *Lim* test in *Woolley*. Gleeson CJ and Gummow, Kirby and Callinan JJ all endorsed the test in that very same case.[288] The continued relevance of the *Lim* test has been demonstrated in subsequent cases. In *Plaintiff M76*, for example, Crennan, Bell and Gageler JJ applied and affirmed the test in the course of their majority judgment.[289]

---

[279] *Plaintiff M47* (2012) 251 CLR 1, 61 [120] (Gummow J), 193 [534] (Bell J).   [280] Ibid 138 [351].
[281] *Al-Kateb* (2004) 219 CLR 562, 648–9 [257]–[261] (Hayne J), 584–5 [44]–[46] (McHugh J).
[282] *Lim* (1992) 176 CLR 1, 33.
[283] *Al-Kateb* (2004) 219 CLR 562, 648 [255] (Hayne J), 583 [41] (McHugh J), 662 [303] (Heydon J concurring with Hayne J's analysis on this point). Callinan J, the fourth member of the majority, did not directly address the question.
[284] Ibid 648 [255].   [285] (2004) 225 CLR 1.   [286] Ibid 24–7 [56]–[62].   [287] Ibid 30–1 [71]–[72].
[288] Ibid 13–14 [21] (Gleeson CJ), 51–2 [133]–[134] (Gummow J), 84–5 [257], [260] (Callinan J), 63 [175] (Kirby J).
[289] *Plaintiff M76* (2013) 251 CLR 322, 369–70 [137]–[140].

Moreover, the *Lim* test featured front and centre in the reasoning of the High Court's unanimous decision in *Plaintiff S4/2014 v MIBP* ('*Plaintiff S4*').[290]

Plaintiff S4 concerned a challenge to the validity of the Minister's grant of a restricted temporary visa. The plaintiff, an asylum seeker from Myanmar, was detained for two years while his claim for a permanent protection visa was assessed. He was found to engage Australia's protection obligations under the *Refugee Convention*.[291] However, the Minister decided not to grant a protection visa, and instead issued two temporary permits. The combined effect of these permits was that the plaintiff could remain in Australia for three years, but was barred from applying for a permanent visa.[292] In finding the grant of these visas invalid, the High Court focused on the character and purpose of the plaintiff's detention.

In a unanimous judgment, the Court expressly affirmed and applied the *Lim* test, holding that detention provisions in the *Migration Act* are only valid to the extent that they are 'reasonably capable of being seen as necessary' to achieve three limited purposes. These were 'the purpose of removal from Australia; the purpose of receiving, investigating and determining an application for a visa permitting the alien to enter and remain in Australia; or, in a case such as the present, the purpose of determining whether to permit a valid application for a visa'.[293] As detention in this case was for the purpose of determining whether to permit a valid protection visa application to be made, it was not lawful for the Minister to then grant a different visa which effectively prevented the plaintiff from applying for a protection visa.[294]

Not only did the Court affirm the continued relevance of the *Lim* test, but it also went on to spell out the implications of this test for the permitted duration of detention:

> The duration of any form of detention, and thus its lawfulness, must be capable of being determined at any time and from time to time. Otherwise, the lawfulness of the detention could not be determined and enforced by the courts, and, ultimately, by this Court. And because immigration detention is not discretionary, but is an incident of the execution of particular powers of the Executive, it must serve the purposes of the [Migration] Act and its duration must be fixed by reference to what is both necessary and incidental to the execution of those powers and the fulfilment of those purposes. These criteria, against which the lawfulness of detention is to be judged, are set at the start of the detention.[295]

Although the Court did not cite Gummow J's dissenting judgment in *Al-Kateb*, the requirement of a temporal limitation to the detention powers in question echoes His Honour's sentiment on this point. In *Al-Kateb*, Gummow J emphasised the constitutional requirement that administrative detention have a duration capable of ascertainment at any time, so as to allow the Court to determine that detention is serving a constitutional purpose. His Honour stated:

---

[290] (2014) 253 CLR 219.

[291] *Convention Relating to the Status of Refugees*, opened for signature 28 July 1951, 189 UNTS 137 (entered into force 22 April 1954) ('*Refugee Convention*').

[292] The first visa was a Temporary Safe Haven visa valid for seven days. This visa was subject to a legislative bar that prevented an applicant from applying for a permanent visa: see *Migration Act*, s 91K. The second visa was a Temporary Humanitarian Concern visa valid for three years.

[293] *Plaintiff S4* (2014) 253 CLR 219, 231 [26]. [294] Ibid 237 [47].

[295] Ibid 232 [29] (footnotes omitted).

> The continued viability of the purpose of deportation or expulsion cannot be treated by the legislature as a matter purely for the opinion of the executive government. The reason is that it cannot be for the executive government to determine the placing from time to time of that boundary line which marks off a category of deprivation of liberty from the reach of Ch III. The location of that boundary line itself is a question arising under the Constitution or involving its interpretation.[296]

While not directly overturning *Al-Kateb*, the High Court's decision in *Plaintiff S4* does signal a willingness of the Court to place both *purposive* and *temporal* limits on the scope of the executive's detention powers. In terms of *purpose*, it is important to note that 'exclusion' and 'segregation', which Hayne and McHugh JJ viewed as being constitutionally valid purposes for detaining non-citizens in *Al-Kateb*,[297] are absent from the list of permitted purposes articulated in *Plaintiff S4*. In terms of the *temporal* limitation, *Plaintiff S4* imposes two related requirements.[298] First, the duration of any form of detention must be capable of being determined at any time. This means it must be carried out with respect to clear and objective criteria, rather than at the discretion of the executive. Second, the duration of detention must be limited to what is 'necessary' and 'incidental' to a constitutionally valid purpose. Time will tell how this will be applied to any future assessment of the lawfulness of the detention of persons subject to post-deportation order detention in an analogous position to Mr Al-Kateb. As the relevant legislative provisions prescribe clear guidelines as to when detention of such persons will come to an end (issuance of a visa or removal), the Court will likely accept, as it did in *Al-Kateb*, that detention is carried out pursuant to objective criteria against which the duration of detention can be assessed from time to time. However, it is questionable whether continued detention where removal is not reasonably practical can be validly construed as 'necessary' or 'incidental' to one of the constitutionally permissible purposes of detention.

The cases examined in this chapter demonstrate that there is an outer constitutional limit to the government's power to detain non-citizens in the United States and Australia. However, pinpointing the contours of that limit is no easy task. The judiciary's approach in both countries to determining the scope of rights which ought to be afforded to detained non-citizens has waxed and waned over the years. This has in part been facilitated by the interpretive leeway created by the special status of non-citizens, who are seen to fall outside usual constitutional norms. This inconsistency makes it difficult to predict the legal success or failure of transfers of restrictive detention measures between the United States and Australia. As we will explore in the next two chapters on maritime interdiction and extraterritorial processing, these legal ambiguities are further heightened when government action against non-citizens occurs outside a state's territorial boundaries.

---

[296] *Al-Kateb* (2004) 219 CLR 562, 613 [140].
[297] Heydon J concurred with Hayne and McHugh JJ, endorsing the power to legislate to segregate aliens from the community: ibid 584 [45]. Callinan J, the fourth member of the majority, did not directly address the question.
[298] These requirements have been affirmed and applied in later cases, including in *North Australian Aboriginal Justice Agency* (2015) 256 CLR 569, 612 [99]–[103]; *CPCF v Minister for Immigration and Border Protection* (2015) 255 CLR 514, 625 [374]; *Plaintiff M68/2015 v MIBP* (2016) 257 CLR 42, 71–2 [46], 130–1 [262]; *Plaintiff M96A/2016 v Commonwealth* [2017] HCA 16 (3 May 2017) [31].

4

Maritime Interdiction

> Now the Australian government is prepared to turn boats around, we've been able to do it safely and effectively and I am not surprised that other countries are now doing likewise.
> Former Australian Prime Minister Tony Abbott, May 2015

Maritime interdiction is one of the most controversial measures used by states in their bids to control their borders. In the context of boat migration, it refers to any 'action taken by states to prevent sea-borne migrants from reaching their intended destination'.[1] This generally involves two distinct phases of action. First, a vessel is physically intercepted and boarded or inspected. The second stage involves the deflection or 'taking' of the vessel and/or the passengers to some location. This location could be within or outside the territory of the interdicting state. It could be the point of embarkation, international waters, territorial waters of another nation, a third country or an external territory.

Interdiction at sea and the return of boat migrants without screening asylum claims has been called the 'ultimate' barrier or deterrent.[2] The US Coast Guard explains that '[i]nterdicting migrants at sea means they can quickly be returned to their countries of origin without the costly process required if they successfully enter the United States'.[3] By relying on a view that the *Refugee Convention* has no extraterritorial effect, its *non-refoulement* obligations are said not to apply.[4] A similar argument is employed in an attempt to avoid judicial enforcement of constitutional and statutory rights that migrants may enjoy if they enter the nation's territory. Interdiction coupled with some form of screening for asylum claims strikes a more balanced (but still problematic) approach between border control concerns and protection outcomes. Screening may take place on board Navy or Coast Guard vessels at sea or in a third country or external territory.[5] This practice, known as extraterritorial or offshore processing, is examined in Chapter 5.

---

[1] Bernard Ryan, 'Extraterritorial Immigration Control: What Role for Legal Guarantees?' in Bernard Ryan and Valsamis Mitsilegas (eds), *Extraterritorial Immigration Control: Legal Challenges* (Martinus Nijhoff Publishers, 2010) 3, 22.
[2] David Martin, 'The New Asylum Seekers' in David Martin (ed), *The New Asylum Seekers: Refugee Law in the 1980s* (Kluwer, 1988) 1, 6.
[3] US Coast Guard, *Alien Migrant Interdiction* (31 October 2014) www.uscg.mil/hq/cg5/cg531/AMIO/amio.asp (site down at the time of writing, copy on file with author).
[4] *Convention Relating to the Status of Refugees*, opened for signature 28 July 1951, 189 UNTS 137 (entered into force 22 April 1954) ('*Refugee Convention*'); the validity of this claim is questioned below at nn 37–57, 164–71 and accompanying text, and in Chapter 6.
[5] In this context, the term 'external territory' is used to describe a territory outside the traditional geographic boundaries of country, over which the country's government exercises control, but which is designated as an area in which regular domestic laws are said not to apply.

4.1 US Coast Guard Alien Migrant Interdiction Program

For the most part, US interdiction policies have targeted sea-borne asylum seekers from Haiti and Cuba.[6] The Haitian interdiction program began in 1981. The Coast Guard was authorised to intercept and search vessels suspected of transporting undocumented Haitians. These early measures included summary asylum screening carried out aboard US Coast Guard cutters. Those found to have a 'credible fear' of persecution were transferred to the United States to pursue their claim, while the others were returned to Haiti. The interdiction program and screening procedures were carried out pursuant to a bilateral treaty between the United States and Haiti,[7] INS Interdiction Guidelines,[8] and Executive Order 12324.[9]

The interdiction program has operated continuously to this day.[10] While the interception component has remained largely the same, the actions taken against migrants after they come under the control of the US Coast Guard has varied over the years. The first major policy change occurred in November 1991, when screening procedures for Haitian asylum seekers were suspended. A violent military coup in Haiti replaced the democratically elected President Jean-Bertrand Aristide with a military junta. Reports of widespread politically motivated violence and the US administration's public condemnation of the coup made it difficult for the United States to summarily dismiss asylum claims by interdicted Haitians. But the administration of George HW Bush was reluctant to admit the large number of asylum seekers attempting to reach the United States by boat (more than 38,000 Haitians were interdicted in the eight-month period following the coup).[11] For a brief period, all interdicted Haitians were held on Coast Guard cutters outside US territorial waters. The Bush Administration attempted to frame the issue as a regional problem and negotiated with other Caribbean nations to take some of the Haitians held on US ships. On the whole, these efforts were unsuccessful. Although Belize, Honduras, Venezuela, and Trinidad and Tobago agreed to offer temporary shelter to small numbers in UN-administered camps, the combined intake of 550 places was not enough to defuse the crisis.[12] By late November 1991, 2,200 Haitians were being held in custody and all available Coast Guard cutters were at capacity.[13]

The Bush Administration responded by resuming summary screening at sea and repatriating those who were deemed not to have a credible fear of persecution. A series of injunctions issued by the US District Court for the Southern District of Florida at the end of 1991, temporarily prevented the United States from returning Haitians to their

---

[6] For a detailed analysis of political and historic background of Haitian and Cuban sea-borne migration to the United States, see Azadeh Dastyari, *United States Migrant Interdiction and the Detention of Refugees in Guantánamo Bay* (Cambridge University Press, 2015) 13–52.

[7] *Agreement Effected by Exchange of Notes Regarding Migrants and Interdiction*, US–Haiti, 33 UST 3599, TIAS 10241 (signed and entered into force 23 September 1981).

[8] INS Interdiction Guidelines, 'INS Role in and Guidelines for Interdiction at Sea' (6 October 1981, revised 24 September 1982).

[9] Exec Order No 12324, 46 Fed Reg 48109 (1 October 1981).

[10] For a detailed account of the development of the policy, see Dastyari, above n 6, 13–57.

[11] 'Islands of Inequality', *Washington Post* (4 November 1992) A18, cited in Arthur Helton, 'The United States Government Program of Intercepting and Forcibly Returning Haitian Boat People to Haiti: Policy Implications and Prospects' (1993) 10 *New York Law School Journal of Human Rights* 325, 330.

[12] Vernon Briggs, 'US Asylum Policy and the New World Order' (1993) 1 *People and Place* 1, 3.

[13] Ibid 3.

home country.[14] Unwilling to let the Haitians enter the United States, and with no space left on the Coast Guard cutters, the US government decided to transfer the asylum seekers to a hastily built camp on the US-controlled territory of Guantánamo Bay in Cuba.[15] Although better known in recent times as an exceptional space created to exclude enemy combatants from the protections of the US justice system,[16] Guantánamo was used first as a holding and processing centre to bar interdicted asylum seekers from accessing these same legal protections. Between November 1991 and May 1992, all interdicted Haitians were taken to Guantánamo for processing. Those found to have a credible fear of persecution were transferred to the United States to pursue an asylum claim.[17] Those found not to exhibit such a fear were forcibly returned to Haiti. Even these streamlined procedures, however, could not keep up with the steady flow of arrivals, and the makeshift camp at Guantánamo quickly reached its 12,500-person capacity.

With the facilities at Guantánamo full, President Bush issued the 'Kennebunkport Order' on 24 May 1992.[18] The new policy provided for the interdiction and summary return of all Haitians leaving Haiti by boat. The order expressly declared that US *non-refoulement* obligations under the *Refugee Convention* and *Protocol* did not extend outside US territory.[19] Despite criticising the policy during the 1992 presidential election and promising to repeal it, President Bill Clinton maintained the policy of interdiction and return without screening when he came to office. In 1993, in *Sale v Haitian Centers Council*, the Supreme Court tacitly upheld the no-screening policy.[20] It affirmed the government's stance that neither the *non-refoulement* obligations in the *Refugee Convention* and *Protocol* nor the United States implementing legislation prohibited the return of refugees intercepted on the high seas. This decision is examined in detail later in this section.

President Clinton suspended the no-screening policy in May 1994, apparently deciding that Haiti was, in fact, too dangerous a place to return the asylum seekers to.[21] Initially, all Haitians were subject to full status determination procedures. These took place aboard US Coast Guard vessels on the high seas, in the territorial waters of third countries or in Guantánamo Bay.[22] Those who satisfied the more stringent 'well-founded fear of persecution' test (rather than the 'credible fear' test) were resettled in the United States. The number of Haitians arriving quickly outstripped the processing capabilities, and the refugee

---

[14] *Haitian Refugee Center, Inc v Baker*, 789 F Supp 1552, 1576–1577 (SD Fla, 1991) ('*Baker*'); *Haitian Refugee Center, Inc. v Baker*, 789 F Supp 1579 (SD Fla, 1991). These were overturned in *Haitian Refugee Center v Baker* ('*Baker II*') 949 F 2d 1109 (11th Cir, 1991) and *Haitian Refugee Center v Baker* ('*Baker III*') 953 F 2d 1498 (11th Cir, 1992). These cases are examined in detail in Chapter 5.

[15] See Chapter 5, nn 19–50 and accompanying text. For a historical overview of US interests in Guantanamo Bay, see Dastyari, above n 6, 6–8.

[16] Fleur Johns, 'Guantanamo Bay and the Annihilation of the Exception' (2005) 16 *European Journal of International Law* 613.

[17] Note that persons who were found to have a credible fear but were HIV positive were not transferred to the US, but were detained in a special section of the Guantanamo Bay facility: see Chapter 5.

[18] Exec Order No 12807, 57 Fed Reg 23 133 (1 June 1992).

[19] *Protocol Relating to the Status of Refugees*, opened for signature 31 January 1967, 606 UNTS 267 (entered into force 4 October 1967) ('*Protocol*').

[20] 509 US 155 (1993).

[21] Bill Frelick, 'US Refugee Policy in the Caribbean: No Bridge Over Troubled Waters' (1996) 20 *Fletcher Forum of World Affairs* 67, 67.

[22] For an examination of the processing of asylum claims in third countries, see Chapter 5, nn 78–79 and accompanying text.

adjudication procedures were suspended. From July 1994 onwards, Haitians were instead extended 'safe haven' in either Guantánamo or one of a number of participating Caribbean nations.[23] In August 1994, the interdiction and safe haven policy was extended to Cuban arrivals. Up until then, US policy had presumed all persons fleeing Cuba to be refugees, and those that made it to sea had been rescued and brought to the United States.[24] A large spike in the number of Cubans making the journey prompted a rethink of this approach.[25] The safe haven policy came to an end in 1995. Reinstituting a policy of presumptive ineligibility, the United States repatriated nearly all the remaining Haitian asylum seekers held at Guantánamo in January 1995.[26] The Cubans on Guantánamo were more lucky. Those remaining in the camp were transferred to the United States in May 1995. But future arrivals were subject to the same presumptive ineligibility as Haitians. They were to be interdicted and returned to Cuba, except where they could show shipboard adjudicators a 'genuine need for protection; that could not be satisfied by applying for refugee status with the US Interests Section in Havana'.[27]

The US interdiction program has also targeted migrants from a range of other countries, including the Dominican Republic, Ecuador and China. Current operations are carried out pursuant to Executive Order 13276, which was issued by President George W Bush in 2002.[28] This authorises the Attorney General to detain, at any location she or he deems appropriate, any undocumented aliens she or he has reason to believe are seeking to enter the United States and who are intercepted in the Caribbean region. In the 2016 financial year, there were a total of 6,346 migrants interdicted.[29] Interdicted migrants undergo basic screening at sea. The vast majority are 'screened out' and returned to their point of departure, but a small number continue to be transferred to Guantánamo Bay for processing.[30]

The leading Supreme Court case on the legality of the US migrant interdiction program is *Sale v Haitian Centers Council* ('*Sale*').[31] This case involved a challenge to President George HW Bush's 'Kennebunkport Order' of 24 May 1992, which authorised the interdiction and repatriation of all Haitians attempting to reach the United States by boat without any screening for asylum claims.[32] The main issue in *Sale* was whether these actions violated the *non-refoulement* obligation in art 33 of the *Refugee Convention*,[33] or section 243(h) of the *Immigration and Nationality Act* ('*INA*'), which implemented a similar obligation into US law.[34] Prior to the Supreme Court's decision, several circuit courts had considered this issue in the context of the Haitian interdiction program. The District of Columbia and Eleventh Circuit found that the US government's *non-refoulement* obligations under the

---

[23] See Chapter 5, nn 47–50, 82–4 and accompanying text.   [24] Frelick, above n 21, 68.
[25] This was precipitated by an announcement by the Cuban government on 6 August 1994 that they would no longer interfere with efforts of those who desired to emigrate to the United States: Thomas David Jones, 'A Human Rights Tragedy: The Cuban and Haitian Refugee Crises Revisited' (1995) 9 *Georgetown Immigration Law Journal* 479, 492; The similarities to the Mariel boat lift in 1981 led some to label the incident as Mariel II: Carlos Verdecia, 'Wily Castro Again Sends His Problems North', *Christian Science Monitor* (12 September 1994) 19; See also Appendix, Table A.1.
[26] Frelick, above n 21, 67.   [27] Ibid 72.
[28] Exec Order No 13276, 67 Fed Reg 69985 (19 November 2002).   [29] See Appendix, Table A.1.
[30] See Chapter 5, nn 67–9.   [31] 509 US 155 (1993).   [32] See above n 18 and accompanying text.
[33] Note that the United States is not party to the Convention but in effect assumed the obligations under it when it acceded to the Protocol.
[34] In 1996, Congress repealed § 243(h) and inserted similar provisions in § 241(b)(3) of the *INA*: see *Illegal Immigration Reform and Immigrant Responsibility Act of 1996*, Pub L No 104-208, 100 Stat 3009-546.

Refugee Convention and the *INA* only extended to aliens who were physically present in the United States.[35] The Second Circuit took the contrary view, interpreting art 33 and the relevant legislative provisions as having extraterritorial effect.[36]

In *Sale*, the US Supreme Court adopted the restrictive interpretation of the *non-refoulement* obligations as only applying within the territorial boundaries of the United States.[37] Stevens J, writing for the majority, began by examining the meaning of the relevant provisions of the *INA*. Section 243(h) provided, subject to a number of exceptions, that 'the Attorney General shall not deport or return any alien ... to a country if the Attorney General determines that such alien's life or freedom would be threatened in such country on account of race, religion, nationality, membership of a particular social group, or political opinion'.

Through an examination of the language and legislative history of this provision, the Court interpreted two main restrictions to its operation. First, as the language only referred to the Attorney General, it could not be interpreted as placing any limitations on the President's authority to repatriate aliens interdicted in international waters.[38] Second, the provision was interpreted as not having any extraterritorial applicability. This was grounded in a view that the protection only extended to regulating actions of the Attorney General authorised under the Act. The Act only authorised the operation of deportation and exclusion proceedings within the United States. Stevens J reasoned, therefore, that '[s]ince there is no provision in the statute for the conduct of such proceedings outside the United States ... we cannot reasonably construe § 243(h) to limit the Attorney General's actions in geographic areas where she has not been authorised to conduct such proceedings'.[39] His Honour also relied on the presumption that acts of Congress do not ordinarily apply outside US borders to support the interpretation of § 243(h) as only applying within US territory.

Having rejected the proposition that the *INA* created any extraterritorial *non-refoulement* obligations, Stevens J turned his attention to the possibility that the *Refugee Convention* may create such an obligation. If that were the case, under the Supremacy Clause of the *US Constitution*, the broader treaty obligation might provide the controlling rule of law.[40] The Court decided, however, that neither a textual analysis nor the negotiating history of the treaty supported the position that art 33 is applicable on the high seas or extraterritorially.

Article 33 of the *Refugee Convention* states:

1. No Contracting State shall expel or return (*'refouler'*) a refugee in any manner whatsoever to the frontiers of territories where his life or freedom would be threatened on account of his race, religion, nationality, membership of a particular social group or political opinion.
2. The benefit of the present provision may not, however, be claimed by a refugee whom there are reasonable grounds for regarding as a danger to the security of *the country*

---

[35] *Haitian Refugee Center v Gracey*, 809 F 2d 794 (DC Cir, 1987); *Haitian Refugee Center v Baker*, 949 F 2d 1109 (11th Cir, 1991); *Haitian Refugee Center v Baker*, 953 F 2d 1498 (11th Cir, 1992).
[36] *Haitian Centers Council v McNary*, 969 F 2d 1350 (2nd Cir, 1992).
[37] 509 US 155 (1993) (Stevens, White, O'Connor, Scalia, Kennedy, Souter, and Thomas JJ and Rehnquist CJ; Blackmun J dissenting).
[38] Ibid 172.   [39] Ibid 173.   [40] Ibid 178.

in which he is, or who, having been convicted by a final judgement of a particularly serious crime, constitutes a danger to the community of that country.[41]

Steven J's first textual argument stemmed from the geographic limitation included in art 33(2). The effect of that provision is that a refugee cannot claim the benefit of the *non-refoulement* obligation if he poses a threat to the country *in which he is located.* His Honour reasoned that

> [i]f the first paragraph did not apply to the high seas, no nation could invoke the second paragraph's exception with respect to an alien there: An alien intercepted on the high seas is in no country at all. If Article 33.1 applied extraterritorially, therefore, Article 33.2 would create an absurd anomaly: Dangerous aliens on the high seas would be entitled to the benefits of 33.1 while those residing in the country that sought to expel them would not.[42]

Steven J's second textual argument related to the meanings of the terms 'expel' and 'return' in art 33(1). The Court ruled that these terms paralleled the phrase 'deport or return' found in § 243(h)(1) of the *INA*. 'Expel' was interpreted as having the same meaning as 'deport', referring to the deportation or expulsion of an alien who is already present in the host country. The term 'return' (*refouler*) was interpreted as being limited to the exclusion of aliens who are 'on the threshold of initial entry'.[43] The Court reasoned that the inclusion of the term '*refouler*' following 'return' narrows the meaning of the term, as '*refouler*' is not a synonym for 'return'.[44] Stevens J referred to two English–French dictionaries translating '*refouler*' as 'repulse', 'drive back' or 'expel'. His Honour concluded that these translations imply that in the context of art 33(1), '"return" means a defensive act of resistance or exclusion at the border rather than an act of transporting someone to a particular destination'.[45] The Court also found that this interpretation of the terms 'expel' and 'return' (as applying only to refugees who have entered the host country) was also supported by the *travaux préparatoires* of the *Refugee Convention*. The Court cited statements by the Swiss and Dutch delegates supporting such an interpretation.[46] Thus, the Supreme Court held that art 33 does not have extraterritorial effect.

Blackmun J delivered a powerful dissent, finding that the duty of *non-refoulement* in both the *Refugee Convention* and the *INA* applied extraterritorially. In relation to art 33 of the *Refugee Convention*, His Honour's starting point was the principle that a treaty must be construed according to its 'ordinary meaning'.[47] The majority's attempt to give the term 'return' a more narrow legal meaning was inconsistent with this accepted canon of statutory interpretation. Blackmun J found that the ordinary meaning of 'return' is 'to bring, send, or put (a person or thing) back to or in a former position', and that was exactly what the US government was doing to the Haitians.[48] His Honour was critical of the majority's attempt to construe the term *refouler* in the text of art 33(2) as somehow limiting the meaning of 'return' in that provision. Blackmun J noted that even if the majority's translation of *refouler* as 'repulse', 'repel' and 'drive back' was accepted, none of these terms necessitated the

---

[41] *Refugee Convention* art 33 (emphasis added).   [42] *Sale*, 509 US 155, 180 (1993).
[43] Ibid 180, quoting *Shaughnessy v United States ex rel Mezei*, 345 US 206, 212 (1953).   [44] Ibid.
[45] Ibid 182.   [46] Ibid 184–7.
[47] Ibid 191, citing the *Vienna Convention on the Law of Treaties*, opened for signature 23 May 1969, 1155 UNTS 331 (entered into force 27 January 1980) art 31(1).
[48] Ibid.

conclusion that the term should be read down to only mean exclusion at the border. A person can be repulsed, repelled or driven back on the high seas.

Next, Blackmun J dismissed the majority's argument relating to the inclusion of the geographical limitation in art 33(2). For His Honour, the fact that the drafters of the Convention decided to allow nations to deport criminal aliens who have entered their territory hardly suggested an intent to permit the apprehension and return of non-criminal aliens who have not entered their territory.[49] Blackmun J was also very critical of the majority's reliance on the *travaux préparatoires*, and in particular the oral statements of Swiss and Dutch delegates. Such reference, he argued, should only be made as a last resort when there is ambiguity in the language.[50] They could not be used to change the plain meaning of the text. Moreover, there is no evidence that the statements relied upon reflected the views of other delegates, as they were not 'agreed to' or 'adopted' as official amendments to the Convention.[51]

In relation to § 243(h) of the *INA*, Blackmun J reasoned that the provisions are both syntactically and grammatically unambiguous in their extraterritorial effect. His Honour argued that such an interpretation was supported by a correct reading of the legislative history. He criticised the majority's reliance on the presumption against the extraterritorial applicability of US law. The presumption, he argued, only operates where congressional intent is 'unexpressed'. The language of the provisions in this case clearly expressed an extraterritorial effect. Even if the congressional intent was unexpressed, the international subject matter of the legislation (immigration, nationalities and refugees) created a presumption of extraterritorial applicability. Blackmun J also dismissed the argument that as § 243(h) only purports to constrain the actions of the Attorney General, the provision did not apply to the Haitian interdiction program as it was carried out pursuant to a Presidential Order. His Honour concluded that '[t]here can be no doubt that the Coast Guard is acting as the Attorney General's agent when it seizes and returns undocumented aliens'.[52]

The overwhelming weight of academic opinion backs Blackmun J's dissent. The majority's reasoning in *Sale* is subject to almost universal criticism by US,[53] as well as international, legal scholars.[54] The Executive Committee of UNHCR was also quick to condemn the outcome of the case: 'UNHCR considers the Court's decision a setback to modern international refugee law which has been developing for more than forty years, since the end of World War II. It renders the work of the Office of the High Commissioner in its global refugee protection role more difficult and sets a very unfortunate example.'[55]

---

[49] Ibid 193.   [50] Ibid 194–5.   [51] Ibid 197.   [52] Ibid 201.

[53] See, eg, Thomas David Jones, 'Sale v Haitian Centers Council, Inc' (1994) 88 *American Journal of International Law* 114; Harold Hongju Koh, 'Reflections on *Refoulement* and *Haitian Centers Council*' (1994) 35 *Harvard International Law Journal* 1; Stephen Legomsky, 'The USA and the Caribbean Interdiction Program' (2006) 18 *International Journal of Refugee Law* 677, 687–92.

[54] See, eg, Thomas Gammeltoft-Hansen, *Access to Asylum: International Refugee Law and the Globalisation of Migration Control* (Cambridge University Press, 2011) 122; James Hathaway, *The Rights of Refugees under International Law* (Cambridge University Press, 2005) 336–9; Guy Goodwin-Gill, 'The Haitian Refoulement Case: A Comment' (1994) 6 *International Journal of Refugee Law* 103, 103–9.

[55] 'UN High Commissioner for Refugees Responds to US Supreme Court Decision in Sale v Haitian Centers Council' (1993) 32 *International Legal Materials* 1215. For an elaboration of the UNHCR position, see Executive Committee of the High Commissioner's Programme, *Interception of Asylum-Seekers and Refugees: The International Framework and Recommendations for a Comprehensive Approach*, 18th standing mtg, UN Doc EC/50/SC/CRP.17 (9 June 2000) [10].

A similar view was affirmed by the Inter-American Commission on Human Rights when it was called upon to determine the legality of the US Haitian interdiction program. The Commission rejected the Supreme Court's approach in *Sale*, interpreting art 33 of the *Refugee Convention* as operating extraterritorially in the context of migrant interdiction on the high seas.[56] The decision in *Sale* also directly contradicts advice provided to the government by its own Office of Legal Counsel back in 1981 when the Haitian interdiction program was established. This advice concluded that even on the high seas, art 33 created an obligation for the United States to ensure that interdicted Haitians 'who claim they will be persecuted ... [are] given an opportunity to substantiate their claims'.[57]

The widespread criticism of the legal reasoning adopted in the case, the fact that the outcome contradicted the government's earlier legal advice and the plausibility of the construction put forward in Blackmun J's dissent all indicate that the alternative interpretation recognising the extraterritorial effect of the *non-refoulement* obligations under the *Refugee Convention* and *INA* was at the very least open to the judges in *Sale*.

In the immediate aftermath of the Supreme Court's decision in *Sale*, concerns were raised that it would provide a green light for other nations to engage in push-back operations. *The New York Times* queried whether 'this ruling by one of the most influential courts in the world [could] set a tempting precedent, particularly for developing nations? If the United States, with the imprimatur of its highest court, appears to put the protection of its borders above its responsibilities under international law, will others be enticed to follow suit?'[58]

This concern turned out to be well founded. But it is interesting to note that the *New York Times* was wrong to single out 'developing nations', with the influence of the US interdiction practices having the most direct influence on wealthy liberal democracies such as Australia.

4.2 Australia's Interdiction and 'Push-Back' Operations

Australia's reaction to its first large-scale experience of asylum-seeker boat arrivals was relatively restrained. The asylum seekers from Vietnam, who arrived in Australia from 1976 to 1981, were provided with hostel accommodation and generous settlement services. The second group of boat arrivals to reach Australia mostly consisted of Cambodian, Sino-Vietnamese and Chinese nationals, who travelled to Australia between 1989 and 1995. As discussed in Chapter 3, the Australian government's response to these arrivals was to introduce a system of mandatory immigration detention. The introduction of maritime

---

[56] *Haitian Center for Human Rights v United States*, Case 10.675, Inter-Am Comm'HR, Report No 51/96, OEA/Ser.L/V/II.95, doc 7 rev ¶ 550 (1997) [156]–[157]. For an analysis of this case, see Itamar Mann, 'Dialectic of Transnationalism: Unauthorised Migration and Human Rights, 1993–2013' (2013) 54 *Harvard International Law Journal* 315, 356–7.

[57] 'Proposed Interdiction of Haitian Flag Vessels' (1981) 5 *Opinions of the Office Legal Counsel of the United States Department of Justice* 242, 248. Note, however, that after contrary views were expressed by the legal advisor to the State Department, this Office of Legal Counsel opinion was withdrawn: see Lory Rosenberg, 'International Association of Refugee Law Judges Conference: The Courts and Interception – The United States' Interdiction Experience and its Impact on Refugees and Asylum Seekers' (2003) 17 *Georgetown Immigration Law Journal* 199, 201.

[58] Deborah Sontag, 'Reneging on Refuge: The Haitian Precedent', *New York Times* (online), 27 June 1993 www.nytimes.com/1993/06/27/weekinreview/reneging-on-refuge-the-haitian-precedent.html.

interdiction and extraterritorial processing measures can be broadly viewed as a response to a new flow of boats carrying asylum seekers from Iraq and Afghanistan. The immediate trigger for the policy change was the rescue at sea of 433 asylum seekers by a Norwegian-registered container ship, *MV Tampa*, in August of 2001.[59] A diplomatic row erupted over where the rescuees should be delivered. Reflecting the climate of public unease with the increasing number of unauthorised arrivals, Prime Minister John Howard decided to prevent the delivery of the rescuees to Australia. When initial negotiations failed to convince the ship's captain to change course, Australian Special Air Service troops were deployed to board the vessel and prevent it from entering Australian territorial waters. After a five-day stand-off, the crisis was resolved when agreements were reached with New Zealand and Nauru for rescuees to be transferred to those countries to have their protection claims assessed.

At the time, the Australian government did not have statutory powers that authorised the actions that were taken against the passengers of the *MV Tampa*. Two years earlier, the *Border Protection Legislation Amendment Act 1999* (Cth) had inserted provisions into the *Migration Act 1958* (Cth) ('*Migration Act*') authorising maritime interdiction activities.[60] However, these provisions only allowed interdicted persons to be detained at sea and brought to Australia. The provisions did not authorise transfer to locations outside Australia.[61] Given the absence of statutory authority, the government purported to be acting pursuant to the executive's 'prerogative power'. This claim was challenged in *Ruddock v Vadarlis*, which is examined later in this section.[62]

In the immediate aftermath of the *Tampa* incident, the Australian Parliament enacted a series of legislative reforms that retrospectively validated the executive's response,[63] and introduced new provisions to deprive future unauthorised boat arrivals of access to regular Australian asylum procedures. The scheme, which became known as the 'Pacific Solution' and later the 'Pacific Strategy', involved two main initiatives. The first was the offshore processing regime established in Nauru and Manus Island. This is explored in detail in Chapter 5. The second strategy was a maritime interdiction program dubbed 'Operation Relex'. The Royal Australian Navy was deployed to intercept unauthorised boats attempting to enter Australia. Interceptions took place when boats entered Australia's contiguous zone, which extends twenty-four nautical miles from the Australian coast. The Navy would then attempt to tow or escort intercepted vessels back to the edge of Indonesian territorial waters. If these attempts failed, the asylum seekers aboard the vessels were transferred to Manus Island or Nauru for processing of their claims. The so-called 'push-back' operations

---

[59] For a detailed analysis of the incident, see Mary Crock and Daniel Ghezelbash, 'Do Loose Lips Bring Ships?: The Role of Policy, Politics and Human Rights in Managing Unauthorised Boat Arrivals' (2010) 19 *Griffith Law Review* 238; Mary Crock, 'In the Wake of *Tampa*: Conflicting Visions of International Refugee Law in the Management of Refugee Flows' (2003) 12 *Pacific Rim Law & Policy Journal* 49; Chantal Marie-Jeanne Bostock, 'The International Legal Obligations Owed to the Asylum Seekers on the MV Tampa' (2002) 14 *International Journal of Refugee Law* 279.

[60] *Migration Act* pt 2 div 12A.

[61] See former s 245F(9) of the *Migration Act*, inserted by the *Border Protection Legislation Amendment Act 1999* (Cth).

[62] *Ruddock v Vadarlis* (2001) 110 FCR 491.

[63] *Border Protection (Validation and Enforcement Powers) Act 2001* (Cth) ss 5 and 6 (providing that any action taken between 27 August 2001 and 27 September 2001 by the Commonwealth in relation to the MV Tampa and other vessels carrying passengers attempting 'to enter Australia unlawfully' and any person who was on board such a vessel 'is taken for all purposes to have been lawful when it occurred').

were carried out pursuant to amendments to the *Migration Act* that authorised the transfer of interdicted vessels and their passengers 'to a place outside Australia'.[64]

There is ample evidence demonstrating that both the interdiction and extraterritorial processing elements of the Pacific Solution were modelled on US policy. The similarities in the extraterritorial processing regimes are examined in Chapter 5. In relation to interdiction, Operation Relex operated in a very similar way to the US interdiction program that was in force from March 1992 to March 1994, during which boats carrying Haitian asylum seekers were intercepted and returned to their point of departure with no screening of asylum claims. The clear similarities between Operation Relex and the US interdiction program raise a strong presumption that legal and policy transfer has occurred. Such a view is supported by evidence that policymakers in Australia had direct knowledge of the US precedent. The bilateral and multilateral forums discussed in Chapter 3 provided ample *opportunity* for US and Australian policymakers to meet and share information on interdiction activities. The key forums discussed there were networks operating within international organisations (as well as the informal bilateral discussions that occur on the sidelines of these meetings); Regional Consultative Processes such as the Five Country Conferences and the Intergovernmental Consultations on Asylum; and bilateral avenues of communication such as ad hoc meetings, staff exchanges, fact-finding missions and migration policy attachés based in the Australian Embassy in Washington and the US Embassy in Canberra. In terms of direct evidence of legal and policy transfer, the Bills Digest accompanying the *Border Protection (Validation and Enforcement Powers) Act 2001* refers to the US precedent.[65] This Act was the first of a series passed in the immediate aftermath of the *Tampa* incident to retrospectively authorise the actions taken against that vessel and establish the legislative framework underpinning interdiction and offshore processing. The Bills Digest includes a section titled 'United States Analogy', which sets out a detailed history of US interdiction and extraterritorial processing.[66]

A senior US policymaker interviewed by the author confirmed that they had provided Australian policymakers extensive advice relating to the US experience with interdiction and extraterritorial processing in the immediate lead-up to the introduction of the Pacific Solution.[67] This interview subject was a former senior bureaucrat who had been one of the key architects of the US extraterritorial processing policies in the Caribbean in the 1990s. The policymaker reported sharing detailed advice relating to the US experience with Haitian arrivals with officials from Australia's Department of Foreign Affairs and Trade and the Department of Immigration, as well as with the Australian Ambassador in Geneva. The policymaker was based in Geneva at the time the *Tampa* crisis unfolded, and was consulted on a daily basis by Australian officials in the immediate aftermath of the incident.

Operation Relex operated from 28 August 2001 to 12 March 2002. During this time, a total of twelve asylum-seeker boats were intercepted by the Australian Navy.[68] Of these, 4 boats, with some 600 asylum seekers on board, were successfully forced back to Indonesia.

---

[64] See *Migration Act* ss 245F(9) and (9A), amended by the *Border Protection (Validation and Enforcement Powers) Act 2001* (Cth).

[65] Nathan Hancock, '*Border Protection (Validation and Enforcement Powers) Bill 2001*' (Bills Digest No 62 2001–02, Parliamentary Library, Parliament of Australia, 2001) 14–16.

[66] Ibid.   [67] USB19.

[68] For a detailed account of what happened to each of these vessels, see Adreas Schloenhardt and Colin Craig, 'Turning Back the Boats: Australia's Interdiction of Irregular Migrants at Sea' (2015) 27 *International Journal of Refugee Law* 536.

The other eight were intercepted but could not safely make the journey back, either because they had broken down or because they had been sabotaged by asylum seekers in an attempt to stop their return. The passengers aboard these vessels were transferred to Nauru or Manus Island. Operation Relex was replaced by Operation Relex II, which continued until 16 July 2006. This operation only involved the successful return of one vessel to Indonesia.

Maritime interdiction continued under the Rudd Labor government, which came to power in late 2007. But the policy of returning vessels to Indonesia was abandoned. Instead, vessels were issued with warnings about the penalties attached to migrant-smuggling offences in Australia and told to return to Indonesia. Where these warnings failed to dissuade the migrant vessel from continuing its journey (as they often did), the boat would be boarded and escorted to Christmas Island, an Australian territory in the Indian Ocean.

Over the next few years the number of asylum seekers attempting to reach Australia began to increase. Consisting of mostly Iranian, Sri Lankan, Afghani and Syrian asylum seekers, the size of this new group of arrivals soon outstripped anything Australia had experienced before. More than 50,000 asylum seekers travelled by boat to Australia between 2009 and 2013.[69] The Coalition government was elected in September 2013 on a policy platform which promised to 'stop the boats'. Immediately upon coming to office, Prime Minister Tony Abbott launched Operation Sovereign Borders, a military-led initiative to deter and prevent asylum seekers reaching Australia by sea. Turn-backs were to be used alongside a suite of other policies aimed at containing and deterring unauthorised boat arrivals. As of April 2017, the government had intercepted and returned thirty boats carrying approximately 765 people as part of Operation Sovereign Borders.[70]

The majority of these turn-back operations involved the return of asylum-seeker boats to the edge of Indonesia's waters, often without the cooperation of the Indonesian government. There have also been at least four reports of asylum-seeker vessels being intercepted en route to Australia from Sri Lanka and their passengers being handed over to Sri Lankan authorities on the high seas.[71] Whereas the asylum seekers returned to Indonesia have not been subject to any screening processes, the Sri Lankan asylum seekers were subject to

---

[69] See Appendix, Table A.2.

[70] Interview with Peter Dutton and AVM Stephen Osborne, Commander JATF (Press conference, Austal Ship Yard, Western Australia, 7 April 2017) www.minister.border.gov.au/peterdutton/2017/Pages/press-conference-07042017.aspx.

[71] Forty-one Sri Lankan asylum seekers were intercepted and handed over to Sri Lankan authorities in June 2014: Daniel Hurst, 'Australia Returns Asylum Seekers to Sri Lanka in Sea Transfer', *The Guardian* (online), 7 July 2014, www.theguardian.com/world/2014/jul/07/australia-asylum-seekers-sri-lanka-sea-transfer. Thirty-seven Sri Lankan asylum seekers were intercepted near the Indonesian coast by Australian authorities and handed over to the Sri Lankan navy in November 2014: Nick Pedley, 'Australian Authorities Turn Back 37 Sri Lankan Asylum Seekers Near Indonesian Coast', *ABC News* (online), 29 November 2014 www.abc.net.au/news/2014-11-29/australian-authorities-turn-back-37-sri-lankan-asylum-seekers/5927436. Four Sri Lankan asylum seekers were similarly returned to Sri Lankan authorities after the boat they were travelling on was intercepted in February 2015: Louise Yaxley, 'Government Defends Decision to Send Four Men Back to Sri Lanka Whose Boat Was Intercepted as Part of "People Smuggling Venture"', *ABC News* (online), 20 February 2015 www.abc.net.au/news/2015-02-20/federal-govt-defends-sending-four-men-back-to-sri-lanka/6155204. Additionally, twelve Sri Lankan asylum seekers were returned on 6 May 2016 after reaching Australia's Cocos Islands, a remote group of islands between Sri Lanka and the west coast of Australia: 'Australia Sends Back Sri Lankan Asylum Seekers', *BBC News* (online), 9 May 2016 www.bbc.com/news/world-australia-36222959.

summary screenings at sea via teleconference.[72] In this regard, there are clear parallels with the current iteration of the US interdiction program (operating since 1995) where asylum seekers are subject to summary screening procedures at sea.

The Australian government has also invested in purchasing vessels to be used in the return of migrants in situations where interdicted vessels are unseaworthy and cannot make the journey back to Indonesia. These are presumably to prevent the sabotage of vessels and associated loss of life that marred Operation Relex.[73] Initially, custom-built orange life boats were used, but recent reports indicated that these have been replaced by a fleet of Vietnamese-built wooden vessels, resembling Asian fishing boats.[74] The need for such vessels underscores one of the differences between the Australian and US interdiction operations. The United States has entered into various bilateral agreements which authorise the US Coast Guard to enter the territorial waters of certain Caribbean nations for the purpose of carrying out interdiction activities and returning interdicted vessels.[75] Australia does not have any equivalent agreement with Indonesia. As such, vessels are left at the edge of Indonesia's territorial sea and must be sea-worthy to undertake the twelve-nautical-mile trip to the coastline.[76] Sri Lanka and Vietnam have been more willing to cooperate with Australia in relation to accepting the return of interdicted migrants.

Another important distinction between US and Australian interdiction activities relates to the location of interception. The United States generally intercepts and returns boats before they reach US waters (either in international waters, or the territorial sea of other nations).[77] In contrast, there are numerous reports of Australian authorities returning boats intercepted in Australian territorial waters, and in some cases, boats that had reached Australia's northern outlying islands.[78] This distinction has important ramifications under international law, which are explored in Chapter 6.

The statutory basis for the current interdiction regime is the *Maritime Powers Act 2013* (Cth) ('*MPA*'). This Act consolidates the Commonwealth's existing maritime enforcement powers, including those previously included in the *Migration Act*,[79] into a single framework.[80] The key relevant provision, s 72(4), states that where a maritime officer suspects a vessel has been involved in a contravention of Australian law, including the *Migration Act*,

---

[72] See Chapter 5, n 225 and accompanying text. [73] Schloenhardt and Craig, above n 68, 562–3.
[74] Ben Doherty and Helen Davidson, 'Orange Lifeboats Used to Return Asylum Seekers to Be Replaced by "Fishing Boats"' *The Guardian* (online) 4 March 2015 www.theguardian.com/australia-news/2015/mar/05/orange-lifeboats-used-to-return-asylum-seekers-to-be-replaced-by-fishing-boats.
[75] See, eg, *Agreement Effected by Exchange of Notes Regarding Migrants and Interdiction*, US–Haiti, 33 UST 3559, TIAS 10241 (signed and entered into force 23 September 1981); *Agreement Concerning Cooperation in Maritime Migration Law Enforcement*, US–Dominican Republic, TIAS 03-520 (signed and entered into force 20 May 2003); *Agreement Concerning Cooperation in Maritime Law Enforcement*, US–Dominican Republic, TIAS 04-629 (signed and entered into force 29 June 2004).
[76] Schloenhardt and Craig, above n 68, 565.
[77] Dastyari, above n 6, 3. The US has in the past returned asylum seekers intercepted in its territorial sea who have not yet made landfall. A 1993 legal opinion issued by the Department of Justice's Office of Legal Counsel concluded that such migrants were not covered by the *non-refoulement* obligations in the *Refugee Convention* or municipal US law: 'Immigration Consequences of Undocumented Aliens' Arrival in United States Territorial Waters' (1993) 17 *Opinions of the Office of Legal Counsel of the United States Department of Justice* 77.
[78] Schloenhardt and Craig, above n 68, 549–50.
[79] See former pt 2 div 12A of the *Migration Act*; see above nn 60–1 and accompanying text.
[80] Explanatory Memorandum, Maritime Powers Bill 2012 (Cth) 1.

a maritime officer may detain the person and take them to a place inside or outside Australia's migration zone.[81]

In response to the *CPCF v MIBP* litigation examined later in this section,[82] the government passed the *Migration and Maritime Powers Legislation Amendment (Resolving the Asylum Legacy Caseload) Act 2014* (Cth) ('*Legacy Caseload Act*'), which included a raft of changes to the *MPA* that greatly expanded the executive's powers to interdict, detain and transfer asylum seekers at sea.[83] Most significantly, the amendments stipulate that when carrying out maritime powers, an authorising officer is not required to consider Australia's international obligations, or the international obligations or domestic law of another country.[84] Additionally, the amendments stipulate that authorisation of maritime powers under the Act is not invalid if inconsistent with Australia's international obligations.[85] As such, there are no legal safeguards in place to ensure that Australia does not breach its *non-refoulement* obligations by returning a person to a place where they face persecution contrary to the *Refugee Convention*, or to a situation where they are in danger of death, torture or other mistreatment. Other amendments authorise potentially long-term detention at sea;[86] restrict the application of the rules of natural justice from applying to most maritime powers under the Act;[87] and restrict the capacity of the courts to review government actions at sea in a number of other ways.[88] The government continues to claim that its interdiction activities are also authorised under its non-statutory prerogative power.

Ruddock v Vadarlis dealt with the actions of the Australian government against the passengers of the *MV Tampa* in 2001.[89] The case was heard while the vessel was under the control of Australian Special Armed Service troops off Christmas Island. Eric Vadarlis and the Victorian Council for Civil Liberties commenced proceedings in the Federal Court against the Minister for Immigration and a number of other Commonwealth officers in an attempt to force the government to bring the asylum seekers to shore.[90] The first hurdle to overcome was the issue of standing. While the lawyers had received a letter from the rescuees, they were unable to obtain direct instructions for the purpose of mounting a legal challenge under the *Migration Act*.[91] Given the lack of direct instructions, the public

---

[81] These provisions reflect the former s 245F(9)–(9A) of the *Migration Act*. [82] (2015) 255 CLR 514.
[83] *Legacy Caseload Act* sch 1.   [84] *MPA* s 22A(1)(a).   [85] *MPA* s 22A(1)(c).
[86] The Minister is authorised to detain passengers of an interdicted vessel for as long as a decision is made on where the indertictees should be transferred: *MPA* s 75A(1)(c).
[87] *MPA* s 22B, which relates to the authorisation powers under pt 2 div 2, and s 75B, which relates to the exercise of powers under ss 69, 69A, 71, 72, 72A, 74, 75D, 75F, 75G or 75H.
[88] These include exclusion of review by the Federal Court under the *Administrative Decisions (Judicial Review) Act 1977* (Cth) of certain decisions (see, eg, new ss 75D and 75H) and the provisions discussed above which state that the exercise of certain maritime powers are not invalid due to a failure to consider, or inconsistency with, Australia's international obligations.
[89] (2001) 110 FCR 491.   [90] *Victorian Council for Civil Liberties v MIMA* ('*VCCL*') (2001) 110 FCR 452.
[91] Vadarlis argued that s 245F(9), which confers on officers the power to board ships, applies to the rescuees and requires the government to bring the rescuees to mainland Australia. He contended further that the mandatory detention provisions contained in s 189 of the Act applied to the rescuees and required the respondents to take the rescuees into detention. The application for mandamus to compel the respondents to perform these statutory duties was dismissed on the grounds that Vadarlis did not have standing: *VCCL* (2001) 110 FCR 452, 467–68 [45]–[48] (North J); *Ruddock v Vadarlis* (2001) 110 FCR 491, 529–30 [151]–[152] (French J). Vadarlis also claimed that the government's refusal to give him access to the rescuees constituted a breach of his implied constitutional right to freedom of communication. He

advocates only had standing to seek an order in the nature of habeas corpus, requiring the respondents to bring the rescuees to Australia.[92] Two requirements had to be met for the writ to issue. First, the rescuees had to be 'detained' by the government. This required a determination that the government was imposing total restraint on their movement. Second, it needed to be shown that this detention was not authorised by law. The government purported to be acting outside of the statutory regime set up by the *Migration Act*. This was because if this Act was to apply, the rescuees would have to be transferred into immigration detention in Australia and afforded an opportunity to claim asylum.[93] Instead, the government argued that the executive had a non-statutory 'prerogative power' which authorised its actions. The determinative question in this regard was whether such a power existed.

The trial judge, North J, held that the circumstances amounted to a total restraint on the freedom of the rescuees attributable to the government. On the second question, North J concluded that there was no non-statutory prerogative power to detain non-citizens for the purpose of expulsion. If there ever had been such a power, North J reasoned that it was extinguished by the comprehensive provisions contained in the *Migration Act* dealing with the subject. Detention could only be authorised if it was pursuant to the *Migration Act*, and to the extent that the government purported to be acting outside the Act, detention was unlawful. Accordingly, orders were made directing the Commonwealth to bring ashore and release the asylum seekers.

In *Ruddock v Vadarlis*, the Full Federal Court overturned the primary judge's ruling in a 2:1 majority decision.[94] Black CJ, in dissent, would have dismissed the appeal on similar grounds relied upon in the primary decision. French J, joined by Beaumont J, disagreed with North J's and Black CJ's analysis of the two key questions. On the question of whether the rescuees were being detained by the government, French J invoked the 'three walled prison' concept constructed by the High Court in *Chu Kheng Lim v MILGEA* ('*Lim*').[95] His Honour reasoned that the rescuees were not being detained as they were free to travel anywhere they wished, except to Australia.[96] French J went on to conclude that even if the rescuees were being detained, such detention would be authorised pursuant to the government's executive power conferred by s 61 of the *Australian Constitution*.[97] His Honour distinguished between the old royal prerogative powers and the constitutional executive power, finding that the former had been subsumed by the latter upon the creation of the

---

unsuccessfully sought an injunction and mandamus to allow him to give legal advice to the rescuees: *VCCL* (2001) 100 FCR 452, 489–90 [162]–[168] (North J).

[92] *VCCL* (2001) 110 FCR 452, 469 [56] (North J); *Ruddock v Vadarlis* (2001) 110 FCR 491, 509 [66] (Black CJ), 518 [108] (Beaumont J). The *Federal Court of Australia Act 1976* (Cth), which sets out the powers of the Federal Court, does not explicitly mention the writ of habeas corpus. This has led to divided opinions as to whether the Court has the power to issue such a writ: see David Clark, 'Jurisdiction and Power: Habeas Corpus and the Federal Court' (2006) 32 *Monash University Law Review* 275 (arguing that the Federal Court judges have been incorrect in their conclusion that they do not have the power to issue habeas corpus writs). It is accepted, however, that the Court has the power to issue a writ *in the nature* of habeas corpus, which is essentially a mandatory injunction: *Ruddock v Vadarlis* (2001) 110 FCR 491, 518 [107] (Beaumont J).

[93] See above nn 60–1 and accompanying text.   [94] (2001) 110 FCR 491.

[95] (1992) 176 CLR 1, 34 (Brennan, Deane and Dawson JJ); see Chapter 3, n 207 and accompanying text.

[96] *Ruddock v Vadarlis* (2001) 110 FCR 491, 548 [214].

[97] Section 61 of the *Australian Constitution* provides that 'the executive power of the Commonwealth is vested in the Queen and is exercisable by the Governor-General'.

Australian Constitution. The executive power authorises the executive to prevent the entry of non-citizens and to do all things necessary to effect such exclusion (including detention). Whereas the old prerogative power could be superseded by legislation which operates in the same area, the executive power could only be displaced by clear and unambiguous legislative intention.[98] This is particularly so in cases where the executive power is of great significance to national sovereignty.[99] While detailed and comprehensive, the provisions of the *Migration Act* dealing with the entry and removal of non-citizens were construed as not demonstrating an intention to override the executive of its non-statutory power to prevent the entry of non-citizens into Australian waters.[100] Vadarlis sought leave to appeal to the High Court. However, the Court declined to entertain the appeal, as by that stage, the rescuees had been transferred to Nauru and New Zealand.[101]

Much like the *Sale* decision in the United States, the majority's decision in *Ruddock v Vadarlis* has been the subject of intense academic criticism.[102] In reaching the conclusion that the rescuees were not detained as they were free to go anywhere other than Australia, French J relied on the High Court's decision in *Lim*. As Mary Crock points out, however, that characterisation of immigration detention in *Lim* had been repeatedly and roundly rejected by the UN Human Rights Committee and by the European Court of Human Rights.[103] This point is also made by Black CJ in his dissenting opinion.[104]

The majority's broad construction of the executive power is also questionable. French J's assertion that the boundaries of the Commonwealth executive power should not be determined with reference to the content of the prerogative power deviates from precedent.[105] The approach is also at odds with the context of imperial and colonial history in which the constitutional provision was drafted.[106] George Winterton argues that French J's approach

---

[98] *Ruddock v Vadarlis* (2001) 110 FCR 491, 540-1 [183]–[185], 545-6 [204] (French J).
[99] Ibid 543 [193], 545 [202] (French J).   [100] Ibid 545 [202] (French J).
[101] Transcript of Proceedings, *Vadarlis v MIMA* [2001] HCATrans 625 (27 November 2001).
[102] See, eg, George Winterton, 'The Relationship Between Commonwealth Legislative and Executive Power' (2004) 25 *Adelaide Law Review* 21; Bradley Selway, 'All at Sea: Constitutional Assumptions and "The Executive Power of the Commonwealth"' (2003) 31 *Federal Law Review* 495; Simon Evans, 'The Rule of Law, Constitutionalism and the MV Tampa' (2002) 13 *Public Law Review* 94; Mary Crock, 'Durable Solutions or Politics of Misery: Refugee Protection in Australia after Tampa' in Natalie Bolzan, Michael Darcey and Jan Mason (eds), *Fenced Out, Fenced In: Border Protection, Asylum and Detention in Australia* (Common Ground Publishing, 2006) 23; Mary Crock, 'In the Wake of *Tampa*', above n 59; Peter Gerangelos, 'The Executive Power of the Commonwealth of Australia: Section 61 of the Commonwealth Constitution, "Nationhood" and the Future of the Prerogative' (2012) 12 *Oxford University Commonwealth Law Journal* 97.
[103] Mary Crock and Laurie Berg, *Immigration, Refugees and Forced Migration: Law, Policy and Practice in Australia* (Federation Press, 2011) 52, 97; referring to Human Rights Committee, *Views: Communication No 560/1993*, 59th sess, UN Doc CCPR/C/59/D/560/1993 (30 April 1997) ('*A v Australia*') and *Amuur v France* [1996] III Eur Court HR 826.
[104] *Ruddock v Vadarlis* (2001) 110 FCR 491, 510 [73].
[105] Selway, above n 102, 501, referring to the High Court decision in *Re Residential Tenancies Tribunal (NSW); Ex parte Defence Housing Authority* (1997) 190 CLR 410, 438 as authority for this point. There, Dawson, Toohey and Gaudron JJ held that the power conferred by s 61 included 'the prerogative of the Crown because the setting in which the Crown is invested with the executive power is that of the common law and the prerogatives of the Crown are those rights, powers, privileges and immunities it possesses at common law.' See also Winterton, above n 102, 35; Gerangalos, above n 102, 116 (noting that *Vadarlis* 'constitutes a decisive step beyond what may have been suggested in earlier cases').
[106] Selway, above n 102, 505. See also Evans, above n 102, 97.

involves abandoning the long-standing principle that the common law should be used to interpret both statutes and constitutions.[107] For Winterton, the prerogative, despite its uncertainty, 'constitutes a substantial body of principles, rules and precedents, established over hundreds of years'.[108] Such principles provide clearer guidance than vague notions of sovereignty and what is 'appropriate' for national governments.[109]

The second line of criticism targets French J's conclusion that the executive power to prevent the entry of non-citizens had not been abrogated by the passage of the *Migration Act*.[110] Again, this conclusion is not derived from any precedent[111] and 'ignores the history of the executive power since the 17th century [which] demonstrates progressive constitutionalisation, moderation, and republicanisation'.[112] This history supports the conclusion that even if the executive power encompassed a power to detain non-citizens for the purpose of exclusion at federation, this power was abrogated by the legislative action of passing the relevant provisions on interdiction and exclusion contained in the *Migration Act*. Simon Evans argues that this position is correct when one considers the legislative intention behind the passage of those provisions, querying whether it is 'realistic to imagine that the Parliament intended to enact in clear and general terms that a person attempting to enter Australia unlawfully must be taken into immigration detention by an officer, but to leave open to the officer an alternative non-statutory option with none of the safeguards of immigration detention?'[113]

This criticism, combined with the fact that two out of the four judges who heard the case at trial and appeal upheld the habeas challenge (including the most senior judge of the group, Black CJ), illustrates that, at the very least, a reasonable alternative construction was available to that which was adopted by the majority of the Full Federal Court.

The High Court had an opportunity to examine some of the issues raised in *Ruddock v Vadarlis* in its 2015 decision in *CPCF v MIBP* ('*CPCF*').[114] The case concerned a challenge to the detention at sea of one of a group of 157 Sri Lankan asylum seekers interdicted en route to Australia. The Indian-flagged vessel on which the group was travelling was intercepted on 29 June 2014 by an Australian Customs vessel in Australia's contiguous zone. The asylum seekers were transferred to the Australian vessel, where they were detained while diplomatic negotiations were undertaken to return them to India. They remained aboard the Customs vessel until 27 July 2014, when a decision was made to disembark the passengers to Cocos (Keeling) Island, an Australian territory in the Indian Ocean. Subsequently, the asylum seekers were moved to the offshore processing facility on Nauru.

---

[107] Winterton, above n 102.   [108] Ibid 35.
[109] Note that French J went on to become the Chief Justice of the High Court. Under his leadership, the Court further developed and implemented His Honour's expansive view of the executive power. See *Pape v Commissioner of Taxation* (2009) 238 CLR 1, and follow-up discussion in *Williams v the Commonwealth* (2012) 248 CLR 156 and *Williams v the Commonwealth* (2014) 252 CLR 416 (finding the executive power includes a power to engage in actions peculiarly adapted to a national government and that these powers exist separately from those derived from the prerogative, statute and its capacities as a person.)
[110] See *Ruddock v Vadarlis* (2001) 110 FCR 491, 540 [183].
[111] Winterton, above n 102, 47 (arguing that 'it may be doubted whether the cases upon which French J relied upon [to reach this conclusion] represent current Australian authority').
[112] Evans, above n 102, 98.   [113] Ibid.   [114] (2015) 255 CLR 514.

The key legal issue was that of wrongful imprisonment, namely whether the detention of the plaintiff for almost one month on the Australian vessel was lawful. As already discussed, following *Ruddock v Vadarlis*, the government had introduced a comprehensive legislative framework for maritime interdiction activities.[115] This was later consolidated into the *Maritime Powers Act 2013* (Cth) ('*MPA*'). The Commonwealth's argument was that its actions were authorised under s 72(4) of the *MPA*, which provided that where a maritime officer suspects a vessel has been involved in a contravention of an Australian law (including the *Migration Act*):[116]

> A maritime officer may detain the person and take the person, or cause the person to be taken:
>
> (a) To a place in the migration zone; or
> (b) To a place outside the migration zone, including a place outside Australia.[117]

In the alternative, the Commonwealth argued that detention was authorised by the non-statutory executive power of the Commonwealth derived from s 61 of the *Australian Constitution*. This drew on the majority's reasoning in *Ruddock v Vadarlis*, where French J noted that the Commonwealth executive power included the power 'to prevent the entry of non-citizens and to do such things as necessary to effect such exclusion'.[118]

The plaintiff argued that his detention was not authorised by the *MPA* as the decision to take him to India was invalid. He contended that detention was unlawful because there was no assurance he would be allowed to disembark in India. The plaintiff sought to rely on the High Court's ruling in *Lim* that a Commonwealth statute authorising executive detention must limit the duration of incarceration to what is reasonably capable of being seen as necessary to effect an identified statutory purpose which is reasonably capable of being achieved.[119] The lack of agreement with India for disembarkation created uncertainty regarding the possible duration of detention. It was argued that this took the duration of the plaintiff's detention beyond something reasonably capable of being seen as necessary to effect removal. The plaintiff's second argument relied on the fact that there was no legal guarantee of *non-refoulement* by India. Finally, the plaintiff contended that the majority's ruling on the executive power in *Ruddock v Vadarlis* was incorrect, arguing that even if an executive power to detain on the high seas had ever existed, it was extinguished by the *MPA*.[120]

By a narrow 4:3 majority, the High Court found that the detention of the plaintiff was authorised under s 72(4) of the *MPA*. Almost all the judges cited with approval the constitutional principle in *Lim*. That is, statutory detention provisions must be limited to what is reasonably capable of being seen to be necessary to effect an identified statutory purpose which is reasonably capable of being achieved.[121] However, they split on how

---

[115] See former div 12A of the *Migration Act*.   [116] See *MPA* ss 9, 17 and 18.
[117] These provisions reflect the former s 245F(9)–(9A) of the *Migration Act*.
[118] *Ruddock v Vadarlis* (2001) 110 FCR 491, 543 [193].
[119] *Lim* (1992) 176 CLR 1, 33–4 (Brennan, Deane and Dawson JJ); *CPCF v Minister for Immigration and Border Protection* (2015) 255 CLR 514 [196] (Crennan J) ('*CPCF*').
[120] A third argument alleged that the maritime officer responsible for detaining him and taking him towards India made the decision to do so at the dictation of the National Security Committee without exercising independent discretion as to where he should be taken. This argument was dismissed by all members of the Court and is beyond the scope of the present analysis.
[121] See, eg, *CPCF* (2015) 255 CLR 514, 579–80 [196], 584 [215]–[216] (Crennan J), 599 [273] (Kiefel J), 625 [374] (Gageler J).

this principle should be applied to the facts before them. The majority consisted of four separate judgments delivered by French CJ and Crennan, Keane and Gageler JJ. All rejected the plaintiff's argument that *Lim* created an implicit requirement in s 72(4) that detention be authorised only when the detainee has an existing right to disembark in the destination country.

French CJ noted that the statute could not be construed as authorising 'futile or entirely speculative taking'. However, it did authorise detention when there is knowledge or reasonable belief that the destination country would allow the person to enter its territory.[122] The ongoing diplomatic negotiations between Australian and Indian officials were sufficient to support this requisite reasonable belief. Crennan J found that while removal must be to a reasonable place and within a reasonable time, s 72(4) did not require certainty of disembarkation at a specific destination.[123] Gageler J adopted a similar approach, finding that the only limitation on the power was that it be exercised reasonably, in good faith and in accordance with the objects of the Act.[124]

The fourth member of the majority, Keane J, took a slightly different approach, but reached a similar conclusion. For Keane J, the decision to take the plaintiff and the other passengers to India was not made under the Act. Keane J interpreted s 72(4) as authorising only actions taken by a maritime officer. The decision to take the plaintiff to India was made by the Minister in consultation with the National Security Committee ('NSC'), not the maritime officer aboard the Australian Customs vessel. As s 72(4) was not a source of the decision-making power exercised by the executive, it was not a source of constraint on the power of the executive.[125] Instead, Keane J found the decision of the Minister and the NCP to take the plaintiff to India was authorised under the executive powers conferred by ss 61 and 64 of the *Australian Constitution*.[126] His Honour did stipulate, however, that the implementation of that decision was 'subject to such constraints as are expressed by, or necessarily implicit in, s 72(4)'.[127] This included requirements that the power be exercised with reference to the scope and purpose of the Act, and that 'taking' under s 72(4) be carried out in a reasonable time.[128] His Honour concluded that these constraints had not been breached in this case.

The dissenting judges held that s 72(4) of the *MPA* only authorised the removal of a person to a destination when, at the time the destination is chosen, the person taken has a right or permission to enter.[129] In addition to the *Lim* test, Hayne and Bell JJ (in a joint judgment) and Kiefel J referred to the High Court's ruling in *Plaintiff S4/2014 v MIBP* ('*Plaintiff S4*').[130] There, the Court said '[t]he duration of any form of detention, and thus its lawfulness, must be capable of being determined at any time and from time to time. Otherwise, the lawfulness of the detention could not be determined and enforced by the courts, and, ultimately by this Court'.[131]

Hayne and Bell JJ reasoned that the duration of detention was not capable of determination where uncertainty surrounds a person's right to enter a place chosen for the purposes of s 72(4). In such circumstances, 'the length of detention would depend upon the particular (unconstrained) decision to choose as the destination to which a person subject to s 72 of

---

[122] Ibid 540- 1 [46]–[50]. [123] Ibid 582 [205]–[207]. [124] Ibid 620 [360]–[361].
[125] Ibid 641 [450]. [126] Ibid 636 [423]. [127] Ibid 641 [450]. [128] Ibid 641-2 [450]–[453].
[129] Ibid 547 [71], 552 [92], 554 [99], 560-1 [123], 564 [135] (Hayne and Bell JJ); 609 [318] (Kiefel J).
[130] Ibid 553 [97] (Hayne and Bell JJ); 610 [321] (Kiefel J).
[131] *Plaintiff S4* (2014) 253 CLR 219, 232 [29]. See Chapter 3, nn 290–8 and accompanying text.

the [*MPA*] should be taken a place (or succession of places) which that person has no right or permission to enter'.[132]

They went on to reason that a construction of the statute that would authorise detention where there is a *hope* that a person may be allowed to land would raise serious concerns:

> How is a court (and ultimately this Court) to judge whether that hope has been explored with sufficient diligence to make the consequential detention not unduly, and thus not unlawfully prolonged? If neither a right to land nor an existing permission to do so is required, and hope of landing will do, what level of hope must exist?[133]

The difficulties in answering these questions make it impossible for a court to determine whether the person has been detained for longer than was reasonably necessary to be taken to his or her destination.

Kiefel J agreed that the valid exercise of the detention power under s 72(4) required certainty about the choice of place to which the plaintiff would be removed. A decision under s 72(4) must be 'limited to one place, which is identified at the time the decision is made as one where it is known that the detained person may be disembarked'.[134] To hold otherwise would result in a situation where the length of a person's detention is unknown. Such detention would fall foul of the principles from *Lim* and *Plaintiff S4* discussed previously in this chapter.

On the facts before them, most of the Justices found it unnecessary to address the question of whether the power to detain and transfer a person under s 72(4) was constrained by the *non-refoulement* provisions of the *Refugee Convention* and other human rights treaties. This was because there was no evidence before the Court that the plaintiff faced any risk of *refoulement* if returned to India. Nevertheless, the Justices provided some hints about how they would approach this question if the fact scenario was different.

French CJ and Keane and Gageler JJ all indicated that there was no basis for adopting a construction that limited the power conferred by s 72(4) by reference to Australia's *non-refoulement* obligations.[135] Given the dualist nature of Australia's legal system, international law does not form part of Australian law until it has been enacted in legislation. However, it is an accepted principle of statutory construction that 'a statute is to be interpreted and applied, as far as its language permits, so that it is in conformity and not in conflict with the established rules of international law'.[136] French CJ and Keane and Gageler JJ all indicated that this principle does not assist the plaintiff in this case, as both the text of the relevant provisions and the scope and purpose of the Act are clear and unambiguous.[137]

The judgments of Kiefel and Crennan JJ and the joint judgment delivered by Hayne and Bell JJ all leave open the possibility that the power under s 72(4) may be limited by Australia's *non-refoulement* obligations. Interestingly, it was Crennan J, who formed part of the majority in upholding the legality of the detention of the plaintiff, who gave the strongest indication that Australia's *non-refoulement* obligations may limit the power to transfer detainees under s 72(4). Her Honour stated that

> [t]he Refugees Convention is part of the context of the Act, considered widely. If the s 72(4)(b) power had been invoked to return the plaintiff to Sri Lanka or to take the

---

[132] *CPCF* (2015) 255 CLR 514, 554 [99]. [133] Ibid 554–5 [101]. [134] Ibid 609 [318].
[135] Ibid 528 [11] (French CJ); 604 [296] (Kiefel J); 627 [384] (Gageler J); 643–4 [462] (Keane J).
[136] *MIEA v Teoh* (1995) 183 CLR 273, 287, cited at ibid 627 [385] (Gageler J).
[137] *CPCF* (2015) 255 CLR 514, 528 [11] (French CJ), 627–8 [385]–[387] (Gageler J), 643–4 [462] (Keane J).

plaintiff to a place outside the migration zone which was not safe, questions might have arisen about an interpretation of s 72(4)(b) consistent with Australia's obligation under the Refugees Convention.[138]

A number of the Justices also noted that statutory protections included in the *MPA* impose similar protections to the *non-refoulement* obligations of the *Refugee Convention* and other human rights instruments. The power to detain and transfer a person under s 72(4) is limited by s 74 of the *MPA*, which provides that '[a] maritime officer must not place ... a person in a place, unless the officer is satisfied, on reasonable grounds that it is safe for the person to be in that place'. For Hayne and Bell JJ, this safeguard provides a similar scope of protection as found in the *Refugee Convention*:

> The reference in s 74 to a person being 'safe' in a place must be read as meaning safe from risk of physical harm. A decision-maker who considers whether he or she is satisfied, on reasonable grounds, that it is safe for a person to be in a place must ask and answer a different question from that inferentially imposed by the Refugees Convention. But there is a very considerable factual overlap between the two inquiries. Many who fear persecution for a Convention reason fear for their personal safety in their country of nationality.[139]

French CJ makes a similar observation, stating:

> [t]he content of the term 'safe for the person to be in that place' in s 74 may be evaluative and involve a risk assessment on the part of those directing or advising the relevant maritime officers. A place which presents a substantial risk that the person, if taken there, will be exposed to persecution or torture would be unlikely to meet the criterion 'that it is safe for the person to be in that place'. The constraint imposed by s 74 embraces risks of the kind to which the *non-refoulement* obligations under the Refugees Convention and Convention against Torture are directed. The existence of such risks may therefore amount to a mandatory relevant consideration in the exercise of the power under s 72(4) because they enliven the limit on that power which is imposed by s 74 at the point of discharge in the country to which the person is taken.[140]

Kiefel J took a slightly different approach, finding that s 74 only requires that a point of disembarkation for a person is, 'in its immediate physical aspects ... safe'.[141] It does not require that a maritime officer be satisfied that that place is one in which the person will not face a real risk of harm more generally. Meeting such an obligation would involve wider considerations than what is necessary to a decision under s 72(4).[142]

Only four out of the seven Justices in the case addressed the question of whether the executive power in s 61 of the Constitution extended to detention and removal of non-citizens seeking to enter Australia without authorisation. Having found that the detention of the plaintiff was authorised under the *MPA*, French CJ and Crennan and Gageler JJ indicated that it was not necessary to address this question.[143] The fourth member of the majority, Keane J, agreed that it was not strictly necessary to answer this question.[144] However, His Honour went on to do so at length in obiter dictum. Keane J endorsed the

---

[138] Ibid 585 [219].   [139] Ibid 556 [109].   [140] Ibid 528 [12].   [141] Ibid 604 [296].   [142] Ibid.
[143] Ibid 538–9 [42] (French CJ), 587 [229] (Crennan J), 630 [392] (Gageler J). Note that Gageler J rejected the claim that executive power extends to detaining non-citizens in the absence of statutory authority in *Plaintiff M68/2015 v MIBP* (2016) 257 CLR 42, 105–7 [162]–[166] ('*Plaintiff M68*').
[144] Ibid [476].

approach of the majority in *Ruddock v Vadarlis*.[145] He found that the Commonwealth had a non-statutory executive power to prevent non-citizens from entering Australia and to detain them for that purpose.[146] This power had not been abrogated by the *MPA* or the *Migration Act*.[147] Finally, this power to detain and remove was not constrained by Australia's *non-refoulement* obligations or the requirement of certainty of destination.[148]

Having found that the detention of the plaintiff was not authorised under the *MPA*, the three dissenting Justices all rejected the government's contention that the detention was authorised under the non-statutory executive power of the Commonwealth. Kiefel J adopted similar reasoning to Black CJ's dissent in *Ruddock v Vadarlis*. Her Honour found it doubtful that such a power ever existed in Australia,[149] but even if it did, it had since been displaced by the *MPA*.[150] Hayne and Bell JJ rejected the need to analyse the broad historical questions of whether the government has the inherent power to regulate who enters the nation's territory and to repel those who seek to do so without authority. Even if such a power is conceded, such considerations 'do not answer the questions about the scope of the power and the organ or organs of government which must exercise it'.[151] Instead, Their Honours asked more narrowly whether the 'executive power of the Commonwealth of itself provides legal authority for an officer of the Commonwealth to detain a person and thus commit a trespass?'[152] In answering this question in the negative, Hayne and Bell JJ relied on the following passage from the High Court's decision in *Lim*:

> Neither public official nor private person can lawfully detain [an alien who is within this country, whether lawfully or unlawfully] or deal with his or her property except under and in accordance with some positive authority conferred by the law. Since the common law knows neither letter de cachet nor other executive warrant authorising arbitrary arrest or detention, any officer of the Commonwealth Executive who purports to authorise or enforce the detention in custody of such an alien without judicial mandate will be acting lawfully only to the extent that his or her conduct is justified by valid statutory provisions.[153]

Like most of the cases examined in this book, the outcome in *CPCF* could easily have gone the other way. It was decided by a tight 4:3 majority and there was a lack of a uniform approach amongst the majority Justices. The majority consisted of four separate judgments. Keane J adopted a construction of the power conferred by the relevant statutory provisions that was significantly different from the other majority judges. French CJ and Gageler and Crennan JJ construed s 72(4) as the relevant source of power for both the maritime officers involved and the NSC that gave the order for removal. Keane J construed s 72(4) as only authorising actions of the maritime officers, finding that the decision of the NSC was made under the executive's non-statutory powers. There was also no clear ratio on the relevance of the *non-refoulement* obligations under the *Refugee Convention* and other Human Rights instruments or on the scope of the executive's non-statutory powers.

---

[145] Keane J quotes passages from French J's judgment in *Ruddock v Vadarlis* (2001) 110 FCR 491 with approval at ibid 648 [482] and 650 [489].
[146] *CPCF* (2015) 255 CLR 514, 647-50 [478]-[487].   [147] Ibid 650-1 [488]-[492].
[148] Ibid 651-2 [493]-[495].   [149] Ibid 599 [271].   [150] Ibid 600 [277], 601 [280].
[151] Ibid 565-6 [143] (footnotes omitted) (Hayne and Bell JJ).   [152] Ibid 567 [147].
[153] *Lim* (1992) 176 CLR 1, 19 (Brennan, Deane and Dawson JJ) (footnotes omitted), cited at ibid 567 [148].

4.3 Comparing the US and Australian Jurisprudence

The decisions in *Sale*, *Ruddock v Vadarlis* and *CPCF* were and remain highly contentious. This is a reflection of the fact that the relevant legal principles were far from clear in each case. This gave substantial discretionary leeway to the presiding judges when deciding whether to uphold the validity of interdiction activities. But as they stand, the majority judgements in each case share a number of similarities. In all three instances, it was held that the executive had broad powers to intercept and deflect asylum seekers attempting to enter their respective jurisdictions without authorisation. In the US case of *Sale*, the interdiction program was explicitly authorised in an Executive Order issued by the President.[154] The order was made pursuant to INA § 212(f), which confers authority on the President to suspend the entry of any class of aliens, or to impose on the entry of aliens any restrictions that the President may deem appropriate. In *Ruddock v Vadarlis*, the government's authority to carry out the interdiction program was less explicit. The majority accepted the government's claims that its activities were authorised under the executive power in s 61 of the *Australian Constitution*. Moreover, in both cases, the executive power was found not to be subject to the constraints of domestic statutory law. Both the *INA* and the *Migration Act* afforded certain protections for asylum seekers. In both cases, it was found that those protections did not apply to the interdicted asylum seekers.[155] By the time of the High Court's decision in *CPCF*, the government had introduced a new statutory regime with explicit interdiction powers. By a narrow majority, the Court found that the interdiction and detention at sea challenged in that case were authorised under this statutory framework. The *MPA* contained certain protections for interdicted persons, the most significant being that these people could be disembarked only at a 'place of safety'.[156] While the government responded to the *CPCF* litigation with legislation strengthening its interdiction powers under the *MPA*,[157] the requirement that a person must not be taken to a place which is unsafe remains. No such limitations were read into the executive powers to interdict, detain and remove as construed by the US Supreme Court in *Sale* or by the Full Bench of the Australian Federal Court in *Ruddock v Vadarlis*.

There are also parallels in the way the US Supreme Court and the Australian Federal and High Court dealt with the issue of international law. In all three cases, a majority of the Justices indicated that nothing in international law constrained the actions of the executive. On this point, the approach taken in the Australian cases is more understandable. As discussed, Australia adheres to a dualist system of international law where international treaties ratified by the executive do not become binding at a domestic level unless translated through Parliament or legislation.[158] As Parliament had not directly enacted the terms of the *Refugee Convention*,[159] the Court was not called upon to determine the compatibility of

---

[154] Exec Order No 12807, 57 Fed Reg 23133 (1 June 1992).
[155] Note that in *Ruddock v Vadarlis*, this question was not dealt with directly as there was no standing to bring claims under the *Migration Act*.
[156] *MPA* s 74.   [157] See above nn 83–8 and accompanying text.
[158] See above nn 135–6 and accompanying text; and Chapter 1, n 85 and accompanying text.
[159] At the time *Ruddock v Vadarlis* and *CPCF* were decided, the *Migration Act* incorporated the *Refugee Convention* definition of a refugee into s 36 of the Act (stating 'a person is qualified for a Protection visa if they are one to whom Australia owes obligations under the Convention'), but the Act did not incorporate the remainder of the Convention. The reference to the *Refugee Convention* in s 36 of the

the government's actions with the Convention. The only scope for considering Australia's obligations under the *Refugee Convention* was in the course of applying the accepted principle of statutory construction that requires statutes to be interpreted, as far as their language permits, in a manner which conforms to international law.[160] However, neither the Federal Court in *Ruddock v Vadarlis* nor the High Court in *CPCF* addressed this point, as the facts before them did not give rise to any *non-refoulement* considerations. In *Ruddock v Vadarlis*, French J found that 'nothing done by the Executive on the face of it amounts to a breach of Australia's obligations in respect of *non-refoulement* under the Convention'.[161] This was because the rescuees were not being returned to their home countries; rather, the Australian government had concluded agreements with New Zealand and Papua New Guinea to transfer the asylum seekers to those countries for the processing of their claims. In *CPCF*, the challenge related to the legality of attempts by Australian officials to take the plaintiff to India, and there was no evidence before the Court indicating risk of harm or secondary *refoulement*.[162] In this regard, the decision in *Sale* is of greater concern. There, the intercepted asylum seekers faced summary return to Haiti without any consideration of their protection needs. Further, the Court proceeded on the assumption that the Convention's *non-refoulement* may have the force of law in the US domestic legal system.[163] Nevertheless, the Court concluded that the actions of the executive did not breach the *Refugee Convention*. This was thanks to a somewhat questionable interpretation of the *non-refoulement* provision as having no extraterritorial effect.

The Full Federal Court in *Ruddock v Vadarlis* and the High Court in *CPCF* did not have to directly deal with the question of whether the *Refugee Convention* constrained the power of the executive when carrying out interdiction activities. Accordingly, they avoided the question of whether the Convention's *non-refoulement* obligations had extraterritorial effect. It would have been a moot point in *Ruddock v Vadarlis* given the fact that the asylum seekers were intercepted inside Australian territorial waters. French CJ and Keane J did address the issue briefly in *CPCF*. Their Honours noted that there is judicial authority in Australia, the United Kingdom and the United States supporting the proposition that the Convention's *non-refoulement* obligation only extends to refugees within a state's territory.[164] *Sale* is the US authority cited by both Justices, and as discussed, that case clearly supports such an interpretation. The Australian and UK cases cited for the proposition by the two Justices are more problematic. Both French CJ and Keane J refer to comments by McHugh and Gummow JJ in *MIMIA v Khawar* ('*Khawar*') as Australian authority

---

Migration Act was removed with the passage of the *Legacy Caseload Act* which came into effect on 18 April 2015.

[160] *MIEA v Teoh* (1995) 183 CLR 273, 287, cited in *CPCF* (2015) 255 CLR 514, 627 [385] (Gageler J).

[161] *Ruddock v Vadarlis* (2001) 110 FCR 491, 545 [203]; Beaumont J echoed a similar sentiment, referencing the *non-refoulement* obligation of the *Refugee Convention*, but noting that international law imposes no obligation to settle those who are rescued: 521 [126].

[162] See *CPCF* (2015) 255 CLR 514, 529 [13] (French CJ), 645 [470] (Keane J).

[163] US courts have distinguished between 'self-executing' treaties and 'non-self-executing treaties'. Whereas the former have automatic domestic effect, the latter must be enacted through implementing legislation to have effect domestically. While the lower courts found that art 33 of the *Refugee Convention* was not self-executing, the Supreme Court carefully avoided addressing the issue in *Sale*. Instead, the Court reasoned that regardless of its status under US municipal law, art 33 would not assist in this case as it did not apply extraterritorially: *Sale*, 509 US 155, 178 (1993).

[164] *CPCF* (2015) 255 CLR 514, 527–8 [10] (French CJ) (note that French CJ does go on to note the contrary position put forward by UNHCR in their amicus curiae brief); 643 [461] (Keane J).

supporting the lack of extraterritorial applicability of the *Refugee Convention*'s *non-refoulement* obligations.[165] However, this case did not deal with any issues of extraterritoriality.[166] The comments relied upon were made in the context of a general introduction to the *Refugee Convention*. In that case, McHugh and Gummow JJ stated

> The term 'asylum' does not appear in the main body of the text of the Convention; the Convention does not impose an obligation upon Contracting States to grant asylum or a right to settle in those States to refugees arriving at their borders. Nor does the Convention specify what constitutes entry into the territory of a Contracting State so as to then be in a position to have the benefits conferred by the Convention. Rather the protection obligations imposed by the Convention upon Contracting States concern the status and civil rights to be afforded to refugees who are within Contracting States.[167]

Nothing here indicates that the *non-refoulement* obligations in the *Refugee Convention* do not apply extraterritorially. Rather, the claim relates to the absence of an obligation to provide asylum. The provision of asylum is qualitatively different to *non-refoulement* protection. The grant of asylum allows a person to stay in the receiving country's territory. *Non-refoulement* does not necessarily require this. All that is required is that the person is not sent back to a place where they will be subject to certain prescribed harms. French CJ also refers to Gummow J's comments in *MIMA v Haji Ibrahim* ('*Ibrahim*'), where His Honour cites *Sale* with approval stating that 'provisions of the Convention assume a situation in which refugees, possibly by irregular means, have somehow managed to arrive at or in the territory of the contracting State'.[168] Again, these comments appear in a general background to the *Refugee Convention* in a case that does not deal with issues of extraterritorial applicability. It is a long bow to draw to conclude this statement supports a restrictive interpretation of *non-refoulement* obligations.

In *CPCF*, French CJ and Keane J also reference the House of Lords decision in *R (European Roma Rights Centre) v Immigration Officer at Prague Airport* as UK authority for the non-extraterritorial applicability of the Convention's *non-refoulement* obligations.[169] That case challenged the practice of stationing UK immigration officials at Prague Airport to 'pre-clear' passengers before they boarded flights to the United Kingdom. Lord Bingham of Cornhill delivered the lead judgment on the issue of whether this practice was in contravention of the *Refugee Convention*. The key determining factor in finding that the policy in question did not violate the *Refugee Convention* was that the would-be asylum seekers had not left their country of origin or habitual residence. Hence, they could not meet the art 1A definition of a refugee.[170] This was a very different situation to those which occurred in *Sale*, *Vadarlis* and *CPCF*, where the asylum seekers were intercepted on the high seas or in the contiguous zone of the intercepting state. Lord Bingham does, however, cite a number of authorities supporting the view that the *non-refoulement* obligations of the

---

[165] (2002) 2010 CLR 1, 15 [42]; *CPCF* (2015) 255 CLR 514, 527–8 [10] (French CJ), 643 [461] (Keane J).
[166] Rather, the main issue related to the meaning of the term 'particular social group' in the Convention definition of the term 'refugee' and whether it could encompass victims of domestic violence in certain cases.
[167] *Khawar* (2002) 210 CLR 1, 15 [42] (footnotes omitted).
[168] *Ibrahim* (2000) 204 CLR 1, 45 [136] (footnotes omitted).
[169] [2005] 2 AC 1, cited in *CPCF* (2015) 255 CLR 514, 527–8 [10] (French CJ), 643 [461] (Keane J).
[170] *R (European Roma Rights Centre) v Immigration Officer at Prague Airport* [2005] 2 AC 1, 29–30, 33 (Lord Bingham).

Refugee Convention do not apply extraterritorially. Interestingly, Lord Bingham's analysis on this point makes repeated references to the Australian High Court's decisions in *Khawar* and *Ibrahim*.[171] Again, as discussed, these cases are not sound authority for the non-extraterritorial applicability of art 33(2). It appears that in *CPCF*, French CJ and Keane J may have relied on Lord Bingham's reference to *Khawar* and *Ibrahim* when citing these cases as authority for the lack of extraterritorial applicability of art 33. This represents an interesting example of the mischief that can be caused by the use of foreign case law, and, in particular, foreign interpretations of domestic case law.

Another interesting parallel between the US and Australian case law relates to the way in which each jurisdiction deals with the issue of whether the scope of rights afforded to non-citizens changes based on whether they are inside or outside the state's territory. US law has long tied constitutional protections to the degree of connection a non-citizen has with the United States. As discussed in Chapter 3, the plenary power doctrine provides for differentiated treatment of non-citizens seeking entry into the United States and non-citizens who have effectuated entry and are subsequently being removed. While the former have no constitutional rights, the latter may have limited recourse to such protections. Given that even non-citizens physically present in the United States seeking entry cannot avail themselves of constitutional protections, it is no surprise that interdicted asylum seekers, who are outside US territory, are similarly excluded.

Australian law on this point is not as clear-cut. Three Justices directly addressed this issue in *CPCF* in the context of whether the constitutional limitations contained in *Lim*, in regard to the detention of non-citizens inside Australia, should also apply to non-citizens detained outside Australia's territorial boundaries. Keane J appeared sympathetic to the US approach, explicitly limiting the applicability of the constitutional holding in *Lim* to non-citizens within Australia.[172] Hayne and Bell JJ took a different approach:

> This case concerns actions taken beyond Australia's borders. But why should some different rule apply there, to provide an answer to a claim made in an Australian court which must be determined according to Australian law? ... To hold that the Executive can act outside Australia's borders in a way that it cannot lawfully act within Australia would stand legal principle on its head.[173]

The High Court revisited the issue in 2016 in *Plaintiff M68*.[174] The case, which is examined in depth in Chapter 5, challenged Australia's involvement in the offshore detention arrangements in Nauru. A majority of the Court found that the *Lim* test did not apply because the plaintiff was being held by the Nauruan rather than the Australian government.[175] In reaching this conclusion, they did not directly address the issue of extraterritorial applicability; rather, the focus was on who was exercising control over the detention of the plaintiff. However, Bell, Gageler and Gordon JJ all found that the *Lim* test did apply extraterritorially to detention on Nauru (although only Gordon J found the test's requirements to be infringed).[176] This is an issue that will no doubt be explored in future cases.

Attempts by the United States and Australia to circumvent obligations owed to asylum seekers through maritime interdiction activities have by and large been upheld in domestic

---

[171] Ibid 30, 31, 38 (Lord Bingham). [172] *CPCF* (2015) 255 CLR 514, 648 [483].
[173] Ibid 567–8 [149]–[150]. [174] (2016) 257 CLR 42.
[175] Ibid 70 [41] (French CJ, Kiefel and Nettle JJ), 124 [239] (Keane J).
[176] Ibid 84–7 [93]–[99] (Bell J), 111 [184] (Gageler J); 164–6 [395]–[401] (Gordon J).

courts. This outcome has not been without controversy, and the judicial reasoning in the leading cases in both Australia and the United States has been the subject of much criticism. In upholding government interdiction activities, the courts have relied on two layers of ambiguity relating to the rights of asylum seekers subject to such action. First is the general exceptional status afforded under statutory and constitutional law to unauthorised non-citizens seeking entry. This was explored at length in Chapter 3. Second is the ambiguity that arises when applying constitutional and statutory principles to non-citizens encountered outside a state's territory. In the following chapter, I turn my attention to extraterritorial processing. As we will see, this practice can in some instances add a third layer of obfuscation by diffusing responsibility for the treatment of asylum seekers across multiple governments.

5

Extraterritorial Processing

> We are victims of political propaganda and should be understood as political prisoners. Australia put [us] up in a hell prison camp under a regime of systematic torture. I wanted to show that this policy is cruel, inhumane, unjust and a modern form of slavery. We were forcibly transported from Australia to their black site on Manus Island and are subject to a regime of systematic torture. I hope that this action will encourage people to think more about the Australian Guantánamo in the heart of the Pacific Ocean.
>
> Behrouz Boochani, refugee journalist detained at Manus Island justifying his non-violent protest against his treatment, April 2016

In their bid to maximise control over access to their territories, the US and Australian governments have had recourse to various forms of extraterritorial processing. Extraterritorial processing refers to any process for screening or assessing asylum claims carried out beyond a state's traditional geographic boundaries. The practice is often paired with maritime interdiction activities. As discussed in Chapter 4, at times, interdicted migrants have been summarily returned to their point of departure without any screening for asylum claims. Interdiction coupled with some form of extraterritorial processing strikes a slightly more balanced approach between control and the rights of asylum seekers. Rather than being summarily returned, interdicted persons are subject to procedures to identify those who may have an asylum claim. These have taken the form of crude screening measures aboard government vessels on the high seas, as well as more formal status determination procedures in external territories or third countries. This approach adheres to the letter (if not the spirit) of the *non-refoulement* obligations by providing mechanisms to identify persons who may be refugees and not returning such persons to a place where they may face harm on a convention ground. However, in practice, the procedures are often inadequate and have resulted in *refoulement*.[1] The extraterritorial nature of these procedures purports to place them beyond the reach of domestic statutory and constitutional protections. Control over access to the territory of the state is also maintained, with those recognised as refugees not automatically granted access to a state's territory, and instead often held for long periods of time awaiting resettlement in a third country.

Extraterritorial processing was pioneered by the United States, which began screening for asylum claims at sea in 1981. Since the early 1990s, certain asylum seekers interdicted at sea have been sent to the US territory of Guantánamo Bay. The United States has also entered into arrangements with third countries to accept the transfer of certain interdicted

---

[1] See Robert Manne and David Corlett, 'Sending Them Home: Refugees and the New Politics of Indifference' (2003) 13 *Quarterly Essay* 1.

migrants. The US interdiction and extraterritorial processing regime provided the blueprint for Australia's Pacific Solution, introduced in 2001, which coupled maritime interdiction activities with the use of extraterritorial processing camps in Manus Island in Papua New Guinea and the tiny Pacific state of Nauru. The policy of transferring interdicted asylum seekers to Papua New Guinea and Nauru was abandoned in 2007, only to be reintroduced in a modified form in 2012.

The United States and Australia have exerted varying degrees of control over extraterritorial status determination procedures. At times, the governments have maintained full control and responsibility over these procedures. The United Nations High Commissioner for Refugees ('UNHCR') refers to this as 'out of country' processing.[2] This is where the intercepting state processes claims on the high seas, in the territory of another state or in a location within the territory of the intercepting state which has been designated as 'extraterritorial' for migration or other purposes under national law.[3] At other times, there have been attempts to outsource responsibility for processing to third countries. I refer to this practice as 'third country transfers'. In reality, the line between out of country processing and third country transfers is often blurred, as the first state generally exerts some degree of control over processing in the third state.

5.1 Extraterritorial Processing in the United States

Since its inception in 1981, the US maritime interdiction program has been accompanied by a number of different forms of extraterritorial processing. These can be divided into three main categories: processing at sea; the use of the Migrant Operations Centre ('MOC') on the US territory of Guantánamo Bay; and third country transfers to Caribbean and South American nations. The political context surrounding the changes in policy was examined in Chapter 4. Here, I examine the details of the extraterritorial mechanisms, and, where relevant, the judiciary's response to these policies.

5.1.1 Processing at Sea

From its launch in 1981 through to November 1991, the Haitian maritime interdiction program was accompanied by crude extraterritorial processing at sea, with summary screening carried out aboard US Coast Guard cutters. Officers from the Immigration and Naturalization Service ('INS') assessed interdicted individuals to determine if any had a credible fear of persecution.[4] Those found to have such a fear were transferred to mainland United States for full refugee status determination procedures, while the others were returned to Haiti. Section 3 of Executive Order 12324 authorising the interdiction program required that the Attorney General 'take whatever steps are necessary to ensure ... the strict observance of our international obligations concerning those who genuinely flee

---

[2] UNHCR, 'Maritime Interception Operations and the Processing of International Protection Claims: Legal Standards and Policy Considerations with Respect to Extraterritorial Processing' (Protection Policy Paper, November 2010) 12.
[3] Ibid.
[4] For a critique of the 'credible fear' test, see Bill Frelick, 'US Refugee Policy in the Caribbean: No Bridge over Troubled Waters' (1996) 20(2) *Fletcher Forum of World Affairs* 67, 72–4.

persecution in their homeland'.[5] This was operationalised through the INS Interdiction Guidelines, which advised INS officers to be 'constantly watchful of any indication that ... persons on board ... may qualify as refugees under the Protocol'.[6] In practice, the screening was carried out in a 'superficial' and 'haphazard' manner.[7] A study by the Lawyers Committee for Human Rights (now Human Rights First) found that out of 23,000 Haitians interdicted by the United States between 1981 and 1990, only 6 passengers were found to have claims strong enough to warrant a full asylum hearing.[8] Stephen Legomsky notes that '[g]iven the high incidence of serious human rights violations in Haiti during that period, there was ample reason to worry that the rarity of cases found to justify full hearing said more about the procedural adequacy of interviews than about the merits of the claims'.[9]

The legality of these procedures for screening asylum claims at sea was challenged in *Haitian Refugee Center v Gracey* in 1985.[10] The Haitian Refugee Centre ('HRC'), a US-based NGO, launched a challenge in the District Court of the District of Columbia, arguing that the US government's *non-refoulement* obligations under the *Refugee Convention*,[11] as well as under the *INA*, applied to refugees outside the United States and that the procedures for screening at sea violated the due process requirements of the Fifth Amendment of the *US Constitution*. Both these arguments were rejected by the District Court.[12] The HRC appealed to the US Court of Appeals for the Eleventh Circuit. The Court of Appeals affirmed the decision of the District Court, but did so on the basis that the HRC had no standing, and as such did not deal with the substantive grounds of the challenge.[13]

After a brief hiatus, basic pre-screening procedures at sea were reintroduced in 1995. This process is currently governed by Executive Order 12807 ('Kennebunkport Order') as amended by Executive Order 13286.[14] This gives the Secretary of Homeland Security an unreviewable discretion to determine that a person is a refugee and as such should not be returned. The vast majority of interdicted asylum seekers are 'screened out' and returned to their point of departure, but a small number are transferred to Guantánamo Bay for processing. Screening procedures are reported to vary depending on the nationality of the arrival. Cubans are subject to individual 'credible fear' screenings aboard Coast Guard

---

[5] Exec Order No 12324, 46 Fed Reg 48109 (1 October 1981).
[6] INS Interdiction Guidelines, 'INS Role in and Guidelines for Interdiction at Sea' (6 October 1981, revised 24 September 1982).
[7] A G Mariam, 'International Law and the Preemptive Use of State Interdiction Authority on the High Seas: The Case of Suspected Illegal Haitian Immigrants Seeking Entry into the US' (1988) 12 *Maryland Journal of International Law* 211, 237–8.
[8] Lawyers Committee for Human Rights, *Refugee Refoulement: The Forced Return of Haitians under the US–Haitian Interdiction Agreement* (1990) 4; cf Ruth Ellen Wasem, 'US Immigration Policy on Haitian Migrants' (Report for Congress, Congressional Research Service, 17 May 2011) 4; Frank Brennan, *Tampering with Asylum: A Universal Humanitarian Problem* (University of Queensland Press, 2003) 77 (both putting the number of interdicted Haitians recognised as refugees during this period at eleven).
[9] Stephen Legomsky, 'The USA and the Caribbean Interdiction Program' (2006) 18 *International Journal of Refugee Law* 677, 679.
[10] See *Haitian Refugee Center v Gracey*, 809 F 2d 794 (DC Cir, 1987).
[11] *Convention Relating to the Status of Refugees*, opened for signature 28 July 1951, 189 UNTS 137 (entered into force 22 April 1954) ('Refugee Convention').
[12] *Haitian Refugee Center v Gracey*, 809 F 2d 794 (DC Cir, 1987). [13] Ibid.
[14] Exec Order No 12807, 57 Fed Reg 23133 (1 June 1992); Exec Order No 13286, 68 Fed Reg 10619 (3 May 2003).

cutters where they are explicitly asked whether they have a fear of returning to Cuba.[15] All other interdicted migrants, such as Haitians, are not questioned about whether they fear being returned, but are required to vocalise a 'manifestation of fear' independently.[16] A US Department of State official described this policy as 'shout and you get an interview'.[17] Regardless of nationality, when a person is found to have a credible fear, they are transferred to Guantánamo Bay. Very few migrants are 'screened in'. Between 1996 and 2014, only 425 individuals were transferred to Guantánamo Bay for further processing.[18]

5.1.2 Guantánamo Bay

The United States has used Guantánamo Bay as a site for processing and holding asylum seekers interdicted at sea since November 1991. Guantánamo Bay is a territory nominally owned by Cuba, but controlled by the US government.[19] The United States first occupied the area in 1898, during the Spanish–American war, for the purpose of establishing a naval base. Its control over the territory was formalised by a lease agreement entered into with the Cuban government in 1903. This agreement recognised 'the continuance of the ultimate sovereignty of the Republic of Cuba'. However, it went on to stipulate that the 'United States shall exercise complete jurisdiction and control' over the territory.[20] A subsequent treaty in 1934 renewed the lease agreement '[u]ntil the two contracting parties agree to the modification or abrogation of the stipulations'.[21] The effect was to give the United States a perpetual lease over Guantánamo Bay. The arrangement has given rise to jurisdictional ambiguities in the context of rights protection, with the territory described as an 'anomalous legal zone'[22] and a 'legal black hole'.[23]

---

[15] Alexander Aleinikoff, 'YLS Sale Symposium: International Protection Challenges Occasioned by Maritime Movement Asylum Seekers', *Opinio Juris* (online), 16 March 2014 http://opiniojuris.org/2014/03/16/sale-symposium-international-protection-challenges-occasioned-maritime-movement-asylum-seekers/.

[16] Ibid.

[17] Women's Commission for Refugee Women and Children, *Refugee Policy Adrift: The United States and Dominican Republic Deny Haitians Protection* (January 2003) 18.

[18] Azadeh Dastyari, *United States Migrant Interdiction and the Detention of Refugees on Guantánamo Bay* (Cambridge University Press, 2015) 5.

[19] For a detailed history of the US presence in Guantanamo Bay see Ernesto Hernández-López, 'Guantanamo as Subordination: Detainees as Resisting Empire' (2010) 104 *Proceedings of the Annual Meeting (American Society of International Law)* 472 (explaining the establishment and development of the base as a manifestation of US imperial ambition); Joseph Sweeney, 'Guantanamo and US Law' (2007) 30 *Fordham International Law Journal* 673; Amy Kaplan, 'Where is Guantanamo?' (2005) 57 *American Quarterly* 831.

[20] *Agreement between the United States of America and the Republic of Cuba for the Lease to the United States of Lands in Cuba for Coaling and Naval Stations*, TS No 418 (signed and entered into force 23 February 1903).

[21] *Treaty between the United States of America and Cuba Defining Their Relations*, signed 29 May 1934, TS No 866 (entered into force 9 June 1934).

[22] Gerald Neuman, 'Anomalous Zones' (1996) 48 *Stanford Law Review* 1197, 1201 (defining an anomalous zone as 'a geographical area in which certain legal rules, otherwise regarded as embodying fundamental policies of the larger legal system, are locally suspended'); Gerald Neuman, 'Closing the Guantanamo Loophole' (2004) 50 *Loyola Law Review* 1 (examining how Guantanamo's designation as an anomalous zone influences the detention of enemy combatants).

[23] See Johan Steyn, 'Guantanamo Bay: The Legal Black Hole' (2004) 53 *International and Comparative Law Quarterly* 1; Ernesto Hernández-López, 'Guantánamo as a "Legal Black Hole": A Base for Expanding Space, Markets, and Culture' (2011) 45 *University of San Francisco Law Review* 141.

It is precisely these legal ambiguities which have made Guantánamo Bay an attractive location for holding asylum seekers and, more recently, enemy combatants captured in the course of the so-called war on terror. When establishing the MOC on Guantánamo Bay in 1991, the administration of George HW Bush created a special process for assessing refugee claims, which was procedurally inferior to that available to persons seeking asylum within mainland America. Guantánamo Bay fell outside of the statutory definition of 'the United States' under the *Immigration and Nationality Act* ('*INA*'), and hence the statutory protections contained in that statute did not apply there.[24] A similar extraterritorial argument was used to frame the Guantánamo detainees as having no rights under the *US Constitution*. This left the executive free to streamline the screening process, 'dispensing with such complications as the assistance of lawyers, administrative appeals, and judicial review'.[25] Those found to have a credible fear of persecution were transferred to the United States to pursue an asylum claim.[26] Those found not to exhibit such a fear were forcibly returned to Haiti.

These procedures were challenged in *Haitian Refugee Center v Baker* ('*Baker*').[27] The HRC initiated litigation against US government officials in an attempt to block the practice of returning 'screened-out' Haitians without sufficient process. These were those who, upon initial inspection, were found not to possess a credible fear of persecution. The constitutional claim asserted was a First Amendment right of association on the part of attorneys seeking to provide pro bono representation to 'screened-out' Haitian asylum applicants at Guantánamo.[28] The relevant part of the First Amendment states that 'Congress shall make no law ... abridging the freedom of speech, or of the press; or the right of the people to peaceably assemble, and to petition the Government for redress of grievances'.[29] The HRC also argued that protection in the *INA* and the *Refugee Convention* applied to the status determination procedures on Guantánamo Bay. While the HRC was successful in securing a number of temporary restraining orders in the US District Court for the Southern District of Florida, the Court of Appeals for the Eleventh Circuit dismissed the case.[30] With little analysis, the Court concluded that Guantánamo Bay was 'outside the United States' and rejected the argument that aliens located there could claim rights under the First Amendment of the Constitution, the *Refugee Convention* or the *INA*.[31] The HRC petitioned the Supreme Court to hear an appeal, but this request was denied.[32] Thomas J, in concurring with the decision to deny a writ of certiorari, expressed deep concern about the treatment of Haitians returned to Haiti, but reasoned that the matter should be dealt with by the political branches.[33]

---

[24] 8 USC §1101(a)(38) (1994) (defining 'United States' as limited to the continental United States, Alaska, Hawaii, Puerto Rico, Guam and the Virgin Islands); See also Neuman, 'Anomalous Zones', above n 22, 1229.
[25] Neuman, 'Anomalous Zones', above n 22, 1229.
[26] Note that persons who were found to have a credible fear but were HIV positive were not transferred to the US, but were detained in a special section of the Guantanamo Bay facility. See below nn 41–6 and accompanying text.
[27] 953 F 2d 1498 (11th Cir, 1992). [28] Ibid 1503. [29] *US Constitution* amend I.
[30] 953 F 2d 1498 (11th Cir, 1992). [31] Ibid 1513.
[32] *Haitian Refugee Center v Baker*, 502 US 1122 (1992).
[33] Ibid 1123. Blackmun J, in dissent, argued that the issues raised in the case were difficult and susceptible to competing interpretations, as evidenced by the different approaches adopted by the four federal judges who considered the claims: at 1123.

Haitian Centers Council v McNary ('*McNary*')[34] involved similar issues to those raised in the *Baker* litigation, but concerned 'screened-in' asylum seekers. 'Screened-in' Haitians were those found to possess a credible fear of persecution and who were, according to policy, to be brought to the United States to apply for asylum. In March 1992, the INS decided that they would no longer transfer 'screened-in' Haitians to the United States for processing.[35] Instead, full asylum interviews would be carried out in Guantánamo Bay. When the litigation was initiated, some 3,000 'screened-in' Haitians were being held at Guantánamo Bay.[36] A challenge was brought on behalf of the Haitian asylum seekers and several Haitian service organisations. The asylum-seeker plaintiffs asserted a due process right to counsel before being returned to persecution, while the Haitian service organisations asserted a reciprocal First Amendment right of access to Guantánamo Bay for the purpose of providing legal advice to the Haitian detainees. The District Court for the Eastern District of New York granted a preliminary injunction based on both the First Amendment and due process claims.[37] The Second Circuit affirmed the preliminary injunction, finding that there were serious questions going to the merits of the claim that Haitian refugees held on Guantánamo Bay were protected by the Due Process Clause.[38] The Court found that the Guantánamo Bay Naval Base was under the jurisdiction of the United States, making protections of the Due Process Clause applicable to aliens held there.[39] Following Bush's 'Kennebunkport Order' in May 1992, directing the return of all Haitians interdicted on the high seas without screening, the *McNary* litigation was broken up. The question of whether Haitian interdictees were covered by the *non-refoulement* provisions in art 33 of the *Refugee Convention* or § 243(h) of the *INA*, was ultimately resolved in *Sale v Haitian Centers Council* ('*Sale*')[40] (examined in Chapter 4) and the Second Circuit's injunction in *McNary* was vacated.

The question of the rights of 'screened-in' asylum seekers still held at Guantánamo Bay was returned to the District Court and dealt with in *Haitian Centers Council v Sale* ('*Haitian HIV case*').[41] By this stage, there were still around 300 Haitian men, women and children held at Guantánamo Bay who had been 'screened in' as having a 'credible fear' of return to Haiti. They had been barred from entering the United States because they had tested positive for human immunodeficiency virus ('HIV'). The refugees' claims were reformulated to focus on the illegality of the HIV detention camp, rather than on their original right-to-counsel claim. In a scathing opinion, Judge Sterling Johnson Jr issued a permanent injunction, ordering that the Guantánamo Bay Haitians be immediately released and declaring their confinement illegal.[42] Johnson J reasoned that the US Naval Base at Guantánamo Bay is 'subject to the exclusive jurisdiction and control of the United States where the criminal and civil laws of the United States apply'.[43] The plaintiffs were held to

---

[34] 969 F 2d 1326 (2nd Cir, 1992).   [35] *McNary*, 969 F 2d 1326, 1332–3 (2nd Cir, 1992).
[36] Harold Hongju Koh, 'Refugees, the Courts, and the New World Order' [1994] (3) *Utah Law Review* 999, 1001.
[37] *Haitian Centers Council v McNary* (ED NY, No 92 CV 1258, 6 April 1992) Preliminary Injunction Order (Johnson J).
[38] *McNary*, 969 F 2d 1326 (2nd Cir, 1992).   [39] Ibid 1347.   [40] 509 US 155 (1993).
[41] 823 F Supp 1028 (ED NY, 1993) ('*Haitian HIV case*') (vacated per settlement agreement). The story of this litigation is recounted in Brandt Goldstein, *Storming the Court: How a Band of Yale Law Students Sued the President – and Won* (Simon & Schuster, 2005); Victoria Clawson, Elizabeth Detweiler and Laura Ho, 'Litigating as Law Students: An Inside Look at Haitian Centers Council' (1994) 103 *Yale Law Journal* 2337.
[42] 823 F Supp 1028 (ED NY, 1993).   [43] Ibid 1041 (citations omitted).

have constitutional due process rights. These included a right to counsel during status determination interviews, access to adequate medical care and a liberty interest in not being arbitrarily or indefinitely detained. For Johnson J, to hold otherwise would be unacceptable: 'If the Due Process Clause does not apply to the detainees at Guantánamo, Defendants would have discretion deliberately to starve or beat them, to deprive them of medical attention, to return them without process to their persecutors, or to discriminate among them based on the color of their skin.'[44]

Further, Johnson J rejected the government's contention that status determination procedures on Guantánamo Bay were undertaken pursuant to executive authority and operated outside the *INA*. As such, the plaintiffs were held to possess the same statutory rights as those processed on the US mainland. The government decided to settle, rather than appeal the decision.[45] The settlement allowed the asylum seekers to enter the United States, but resulted in the District Court decision being vacated.[46]

In July 1994 a new policy was implemented pursuant to which interdicted Haitians would be provided 'safe haven' at Guantánamo Bay and in other Caribbean countries. Asylum seekers would not be returned automatically to their country, nor would they be offered the option of entering the United States as refugees or to pursue asylum claims. In August 1994, the 'safe haven' policy was expanded to include interdicted Cubans. This was challenged in the *Cuban American Bar Association v Christopher* ('*CABA*') litigation.[47] A class action was brought on behalf of a group of Cuban asylum seekers and Cuban refugee service organisations.[48] The plaintiffs claimed that the US government was violating the First and Fifth Amendment rights of both the Cuban refugees and the service organisations. The service organisations contended that they had a right to associate with refugee clients at Guantánamo Bay and that the Cuban refugees had a correlative right to counsel. The District Court was sympathetic to these arguments, and issued a temporary restraining order compelling the government to give service organisations access to their refugee clients on Guantánamo Bay and prohibiting further involuntary repatriation of refugee plaintiffs to Cuba prior to reasonable access to their lawyers.[49] The Court ruled that the government's complete control and jurisdiction over Guantánamo Bay effectively made it a US territory. Hence asylum seekers detained there could avail themselves of US constitutional protections. The US Supreme Court's decision in *Sale* was distinguished as the Haitian plaintiffs in that case were interdicted by US Coast Guard vessels on the high seas and as such were 'not already within the

---

[44] Ibid 1042.

[45] The plaintiffs agreed to have the trial orders vacated in return for the freedom of the Haitians held at Guantanamo, a government decision not to appeal and a compensatory award of fees and costs totalling $643,100: see *Haitian Centers Council v Meissner* (ED NY, No 92-1258, 22 February 1994) Stipulated Order Approving Class Action Settlement Agreement; Koh, 'Refugees, the Courts, and the New World Order', above n 36, 1011.

[46] *Haitian Centers Council v Meissner* (ED NY, No 92-1258, 22 February 1994) Stipulated Order Approving Class Action Settlement Agreement.

[47] (SD Fla, No 94-2183-CV-CCA, 31 October 1994) Temporary Restraining Order; 43 F 3d 1412 (11th Cir, 1995).

[48] The two service organisations involved in the litigation were the Cuban American Bar Association and the Cuban Legal Alliance and Due Process, Inc.

[49] *Cuban American Bar Association v Christopher* (SD Fla, No 94-2183-CV-CCA, 31 October 1994) Temporary Restraining Order.

United States territory, [and] not yet admitted'. Subsequent to its original ruling, the District Court allowed the Haitian Refugee Center to intervene in the case.

The US Court of Appeals for the Eleventh Circuit reversed the District Court decision. The Justices reasoned that jurisdiction and control over Guantánamo Bay were not synonymous with the concept of state sovereignty. As the United States did not exercise legal sovereignty over the territory, asylum seekers had no legally cognisable rights under the INA or the *Refugee Convention*. This in effect affirmed the Court's earlier approach to this question in *Baker*. The Court of Appeals also ruled that the service organisations had no First Amendment right of association with the asylum seekers. As the Haitian and Cuban migrants had no legal rights under domestic or international law, the legal organisations could not have a right of association for the purpose of counselling them. The plaintiffs appealed to the US Supreme Court, but the Court declined to hear the case.[50] Accordingly, the only decisions of any precedential value resulting from the asylum-seeker litigation in the 1990s, *Baker* and *CABA*, clearly affirm the proposition that non-citizens held at Guantánamo Bay were outside the reach of US statutory and constitutional protections.

This approach appears to be at odds with that taken by the Supreme Court in later years in relation to the rights of enemy combatants held at Guantánamo Bay. Beginning in 2002, some 660 persons captured by US and allied forces, in the course of military operations against the Taliban regime in Afghanistan, were transferred to military prisons in Guantánamo Bay. The location was selected for the same reasons as it had been selected to house asylum seekers: it was under the complete control of the US government, but purportedly beyond the reach of US courts.[51] In selecting Guantánamo Bay, US authorities relied on legal advice that Federal District Courts would likely not have jurisdiction to entertain a petition for a writ of habeas corpus filed on behalf of enemy combatants transferred there.[52] In the World War II-era case of *Johnson v Eisentrager*,[53] the Supreme Court held that federal courts did not have authority to entertain an application for habeas corpus relief filed by an enemy alien who had been seized and held outside the territory of the United States.[54] Government lawyers relied on the finding in *CABA* that Guantánamo Bay was not US sovereign territory, to advise the George W Bush Administration that the writ of habeas corpus would likely not apply there.[55]

This advice ultimately proved incorrect. In *Rasul v Bush*,[56] the Supreme Court affirmed the statutory right to habeas corpus for Guantánamo Bay detainees. In reaching this decision, the Court characterised Guantánamo Bay as within 'the territorial jurisdiction' of the United States and emphasised the fact that the government exercised 'complete

---

[50] *Cuban American Bar Association v Christopher*, 516 US 913 (1995).
[51] Daniel McCallum, 'Why GTMO?' (unpublished seminar paper, National War College, 2003) www.pegc.us/archive/Authorities/McCallum_why_gtmo.pdf 5–6 (citing seven factors that were considered by US officials when deciding where to detain the enemy combatants: (1) Impact on US Foreign Relations, (2) Impact on Domestic Security, (3) Facility Security, (4) Facility Size, (5) Remoteness of the Locations, (6) Litigation Risks and (7) Logistics).
[52] See Deputy Assistant Attorney Generals Patrick Philbin and John Yoo, 'Memo 3 – Memorandum for William J. Haynes II, General Counsel, Department of Defense: Possible Habeas Jurisdiction over Aliens Held in Guantanamo Bay, Cuba' (28 December 2001) reproduced in Karen Greenberg and Joshua Dratel (eds), *The Torture Papers: The Road to Abu Ghraib* (Cambridge University Press, 2005) 29; McCallum, ibid 6.
[53] 339 US 763 (1950).   [54] Ibid 768–78.   [55] Philbin and Yoo, above n 52, 4.
[56] 542 US 466 (2004).

jurisdiction and control' over the naval base, 'and may continue to exercise such control permanently if it chooses'.[57] Following the Supreme Court's decision in *Rasul*, Congress introduced statutory amendments that purported to strip federal courts of jurisdiction to hear habeas corpus petitions from Guantánamo detainees.[58] In *Boumediene v Bush*, the Supreme Court examined the constitutionality of the jurisdiction-stripping provisions.[59] The Suspension Clause of the *US Constitution* states that the 'Privilege of the Writ of Habeas Corpus shall not be suspended, unless when in Cases of Rebellion or Invasion the public Safety may require it'.[60] The central question was whether this constitutional privilege could be claimed by aliens designated by the government as enemy combatants and held at Guantánamo Bay. The government made the same arguments that were accepted in the asylum-seeker cases: that Guantánamo Bay was outside US territory and as such US constitutional protections did not apply there.[61] In a narrow 5:4 decision, the Supreme Court rejected this contention.[62] The majority of the Supreme Court agreed with the government's position (as well as the construction of the judges in *Baker* and *CABA*) that Cuba, not the United States, had sovereignty, in the technical sense of the term, over Guantánamo Bay.[63] However, they reached a different conclusion as to the implications of this lack of formal sovereignty. The majority adopted a 'functional approach' to the reach of the *US Constitution*. The fact that the United States exercised 'complete jurisdiction and control' over Guantánamo Bay was sufficient to extend constitutional protection to certain non-citizens detained there. The Court reached this conclusion by distinguishing between *de jure* sovereignty, which was retained by Cuba, and *de facto* sovereignty, held by the United States. The 'absolute' and 'indefinite'[64] control exercised by the United States over the territory was more important in deciding the scope of the constitutional protection than considerations of 'legal and technical' sovereignty. To hold otherwise would mean that the political branches could surrender formal sovereignty over any unincorporated territory to a third country, enter into a lease that grants total control back to the United States and 'govern without legal constraint'.[65] However, the Circuit Court decision in *Baker* and *CABA* upheld exactly this form of unconstrained power with respect to asylum seekers in Guantánamo Bay. The divergent approaches may be the result of the privileged status the Court gave to the writ of habeas corpus (claimed in *Boumediene*) over rights under the First and Fifth Amendments (claimed in *Baker* and *CABA*).[66] Alternatively, they may represent a broader shift in the willingness of the Supreme Court to accept Guantánamo Bay's status as an extralegal space beyond the reach of the *US Constitution*.

---

[57] Ibid 480–1 (references omitted).

[58] *Detainee Treatment Act of 2005*, enacted pursuant to the *Department of Defense, Emergency Supplemental Appropriations to Address Hurricanes in the Gulf of Mexico, and Pandemic Influenza Act of 2006*, Pub L 109–148, 119 Stat 2680; and *National Defense Authorization Act for the Fiscal Year 2006*, Pub L 109–163, 119 Stat 3136, inserting 28 USC § 2241(e)(1); *Military Commissions Act of 2006*, Pub L 109–366, 120 Stat 2600, amending 28 USC § 2241(e) (2006).

[59] 533 US 723 (2008).   [60] *US Constitution* art 1 § 9 cl 2.   [61] *Boumediene*, 533 US 723, 753 (2008).

[62] Kennedy J wrote the majority opinion, which Stevens, Souter, Ginsburg and Breyer JJ joined. Justice Scalia wrote the primary dissenting opinion dealing with the characterisation of Guantanamo, in which Roberts CJ and Thomas and Alito JJ joined. Roberts CJ also filed a separate dissenting opinion in which Scalia, Thomas and Alito JJ joined.

[63] *Boumediene*, 533 US 723, 754 (2008).   [64] Ibid 768.   [65] Ibid 765.

[66] Dastyari, *United States Migrant Interdiction and the Detention of Refugees on Guantánamo Bay*, above n 18, 146–7.

The United States continues to operate the MOC on Guantánamo Bay. Under the current policy, which has been in place since 1995, asylum seekers undergo initial pre-screening at sea. Those found to meet the credible fear threshold are transferred to the centre to be subject to full status determination procedures. Where a person processed at Guantánamo is found to be a refugee, they are generally not admitted to the United States. Instead, they are resettled in a third country pursuant to bilateral agreements entered into by the Department of State. From 1996 to 2011, 331 persons were resettled to twenty-one countries worldwide.[67] Up-to-date figures on the number of interdicted asylum seekers transferred to the MOC at Guantánamo are not available. The most recent statistics, which are from February 2012, indicate that a total of only thirty-three migrants (all Cuban) were held there at that time.[68] The facility remains ready to respond to future mass migration flows, with a surge capacity of up to 10,000 persons.[69]

Operations are governed by Executive Order 13276, as amended by Executive Order 13286,[70] which gives the Secretary of Homeland Security an unreviewable discretion to detain and carry out status determinations of asylum seekers on the island.[71] The executive orders themselves do not create any enforceable rights for asylum seekers held at Guantánamo Bay.[72] These current arrangements have not yet been the subject of judicial challenge. As such, it remains to be seen whether the Supreme Court will be willing to extend constitutional protections to the migrant population. While the Court in *Boumediene* extended protection under the Suspension Clause to enemy combatants on Guantánamo Bay, the Court was at pains to emphasise that its decision did not extend beyond the specific petitioners before the Court.[73] In *Kiyemba v Obama*, the DC Circuit Court confirmed that the holding in *Boumediene* only applied to the Suspension Clause and not any other constitutional rights.[74] As such, the Circuit Court decisions in *Baker* and *CABA* remain the controlling authority for the fact that the protections of the First and Fifth Amendments of the *US Constitution* do not apply to asylum seekers in Guantánamo Bay. It also remains unclear whether the holding in *Boumediene* regarding access to habeas corpus would be extended to apply to the asylum-seeker population in Guantánamo Bay. However, as Azadeh Dastyari has noted, access to habeas corpus would be of little utility for the asylum-seeker population.[75] Even if an asylum seeker was successful in challenging their detention, at best, this would result in them being released into the community in Guantánamo Bay – a privilege that most asylum seekers already enjoy

---

[67] US Department of State, US Department of Homeland Security, US State Department of Health and Human Services, 'Proposed Refugee Admissions for Fiscal 2012' (Submission to the Committees on the Judiciary of the United States Senate and United States House of Representatives, 2012) 38.
[68] Azadeh Dastyari and Libbey Effeney, 'Immigration Detention in Guantanamo Bay' (2012) 6(2) *Shima: The International Journal of Research into Island Cultures* 49, 58.
[69] Ibid.
[70] Exec Order No 13276, 67 Fed Reg 69985 (19 November 2002); Exec Order No 13286, 68 Fed Reg 10619 (3 May 2003).
[71] Exec Order No 13276, 67 Fed Reg 69985 (19 November 2002) § 1(a)(ii).
[72] Exec Order No 13276, 67 Fed Reg 69985 (19 November 2002) § 3(e) makes it explicit that the order should 'not be construed to require any procedure to determine whether a person is a refugee or otherwise in need of protection'; see also Dastyari, *United States Migrant Interdiction and the Detention of Refugees on Guantánamo Bay*, above n 18, 144.
[73] *Boumediene*, 533 US 723, 795 (2008).   [74] *Kiyemba v Obama*, 555 F 3d 1022 (DC Cir, 2009).
[75] Dastyari, *United States Migrant Interdiction and the Detention of Refugees on Guantánamo Bay*, above n 18, 148–9.

while awaiting assessment of their claim.[76] It would not result in the grant of entry into the United States or any other country.

5.1.3 Third Country Processing and Transfers

The United States has on at least three occasions sought agreement from Caribbean and Central American nations to participate in extraterritorial or third country transfer schemes. In November 1991, the administration of George HW Bush sought the cooperation of countries in the region to provide safe haven for Haitians interdicted at sea. These efforts were, on the whole, unsuccessful. The Dominican Republic and the Bahamas refused the request, while Honduras, Belize and Trinidad and Tobago agreed to take a total of only 550 Haitians.[77] The United States again looked abroad for regional partners when President Clinton decided to suspend the 'Kennebunkport Order', which had authorised the return of Haitians without screening. An agreement was reached with Jamaica that allowed for processing to be carried out on board the US hospital ship *Comfort* in Kingston Harbour.[78] From 15 June to 4 July 1994, interdicted Haitians were transferred there and given access to full status determination procedures. These were carried out under the advisory and review capacity of UNHCR.[79] Those found to be refugees were then transferred to the United States. A separate agreement was reached with the United Kingdom for processing to be carried out in the Turks and Caicos Islands.[80] A facility was constructed on Grand Turk Island, but was never used. Following the adoption of the safe haven policy on 5 July 1994, the Clinton administration sought to supplement capacity on Guantánamo Bay through agreements with countries in the region to provide temporary safe haven for Haitians interdicted at sea. A camp was built by US military engineers in Suriname for this purpose, but like the facility on Grand Turk Island, it was never utilised.[81] After the safe haven policy was extended to Cubans on 19 August 1994, the United States again embarked on efforts to find safe haven locations in the region. While Belize and Honduras offered to assist, a US military installation in Panama was ultimately selected as the site for a camp to house 10,000 Cubans. This camp remained operational until Panama opted not to renew authorisation in February 1995, at which point the remaining 7,000 people housed there were transferred to the Guantánamo facility.[82] The arrangement with Panama is the only aspect of US third country transfer policies which has been examined by the courts. *CABA* examined the rights of asylum seekers held in Guantánamo Bay and Panama. The Court of Appeals for the Second Circuit rejected the claim made by the plaintiffs that the leased

---

[76] Confinement in Guantanamo Bay, even in the community, may amount to detention under international law: see Chapter 6, nn 117–18 and accompanying text.
[77] Vernon Briggs, 'US Asylum Policy and the New World Order' (1993) 1 *People and Place* 1, 4.
[78] *Memorandum of Understanding for the Establishment within the Jamaican Territorial Sea and Internal Waters of a Facility to Process Nationals of Haiti seeking Refuge within or Entry to the United States of America*, US- Jamaica, KAV 3901 (signed and entered into force 2 June 1994).
[79] Brunson McKinley, 'Safe Haven for Boat People in the Caribbean' (1995) 18 *In Defence of the Alien* 203, 206.
[80] *Memorandum of Understanding to Establish in the Turks and Caicos Islands a Processing Facility to Determine the Refugee Status of Boat People from Haiti*, US–UK–Turks and Caicos Islands, KAV 3906 (signed and entered into force 18 June 1994).
[81] McKinley, above n 79, 209.   [82] Ibid.

military base on Panama could be construed as part of US territory for the purposes of applying statutory and constitutional protections.[83] Nor was the Court willing to view these protections as having extraterritorial affect.[84] As such, the Cubans held on Panama were found not to have any cognisable rights under US law.

5.2 Extraterritorial Processing in Australia

Over the years, the Australian government has made a number of attempts at creating its own Guantánamo – a place to hold asylum seekers which is beyond the reach of Australian statutory and constitutional protections. The Pacific Islands of Nauru and Manus Island in Papua New Guinea ('PNG') have proved most effective in achieving this goal. They were used for this purpose from 2001 to 2008,[85] and again from 2012 to the present day. To date, legal challenges in Australian courts to the offshore processing regimes in these locations have proved unsuccessful. Attempts to use two other locations were ultimately frustrated by the courts. The first involved the purported redesignation of Australia's offshore territory of Christmas Island as an extralegal location where processing could be carried out outside the statutory framework that existed on the mainland. This characterisation was firmly rejected by the Australian High Court. The second initiative, which involved the transfer of asylum seekers to Malaysia, was struck down by the High Court before it could be implemented. In recent years, the Australian government has also followed the United States in carrying out limited screening procedures at sea. Australia's approach to extraterritorial processing has not been an exact copy of US policies. Rather, various US policies, from different points in time, have been drawn on and adapted for Australia's purposes.

5.2.1 Pacific Solution Mark I

As discussed in Chapter 4, the so-called Pacific Solution, which operated from 2001 to 2007, was closely modelled on US practices. The extraterritorial processing component involved two main initiatives.[86] The first was the 'excision' of territories from Australia's 'migration zone', with the effect that the migration legislation pertaining to the mainland (including refugee determination procedures) no longer applied in these places.[87] Initially, only the remote territories of Christmas Island, Ashmore Reef, Cartier Island and Cocos Islands were 'excised'. Later, the excision zone was extended to include all territories outside of mainland Australia.[88] A new category of 'offshore entry person' ('OEP') was then created to catch all asylum seekers who landed without a valid visa or authority on an excised territory.[89] Such OEPs were barred from making a valid application for a Protection visa

---

[83] *CABA*, 43 F 3d 1412, 1425 (11th Cir, 1995).   [84] Ibid 1425–6.
[85] The Manus Island facility ceased operating in 2004, while the detention centre on Nauru was closed in February 2008.
[86] The genesis of the Pacific Solution was examined in detail in Chapter 4.
[87] *Migration Amendment (Excision from Migration Zone) Act 2001* (Cth), amending *Migration Act* s 5(1) ('*Migration Act*') (definition of 'migration zone' and 'excised offshore place').
[88] Note that the excision regime was overhauled in 2012: see below n 153 and accompanying text.
[89] *Migration Amendment (Excision from Migration Zone) Act 2001* (Cth), amending *Migration Act* s 5(1) (definition of 'offshore entry person').

unless the Minister exercised a personal, non-compellable discretion to allow it.[90] Provisions were also introduced to prohibit OEPs from accessing the Australian courts.[91]

The second initiative involved the power to remove OEPs to a designated country for their claims to be processed.[92] Hasty agreements were reached first with Nauru,[93] and shortly thereafter with PNG,[94] for the establishment of offshore detention facilities to which OEPs could be transferred. Asylum seekers processed on Nauru and Manus Island in PNG did not have access to the refugee status determination procedures applied on the Australian mainland. Depending on where they were held and when they arrived, their clams were processed by either UNHCR or Australian immigration officials applying processes stated to be in accordance with those of UNHCR. A total of 1,501 asylum seekers were transferred to Manus Island and Nauru for processing under this policy.[95] Individuals found to be refugees were not automatically entitled to resettlement in Australia. They were required to wait until a place was found for them in Australia or another country. In practice, more than 40 per cent of asylum seekers transferred to the processing centres in Nauru and Manus Island during this period were eventually resettled in Australia.[96]

This regime shares striking similarities with those utilised by the United States. The fact that processing was carried out in a third country in collaboration with UNHCR echoes the third country processing regime the United States established in Jamaica in 1994. However, Australian officials would have been aware that this policy had to be abandoned because the prospect of resettlement in the United States proved to be too big a pull factor for Haitian asylum seekers. So they made it clear that recognition as a refugee did not automatically equate to resettlement in Australia. This draws on the approach the United States has adopted since 1995 with respect to refugees on Guantánamo Bay. As the United States had done in both Guantánamo Bay and Jamaica, Australia created an inferior system for asylum determination, outside domestic legal frameworks. This extraterritoriality allowed for the adoption of streamlined procedures that dispensed with essential features of mainland processing such as access to lawyers, administrative review and judicial review.[97] As

---

[90] *Migration Act* s 46A.

[91] *Migration Act* s 494AA (note that s 494AA(3) provides that the section is not intended to affect the original jurisdiction of the High Court).

[92] *Migration Amendment (Excision from Migration Zone) (Consequential Provisions) Act 2001* (Cth), inserting s 198A of the *Migration Act*.

[93] A thirteen-point Statement of Principles and First Administrative Arrangement was signed by Australian and Nauruan representatives on 10 September 2001: Senate Select Committee, Parliament of Australia, *A Certain Maritime Incident* (2002) 296. A new Memorandum of Understanding was signed on 11 December 2001: *Memorandum of Understanding between the Republic of Nauru and the Commonwealth of Australia for Cooperation in the Administration of Asylum Seekers and Related Issues* (Answers to Questions on Notice, Department of Foreign Affairs and Trade, 19 June 2002).

[94] A Memorandum of Understanding was signed with PNG on establishing a processing centre on Manus Island on 11 October 2001: John Howard, Prime Minister of Australia, 'Arrangement with Papua New Guinea to Process Unauthorised Arrivals' (Media Release, 10 October 2001).

[95] Manne and Corlett, above n 1, 45–6.

[96] Sara Davies and Alex Reilly, 'FactCheck: Were 70% of People Sent to Nauru under the Pacific Solution Resettled in Australia?', *The Conversation* (online), 13 August 2013 http://theconversation.com/factcheck-were-70-of-people-sent-to-nauru-under-the-pacific-solution-resettled-in-australia-16947.

[97] Asylum seekers processed in the United States have a right of review of their primary refugee determination before an Immigration Judge at the Executive Office for Immigration Review. Likewise, asylum seekers processed in Australia have a right to review at the Administrative Appeals Tribunal or Immigration Assessment Authority (depending on their mode of arrival). No such review was

discussed in Chapter 4, my interviews revealed that the Australian government was taking advice from senior bureaucrats involved in designing the US extraterritorial policies in the immediate lead-up to the introduction of the Pacific Solution.[98]

The excision of Australia's offshore islands from Australia's migration zone may also have been inspired by US practice. In some ways, it is a logical extension of the 'entry fiction' introduced in the United States in 1891.[99] This legal fiction allows for certain aliens to be physically present inside the territory of the United States, but deemed as not present for the purposes of immigration law. Under the policy of excision, unauthorised arrivals who reached certain offshore territories were prevented from applying for asylum under domestic Australian law. While possibly inspired by certain US practices, the policy had the effect of expanding the application of extraterritorial processing beyond that which had applied in the United States. Whereas the policy had only been applied in the United States to persons who had been intercepted before they reached US territory, excision as introduced as part of the Pacific Solution extended the applicability of extraterritorial processing to asylum seekers who made landfall at Australia's outlying islands. Reforms introduced in 2013 as part of the Pacific Solution Mark II extended extraterritorial processing to all unauthorised boat arrivals, including those who reached mainland Australia.[100]

5.2.2 Christmas Island

The excision policy took on new significance after the 2008 reforms, which moved the location of extraterritorial processing from the Pacific Islands to the territory of Christmas Island. Upon being elected in 2007, the Australian Labor Party began winding down the Pacific Solution. It did not abandon the policy completely, however, maintaining the legislative provisions underpinning the strategy. Australia's offshore territories remained 'excised' from the 'migration zone'. However, following the February 2008 resettlement in Australia of the final group of refugees detained on Nauru, the government adopted a policy of not exercising the power to transfer OEPs to third countries. Instead, asylum seekers interdicted at sea were to be held on the Australian excised territory of Christmas Island pending a decision by the Minister to exercise the non-delegable, non-compellable discretion to allow an application for a Protection visa. As such, OEPs continued to remain barred from mainland status determination procedures and subject to a separate, inferior processing on Christmas Island.[101] The scheme was essentially designed to create Guantánamo-like

---

available for persons under the extraterritorial regimes at Guantanamo Bay and Jamaica, or on Nauru or Manus Island during the original incarnation of the Pacific Solution.

[98] See Chapter 4, n 67 and accompanying text.   [99] See Chapter 3, nn 3–5 and accompanying text.
[100] See below n 153 and accompanying text.
[101] Whereas undocumented asylum seekers who entered mainland Australia (and the 'migration zone') were entitled to apply for a Protection visa under the *Migration Act* s 36, those who arrived at an excised offshore place could only apply for a Protection visa if the Minister exercised a non-reviewable, non-compellable discretion under the *Migration Act* s 46(A)(2). A non-statutory Refugee Status Determination (RSD) process was set up to advise the Minister as to whether or not to exercise this discretion. Under the 'Pacific Solution', OEPs were not afforded any opportunity for merits review of unfavourable decisions. The Rudd government relaxed policies in this area by introducing a non-statutory independent merits review (IMR) carried out by independent contractors.

extralegal space where status determination procedures could be carried out beyond the reach of the Australian courts.

A non-statutory system was established to process claims for refugee status made by persons taken to Christmas Island. New processes were introduced to allow for Refugee Status Assessment ('RSA') and Independent Merits Review ('IMR') of negative rulings. The government purported that these procedures operated outside of the *Migration Act*. The RSA process allowed an OEP, on request, to be assessed to determine whether he or she was a person with respect to whom Australia had protection obligations under the *Refugee Convention*. RSA procedures were carried out by officers of the Department of Immigration, while IMR was conducted by reviewers employed by a private contractor, Wizard People Pty Ltd. Where an asylum seeker was assessed by the officer or independent reviewer to be a refugee, a submission was made recommending that the Minister *consider exercising* the power conferred by s 46A(2) of the Act. This section allowed the Minister to lift the statutory bar on applying for a Protection visa, or alternatively to exercise the related non-compellable discretion under s 195A to grant a Protection visa to an OEP held in detention. In practice, a recommendation by an RSA or IMR officer to 'lift the s 46A bar' was always followed by a decision by the Minister to exercise the discretion contained in s 46A(2) and grant a Protection visa in accordance with s 195A.

The effect was the creation of a parallel system of refugee status determination for persons processed on Christmas Island. The processes were inferior to those that applied to onshore determinations in a number of respects.[102] Most importantly for the current analysis, as the process purported to be non-statutory, the protections of the *Migration Act*, the *Migration Regulations 1994* (Cth) and Australian case law interpreting Australia's obligations under the *Refugee Convention* were seen as not being binding on either the RSA officer or independent reviewer. The result was that there were purportedly no enforceable criteria in place to ensure claims were 'assessed in accordance with, or even taking into account, Australia's international protection obligations'.[103] Also concerning was the fact that the regime operated in a completely discretionary manner. Even when an OEP was found to engage Australia's protection obligations through the RSA or IMR process, the applicant's access to a Protection visa was reliant on the Minister's discretionary power.

This regime was challenged by two Tamil asylum seekers in *Plaintiff M61/2010E v Commonwealth*; *Plaintiff M69 of 2010 v Commonwealth* ('*Offshore Processing Case*').[104] The plaintiffs had arrived by boat and claimed refugee status on the basis that they feared persecution from the Sri Lankan army and paramilitary groups, due to their alleged support for the Tamil Tigers separatist movement. Their protection claims had been rejected at both the RSA and IMR stages. Each plaintiff instituted proceedings in the original jurisdiction of the High Court, naming the Commonwealth, the Minister and others as defendants. The plaintiffs made two main claims. First, they alleged they were not afforded procedural fairness during either the original RSA assessment or the subsequent IMR review. Second, each claimed that the decision-makers who undertook the assessment and the relevant

---

[102] For a detailed analysis of these shortcomings, see Michelle Foster and Jason Pobjoy, 'A Failed Case of Legal Exceptionalism? Refugee Status Determination in Australia's "Excised" Territory' (2011) 23 *International Journal of Refugee Law* 583, 591–9.
[103] Ibid 593.   [104] (2010) 243 CLR 319.

review made errors of law by not treating themselves as bound by relevant provisions of the *Migration Act* and case law interpreting these provisions.[105]

The government sought to rely on the Full Federal Court decision in *Ruddock v Vadarlis* to argue that the RSA and IMR regimes were undertaken in exercise of a non-statutory executive power under s 61 of the *Australian Constitution*.[106] This power, it was submitted, was a prerogative executive power to inquire. While capable of informing the government and shaping the course of executive decisions, the exercise of the power did not in itself directly determine rights. As the inquiry was said to affect neither legal rights nor interests, there was no obligation to afford procedural fairness in conducting the RSA and IMR processes. Nor were the decision-makers undertaking the inquiry bound by certain provisions of the *Migration Act* and associated case law.

The High Court unanimously rejected the government's characterisation of the power exercised by the RSA and IMR decision-makers. Instead, the Court found that the power was *statutory*, being tied to the Minister's consideration of whether to exercise his discretion under s 46A or s 195A(2) of the *Migration Act*. The Court found that the Minister's practice and the published policies governing the RSA and IMR processes indicated that the Minister had made a decision to tie the non-reviewable, non-compellable discretions conferred by ss 46A and 195A to the assessment and review outcomes.

A key factor in the Court's reasoning was the fact that the *Migration Act* required the detention of an OEP for the duration of RSA and IMR processes.[107] The Court expressed a reluctance to accept that a statutory power to detain a person could permit the continuation of that detention at the unconstrained discretion of the executive.[108] Such detention, the Court found, could only be lawful if the relevant assessment and review had some sort of statutory footing.

The Court held that RSA and IMR determinations had to be carried out in accordance with the *Migration Act*. The relevant inquiries were made pursuant to the power to lift the bar under s 46A and permit a claimant to make a valid claim for a Protection visa. The Court determined that the '[e]xercise of that power on the footing that Australia owed protection obligations to the plaintiff would be pointless unless the determination was made according to the criteria and principles identified in the *Migration Act*, as construed by the courts of Australia'.[109]

It followed that the reviewer had made an error of law by treating the *Migration Act* and decided cases as no more than guides to decision-making. The decision did not strike down any aspect of the scheme for processing OEPs. But it did overturn one of the fundamental assumptions underlying the scheme. Whereas the government believed its assessment process was 'non-statutory' and thus unreviewable, the Court found that the process was in fact statutory, and as such, decisions could be reviewed by the courts for compliance with relevant statutory provisions and on procedural fairness grounds.

---

[105] Plaintiff M69 made a further constitutional claim that s 46A of the *Migration Act* was invalid as the provision had the effect of precluding judicial oversight. This argument was rejected by the court. For analysis of this issue, see Mary Crock and Daniel Ghezelbash, 'Due Process and Rule of Law as Human Rights: The Court and the "Offshore" Processing of Asylum Seekers' (2011) 18 *Australian Journal of Administrative Law* 101, 110–11.
[106] (2001) 110 FCR 491.   [107] See *Migration Act* s 189.
[108] *Offshore Processing Case* (2010) 243 CLR 319, 348 [63]–[64].   [109] Ibid 356 [88].

The fact that the decision in the *Offshore Processing Case* was delivered as a single unanimous judgment by the High Court may give the impression that the case involved an uncontroversial application of the relevant legal rules and precedent. However, the decision appears to diverge from previous High Court jurisprudence in its analysis of two key issues. First, the Court's attitude appears to have shifted in regard to the permissibility of discretionary executive detention.[110] The decision to link the right to procedural fairness with the plaintiff's continued detention rested on a view that '[i]t is not readily to be supposed that a statutory power to detain a person permits continuation of that detention at the unconstrained discretion of the Executive'.[111] However, as Rayner Thwaites has noted, this generates a dissonances with the majority reasoning in *Al-Kateb v Godwin* ('*Al-Kateb*'):[112]

> In the *Offshore Processing Case*, the High Court lambasted the idea that a person can continue in detention 'at the unconstrained discretion of the executive'. There were two components to this characterisation of the government's position by the Court in the *Offshore Processing Case*: the means of obtaining release were completely within the control of the executive; and no predictions could be made as to whether, or when, those means would be utilised by the government. These components also served to characterise the power of detention pending removal given legal sanction in *Al-Kateb*. There is the distinction that, in *Al-Kateb*, the ability to effect a detainee's removal from Australia is not 'wholly within the control of the [Australian] executive'. It is dependent on the cooperation of foreign governments. But in a situation where the Australian government cannot effect removal, *Al-Kateb* illustrated that the detainee may be entirely dependent on the government to obtain release. Absent removal, *Al-Kateb* means that any remaining prospect of the detainees' release is 'wholly within the control of the executive'.[113]

Second, the reasoning of the Court represented a shift in approach to the relevance of international law to the statutory construction of the *Migration Act*. In the *Offshore Processing Case*, the Court stated: 'read as a whole, the *Migration Act* contains an elaborated and interconnected set of statutory provisions directed to the purpose of responding to the international obligations which Australia has undertaken in the Refugees Convention and the Refugees Protocol'.[114]

This is a clear departure from earlier case law, which had drawn a much more limited link between the *Migration Act* and the *Refugee Convention*. For example, in *MIMIA v QAAH*, the Court expressed the view that the *Migration Act* should not be construed as an attempt to implement the entirety of the *Refugee Convention* into Australian law.[115] The Court noted that only s 36 of the *Migration Act* related to the *Refugee Convention*, and then only to use its art 1 definition of 'refugee'.[116] As such, the Court was able to uphold the lawfulness of the Temporary Protection visa program operating at that time, despite concerns about the regime's compatibility with the *Refugee Convention*.[117] Gummow ACJ

---

[110] Rayner Thwaites, *The Liberty of Non-Citizens: Indefinite Detention in Commonwealth Countries* (Hart, 2014) 119.
[111] *Offshore Processing Case* (2010) 243 CLR 319, 348 [64].   [112] (2004) 219 CLR 562.
[113] Thwaites, above n 110, 107 (footnotes omitted).   [114] (2010) 243 CLR 319, 339 [27].
[115] (2006) 231 CLR 1.   [116] Ibid 14 [34].
[117] Under the Temporary Protection visa policy in operation from 1999 to 2008, asylum seekers who arrived in Australia without authorisation and were found to be in need of protection were granted temporary visas to stay in Australia for three years, after which their protection claims were reassessed.

and Callinan, Heydon and Crennan JJ stated that 'it is the law of Australia which prevails in case of any conflict between it and the [Refugee] Convention. It is the law of Australia which must first be identified'.[118]

5.2.3 The Malaysian Solution

The decision in the *Offshore Processing Case* resulted in a surge of litigation by OEPs challenging adverse refugee status determinations. This coincided with a significant increase in the number of people arriving by boat.[119] Public opinion began to turn against the government, with a view that the perceived 'softening' of Australia's border protection policies was to blame.[120] In response, the Gillard Labor government moved to introduce a number of measures to stem the flow of new arrivals. First, attempts were made to seek agreements for the creation of a regional processing centre. East Timor was flagged as a possible location, but this plan was abandoned after support within the East Timorese government evaporated.[121] Second, the government entered into an 'arrangement' with Malaysia that involved sending 800 OEPs to that country in exchange for Australia resettling 4,000 UNHCR-recognised refugees from Malaysia ('*Malaysia Arrangement*').[122] This differed from the Pacific Solution as the asylum seekers transferred to Malaysia would not be screened for protection claims. Instead, they were to be issued with temporary permits giving them legal status and work rights in Malaysia for the duration of the four-year deal.

The government sought to rely on s 198A of the *Migration Act* that enabled the transfer of OEPs to a 'declared' country. Section 198A(3)(a) set out the conditions necessary to designate a 'declared' country:

> The Minister may declare in writing that a specified country:
>
> (i) provides access, for persons seeking asylum, to effective procedures for assessing their need for protection; and
> (ii) provides protection for persons seeking asylum, pending determination of their refugee status; and
> (iii) provides protection to persons who are given refugee status, pending their voluntary repatriation to their country of origin or resettlement in another country, and
> (iv) meets relevant human rights standards in providing that protection.[123]

A similar Temporary Protection visa regime was reintroduced in 2014 and remains in force at the time of writing in June 2017.

[118] *MIMIA v QAAH* (2006) 231 CLR 1, 14 [33]. It is a well-established principle in Australian law that statute law takes precedent over international law. See, eg, *Polites v The Commonwealth* (1945) 70 CLR 60, 69 (Latham CJ stating that 'courts are bound by the statute law of their country, even if the law should violate a rule of international law').

[119] See Appendix, Table A.2.

[120] See Mary Crock, 'First Term Blues: Labor, Refugees and Immigration Reform' (2010) 17 *Australian Journal of Administrative Law* 205.

[121] Peter Billings, Anthony Cassimatis and Marissa Dooris, 'Irregular Migration, Refugee Protection and the "Malaysian Solution"' in Angus Francis and Rowena Maguire (eds), *Protection of Refugees and Displaced Persons in the Asia Pacific Region* (Routledge, 2016) 135, 144.

[122] *Arrangement between the Government of Australia and the Government of Malaysia on Transfer and Resettlement*, signed 25 July 2011.

[123] Note that this provision was repealed by the *Migration Legislation Amendment (Regional Processing and Other Measures) Act 2012* (Cth), which amended the *Migration Act 1958* (Cth) by replacing s 198A with a new s 198AA. See below nn 165–70 and accompanying text.

A declaration made by the Minister under this section triggered a corresponding power of removal under s 198A(1) of the *Migration Act*. That power authorised the Department to remove an OEP to a country which is the subject of the declaration. These were the same legislative provisions the Australian government had relied on to transfer OEPs to Nauru and PNG from 2001 to 2007 as part of the Pacific Solution. The validity of a ministerial declaration with respect to Nauru was upheld in a line of Federal Court cases initiated in 2002, referred to here as the *Sadiqi* litigation.[124] The litigation involved a number of complex claims which are beyond the scope of analysis here. The relevant point for our purposes relates to the proper construction of the criteria for making a declaration under s 198A(3)(a). The government had contended that all that was required for the valid exercise of the power was that the Minister 'declare in writing' that a specified country meets the four identified criteria.[125] On this reading, the objective existence of any facts relating to those criteria was not required as a precondition for the exercise of this power. Counsel for the plaintiff proposed an alternative interpretation of s 198A(3)(a) as constituting jurisdictional facts, such that proof of their existence was essential to the valid exercise of the jurisdiction conferred by s 198A upon the Minister. Put simply, a declaration would be invalid if made in respect of a country that did not objectively meet the criteria enumerated in s 198A(3)(a).[126] All three Federal Court judges who addressed this question at various stages of the litigation rejected the argument that the criteria of s 198A(3)(a) should be construed as constituting jurisdictional facts.[127]

It was not until 2011 that the High Court was called upon to determine this issue. *Plaintiff M70/2011 v MIAC* ('*Malaysian Solution Case*')[128] was a challenge to the declaration made under s 198A in respect of Malaysia.[129] A challenge was brought on behalf of two asylum seekers from Afghanistan who were part of the first cohort of OEPs scheduled to be transferred to Malaysia. The plaintiffs sought an injunction against their removal from Australia. Their argument focused on the fact that there were no binding international or domestic legal protections for asylum seekers or refugees in Malaysia. The absence of such protections, it was argued, meant that the criteria in s 198A(3) were not met. As a result, the Minister's declaration under that section was outside the power conferred on the Minister by the Act, and thus invalid.

---

[124] The litigation spanned more than eight years and was comprised of the following cases (collectively '*Sadiqi* litigation'): *WAJC v MIMIA* [2002] FCA 1631 (23 December 2002) (claim for interlocutory relief); *Plaintiff P1/2003 v MIMIA* [2003] FCA 1029 (26 September 2003) (claim for further interlocutory relief); *Plaintiff P1/2003 v MIMIA* [2003] FCA 1370 (26 November 2003) (application for an extension of motion in which to file and serve a notice of appeal); *Plaintiff P1/2003 v Ruddock* (2007) 157 FCR 518 (application by plaintiff to amend statement of claims); *Sadiqi v Commonwealth* [2008] FCA 1262 (18 August 2008) (relating to discovery); *Sadiqi v Commonwealth (No 2)* (2009) 181 FCR 1 ('*Sadiqi (No 2)*') (determination of preliminary legal questions); *Sadiqi v Commonwealth (No 3)* [2010] FCA 596 (11 June 2010) (determination of substantive claim).
[125] *Sadiqi (No 2)* (2009) 181 FCR 1, 47 [218].   [126] Ibid 46 [215].
[127] *Plaintiff P1/2003 v MIMIA* [2003] FCA 1029 (26 September 2003) [49]–[50] (French J); [2003] FCA 1370 (26 November 2003) [14] (Nicholson J); *Sadiqi (No 2)* (2009) 181 FCR 1, 49 [223]–[225] (McKerracher J).
[128] (2011) 244 CLR 144.
[129] *Instrument of Declaration of Malaysia as a Declared Country under Subsection 198A(3) of the Migration Act 1958*, 25 July 2011.

The main legal issue considered by the Court was the same question of statutory construction considered in the *Sadiqi* litigation: what was the relationship between the objective existence of the criteria set out in s 198A(3)(a) and the Minister's power to issue a declaration? The plaintiffs argued two alternative constructions of the provisions. First, they made the same argument put forward in the *Sadiqi* litigation, contending that the criteria in s 198A(3)(a) constituted 'jurisdictional facts' for the exercise of the power to make the declaration. On this construction, the Court had the power to find the declaration invalid if the criteria were not, as a matter of fact, satisfied.[130] In the alternative, the plaintiffs put forward a new argument that as a minimum, the Minister needs to be satisfied of the s 198A(3)(a) criteria, and that whether the Minister had properly reached a state of satisfaction was judicially reviewable.[131]

The government's position was that the only prerequisite for the exercise of the Minister's power was that it be 'exercised in good faith and within the scope and for the purpose of the statute'.[132] The government's submission on this point cited the *Sadiqi* litigation as authority for its position.[133] The outcome of the *Sadiqi* litigation also appears to have played an important role in shaping the legal advice given to the government by the Solicitor-General, which stated that the proposed Malaysian arrangement would withstand judicial scrutiny.[134]

The majority of the High Court rejected the government's submissions. Of the seven judges, five determined that the objective satisfaction of each of the criteria set out in s 198A(3)(a) were jurisdictional facts.[135] In a joint judgment, Gummow, Hayne, Crennan and Bell JJ reasoned that to determine otherwise would 'pay insufficient regard to [s 198A(3)(a)'s] text, context and evident purpose'.[136] In reaching this conclusion, the joint judgment affirmed the position taken in the *Offshore Processing Case* as to the relevance of the *Refugee Convention* in establishing the context and purpose of the *Migration Act*. The majority reasoned that the safeguards included in s 198A(3)(a) 'are to be seen as reflecting a legislative intention to adhere to the understanding of Australia's obligations under the *Refugee Convention and Refugees Protocol* that informed other provisions made by the Act'.[137] Kiefel J concurred with the joint judgment's finding on this point.[138] In a separate judgment, French CJ (who was involved in the *Sadiqi* litigation in his previous role as a Federal Court judge) rejected the notion that the objective fulfilment of the criteria in s 198A(3)(a) was a jurisdictional fact.[139] His Honour, however, accepted the alternative construction put forward by the plaintiffs: that the Minister must be satisfied of the

---

[130] *Malaysian Solution Case* (2011) 244 CLR 144, 193 [105].   [131] Ibid 194 [107].   [132] Ibid 194 [108].
[133] See MIAC, 'Submissions of the Defendants', Submission in the *Malaysian Solution Case*, 18 August 2011, [66]-[67].
[134] Mary Crock and Mary Anne Kenny, 'Rethinking the Guardianship of Refugee Children after the Malaysian Solution' (2012) 34 *Sydney Law Review* 437, 456 (quoting Minister Bowen's statement made on 8 August 2011 that '[s]uffice to say our legal advice remains the same as it has been all the way through. The Commonwealth Government is on very strong legal grounds. Very strong legal grounds in the case').
[135] *Malaysian Solution Case* (2011) 244 CLR 144, 194 [109] (Gummow, Hayne, Crennan and Bell JJ); 236 [255]-[256] (Kiefel J).
[136] Ibid 194 [109].
[137] Ibid 160 [10], quoting the *Offshore Processing Case* (2010) 243 CLR 319, 341 [34].
[138] Ibid 223 [212].   [139] Ibid 180-1 [59].

s 198A(3)(a) criteria, and that the question of whether the Minister had properly reached a state of satisfaction was a jurisdictional fact.

All six of the concurring judges concluded that, for the criteria in s 198A(3)(a) to be met, the protections contained in that section must exist as a matter of law.[140] For the majority, the agreed fact that no such legal protections existed in Malaysia under domestic or international law meant that the relevant jurisdictional facts under s 198A(3)(a) were not met. As such, the Minister's declaration was invalid.[141] For French CJ, the Minister's failure to *consider* whether such legal protections existed meant that a jurisdictional error had occurred.[142]

Heydon J, in dissent, was the only justice to refer directly to the *Sadiqi* litigation.[143] He cited, with approval, the three Federal Court judges' separate pronouncements that the subjective nature of the criteria set out in s 198A(3)(a) evidences a legislative intention that the subject matter of the declaration is for ministerial satisfaction.[144] For Heydon J, all that was required for a valid declaration was that the Minister consider the criteria in s 198A(3)(a) and assert that they exist as a matter of fact. His Honour construed the criteria as requiring practical protections and not legal obligations.[145] The Minister had considered the practical protections enshrined in the *Malaysia Arrangement* and its Operational Guidelines.[146] This was sufficient to form the basis of a valid declaration under s 198A(3).[147]

5.2.4 Return to Offshore Processing: Pacific Solution Mark II

With the Malaysian Solution frustrated by the High Court, the Labor government searched for policy alternatives. It established an expert panel to assist with this task.[148] Based on the recommendations of the panel, the government reversed its opposition to extraterritorial processing on Nauru and Manus Island and moved to reopen the facilities at those locations.[149] The 'Pacific Solution Mark II' was born. The government negotiated new memoranda of understanding ('MOU') with Nauru and PNG to reopen the processing camps on their territories.[150] The first group of asylum seekers were transferred to Nauru

---

[140] *Malaysian Solution Case* (2011) 244 CLR 144, 195 [116] (Gummow, Hayne, Crennan and Bell JJ), 182–3 [64]–[66] (French CJ), 244 [244] (Kiefel J).
[141] Ibid 201–2 [135]–[136] (Gummow, Hayne, Crennan and Bell JJ), 236–7 [255]–[256] (Kiefel J).
[142] Ibid 182 [65].   [143] Ibid 208–10 [161]–[164].
[144] Ibid, referring to French J's comments in *Plaintiff P1/2003 v MIMIA* [2003] FCA 1029 (26 September 2003) [49]; McKerracher J's comments in *Sadiqi v The Commonwealth [No 2]* (2009) 181 FCR 1, 49 [223]. See also *Plaintiff P1/2003 v Ruddock* (2007) 157 FCR 518, 537 [69] (Nicholson J).
[145] *Malaysian Solution Case* (2011) 244 CLR 144, 208–9 [162].
[146] DIAC, *Operational Guidelines to Support Transfers and Resettlement* (Australian Government, 2011).
[147] *Malaysian Solution Case* (2011) 244 CLR 144, 208–9 [162].
[148] Angus Houston, Paris Aristotle and Michael L'Estrange, *Report of the Expert Panel on Asylum Seekers* (Australian Government, 2012).
[149] For a detailed analysis of the reestablishment of offshore processing and its operation between 2012 and 2015, see Madeline Gleeson, *Offshore: Behind the Wire on Manus and Nauru* (NewSouth, 2016).
[150] Julia Gillard, Prime Minister and Chris Bowen, Minister for Immigration, 'Australia Signs Memorandum of Understanding with Nauru' (Media Release, 29 August 2012); Julia Gillard, Prime Minister and Chris Bowen, Minister for Immigration, 'Australia and Papua New Guinea Sign Updated Memorandum of Understanding' (Media Release, 8 September 2012).

on 14 September 2012,[151] and another to the Manus Island facility in PNG on 20 November 2012.[152] The new extraterritorial processing regime differed from the original 'Pacific Solution' in a number of ways. First, amendments to the *Migration Act* expanded the categories of persons liable for transfer to third countries to include all unauthorised boat arrivals, not just those who arrived at an excised offshore place.[153] Consequently, the term 'OEP' was abandoned and replaced with 'unauthorised maritime arrival' ('UMA'). Second, processing on Nauru and Manus Island was seen as a direct pathway to resettlement in Australia. However, asylum seekers who tried to reach Australia by boat were to be subject to the 'no advantage' principle. They would not be given any advantage as compared to asylum seekers waiting for their claims to be processed by UNHCR in countries like Malaysia and Indonesia. Most importantly, asylum seekers would not be issued Protection visas until the same amount of time had passed as would have been the case if they had waited for a place through Australia's offshore resettlement program. Exactly how long this would be was never defined. This incarnation of the offshore processing regime was short-lived. The number of asylum seekers arriving by boat far outstripped capacity on Nauru and Manus Island.[154] Just over three months after the resumption of offshore processing, the facilities were full and the government began releasing new arrivals into the Australian community on bridging visas that forbade them from working.[155] They would be subject to the same 'no advantage' policy and would experience extensive delays in the processing of their protection claims.

The offshore processing policy received a major overhaul when Kevin Rudd was reappointed as Labor leader and Prime Minister. From 19 July 2013, no one who attempted to reach Australia by boat would ever be given the chance to settle in Australia.[156] The 700 or so asylum seekers on Nauru and Manus Island at the time of the announcement were transferred back to Australia. However, all future arrivals would have to remain in PNG or Nauru, or wait for resettlement in a third country. The Australian government negotiated new MOUs with both PNG and Nauru and implemented new procedures that remain in force at the time of writing.[157] Whereas under previous incarnations of the offshore processing policy, refugee status determinations had been carried out by UNHCR or Australian government officials, status determinations under the new regime are administered pursuant to newly enacted domestic refugee legislation in Nauru and PNG, by officials from those countries.[158] The updated MOU signed with PNG allows not only for the transfer of asylum seekers for processing, but also for the settlement in

---

[151] Paige Taylor and Lanai Vasek, 'First Asylum Flight Arrives in Nauru', *The Australian* (online), 14 September 2012 www.theaustralian.com.au/national-affairs/first-asylum-flight-departs-for-nauru/news-story/dc7f9df2348934cf943f3b9933e3b664.

[152] Simon Cullen, 'First Asylum Seekers arrive on Manus Island', *ABC News* (online), 21 November 2012 www.abc.net.au/news/2012-11-21/first-asylum-seekers-arrive-on-manus-island/4383876.

[153] *Migration Amendment (Unauthorised Maritime Arrivals and Other Measures) Act 2012* (Cth).

[154] Appendix, Table A.2.   [155] *Migration Regulations 1994* (Cth) Sch 2 sc 050 (Bridging Visa E).

[156] Interview with Kevin Rudd, Prime Minister of Australia, and Peter O'Neill, Prime Minister of PNG (Joint Press Conference, Brisbane, 19 July 2013).

[157] *Memorandum of Understanding between the Republic of Nauru and the Commonwealth of Australia, relating to the Transfer to and Assessment of Persons in Nauru, and Related Issues*, signed 3 August 2013; *Regional Resettlement Arrangement between Australia and Papua New Guinea*, signed 19 July 2013.

[158] Australian officials are involved behind the scenes in the RSD process in a supervisory capacity: see Chapter 6, n 180 and accompanying text.

PNG of transferees assessed to be refugees. Practical difficulties as well as repeated backflips on this issue by the PNG government have meant that to date, the settlement process has been slow and fraught with problems.[159] Nauru has made it clear that it cannot offer permanent resettlement. Rather, those recognised as refugees are given rolling six-month visas which allow them to live in Nauru temporarily until a third country can be found to resettle them.[160] In September 2014, Australia signed a MOU with Cambodia that allowed for the voluntary resettlement in Cambodia of some of the recognised refugees from Nauru.[161] Initial reports were that up to 1,000 refugees could be transferred under the deal.[162] However, at the time of writing, only six refugees had been resettled in Cambodia and of these, four had decided to return to their home countries, citing unbearable living conditions.[163] This has come at the cost of approximately AUD $55 million for the Australian government in additional aid and direct payment for resettlement services.[164] A recent deal struck between Australia and the United States for the resettlement of some of the refugees on Nauru and Manus Island to the United States is examined in section 5.2.5.

In order to ensure that the new extraterritorial processing arrangements would not be invalidated by the courts, legislation was passed in 2012 to replace the threshold requirements that had been relied on to strike down the Malaysian arrangement.[165] Section 198A of the *Migration Act* was replaced by a new subdivision titled 'Regional Processing'.[166] The statement of intent included in that subdivision made it clear that the purpose of the changes was to side-step the High Court's decision in the *Malaysian Solution Case*:

(i) people smuggling, and its undesirable consequences including the resulting loss of life at sea, are major regional problems which need to be addressed;
(ii) offshore entry persons, including offshore entry persons in respect of whom Australia has or may have protection obligations under the Refugees Convention as amended by the Refugees Protocol, should be able to be taken to any country designated to be a regional processing country;

---

[159] See Chapter 6, nn 126–8 and accompanying text.
[160] *Immigration Regulations 2013* (Nauru) reg 9A (Temporary settlement visa).
[161] *Memorandum of Understanding between the Government of the Kingdom of Cambodia and the Government of Australia, relating to the Settlement of Refugees in Cambodia*, signed 26 September 2014.
[162] Samantha Hawley, 'Scott Morrison to Sign MOU on Refugee Resettlement, Cambodian Government Says', *ABC News* (online), 25 September 2014 www.abc.net.au/news/2014-09-24/scott-morrison-to-head-to-cambodia-to-sign-refugee-resettlement/5766282.
[163] Madeline Gleeson, *In Focus: Resettlement of Refugees from Nauru to Cambodia* (21 November 2016) UNSW Kaldor Centre for International Refugee Law www.kaldorcentre.unsw.edu.au/news/focus-resettlement-refugees-nauru-cambodia.
[164] Madeline Gleeson, 'FactCheck Q&A: How Much Was Spent on the Cambodia Refugee Deal and How Many Were Settled?', *The Conversation* (online), 21 November 2016 https://theconversation.com/factcheck-qanda-how-much-was-spent-on-the-cambodia-refugee-deal-and-how-many-were-settled-68807.
[165] *Migration Legislation Amendment (Regional Processing and Other Measures) Act 2012* (Cth), amending the *Migration Act* by replacing s 198A with a new s 198AA. The new provisions made it clear that the only condition for the exercise of the power to designate a country is that the Minister thinks that it is in the national interest to make such a designation.
[166] *Migration Act* div 8 sub-div B, inserted by *Migration Legislation Amendment (Regional Processing and Other Measures) Act 2012* (Cth).

(iii) it is a matter for the Minister and Parliament to decide which countries should be designated as regional processing countries; and
(iv) the designation of a country to be a regional processing country need not be determined by reference to the international obligations or domestic law of that country.[167]

The subdivision included s 198AB that set out a new process by which the Minister can issue a legislative instrument designating a country as a 'regional processing country'. The only express condition for the exercise of this power is that 'the Minister thinks that it is in the national interest'.[168] In considering the national interest, the Minister is to take into account whether there are assurances in place that persons transferred to that country will not be subject to *refoulement*, and whether the country has processes in place to carry out refugee status determinations.[169] Such assurances need not be legally binding.[170]

Plaintiff S156/2013 v MIBP ('*Plaintiff S156*')[171] concerned a challenge to the designation of PNG as a 'regional processing country' under the new legislative framework.[172] The plaintiff was an Iranian asylum seeker who had been transferred to Manus Island in PNG. He sought to challenge the Minister's designation on both constitutional and statutory grounds. The High Court dismissed the challenge in a short unanimous judgment. The constitutional argument was that the new statutory framework for third country transfer was invalid as it was not supported by the aliens power,[173] or any other of the Commonwealth government's legislative heads of power.[174] The plaintiff acknowledged that legislation excluding or deporting non-citizens falls under the aliens power.[175] However, it was claimed that the regional processing regime goes much further than this by imposing subsequent control, including detention, over the non-citizen in a regional processing country for purposes unconnected to the determination of status or entry under Australian law.

The plaintiff cited the High Court's decision in *Chu Kheng Lim v MILGEA* ('*Lim*') as imposing a 'proportionality' test when determining whether a law is authorised under the aliens power.[176] Reference was made to Gaudron J's comments that laws 'imposing special obligations or special disabilities on aliens ... which are unconnected with their entitlement to remain in Australia and which are not appropriate and adapted to regulating entry or facilitating departure' are not supported by the aliens power.[177] The plaintiff also sought to rely on comments of the majority in *Lim* about the limits placed on executive detention by the exclusive nature of the judicial power in Chapter III of the *Australian Constitution*. Specifically, the plaintiff cited the majority's finding that laws authorising executive detention would be valid only if incarceration could be seen as 'reasonably capable of being seen as necessary for the purposes of deportation or ... an application for an entry permit to be made and considered'.[178] The High Court rejected the relevance of these proportionality considerations by construing the relevant provisions as dealing only with removal, a purpose clearly authorised by the aliens power. The legislation made no provisions for control

---

[167] *Migration Act* s 198AA. This intent was also confirmed in the Revised Explanatory Memorandum to the *Migration Amendment (Regional Processing and Other Measures Act 2012* (Cth).
[168] *Migration Act* s 198AB(2). [169] Ibid s 198AB(3)(a). [170] Ibid s 198AB(4).
[171] (2014) 254 CLR 28. [172] Ibid. [173] *Australian Constitution* s 51(xix).
[174] In particular, the immigration power (s 51(xxvii)) or the external affairs power (s 51(xxix)).
[175] *Plaintiff S156* (2014) 254 CLR 28 43 [26]. [176] (1992) 176 CLR 1. [177] Ibid 57.
[178] Ibid 33 (per Brennan, Deane and Dawson JJ).

beyond deportation. As such, any detention imposed on the non-citizen after removal was not relevant to determining constitutional validity of the removal provisions.[179]

In the alternative to the constitutional argument, the plaintiff challenged the validity of the Minister's declaration of PNG as a 'regional processing country' on the grounds that the Minister had failed to take into account a number of relevant considerations. Section 198AB stated that the Minister 'must' only consider Australia's national interest when deciding whether to designate a country. However, the plaintiff argued that other mandatory considerations could be implied. These included the potential breach of Australia's international law obligations, the potential for arbitrary and indefinite detention and the capacity of PNG to implement its international legal obligations. In support of such a construction, the plaintiffs cited the pronouncement in the *Offshore Processing Case* – affirmed in the *Malaysian Solution Case* – that the *Migration Act*, read as a whole, contains an 'elaborated and interconnected set of statutory provisions directed to the purpose of responding to the international obligations which Australia has undertaken in the Refugees Convention and Refugees Protocol'.[180]

The Court rejected this argument. The Justices pointed to the unambiguous language of the Act.[181] They ruled that in exercising discretion, the Minister is obliged only to consider the matters listed in s 198AB(3)(a). In reaching this conclusion, the Court appears to have retreated from the statements made in respect to the relevance of the *Refugee Convention* in construing the *Migration Act* in the *Offshore Processing* and *Malaysian Solution Cases*. It acknowledged that '[t]here may be some doubt' whether the new legislative framework for third country transfers, which was introduced after those cases, 'can be said to respond to Australia's obligations under the Refugees Convention'.[182] The case underscores the precarious status of legal victories on behalf of asylum seekers and refugees which are based on statutory interpretation. The protections afforded by such decisions can be overturned by the legislature with clear words of necessary intendment. The legislature used the High Court's reasoning in the *Malaysian Solution Case* as a blueprint for drafting new legislative provisions that placed the offshore processing regime beyond judicial scrutiny.

With the door for challenging the designation of regional processing countries seemingly shut by the High Court in *Plaintiff S156*, refugee advocates decided to change tack. In *Plaintiff M68/2015 v MIBP*, the legal team working on behalf of a Bangladeshi asylum seeker sought to challenge the offshore processing regime by questioning the government's involvement in detaining asylum seekers on Nauru.[183] It was argued that the Australian government was funding and substantially participating in the plaintiff's detention in Nauru without lawful authority.[184] The plaintiff's case was weakened by two developments which occurred in the immediate lead-up to the hearing. First, the Australian government passed legislation creating an express power in the *Migration Act* to fund and participate in regional processing arrangements.[185] The new s 198AHA provided a retrospective power to the Commonwealth, in circumstances where it had entered into an arrangement with

---

[179] *Plaintiff S156* (2014) 254 CLR 28, 44 [32]–[33], 46 [38].
[180] *Offshore Processing Case* (2010) 243 CLR 319, 339 [27]; *Malaysian Solution Case* (2011) 244 CLR 144, 160 [10].
[181] *Plaintiff S156* (2014) 254 CLR 28, 46 [40].   [182] Ibid 39 [44].
[183] (2016) 257 CLR 42, 71–2 [46] (French CJ, Kiefel and Nettle JJ), 130–1 [262] (Keane J) ('*Plaintiff M68*').
[184] Ibid 65 [20] (French CJ and Kiefel and Nettle JJ).
[185] Migration Amendment (Regional Processing Arrangements) Act 2015 (Cth).

another country, to 'take, or cause to be taken any action in relation to the arrangement or the regional processing function of the country'. 'Action' was defined as including 'exercising restraint over the liberty of a person'.[186] It also authorised the making of payments to the country for those purposes.[187] Second, the Nauruan government announced that the Regional Processing Centre (RPC) on Nauru would cease to be a closed centre and asylum seekers would be permitted freedom of movement on the island.[188] The relevant question before the Court was hence narrowed to focus on the detention of the plaintiff in the relevant period before the 'open centre' arrangements had come into effect.

The plaintiff's challenge was dismissed by a majority of 6:1. The joint judgment of French CJ and Kiefel and Nettle JJ held that detention was carried out by the Nauruan, rather than the Australian, government.[189] They further found the degree of the Australian government's involvement in the arrangements on Nauru was validly authorised under s 198AHA. Keane J dismissed the case on similar grounds.[190] One of the plaintiff's central arguments was that the detention carried out by the Australian government contravened the constitutional limits placed on executive detention in *Lim*.[191] This was because the detention could not be construed as being carried out for one of the authorised purposes in *Lim*: namely, deportation or considering an application of an entry permit into Australia.[192] Having found the detention was being carried out by the Nauruan rather than Australian government, French CJ and Kiefel, Nettle and Keane JJ concluded that the *Lim* principles were not relevant. However, Their Honours noted that s 198AHA did not give the government an unfettered power to participate in offshore processing arrangements. Australia could only cause or spend public money on detention on Nauru if it served the purpose of processing asylum seekers.[193]

Bell and Gageler JJ, in their separate judgments, considered Australia's involvement in Nauru was sufficient to find that it had substantially participated in the detention of the plaintiff.[194] However, they found that this action was validly authorised under s 198AHA. In relation to the *Lim* argument, Bell J found Australia's involvement in detention valid as it could 'reasonably be seen to be related to Nauru's regional processing functions'.[195] In doing so, Her Honour appears to have added to the exceptions in *Lim* to authorise detention for the processing and removal of aliens not only from Australia, but also from third countries. Gageler J also found the detention to be lawful. In relation to the Chapter III arguments, His Honour applied the more general test for executive detention which he had developed in recent judgments,[196] rather than the *Lim* test which only applies to executive detention of aliens. Executive detention would be invalid unless two conditions were met. First, the duration of detention must be reasonably necessary to implement a purpose which is identified in the statute and is capable of being fulfilled. Second, the duration of detention

---

[186] *Migration Act* s 198AHA(5)   [187] Ibid s 198AHA(2)(b).
[188] *Plaintiff M68* (2016) 257 CLR 42, 64–5 [19].   [189] Ibid 67–8 [32]–[34].
[190] Ibid 124–5 [238]–[240].   [191] (1992) 176 CLR 1.
[192] See *Lim* (1992) 176 CLR 1, 33 (Brennan, Deane and Dawson JJ); see Chapter 3, nn 195–209 and accompanying text.
[193] *Plaintiff M68* (2016) 257 CLR 42, 71–2 [46] (French CJ, Kiefel and Nettle JJ), 130–1 [262] (Keane J).
[194] Ibid 82–5 [83]–[93] (Bell J), 108 [173] (Gageler J).   [195] Ibid 87 [101] (Bell J).
[196] Ibid 111–12 [184], citing, inter alia, *North Australian Justice Agency Ltd v Northern Territory* (2015) 256 CLR 569, 612 [99]; *Plaintiff S4/2014 v MIBP* (2014) 253 CLR 219, 231–2 [25]–[29]; *CPCF v MIBP* (2015) 255 CLR 514, 625 [374].

must be capable of objective determination from time to time. Gageler J was satisfied that detention under s 198AHA met these requirements.[197]

Gordon J, in dissent, applied the *Lim* test more strictly. Her Honour found that the Australian government had detained the plaintiff on Nauru and that s 198AHA, which authorised this detention, was in breach of the separation of the executive and judicial powers set out in Chapter III of the *Australian Constitution*.[198] The detention in this case could not be reasonably construed as falling into the enumerated authorised purposes for the alien detention set out in *Lim*. The detention was not for the purpose of removal from Australia, as this was achieved when the plaintiff was taken to Nauru.[199] Further, it could not be construed as being for the purpose of enabling the making or assessment of an application for an entry permit to Australia, as the plaintiff was unable to make such an application.[200] The decision highlights an ongoing area of contention in relation to the *Lim* test as to whether the enumerated list of exceptions for which detention of aliens is authorised is exhaustive or illustrative. Gordon J explicitly expressed support for an exhaustive construction,[201] while Bell J implicitly endorsed the view that new categories of permissible executive detention of aliens could be created.[202]

There have also been attempts to challenge the lawfulness of detention under the domestic laws of Nauru and PNG. Unlike Australia, Nauru and PNG both have a constitutionally entrenched bill of rights. A constitutional challenge to the detention of asylum seekers in Nauru was dismissed by the Nauruan Supreme Court in June 2013.[203] The *Nauruan Constitution* prohibits the deprivation of personal liberty, subject to a number of enumerated exceptions.[204] Relevantly, detention is authorised where it is 'for the purpose of preventing ... unlawful entry to Nauru, or for the purpose of effecting ... expulsion, extradition or other lawful removal'.[205] Justice von Doussa found that detention in that case fell under this exception and as such was lawful under the *Nauruan Constitution*. However, His Honour left the door open to future challenge by stating that detention may be unconstitutional if there is a long and unreasonable delay in processing claims or releasing persons after a favourable determination of refugee status.[206] Note, however, that this decision dealt with the detention of asylum seekers prior to the introduction of the open centre arrangements in October 2015. It remains to be seen if the Nauruan courts will accept the Australian and Nauruan governments' claim that these arrangements mean asylum seekers and refugees are no longer held in detention.

A 2016 challenge in PNG proved more fruitful, with the PNG Supreme Court finding that the detention of asylum seekers and refugees on Manus Island was unconstitutional.[207] Section 42 of the *PNG Constitution* provides a right to 'personal liberty'. This is subject to a

---

[197] *Plaintiff M68* (2016) 257 CLR 42, 111–12 [185].   [198] Ibid 162 [388].   [199] Ibid 163 [391].
[200] Ibid.   [201] Ibid 165–6 [401] (Gordon J).
[202] See above n 195 and accompanying text. In *Plaintiff M96A/2016 v Commonwealth* [2017] HCA 16 (3 May 2017), the High Court had an opportunity to address government submissions claiming that the list of permissible purposes for executive detention set out in *Lim* is not closed. However, the Court found it unnecessary to do so as detention in that case was characterised as falling under one of the established exceptions.
[203] *AG v Secretary of Justice* [2013] NRSC 10 (18 June 2013).   [204] *Nauruan Constitution* s 5(1).
[205] Ibid s 5(1)(h).   [206] *AG v Secretary of Justice* [2013] NRSC 10 (18 June 2013) [79].
[207] *Namah v Pato* [2016] PJSC 13 (26 April 2016).

number of exceptions. The PNG government sought to rely on two of these to justify the detention in this case. The first, s 42(1)(g), authorised detention 'for the purpose of preventing unlawful entry of a person into Papua New Guinea, or for the purpose of affecting the expulsion of a person from Papua New Guinea'. The five Justices of the Supreme Court unanimously found that this exception did not apply as the asylum seekers had no intention of entering PNG. Rather, at all relevant times, their destination was Australia.[208] The second was s 42(1)(ga), which was introduced by way of a constitutional amendment in 2014 in an apparent attempt to thwart the Supreme Court challenge. This authorised detention 'for the purposes of holding a foreign national under arrangements by Papua New Guinea with another country or with an international organisation that the Minister ... in his absolute discretion, approves'. The Court found this amendment to be invalid, as it did not meet the constitutional requirements for passing laws which restrict rights or freedoms.[209] These include a requirement that the law 'be reasonably justifiable in a democratic society having proper respect for the rights and dignity of mankind'.[210] When inserting s 42(1)(ga), the PNG government made no attempt to comply with these requirements. Given that the purpose of detention could not be found to fall under any of the valid exceptions in s 42(1), it was thus found to be unconstitutional. The Court ordered both the Australian and PNG governments to 'forthwith take all steps necessary to cease and prevent the continued unconstitutional and illegal detention of the asylum seekers' on Manus Island.[211] The day after the judgment was handed down, PNG Prime Minister, Peter O'Neill announced that the Manus RPC would be shut down.[212] At the time of writing in June 2017, the facility was still operational; however, refugees and asylum seekers have been informed that the centre will close on 31 October 2017. Those who have been found to be refugees have been given the option to relocate to the PNG community or the East Lorengau Transit Centre, or voluntarily leave the country. Non-refugees have been offered financial incentives to return home, and have warned that if they do not accept they will be forcibly removed. There are currently no plans to close the RPC on Nauru.

5.2.5 The Australia–United States Resettlement Deals

The parallels in US and Australian extraterritorial processing policies are evident in the resettlement arrangements that have been concluded between the two countries. These arrangements also highlight the fact that the two governments are engaging in ongoing dialogue in relation to the operation of their respective extraterritorial processing and maritime interdiction regimes. The first such agreement was concluded in 2007.[213] Under a MOU entered into on 17 April 2007, the United States was to resettle 200 refugees from

---

[208] Ibid [39]. [209] Ibid [53]–[54], applying ss 38 and 39 of the *PNG Constitution*.
[210] *PNG Constitution* s 38(1). [211] *Namah v Pato* [2016] PJSC 13 (26 April 2016) [74].
[212] Peter O'Neill, Prime Minister of PNG, 'Manus Regional Processing Centre will Close' (News Release, 27 April 2016) www.documentcloud.org/documents/2813891-PNG-PM-Peter-O-Neill-s-statement .html#document/p1.
[213] Kevin Andrews, Minister for Immigration, 'War Crimes MOU and Asylum Agreement Signed' (Media Release, 17 April 2007). For analysis of the agreement see Azadeh Dastyari, 'Swapping Refugees: The Implications of the "Atlantic Solution"' (2007) 9 *UTS Law Review* 93.

the processing centre in Nauru. In return, Australia was to resettle refugees processed in Guantánamo Bay. As such, the policy would act as a form of 'refugee laundering', with Australia taking refugees which the United States had pledged never to resettle, while the United States took refugees from Nauru in respect of which Australia had made a similar pledge. Shortly after the agreement was concluded, the newly elected Australian Labor Party decided to abandon the offshore processing policy. As such, the swap was never carried out, as the remaining refugees on Nauru were brought to Australia.

It appears that the United States and Australia concluded a similar deal in late 2016. In September 2016, Australian Prime Minister Malcolm Turnbull used an address to Barack Obama's UN Leaders' Summit on Refugees to announce that Australia would resettle an undisclosed number of Central American refugees from camps in Costa Rica.[214] These camps were set up pursuant to a protection transfer arrangement ('PTA') between Costa Rica, the United States, UNHCR and the International Organization for Migration ('IOM') in July 2016.[215] Under this arrangement, the US government carries out in-country pre-screening in Guatemala, Honduras and El Salvador of people who are seeking protection. UNHCR and IOM then transfer applicants who are most in need of protection to Costa Rica, where they undergo refugee status determination procedures. Those found to be refugees are then resettled in the United States or a third country.[216] With Prime Minister Turnbull's announcement, Australia became the first participating third country.

Two months later, in November 2016, Malcolm Turnbull announced that the Obama Administration had agreed to resettle an undisclosed number of refugees from Manus Island and Nauru.[217] Upon coming to office, President Donald Trump signalled that he may not honour that agreement, referring to it as a 'dumb deal'. The Trump Administration eventually confirmed that the agreement would go ahead and that the United States would resettle up to 1,250 refugees, but only after a process of 'extreme vetting'.[218] The Australian government has claimed that the two deals are not linked, and hence the arrangement is not a 'refugee swap'. While not a one-for-one swap like the 2007 deal, the two arrangements appear to be contingent on one another. Anne Richard, the former Assistant Secretary of the State for Population, Refugees and Migration in the US State Department, who was one of the chief architects of the deal, is on the record as stating that the two arrangements are informally linked.[219] This was confirmed by Australian Immigration Minister Peter Dutton's comments that the Australian government will not

---

[214] Malcolm Turnbull, Prime Minister, 'Leaders' Summit on Refugees' (Press Release, 21 September 2016) www.pm.gov.au/media/2016-09-21/leaders-summit-refugees-0.

[215] United States Department of Homeland Security, 'U.S. Expands Initiatives to Address Central American Migration Challenges' (News Release, 26 July 2016) www.dhs.gov/news/2016/07/26/us-expands-initiatives-address-central-american-migration-challenges.

[216] Ibid.

[217] Malcolm Turnbull, Prime Minister, 'Refugee Resettlement from Regional Processing Centres' (Press Release, 13 November 2016) www.pm.gov.au/media/2016-11-13/refugee-resettlement-regional-processing-centres.

[218] Ben Doherty, 'White House Says US Will Take Up to 1,250 Refugees under Australian Deal', *The Guardian* (online), 1 February 2017 www.theguardian.com/australia-news/2017/feb/01/white-house-australian-refugees-deal-resettle-extreme-vetting.

[219] Ibid.

resettle refugees from Central America until he receives assurances that the United States will take people from Nauru and Manus Island.[220]

The Australian government has purportedly been assured that the resettlement deal will not be affected by President Trump's revised Executive Order 13780 suspending the US refugee program for 120 days and banning entrants from six Muslim-majority countries for ninety days.[221] Many of the refugees are from Iran, Somalia, Sudan and Syria, all of which are part of the six countries subject to the revised travel ban. The order allows for 'pre-existing international agreements' to be honoured.[222]

Representatives from the US State Department-funded Refugee Admissions Program have reportedly begun interviewing refugees on Nauru and Manus Island.[223] Officers from the Department of Homeland Security ('DHS') visited Nauru and Manus Island in April 2017 to begin the security screening procedures. However, what 'extreme vetting' will mean in practice remains to be seen and it is likely that the confusion around this procedure will cause delays. There are also concerns that the reduction of the total refugee intake, from 110,000 under Obama to 50,000, will result in further delays.[224] What is clear is that a significant number of asylum seekers and refugees on Nauru and Manus Island will miss out on resettlement in the United States. As of March 2017, there were 2,032 refugees and asylum seekers in PNG and Nauru. An additional 458 were temporarily in Australia for medical treatment, but liable to be returned offshore. Therefore, even if the United States fills its quota of 1,250, which it is in no way obliged to do, that would leave almost half of the refugees in limbo.

5.2.6 Processing at Sea

The processing of asylum claims at sea is a relatively new development in Australia, and has only ever been carried out in limited circumstances. Since the resumption of interdiction and push-back operations under Operation Sovereign Borders, the passengers on boats returned to Sri Lanka and Vietnam have reportedly been subject to rudimentary pre-screening at sea. While the government has not made the exact details of these screening measures public, reports indicate that asylum seekers were asked just four basic questions: their name, their country of origin, where they had come from and why they had left.[225]

---

[220] Zoe Daniel and Stephanie March, 'US Refugee Deal: Architect of Deal Says Arrangement Loosely Based on Australia "Doing More"', *ABC News* (online), 22 March 2017 www.abc.net.au/news/2017-03-22/us-refugee-deal-architect-says-based-on-australia-doing-more/8375250.

[221] David Sharaz, 'Turnbull: Refugee Swap Not Affected by US Travel Ban', *SBS News* (online), 7 March 2017 www.sbs.com.au/news/article/2017/03/07/turnbull-refugee-swap-not-affected-us-travel-ban; Exec Order No 13780, 82 Fed Reg 13209 (9 March 2017) ss 1(f), 6(b). At the time of writing, major elements of the order were the subject of a nationwide Temporary Restraining Order issued in *State of Hawai'i v Trump* (D Haw, Civ No 17-00050 DKW-KSC, 15 March 2017); see Chapter 3, n 52.

[222] Exec Order No 13780, 82 Fed Reg 13209 (9 March 2017) s 5(C).

[223] Zoe Daniel, 'Manus Island, Nauru Refugees Fingerprinted as Processing for US-Australia Resettlement Deal Begins', *ABC News* (online), 21 March 2017 www.abc.net.au/news/2017-03-20/refugee-processing-for-us-australia-resettlement-deal-begins/8368574.

[224] Daniel and March, above n 220.

[225] Sarah Whyte, 'Immigration Department Officials Screen Asylum Seekers at Sea "via teleconference"', *Sydney Morning Herald* (online), 2 July 2014 www.smh.com.au/federal-politics/political-news/immigration-department-officials-screen-asylum-seekers-at-sea-via-teleconference-20140702-3b837.html.

Asylum seekers returned to Indonesia are not subject to any screening. This is presumably based on the assumption by the Australian government that these persons do not fear persecution in Indonesia, but are secondary movers who are using Indonesia as a transit point to reach Australia. These practices are examined in further detail in Chapter 6 in the context of an analysis of their compatibility with international law. To date, the legality of these pre-screening procedures at sea have not been challenged in Australian courts.

5.3 Comparing the US and Australian Jurisprudence

As with the cases dealing with long-term immigration detention and maritime interdiction examined in the preceding chapters, the exceptional status of arriving non-citizens in US and Australian law has given rise to significant ambiguity and discretionary leeway to the judiciary when examining extraterritorial processing arrangements. This uncertainty is further heightened by the deliberate jurisdictional ambiguities created when processing is carried out outside the municipal jurisdictional boundaries of a state. When arrangements involve third countries, there is an added layer of complexity related to apportioning state responsibility. These factors have combined to give rise to unpredictable and sometimes contradictory judicial outcomes.

The case law on extraterritorial processing in the United States and Australia has dealt with very different legal issues. The litigation in the United States primarily dealt with the question of whether asylum seekers held at Guantánamo Bay could avail themselves of constitutional or domestic US statutory protections. A series of cases heard in the early 1990s determined this question in the negative. In *Baker*, the Court of Appeals for the Eleventh Circuit rejected a First Amendment claim to legal counsel brought on behalf of Haitians 'screened out' on Guantánamo Bay and facing repatriation to Haiti.[226] In *CABA*, the same court determined that asylum seekers held in 'safe haven' at Guantánamo Bay and other extraterritorial facilities were not entitled to First Amendment rights to legal counsel, or Fifth Amendment due process rights. In both cases, the decisions were based on a view that Guantánamo Bay was 'outside the United States' and that aliens did not have extraterritorial constitutional rights.[227] This outcome is difficult to reconcile with the Supreme Court jurisprudence with respect to enemy combatants held at Guantánamo Bay. In *Boumediene*, the Supreme Court determined that an enemy combatant detained at Guantánamo Bay was entitled to the protection of the Constitution's Habeas Suspension Clause.[228] In reaching this conclusion, the Court adopted a different approach to construing the status of Guantánamo Bay and the impact of this status on the question of whether constitutional rights extended there. Adopting a functional approach to the reach of the *US Constitution*, the majority in that case viewed the fact that the United States had complete jurisdiction and control over Guantánamo Bay as sufficient for some constitutional protections to apply there. *Boumediene* dealt with the Habeas Suspension Clause, rather than the First and Fifth Amendment rights considered in *Baker* and *CABA*. Nevertheless, the case appears to signify a shift in the approach to construing the reach of

---

These procedures are modelled on the 'enhanced screening' policy used with respect to unauthorised air and sea arrivals from Sri Lanka since 2012.
[226] 953 F 2d 1498 (11th Cir, 1992).   [227] 43 F 3d 1412 (11th Cir, 1995).   [228] 533 US 723 (2008).

constitutional protections to non-citizens in Guantánamo Bay. The issue of processing at sea or in third countries has only received limited judicial attention.[229]

The Australian cases challenging extraterritorial processing measures generally turned on narrow questions of statutory interpretation. The *Offshore Processing Case* dealt with the attempt made by the Australian government to create a Guantánamo-like zone on Christmas Island, where the domestic legal framework for status determination was said not to apply.[230] The legal and factual issues examined in that case were very different to those considered in the US context. Christmas Island was clearly Australian sovereign territory and the reach of Australian constitutional protections there was never contested. The case turned upon the reach of the statutory provisions contained in the *Migration Act*. The Court rejected the government's attempt to characterise refugee status determinations carried out on Christmas Island as a discretionary non-statutory process. Rather, the Court found that the power being exercised was a statutory one, and accordingly, the criteria applied in the process should be informed by relevant provisions of the *Migration Act*. The Court also construed the rights at stake in a way that gave rise to a duty of procedural fairness. Although the judgment was a unanimous one, it was by no means an obvious outcome. The Court's decision hinged on contestable assumptions relating to the relationship between the *Migration Act* and the *Refugee Convention*, as well as a view on the undesirability of unconstrained executive discretionary detention that appeared to be at odds with the decision in *Al-Kateb*.[231]

The second line of Australian cases involved statutory challenges to the Minister's power to transfer a person to an extraterritorial processing location. No analogous issue arose in the US extraterritorial processing regime. The US regime only ever applied to asylum seekers interdicted at sea. The usual destination for extraterritorial processing has been Coast Guard cutters or the US-controlled territory of Guantánamo Bay. When third country processing has been used, the presidential executive orders authorising such action did not contain safeguards about the conditions which needed to be met in the third country to which the asylum seekers were transferred. These safeguards were presumably thought to be unnecessary, given the US government's view that the *Refugee Convention* does not apply to its extraterritorial actions. In Australia, certain asylum seekers have been liable to third country transfer even after reaching Australian territory. The extraterritorial processing regime under the original Pacific Solution applied to asylum seekers who made landfall at certain excised offshore places. The offshore processing arrangements introduced in 2012 extended third country transfers to apply to all unauthorised boat arrivals, regardless of their point of arrival. The fact that the asylum seekers have reached Australian territory means that Australia clearly owes them protection obligations under the *Refugee Convention*.

The *Malaysian Solution* and *Sadiqi* litigation dealt with the proper construction of statutory provisions aimed at ensuring that third country transfers did not contravene these obligations.[232] Section 198A(3)(a) of the *Migration Act* sets out the criteria which the Minister had to consider when designating a country as a destination for third country transfers. In the *Sadiqi* litigation, which challenged the declaration made in respect of Nauru, the Federal Court refused to accept that these conditions need to exist as a matter

---

[229] See *Haitian Refugee Center v Gracey*, 809 F 2d 794 (DC Cir, 1987).   [230] (2010) 243 CLR 319.
[231] (2004) 219 CLR 562.
[232] *Malaysian Solution Case* (2011) 244 CLR 144; see above nn 124–7 for details of the *Sadiqi* litigation.

of fact, in order for a declaration to be valid. In the *Malaysian Solution Case*, the High Court took a different approach when considering a declaration made in respect of Malaysia. By construing the existence of the criteria set out in s 198A(3)(a) as jurisdictional facts, the majority found the declaration invalid as the relevant protections did not exist in Malaysia as a matter of law. The different approaches evident in the judicial reasoning undertaken by the Federal Court judges in the *Sadiqi* litigation and the Justices of the High Court in the *Malaysian Solution Case* illustrate the contingency of the outcomes in those cases. The fact that the law was susceptible to competing plausible interpretations was demonstrated by the advice given by the Solicitor-General to the government in the lead-up to the case, stating that the Malaysian Solution would survive judicial challenge. In response to this decision, Parliament introduced a new legislative regime for declaring a country a 'regional processing country'. This regime was upheld in *Plaintiff S156*, one of the few clear-cut cases examined in this chapter.[233] This was the result of the unambiguous parliamentary intent to authorise the arrangements, with amendments introduced to specifically circumvent the reasoning adopted by the Court in the *Malaysian Solution Case*. *Plaintiff M68* sought to challenge the Australian government's power to cause or procure detention on Nauru.[234] While decided by a clear 6:1 majority, there was disagreement among the plurality as to whether Australia was responsible for the detention of asylum seekers on Nauru. The ramifications of the ambiguity and uncertainty of the case law examined here (and in previous chapters) for predicting the legal success or failure of transfers is taken up in Chapter 7.

The analysis thus far has primarily focused on the domestic law of the United States and Australia. In Chapter 6, I shift my focus to international law. As we will see, the policies of long-term mandatory detention, maritime interdiction and extraterritorial processing raise serious concerns under international treaty and customary law. This is, in part, the result of the fact that the exceptional status afforded to arriving non-citizens in the United States and Australia, is not replicated to the same degree in the international legal regime. This is particularly so in relation to international human rights law, which applies without discrimination as to citizenship, immigration status or geographic location.

---

[233] (2014) 254 CLR 28. [234] (2016) 257 CLR 42.

6

International Law

> While refugees and migrants are entitled to protections under international law, too often border, transit, arrival and post-arrival interactions are conducted as though they occur in rights-free zones. It is precisely in times and places where adherence to international law is most needed, that the temptation to circumvent it can be greatest. Respect for human rights and refugee law is essential to securing stability and security; it also benefits host states and communities.
>
> Eleanor Acer, Human Rights First, September 2016

The policies adopted by the United States and Australia to control and deter asylum-seeker flows have pushed the boundaries of what is acceptable under international law. Mandatory detention practices may violate the prohibition of arbitrary detention and in some circumstances amount to cruel, inhuman or degrading treatment, or even torture. These concerns apply to detention carried out within a state's territorial boundaries; however, they are magnified in the context of detention in remote extraterritorial locations. The policies of maritime interdiction and extraterritorial processing can result in both direct and indirect *refoulement*. Interdiction and deflection practices can also violate obligations arising under the international law of the sea, including the duties to protect life at sea and to disembark rescued persons at a place of safety. To the extent that long-term mandatory detention, interdiction and extraterritorial processing policies generally target individuals who seek to enter Australia and the United States without authorisation, they may contravene the non-penalisation provision of the *Refugee Convention*.[1] Further, the fact that they disproportionately affect asylum seekers from particular ethnicities and nationalities may violate prohibitions against discrimination in the *Refugee Convention* and other human rights instruments.

6.1 Mandatory Detention

6.1.1 Arbitrary Detention

International human rights instruments place clear limits on the circumstances in which asylum seekers can be detained. The most important provision is art 9 of the *International Covenant on Civil and Political Rights* ('*ICCPR*'), which prohibits arbitrary detention.[2] The UN Human Rights Committee has interpreted this provision as requiring an individualised

---

[1] *Convention Relating to the Status of Refugees*, opened for signature 28 July 1951, 189 UNTS 137 (entered into force 22 April 1954) ('*Refugee Convention*').

[2] *International Covenant on Civil and Political Rights*, opened for signature 16 December 1966, 999 UNTS 171 (entered into force 23 May 1976) art 9(1).

assessment as to whether detention of an individual is 'reasonable, necessary and proportionate' in a given case.³ The United Nations High Commissioner for Refugees ('UNHCR') describes what this requires:

> The general principle of proportionality requires that a balance be struck between the importance of respecting the rights to liberty and security and freedom of movement, and the public policy objectives of limiting or denying such rights. The authorities must not take any action exceeding that which is strictly necessary to achieve the pursued purpose in the individual case. The necessity and proportionality tests further require an assessment of whether there were less restrictive or coercive measures (that is, alternatives to detention) that could have been applied to the individual concerned and which would be effective in the individual case.⁴

The *Refugee Convention* provides additional protections against detention for asylum seekers in light of their specific vulnerabilities. Recognising the fact that those fleeing persecution are often unable to obtain appropriate travel documents and visas, art 31 prohibits states from penalising refugees and asylum seekers for unauthorised entry or stay. This has been interpreted as creating a presumption against detaining asylum seekers in the absence of compelling reasons to do so.⁵ Blanket and automatic mandatory detention is inherently arbitrary and violates art 9 of the *ICCPR* and art 31 of the *Refugee Convention*. By definition, mandatory detention will always violate the principles of proportionality and necessity because people are detained without individualised assessments as to the need for detention in a given instance.

The common justifications put forward to justify immigration detention policies in Australia and the United States fail to meet the proportionality test. The US and Australian governments have argued that mandatory detention is necessary to ensure public health and safety.⁶ The argument is that persons who have not had their identities verified and who have not undergone health and security checks can pose a risk to public safety. This is

---

³ Human Rights Committee, *General Comment No 35: Article 9 (Liberty and Security of Person)*, 112th sess, UN Doc CCPR/C/GC/35 (16 December 2014) [18] citing Human Rights Committee, *Views: Communication No 560/1993*, 59th sess, UN Doc CCPR/C/59/D/560/1993 (30 April 1997) [9.3]–[9.4] ('*A v Australia*').

⁴ UNHCR, Guidelines on the Applicable Criteria and Standards relating to the Detention of Asylum-Seekers and Alternatives to Detention (2012) [34].

⁵ Guy Goodwin-Gill, 'Article 31 of the 1951 Convention Relating to the Status of Refugees: Non-Penalization, Detention, and Protection' in Erika Feller et al (eds), *Refugee Protection in International Law: UNHCR's Global Consultations on International Protection* (Cambridge University Press, 2003) 185, 195–6.

⁶ DIAC, *Response to the Australian Human Rights Commission report on the Use of Community Arrangements for Asylum Seekers, Refugees and Stateless Persons Who Have Arrived to Australia by Boat* (2012) Australian Human Rights Commission www.humanrights.gov.au/our-work/asylum-seekers-and-refugees/publications/diac-response-australian-human-rights-commission; see also the Australian government's arguments in response to Communications of detained refugees to the UN Human Rights Committee in Human Rights Committee, *Views: Communication No 2094/2011*, 108th sess, UN Doc CCPR/C/108/D/2094/2011 (28 October 2013) ('*FKAG et al v Australia*') [6.1]–[6.7] and Human Rights Committee, *Views: Communication No 2136/2012*, 108th sess, UN Doc CCPR/C/108/D/2136/2012 (28 October 2013) ('*MMM et al v Australia*') [6.1]–[6.7]. In the US, see the US government's arguments in *Ferrer-Mazorra et al v United States* (Merits) (IACHR Report No 51/01, Case 9903, 4 April 2001) [88]–[96]. US law limits the parole of aliens to those who present no 'security risk nor risk of absconding': see 8 CFR § 212.5.

the most plausible of the justifications given for detention and is based, at least in part, on legitimate concerns. Asylum seekers who travel by irregular means arrive on a nation's shores with no pre-screening whatsoever. In some instances, such persons may indeed pose health and/or security risks if released into the community without sufficient scrutiny. Taken at its strongest, the public health and safety justification only supports the use of mandatory detention for the period of time it takes to establish a person's identity and to run health and security checks. Even during this initial screening period, it is difficult to see how detention would be necessary and proportional for all persons. For example, the detention of minors and other vulnerable individuals will rarely be justifiable as a necessary and proportionate measure required to maintain public safety.

A second justification given for mandatory detention is that confinement is necessary to ensure that individuals turn up for their immigration hearings.[7] The logic is that if irregular entrants are released into the community, some (particularly those with weak claims for a substantive visa) will simply abandon the immigration process and live irregularly in the community. The problem with this argument is that it creates a false dichotomy between full-fledged detention and unsupervised release. In reality, governments have a range of alternatives at their disposal that allow for the monitored release of individuals into the community. Many of these measures have a successful track record of ensuring high levels of compliance. In their more intrusive forms, these programs rely on electronic tagging and other forms of electronic reporting.[8] However, it is important to bear in mind the human rights implications of such intrusive measures. These concerns are highlighted by UNHCR in its 2012 Revised Detention Guidelines, which emphasise that such measures should only be used in circumstances where persons would otherwise be *detained*. They should not be used as an alternative to release. Less intrusive options such as community supervision have also proven to be successful. Community supervision combines regular reporting with the delivery of case management and social services. Studies suggest that these programs can produce compliance rates of more than 90 per cent.[9] Given the proven track record of these alternatives to detention in ensuring high rates of appearance at hearings, mandatory detention cannot be viewed as a necessary and proportionate measure to ensure compliance.

Mandatory detention has also been justified on the grounds that it deters future irregular migrants from making the journey to a nation's shores. At times, the US government has explicitly justified the need for mandatory detention, including detention of children, on the grounds of deterrence.[10] The Australian government has been careful to avoid explicit references to deterrence, but this motive is implicit in public statements put forward by

---

[7] See *A v Australia*, UN Doc CCPR/C/59/D/560/1993 [7.1]; see 8 CFR § 212.5.
[8] See Chapter 3, n 127 and accompanying text.
[9] Daniel Ghezelbash, 'The Rise and Rise of Mandatory Immigration Detention' in Mary Crock and Lenni Benson (eds) *Protecting the Migrant Child: Central Issues in the Search for Best Practice* (Edward Elgar, in press); UNHCR, *Summary Conclusions* (Global Roundtable on Alternatives to Detention of Asylum-Seekers, Refugees, Migrants and Stateless Persons, Geneva, Switzerland, 11–12 May 2011) www.ohchr.org/Documents/Issues/Migration/Events/SummaryConclusions.pdf.
[10] A 2015 district court decision found DHS and ICE have been taking deterrence of mass migration into account in making custody determinations, and that such considerations have played a significant role in the large number of Central American families detained since June 2014: *RIL-R v Johnson*, 80 F Supp 3d 164 (D DC, 2015): see Chapter 3, nn 187–9 and accompanying text. See also Re D-J-, 23 I&N Dec 572 (AG 2003) discussed in Chapter 3, nn 41–2 and accompanying text.

successive governments. For example, the minister responsible for formalising the policy of mandatory detention in the early 1990s justified his actions on the grounds of avoiding the 'grave potential for Australia to become an easy target for spontaneous mass movement'.[11] The logic here is clear: making life difficult for asylum seekers will send a message to other potential asylum seekers not to undertake the journey. The use of detention for this purpose will always be arbitrary. As UNHCR reminds state officials:

> detention of asylum-seekers which is applied ... as part of a policy to deter future asylum seekers, or to dissuade those who have commenced their claims from pursuing them, is contrary to the norms of refugee law. It should not be used as a punitive or disciplinary measure for illegal entry or presence in the country.[12]

The need for an appropriate and proportionate justification for detention has been confirmed by UN treaty bodies. The UN Human Rights Committee has repeatedly found that Australia's immigration detention practices have not met this requirement. In *A v Australia*, the Committee found that while it was not per se arbitrary to detain individuals requesting asylum, there needed to be a justification, beyond illegal entry, which was particular to the individual being detained.[13] As Australia had not advanced any grounds particular to the complainant's case, the Committee found the continued detention of the complainant to be arbitrary. As discussed in Chapter 3, both the United States and Australia continue to automatically detain broad classes of arrivals based on their unauthorised entry alone and without individualised findings as to necessity or proportionality. Such practice amounts to arbitrary detention.

6.1.2 Right to Challenge Detention

Mandatory detention provisions may also violate art 9(4) of the *ICCPR*, which requires that anyone deprived of their liberty should be entitled to challenge their detention in the courts. This requires more than just a right to seek review as to whether detention is authorised in domestic law – it also requires that the court be empowered to order the release of the detainee if detention contravenes the *ICCPR*, for reasons of arbitrariness or otherwise.[14] This recognises the fact that under mandatory detention regimes, review under domestic law will generally be of very limited utility. The only basis for challenge is whether the detainee falls into a class of persons prescribed as being subject to mandatory detention. In *A v Australia*, the UN Human Rights Committee made it clear that such review is insufficient. Article 9(4) requires that 'review is, in its effects, real and not merely formal' and must involve consideration of whether detention is compatible with the *ICCPR*.[15]

---

[11] Commonwealth, *Custody of Boat People*, Cabinet Minute Decision No 326 (1992) 9 (Immigration Minister Gerry Hand).

[12] UNHCR, Guidelines on the Applicable Criteria and Standards relating to the Detention of Asylum-Seekers and Alternatives to Detention, above n 4, Appendix F, 128.

[13] *A v Australia*, UN Doc CCPR/C/59/D/560/1993, [9.3]–[9.4]. This position was reaffirmed in a number of subsequent cases where Australian detention practices were found to be arbitrary, including Human Rights Committee, *Views: Communication No 1324/2004*, 88th sess, UN Doc CCPR/C/88/D/1324/2004 (13 November 2006) [7.2] ('*Shafiq v Australia*'); Human Rights Committee, *Views: Communication No 1442/2005*, 97th sess, UN Doc CCPR/C/97/D/D/1442/2005 (23 October 2009) [9.3] ('*Kwok v Australia*').

[14] *A v Australia*, UN Doc CCPR/C/59/D/560/1993, [9.5]. [15] Ibid.

Effective review which meets these requirements is not afforded under current Australian or US mandatory detention policies.

6.1.3 Conditions of Detention

The conditions under which persons subject to mandatory immigration detention are kept, and the treatment they receive, can also raise concerns under international human rights law. Article 10 of the *ICCPR* requires that governments must ensure that all persons who are detained are treated with humanity and respect for their inherent dignity. At a more extreme level, detention may contravene art 16 of the *Convention against Torture and Other Cruel, Inhuman and Degrading Treatment or Punishment* ('*CAT*'), and art 7 of the *ICCPR*, prohibiting cruel, inhuman and degrading treatment.[16] The UN Human Rights Committee found that Australia had committed such a breach in *C v Australia* (2002), which related to the treatment of an Iranian asylum seeker diagnosed with paranoid schizophrenia.[17] His detention had continued for two years, despite medical experts finding a direct link between his detention and his condition and recommending his immediate release. The UN Human Rights Committee found that the government's knowledge and delay in responding to the asylum seeker's serious medical condition and the recommendations for release amounted to a breach of art 7 of the *ICCPR*. The Australian Human Rights Commission has raised concerns about the conditions in many of Australia's immigration detention facilities and has found that many are not appropriate places in which to hold people, especially for prolonged periods of time.[18] In the United States, non-governmental organisations (NGOs) have similarly criticised detention conditions, especially the increasing use of prisons or prison-like facilities, which do not meet basic international standards.[19]

6.1.4 Duration of Detention

Long-term detention, particularly where the duration is undetermined and possibly indefinite, also raises serious concerns under international law. The UN Human Rights Committee has made two adverse findings against Australia relating to the ongoing and potentially indefinite detention of asylum seekers who were found to be refugees but not released from detention on the grounds they posed security risks.[20] In both cases, detention was found to be arbitrary because Australia had not demonstrated that other, less intrusive measures could not have been used instead.[21] The UN Human Rights Committee also found that the indefinite nature of the detention, when combined with the arbitrary nature and difficult

---

[16] *Convention against Torture and Other Cruel, Inhuman or Degrading Treatment or Punishment*, opened for signature 10 December 1984, 1465 UNTS 85 (entered into force 26 June 1987) ('*CAT*').

[17] Human Rights Committee, *Views: Communication No 900/1999*, 76th sess, UN Doc CCPR/C/76/D/900/1999 (28 October 2002) ('*C v Australia*').

[18] See, eg, Australian Human Rights Commission, The Forgotten Children: National Inquiry into Children in Immigration Detention 2014 (November 2015).

[19] Eleanor Acer and Jessica Chicco, 'US Detention of Asylum Seekers: Seeking Protection, Finding Prison' (Report, Human Rights First, June 2009) 29–30.

[20] *FKAG et al v Australia*, UN Doc CCPR/C/108/D/2094/2011; *MMM et al v Australia*, UN Doc CCPR/C/108/D/2136/2012.

[21] *FKAG et al v Australia*, UN Doc CCPR/C/108/D/2094/2011, [9.2]–[9.3]; *MMM et al v Australia*, UN Doc CCPR/C/108/D/2136/2012, [9.3]–[9.4].

conditions of detention as well as the lack of access to information or procedural rights, was inflicting serious psychological harm upon the complainants. This amounted to cruel, inhuman and degrading treatment under art 7 of the *ICCPR*. In *Ferrer-Mazorra et al v United States*,[22] the Inter-American Commission found the long-term and potentially indefinite detention of a group of Cubans by the US government violated the right to liberty under art I of the *American Declaration of the Rights and Duties of Man*, and their right to be detained only when detention was non-arbitrary under art XXV.[23] In both the US and Australian cases, the open-ended and potentially indefinite nature of the detention without meaningful legal avenues of review contributed to a finding that the detention was arbitrary. In both situations, the fact that the state party was unable to expel them or return the detainees to another country was not accepted as a valid excuse for continued detention.

It is noteworthy that Australia and the United States have generally ignored rulings by supranational human rights bodies. The findings of the UN Human Rights Committee are not binding under Australian domestic law and the body lacks coercive powers to ensure states comply with its decisions. Australia's response to the long line of cases condemning its detention practices has been to either outright ignore them or respond by issuing a statement saying it disagrees with the Committee's interpretation of the relevant human rights provisions. The United States is similarly of the view that it is not legally bound by determinations made by the Inter-American Commission of Human Rights. The United States has not ratified the optional protocols to the *ICCPR* and *CAT* that enable the UN Human Rights Committee and Committee against Torture to consider individual complaints of rights violations.

6.2 Maritime Interdiction

There are a number of intersecting international legal regimes which define the scope of governments' power to interdict asylum-seeker vessels at sea. The most important are the law of the sea, the search and rescue regime, and refugee and human rights law. The contestability and complexity of these overlapping legal regimes makes assessing the legality of US and Australian interdiction activities a difficult task. This issue is exacerbated by the secrecy surrounding these activities. The Australian government has gone as far as implementing an explicit policy of not commenting on on-water 'operational activities'.[24] In both the United States and Australia, it is more often than not unclear when, where and how a given boat has been intercepted and/or turned back. This makes it difficult to identify specific breaches of international law. What follows is commentary on the legality of various circumstances in which US and Australian maritime interdiction is likely occurring. My analysis distinguishes between two stages of interdiction. The first is the act of physically stopping and/or inspecting vessels. The relevant principles for this action are found in the international law of the sea, and search and rescue protocols. The second is any subsequent

---

[22] *Ferrer-Mazorra et al v United States (Merits)* (IACHR Report No 51/01, Case 9903, 4 April 2001).
[23] *American Declaration of the Rights and Duties of Man*, OAS Res XXX, adopted by the Ninth International Conference of American States (1948), reprinted in Basic Documents Pertaining to Human Rights in the Inter-American System, OEA/Ser.L.V/II.82 doc.6 rev.1 at 17 (1992).
[24] Emma Griffiths, 'Scott Morrison Says Government Won't Reveal When Asylum Seekers Boats Turned Back', *ABC News* (online), 24 September 2013 www.abc.net.au/news/2013-09-23/government-won27t-reveal-when-boats-turned-back/4975742.

enforcement or other actions taken against the vessel. My focus is on the act of *taking* the vessel and/or those on board to some location other than their intended destination. This act is limited by *non-refoulement* obligations under refugee and international human rights law, the prohibition of collective expulsion, rules relating to disembarkation under the international search and rescue regime and the overriding duty to preserve life at sea. The United States and Australia utilise a variety of other enforcement actions such as the detention, arrest and prosecution of passengers and/or the seizure or destruction of vessels.[25] These actions may also raise concerns under international law, but are beyond the scope of the present analysis.

6.2.1 Stopping Boats

The *United Nations Convention of the Law of the Sea* ('*UNCLOS*') is the key international treaty regulating maritime activities.[26] It is the main instrument relevant to the first stage of interdiction measures: physically stopping boats. The general starting point is the principle of freedom of navigation.[27] However, this principle is subject to a number of exceptions which authorise stopping and/or inspecting boats in certain circumstances. The exceptions differ based on the location of the vessel. The power to stop and inspect boats is broadest within a state's territorial sea. In this zone, which extends up to twelve nautical miles from the coast, states exercise full sovereignty and may thus enact and enforce domestic laws authorising interdiction activities.[28] This is subject to the right of innocent passage, which allows ships from all states to travel through the territorial sea provided that it is not prejudicial to the peace, good order or security of the coastal state.[29] However, the fact that asylum-seeker boats are usually expected to seek to land and disembark on the territory of the destination country means they arguably fall foul of this right, enabling interdiction.[30] As such, the United States and Australia are likely authorised to stop and inspect vessels within their territorial sea. Such actions will also be authorised within their contiguous zone, which extends up to twenty-four nautical miles from the coast.[31] This will be the case to the extent that these actions are aimed at *preventing* violations of immigration or customs laws within its territory or territorial sea.[32]

---

[25] See, eg, the actions taken by the Australian government at issue in *CPCF v MIBP* (2015) 255 CLR 514: Chapter 4, nn 114–52 and accompanying text.

[26] *United Nations Convention on the Law of the Sea*, opened for signature 10 December 1982, 1833 UNTS 3 (entered into force 16 November 1994) ('*UNCLOS*').

[27] Ibid arts 90, 87(1)(a) and 58(1). Under art 90, 'Every State, whether coastal or land-locked, has the right to sail ships flying its flag on the high seas [areas beyond the jurisdiction of any one state]'. Article 87(1)(a) allows for freedom of navigation on the high seas, subject to the conditions set out in *UNCLOS* and other rules of international law; and art 58(1) creates the same right in exclusive economic zones (or contiguous zones).

[28] Ibid arts 2, 3.

[29] Ibid art 17. Note that the right of innocent passage may be suspended by the coastal state for reasons of national security: *UNCLOS* art 25.

[30] Ibid art 19(2)(g); Guy S Goodwin-Gill and Jane McAdam, *The Refugee in International Law* (Oxford University Press, 3rd ed, 2007) 274. Cf Violeta Moreno-Lax, 'The Interdiction of Asylum Seekers at Sea: Law and (mal)practice in Europe and Australia (Policy Brief No 4, Kaldor Centre for International Refugee Law, May 2017) 4 (arguing that the mere fact that a person may request asylum does not render their passage non-innocent).

[31] *UNCLOS* art 33(2).   [32] Ibid art 33(1)(a).

The scope of the government's power to stop and inspect boats beyond its contiguous zone on the high seas is more controversial. The general principle is that on the high seas, states have exclusive authority over vessels flying their flag and may not interfere with vessels flagged to other states.[33] However, there are a number of exceptions to this rule that may be relevant to the interdiction of asylum-seeker vessels. The first relates to stateless vessels. This applies to the majority of asylum-seeker and migrant vessels, which are often small, unseaworthy and not flying a flag.[34] In such circumstances, US and Australian authorities could rely on art 110 of *UNCLOS*, which authorises government vessels to approach, board and search foreign vessels on the high seas where it is suspected that a boat is stateless. The *Migrant Smuggling Protocol* creates a similar right of visit in relation to stateless vessels suspected of engaging in migrant smuggling.[35] In relation to foreign-flagged vessels, such actions will only be authorised on the high seas in circumstances where the flag state has provided consent.[36] This consent can be ad hoc, or stipulated in a bilateral or multilateral treaty.[37] For example, the United States has agreements with the Dominican Republic and the Bahamas authorising interception and enforcement actions against suspected asylum-seeker vessels flagged to those states.[38] These agreements also authorise such actions within the territorial waters of those states in certain circumstances. Any interdiction or enforcement activities in the territorial sea of other nations will generally be unlawful in the absence of such an agreement. Australia's neighbours have not provided any authorisation for Australia to engage in interdiction activities in their territorial waters or to intercept their flagged vessels on the high seas. Nor does the United States currently have such authorisation from Haiti.

In addition to the security-related interdiction powers, government vessels are authorised, and in some circumstances *required*, to intercept asylum vessels for the purpose of rendering assistance in situations of distress at sea. *UNCLOS* and the *International Convention for the Safety of Life at Sea* ('*SOLAS*') both create obligations for states to require masters of ships flying their flags to provide assistance, with all possible speed, to persons in

---

[33] Ibid art 92(1).

[34] See Lisa Marie Komp, 'The Duty to Assist Persons in Distress: An Alternative Source of Protection against the Return of Migrants and Asylum Seekers to the High Seas?' in Violeta Moreno-Lax and Efthymios Papastavridis (eds), *'Boat Refugees' and Migrants at Sea: A Comprehensive Approach* (Brill, 2016) 222, 224.

[35] *Protocol against the Smuggling of Migrants by Land, Sea and Air, Supplementing the United Nations Convention against Transnational Organised Crime* ('*Migrant Smuggling Protocol*'), opened for signature 15 November 2000, 2241 UNTS 480 (entered into force 28 January 2004) art 8(7).

[36] See, eg, ibid art 8(2).

[37] Jasmine Coppens, 'Interception of Migrant Boats at Sea' in Violeta Moreno-Lax and Efthymios Papastavridis (eds), *'Boat Refugees' and Migrants at Sea: A Comprehensive Approach* (Brill, 2016) 199, 209.

[38] See *Agreement Concerning Cooperation in Maritime Migration Law Enforcement*, US–Dominican Republic, TIAS 03-520 (signed and entered into force 20 May 2003); *Agreement Concerning Cooperation in Maritime Law Enforcement*, US–Bahamas, TIAS 04-629 (signed and entered into force 29 June 2004); Azadeh Dastyari, *United States Migrant Interdiction and the Detention of Refugees in Guantánamo Bay* (Cambridge University Press, 2015) 72–7. For a detailed examination of these and other bilateral and multilateral agreements the United States has entered into in relation to maritime interdiction activities, see Niels Frenzen, 'Responses to "Boat Migration": A Global Perspective – US Practices' in Violeta Moreno-Lax and Efthymios Papastavridis (eds), *'Boat Refugees' and Migrants at Sea: A Comprehensive Approach* (Brill, 2016) 279, 289–92.

danger of being lost at sea.[39] Unlike the security-related interdiction powers, the duty to render assistance at sea is not geographically bounded and applies in all maritime zones.[40] These duties apply to all vessels, whether government, commercial or recreational. Given the fact that government vessels regularly patrol the maritime areas in which asylum-seeker vessels are known to travel, they are often called upon to carry out rescue operations. There is ongoing debate as to the meaning of distress within the context of the duty to assist at sea.[41] The narrow view is that distress, and the resulting duty to render assistance, will only arise when a vessel is in grave and imminent danger. The alternate understanding is that distress exists when it is clear that a vessel will get into a dangerous situation at some point in the future. On this broader reading, the unseaworthiness and overcrowding that is common on asylum-seeker vessels is enough to activate search and rescue obligations. The secrecy around interception activities, however, means that in any given instance, it is difficult to determine whether a government purports to be acting under security-related interdiction or search and rescue powers. The danger is that unauthorised security-related activities are being masked as search and rescue operations.[42]

6.2.2 'Taking'

The act of *taking* interdicted migrants to port or some other location generally requires separate authorisation from the act of stopping and/or inspecting vessels examined in the previous section. It is important to first note that any enforcement activities carried out at sea are subject to the overriding duty to prevent loss of life.[43] In terms of more specific guidance as to the legality of taking intercepted asylum seekers to port or some other location for disembarkation, this will depend on two questions. The first is whether the government can point to the existence of an enforcement or other power *authorising* such action. The second is whether disembarkation at a particular location is *prohibited* for any reason.

Given the broad sovereign power states exercise in their territorial sea, enforcement activities such as taking intercepted asylum seekers to port will generally be authorised in this zone.[44] The permissibility of the use of enforcement measures in the contiguous zone is somewhat less clear. Governments are only permitted to exercise the degree of control necessary to prevent violations of their immigration or customs laws. This likely extends to

---

[39] *UNCLOS* art 98(1); *International Convention for the Safety of Life at Sea*, opened for signature 1 November 1974, 1184 UNTS 278, annex, ch V, reg 10(a) ('*SOLAS*').

[40] See, eg, *SOLAS*, annex, ch V, reg 15(a).

[41] The 1979 Search and Rescue Convention defines distress as a 'situation wherein there is a reasonable certainty that a vessel or a person is threatened by grave and imminent danger and requires immediate assistance': *International Convention on Maritime Search and Rescue*, opened for signature 27 April 1979, 1405 UNTS 97 (entered into force 22 June 1985) annex, para 1.13 ('*Search and Rescue Convention*'); see Komp, above n 34, 222.

[42] Daniel Ghezelbash et al, 'Securitization of Search and Rescue at Sea: The Response to Boat Migration in the Mediterranean and Offshore Australia' (2018) 67(2) *International and Comparative Law Quarterly* (forthcoming).

[43] The right to life is set out in a number of international human rights instruments, including art 6 of the *ICCPR*. The Human Rights Committee has recognised that this creates a positive obligation for states to prevent the loss of life: Human Rights Committee, *CCPR General Comment No 6: Article 6 (Right to Life)*, 16th sess, UN Doc HRI/GEN/1/Rev.1 (30 April 1982) [5].

[44] Coppens, above n 37, 199, 201.

actions specifically aimed at preventing passage. It is doubtful if more drastic actions, such as returning boats to countries of origin or transit, could be validly construed as a preventative measure.[45]

Moving on to the high seas, it is again important to distinguish between the right to visit and the authorisation of enforcement powers such as detention, arrest and taking to port. One does not necessarily flow from the other and hence there must be separate authorisation to carry out enforcement activities.[46] There is disagreement over the scope of enforcement powers with respect to stateless vessels. One view is that statelessness creates a legal vacuum allowing a boarding state to assert its laws and enforcement jurisdiction over the vessel.[47] This is likely the position held by the US and Australian governments, as it would justify the broad enforcement powers they carry out against interdicted vessels. A second view is that statelessness in itself is not enough, and there must be some sort of jurisdictional nexus in order to enliven enforcement powers.[48] The protective principle (or security principle), which authorises states to exercise enforcement jurisdiction over aliens for actions done abroad which are prejudicial to the security of the state, may provide the required jurisdictional nexus in relation to asylum-seeker vessels.[49] However, the validity of this argument will depend on the assertion that the arrival of such vessels necessarily constitutes a threat to the security of a state – an issue that is no doubt open to some debate.[50] The *Migrant Smuggling Protocol* does not create a standalone authority for enforcement measures against stateless vessels involved in people smuggling. Rather, it provides that such action will only be authorised 'in accordance with relevant domestic and international law'.[51] In relation to actions undertaken against foreign-flagged vessels pursuant to the consent of the flag state, the scope of enforcement powers, including any power to take vessels and/or passengers to particular locations, will be determined by the content of the consent provided.

When the interception takes place in a search and rescue context, the taking component of interdiction will be governed by a separate legal regime. In such circumstances, rescuees must be taken to a 'place of safety' for disembarkation.[52] The term 'place of safety'

---

[45] Natalie Klein, 'Assessing Australia's Push Back the Boats Policy under International Law: Legality and Accountability for Maritime Interceptions of Irregular Migrants' (2014) 15 *Melbourne Journal of International Law* 414, 420; Claire Higgins, 'The (Un-)sustainability of Australia's Offshore Processing and Settlement Policy' in Violeta Moreno-Lax and Efthymios Papastavridis (eds), *'Boat Refugees' and Migrants at Sea: A Comprehensive Approach* (Brill, 2016) 303, 311–12.

[46] Klein, above n 45, 422.

[47] For support for this position, see Dastyari, *United States Migrant Interdiction and the Detention of Refugees in Guantánamo Bay*, above n 38, 79–82 (citing numerous examples of state practice); Douglas Guilfoyle, *Shipping Interdiction on the Law of the Sea* (Cambridge University Press, 2009) 341–2.

[48] Efthymios Papastavridis, *The Interception of Vessels on the High Seas* (Hart Publishing, 2013) 264–7.

[49] Coppens, above n 37, 215; Klein, above n 45, 422, citing Malcolm N Shaw, *International Law* (Cambridge University Press, 6th ed, 2008) 666–8.

[50] See Klein, above n 45, 422 (arguing that given the fact that people smuggling is commonly perceived as a maritime security threat, then states do have grounds for relying on the protective principle). Cf Efthymios Papastavridis, 'Interception of Human Beings on the High Seas: A Contemporary Analysis under International Law' (2009) 36 *Syracuse Journal of International Law and Commerce* 145, 195 (arguing that it is unlikely for an immigration offence alone to constitute a threat to the security of a state).

[51] *Migrant Smuggling Protocol* art 8(7).

[52] *SOLAS*, annex, Ch V, reg 33, para 1.1; *Search and Rescue Convention*, annex, para 1.3.2.

is not defined in either *SOLAS* or the *Search and Rescue Convention*. Some guidance is provided in the IMO Guidelines on the Treatment of Persons Rescued at Sea ('IMO Guidelines'), which describe a 'place of safety' as being 'a location where rescue operations are considered terminate; where the survivors' safety of life is no longer threatened and their basic human needs can be met; and is a location from which transportation arrangements can be made for their next or final destination'.[53] There is, however, no associated obligation for states to accept disembarkation.[54] This has resulted in incidents where states have denied rescuees access to their territory in a bid to deflect responsibility to other states.[55] The question of the meaning of 'place of safety' and the overlap with protection obligations under refugee and human rights law is examined further in section 6.2.5.

6.2.3 Non-refoulement

Assuming that some form of taking is authorised, there are the additional limitations which prohibit the transfer of interdictees to certain locations. The most important of these are the *non-refoulement* obligations contained in the *Refugee Convention* and human rights treaties. These obligations apply regardless of whether the government purports to be acting under security-related interdiction or search and rescue authority. Additional protections mandating disembarkation at a place of safety apply in the context of search and rescue operations. The US and Australian practice of intercepting and returning/taking asylum seekers back to their country of departure or origin may contravene these protections in certain circumstances.

Non-refoulement obligations prohibit the return of persons to places where they may be subject to certain types of prescribed harm. Article 33 of the *Refugee Convention*, which is described as the cornerstone of the Convention,[56] imposes an obligation on states not to expel or return ('*refouler*') a refugee in any manner whatsoever to the frontiers of territories where his or her life or freedom would be threatened on account of his or her race, religion, nationality, membership of a particular social group or political opinion. In 2001, States Parties to the *Refugee Convention* issued a Declaration reaffirming their commitment to the 1951 Convention and its 1967 Protocol, and recognising that the principle of *non-refoulement* is binding customary international law.[57] Its customary law status is reinforced by the fact that the *Refugee Convention* does not permit derogation from or reservation of

---

[53] Maritime Safety Committee, International Maritime Organization, *Report of the Maritime Safety Committee on Its Seventy Eighth Session*, 78th sess, Agenda Item 26, IMO Doc MSC 78/26/Add.2 (4 June 2004) annex 34, para 6.12 ('*Resolution MSC.167(78) – Guidelines on the Treatment of Persons Rescued at Sea*').

[54] Papastavridis, *The Interception of Vessels on the High Seas*, above n 48, 299–300.

[55] See, for example, the Australian government's response to the *MV Tampa*: Chapter 4, nn 59–60 and accompanying text.

[56] Brief of the Office of the UNHCR as Amicus Curiae in Support of Petitioner, *Ali v Achim* (Supreme Court of the United States, No 06-1346, Nov 2007) 5.

[57] *Declaration of States Parties to the 1951 Convention and/or its 1967 Protocol Relating to the Status of Refugees*, Ministerial Meeting of States Parties, Geneva, Switzerland, 12–13 December 2001, UN Doc HCR/MMSP/2001/09 (16 January 2002). The Declaration was adopted by the UN General Assembly in *Office of the United Nations High Commissioner*, GA Res 57/187, UN GAOR, 57th sess, Agenda Item 104, UN Doc A/RES/57/187 (6 February 2003) [3].

this principle.[58] Complementary *non-refoulement* obligations are contained in a number of international human rights treaties. Article 3(1) of the *CAT* contains an express prohibition against the expulsion, return or extradition of a person to a place where he or she would be in danger of being subjected to torture. The *ICCPR* contains an implied prohibition against the expulsion or return of a person to a territory where they face a real risk of irreparable harm, such as a threat to the right to life (art 6) or torture or other cruel, inhuman, or degrading treatment or punishment (art 7).[59] The *Convention on the Rights of the Child* (*'CRC'*) has also been interpreted as containing an implied *non-refoulement* obligation preventing the return of a child to a country where there are substantial grounds for believing that they may face a real risk of irreparable harm.[60]

The application of the principle of *non-refoulement* where interception occurs in the territorial waters of the intercepting state is beyond doubt. There is some debate about whether the obligation applies to actions taken extraterritorially, in the contiguous zone or on the high seas or the territorial seas of other nations. The governments of the United States and Australia have both taken the position that the *non-refoulement* provision of the Refugee Convention does not apply extraterritorially.[61] This position was upheld by the US Supreme Court in *Sale* in 1993. That decision turned on a close reading of the text of the provision, as well as selective use of the discussions of the delegates in the lead-up to the drafting of the Convention.[62] The issue has not directly been addressed in Australian jurisprudence, but a number of judges have expressed sympathy for the US approach.[63]

This position is at odds with state practice in other jurisdictions and the overwhelming majority of international judicial and academic opinion.[64] UNHCR has repeatedly affirmed its view as to the extraterritorial applicability of art 33(1), noting that it establishes 'an obligation not to return a refugee or asylum-seeker to a country where he or she would

---

[58] *Refugee Convention* arts 7(1), 42(1).

[59] Human Rights Committee, *General Comment No 20: Art 7 (Prohibition of Torture, or other Cruel, Inhuman or Degrading Treatment or Punishment)*, 44th sess, UN Doc HRI/ GEN/1/Rev.7 (10 March 1992) [9]; Human Rights Committee, *General Comment No 31: Nature of the General Legal Obligation Imposed on States Parties to the Covenant*, 80th sess, UN Doc CCPR/C/21/Rev.1/Add.13 (29 March 2004) [12]; Human Rights Committee, *Views: Communication No 692/1996*, 60th sess, UN Doc CCPR/C/60/D/692/1996 (11 August 1997) [6.8]–[6.9] (*'ARJ v Australia'*); *R v Special Adjudicator* [2004] UKHL 26, [21]–[24] (Lord Bingham of Cornhill).

[60] *Convention on the Rights of the Child*, opened for signature 20 November 1989, 1577 UNTS 3 (entered into force 2 September 1990); United Nations Committee on the Rights of the Child, *General Comment No 6: Treatment of Unaccompanied and Separated Children outside Their Country of Origin*, 39th sess, UN Doc CRC/GC/2006/6 (2005) [27]. This obligation is implied from the protections provided for in art 6 (a child's right to life) and art 37 (a child's right to be free from torture, or other cruel, inhuman or degrading treatment or punishment; right to liberty; and humane treatment in detention).

[61] Minister for Immigration and Border Protection, 'Submission of the Defendants', Submission in *CPCF v MIBP*, No S169/2014, 30 September 2014, [20]. This position was successfully argued by the US government in *Sale*: see Chapter 4, nn 31–52 and accompanying text. For a more recent reassertion of this position see US Mission to the United Nations and other International Organisations in Geneva, *Observations of the United States on the Advisory Opinion of the UN High Commissioner for Refugees on Extraterritorial Application of Non-Refoulement Obligations under the 1951 Convention Relating the Status of Refugees and Its 1967 Protocol* (28 December 2007).

[62] See Chapter 4, nn 31–52 and accompanying text.

[63] See Chapter 4, nn 164–71 and accompanying text.

[64] See Chapter 4, nn 53–7 and accompanying text. See also Dastyari, *United States Migrant Interdiction and the Detention of Refugees in Guantánamo Bay*, above n 38, 111–12.

be at risk of persecution or other serious harm, which applies wherever a State exercises jurisdiction, including at the frontier, on the high seas or on the territory of another State'.[65]

This position is supported in the IMO Guidelines, which prohibit disembarkation of persons rescued at sea (whether on the high seas or any other location) in 'territories where the lives and freedoms of those alleging a well-founded fear of persecution would be threatened'.[66]

The United States has also argued for the non-extraterritorial applicability of *non-refoulement* and other obligations under human rights treaties. For example, it has repeatedly made the case that the *ICCPR* does not apply outside its territory.[67] This stands in contrast to the vast majority of state practice, international jurisprudence and expert opinion. The UN Human Rights Committee has stated that '[a] State party must respect and ensure the rights laid down in the [ICCPR] to anyone within *the power or effective control* of the State Party, even if not situated within the territory of the State Party'.[68] A similar test relating to whether a state exercises 'effective control' has been accepted in relation to establishing the extraterritorial reach of other human rights treaties. For example, the UN Committee against Torture has stated that a state party's jurisdiction under the *CAT* 'includes all areas where the state party exercises, directly or indirectly, in whole or in part, *de jure or de facto effective control*, in accordance with international law'.[69] The Australian government appears to accept this position, conceding that its human rights obligations will apply wherever it exercises 'effective control'.[70]

---

[65] UNHCR, *Extraterritorial Application of Non-Refoulement Obligations under the 1951 Convention relating to the Status of Refugees and its 1967 Protocol (Advisory Opinion)* (26 January 2007) [24]; see also UNHCR Executive Committee, Conclusion No 97: Conclusion on Protection Safeguards in Interception Measures, 58th sess, UN Doc A/58/12/Add.1 (10 October 2003) [22(a)].

[66] *Resolution MSC.167(78) – Guidelines on the Treatment of Persons Rescued at Sea*, IMO Doc MSC 78/26/Add.2, annex 34, para. 6.17; see also Council of European Union, *Council Decision supplementing the Schengen Borders Code as regards the Surveillance of the Sea External Borders in the Context of Operational Cooperation Coordinated by the European Agency for the Management of Operational Cooperation at the External Borders of the Member States of the European Union*, 2010/252/EU (26 April 2010) annex, 1.2, which creates similar obligations for Frontex operations.

[67] See, eg, US Department of State, *Opening Statement by Matthew Waxman on the Report Concerning the International Covenant on Civil and Political Rights (ICCPR)* (Opening Statement to the UN Human Rights Committee, Geneva, Switzerland, 17 July 2006) https://2001-2009.state.gov/g/drl/rls/70392.htm. This continues to be the US position, despite legal advice to the contrary. See Dastyari, *United States Migrant Interdiction and the Detention of Refugees in Guantánamo Bay*, above n 38, 97.

[68] Human Rights Committee, *General Comment No 31: Nature of the General Legal Obligation Imposed on States Parties to the Covenant*, 80th sess, UN Doc CCPR/C/21/Rev.1/Add.13 (29 March 2004) [10] (emphasis added); see also *Legal Consequences of the Construction of a Wall in the Occupied Palestinian Territory (Advisory Opinion)* [2004] ICJ Rep 136, [108]–[109].

[69] UN Committee against Torture, *General Comment No 2: Implementation of Article 2 by States Parties*, UN Doc CAT/C/GC/2 (24 January 2008) [7], [16]; Human Rights Committee, *General Comment No 31: Nature of the General Legal Obligation Imposed on States Parties to the Covenant*, 80th sess, UN Doc CCPR/C/21/Rev.1/Add.13 (29 March 2004) [10] (emphasis added). This position was also reaffirmed in Committee against Torture, Communication No 323/2007, UN Doc CAT/C/41/D/323/2007 (21 November 2008) ('*PK et al v Spain*'); see also UNHCR, *Extraterritorial Application of Non-Refoulement obligations under the 1951 Convention relating to the Status of Refugees and its 1967 Protocol (Advisory Opinion)*, above n 65, [35].

[70] Human Rights Committee, Replies to the List of Issues (CCPR/C/AUS/Q/5) To Be Taken up in Connection with the Consideration of the Fifth Periodic Report of the Government of Australia (CCPR/C/AUS/5), UN Doc CCPR/C/AUS/Q/5/Add.1 (21 January 2009), 4 (but note the clarification

The question of whether the degree of control exercised over asylum seekers in interdiction activities satisfies this test must be determined by reference to the particular facts of each case. There is no doubt that effective control will exist in circumstances where asylum seekers are transferred onto government vessels,[71] or where government forces board and take control of a vessel.[72] It has been suggested that state vessels preventing passage or diverting vessels through 'contactless measures', such as warnings, blockades or the threat of physical force, would also suffice.[73] As such, any action taken by the United States and Australia against vessels at sea that results in the return of asylum seekers to the frontiers of a territory where they face persecution or serious harm will amount to *refoulement*. This is regardless of whether such return is carried out aboard government vessels, the original asylum-seeker vessel or a vessel provided by the interdicting state.

The application of the principle of *non-refoulement* does not translate to a general right to asylum or entry.[74] However, in order to comply with the principle, the United States and Australia must have procedures in place to identify persons in need of protection.[75] The United States and Australia have violated this requirement by, at times, carrying out push-back operations without any screening whatsoever. This was the approach the United States took towards Haitian migrants from 1992 to 1993, directly returning refugees to the country from which they were fleeing harm. It is also the current approach taken in regards to persons intercepted in the territorial waters of states with which the United States has maritime enforcement treaties.[76] Such persons are reportedly summarily returned with no screening for protection claims.[77] While it is relevant that a number of these enforcement treaties have explicit provisions prohibiting *refoulement*, UNHCR has expressed concern that there is 'no evidence that these provisions are monitored or enforced'.[78]

Current Australian policy involves the return of interdicted asylum seekers to Indonesia without screening for asylum claims. Australia presumably justifies this on the grounds that

---

that 'Australia believes that a high standard needs to be met before a State could be considered as effectively controlling territory abroad. It is not satisfied in all, or necessarily any, cases in which Australian officials may be operating beyond Australia's territory from time to time').

[71] See, eg, *PK et al v Spain*, UN Doc CAT/C/41/D/323/2007, [8.2]; *Jamaa v Italy* (European Court of Human Rights, Grand Chamber, Application No 27765/09, 23 February 2012).

[72] *Medvedyev v France* (European Court of Human Rights, Grand Chamber, Application No 3394/03, 29 March 2010).

[73] Violeta Moreno-Lax and Mariagiulia Giuffré, 'The Rise of Consensual Containment: From "Contactless Control" to "Contactless Responsibility" for Migratory Flows', in Satvinder Juss (ed), *Research Handbook on International Refugee Law* (Edward Elgar, 2017) (forthcoming); Andreas Fischer-Lescano, Tillmann Löhr and Timo Tohidipur, 'Border Controls at Sea: Requirements under International Human Rights and Refugee Law' (2009) 21 *International Journal of Refugee Law* 256, 275; Klein, above n 45, 435.

[74] James Hathaway, *The Rights of Refugees under International Law* (Cambridge University Press, 2005) 300–1; Goodwin-Gill and McAdam, above n 30, 215.

[75] Goodwin-Gill and McAdam, above n 30, 277.

[76] *Agreement concerning Cooperation in Maritime Migration Law Enforcement*, US–Dominican Republic, TIAS 03-520 (signed and entered into force 20 May 2003); *Agreement concerning Cooperation in Maritime Law Enforcement*, US–Bahamas, TIAS 04-629 (signed and entered into force 29 June 2004); Frenzen, above n 38, 289–92.

[77] T Alexander Aleinikoff, 'YLS Sale Symposium: International Protection Challenges Occasioned by Maritime Movement of Asylum Seekers', *Opinio Juris* (16 March 2014) http://opiniojuris.org/2014/03/16/sale-symposium-international-protection-challenges-occasioned-maritime-movement-asylum-seekers/.

[78] Ibid.

the asylum seekers are from third countries and do not fear harm from the Indonesian government, but rather from the governments of their countries of origin. Transfers to third countries will not amount to *refoulement*, provided that the asylum seekers will be afforded effective protection in that location. Effective protection requires 'guarantees of protection from *refoulement*, fair and efficient procedures for the determination of refugee status, and respect for human rights'.[79] It is unlikely that Indonesia can be considered to offer such protection.[80] While Indonesia does not systematically *refoule* refugees, it has not signed the *Refugee Convention*, nor does it have any procedures for processing refugee claims. Further, there have been a number of reports of forced returns out of Indonesia where asylum seekers have been removed to situations where they face serious risk of harm.[81]

Current practice in both Australia and the United States is to carry out pre-screening procedures at sea in the case of some asylum seekers who are to be returned directly to their country of origin. This in itself may be taken as implicit acceptance of the extraterritorial applicability of the *non-refoulement* principle, although in the case of the United States, the government has made it clear that it considers these procedures to be discretionary and not required by the *Refugee Convention*.[82] The details of the pre-screening procedures carried out by Australian and US authorities are difficult to identify, given the secrecy and lack of independent oversight over interdiction activities. The available information suggests that the procedures are woefully inadequate and not capable of screening for individual protection claims or vulnerabilities. As discussed in Chapter 5, the United States has separate procedures for Cubans and other nationals.[83] All Cubans intercepted at sea are subject to screening interviews conducted by a Protection Screening Officer from the United States Citizenship and Immigration Service. Non-Cubans are not informed of their right to seek asylum or made subject to screening interviews unless they manifest a fear of returning home. This fear can be communicated verbally or through physical manifestations such as evidence of injury.[84] It is unreasonable to expect those in need of protection to be able to manifest this in the difficult conditions at sea. UNHCR has expressed concerns about the efficacy of both procedures and raised concerns that the US interdiction program in the

---

[79] Andreas Schloenhardt and Colin Craig, '"Turning Back the Boats": Australia's Interdiction of Irregular Migrants at Sea' (2015) 27 *International Journal of Refugee Law* 536, 568; See also Stephen H Legomsky, 'Secondary Refugee Movements and the Return of Asylum Seekers to Third Countries: The Meaning of Effective Protection' (2003) 15 *International Journal of Refugee Law* 567, 629–64. These principles are also set out by UNHCR: see UNHCR, *Summary Conclusions on the Concept of 'Effective Protection' in the Context of Secondary Movements of Refugees and Asylum-Seekers* (Lisbon Expert Roundtable, 9–10 December 2002) (February 2003). This Roundtable drew on Legomsky's recommendations, as set out in an earlier background paper, commissioned by UNHCR. This document uses the expression 'real risk' when dealing with the elements of effective protection.

[80] See Schloenhardt and Craig, above n 79, 568–9; UNHCR, 'UNHCR's Views on the Concept of Effect Protection as It Relates to Indonesia' (Effective Protection Update, UNHCR, 2 December 2004).

[81] Nikolas Feith Tan, 'The Status of Asylum Seekers and Refugees in Indonesia' (2016) 28 *International Journal of Refugee Law* 365, 372–3; Amnesty International, 'Indonesia: Briefing to the UN Committee against Torture' (Report, 14 April 2008) 18–19.

[82] See Exec Order No 13276, 67 Fed Reg 69985 (19 November 2002) as amended by Exec Order No 13286, 68 Fed Reg 10619 (3 May 2003) (stating '[t]his order shall not be construed to require any procedure to determine whether a person is a refugee or otherwise in need of protection'.)

[83] See Chapter 5, nn 15–17 and accompanying text.

[84] Dastyari, *United States Migrant Interdiction and the Detention of Refugees in Guantánamo Bay*, above n 38, 140.

Caribbean is resulting in *refoulement*.[85] In Australia, a form of 'enhanced screening' at sea has been carried out with respect to passengers on boats returned to Sri Lanka and Vietnam. Asylum seekers have been interviewed by officials from Australia's Department of Immigration, either onboard an Australian vessel or via Skype. Some asylum seekers have reported only being asked four basic questions by immigration officers via video-link.[86] Schloenhardt and Craig describe the experience of asylum seekers on one particular boat from Sri Lanka: 'Passengers reported that they had difficulty understanding and hearing the immigration officials conducting the determinations. The refugee status determinations were also conducted in front of other passengers and several passengers reported that this prevented them from speaking freely about the persecution they had suffered in Sri Lanka.'[87]

The procedures carried out at sea by both Australia and the United States fall well short of the minimum standards articulated by UNHCR, which include the right to have a reasonable opportunity to prepare a claim, the right to access legal counsel, the right to receive a reasoned written decision and the right to seek independent review of an adverse determination.[88] Moreover, it is likely that conditions at sea are such that effective screening of protection claims may be impossible.[89] Additional challenges to those already outlined include a lack of access to adequate information and legal advice, sickness, fatigue and overcrowding.[90] UNHCR recognises that extraterritorial pre-screening can be a useful tool in satisfying the *non-refoulement* obligations, particularly with respect to early identification of vulnerable groups.[91] However, it emphasises that such procedures should not replace full refugee status determination ('RSD') procedures, which generally cannot be carried out at sea.[92] The shortcomings of the screening procedures carried out at sea place the United States and Australia in breach of *non-refoulement* obligations. The UN Committee against Torture has affirmed this in relation to Australia's turn-back policy,

---

[85] Aleinikoff, above n 77.
[86] Sarah Whyte, 'Immigration Department Officials Screen Asylum Seekers at Sea "via teleconference"', *Sydney Morning Herald* (online), 2 July 2014 www.smh.com.au/federal-politics/political-news/immigration-department-officials-screen-asylum-seekers-at-sea-via-teleconference-20140702-3b837.html.
[87] Schloenhardt and Craig, above n 79, 570 (footnotes omitted).
[88] Executive Committee of the UNHCR, *Determination of Refugee Status*, 28th sess, Supp No 12A, UN Doc A/32/12/Add.1 (12 October 1977); UNHCR, 'Procedural Standards for Refugee Status Determination under UNHCR's Mandate' (Report, September 2005); UNHCR, *Global Consultations on International Protection/Third Track: Asylum Processes (Fair and Efficient Asylum Procedures)*, UN Doc EC/GC/01/12 (31 May 2001).
[89] UNHCR, Maritime Interception Operations and the Processing of International Protection Claims: Legal Standards and Policy Considerations with Respect to Extraterritorial Processing (Protection Policy Paper, November 2010) [55]; UNHCR, High Commissioner's Dialogue on Protection Challenges: Protection at Sea (Background Paper, 11 November 2014) [18]; Schloenhardt and Craig, above n 79, 570; Maria-Giulia Giuffré, 'Access to Asylum at Sea? Non-Refoulement and a Comprehensive Approach to Extraterritorial Human Rights Obligations' in Violeta Moreno-Lax and Efthymios Papastavridis (eds), *'Boat Refugees' and Migrants at Sea: A Comprehensive Approach* (Brill, 2016) 248, 265.
[90] Elspeth Guild et al, New Approaches, Alternative Avenues and Means of Access to Asylum Procedures for Persons Seeking International Protection (Study, LIBE Committee, European Parliament, October 2014) 45.
[91] UNHCR, Maritime Interception Operations and the Processing of International Protection Claims: Legal Standards and Policy Considerations with Respect to Extraterritorial Processing, above n 89, [14]–[17].
[92] Ibid [55].

finding that it has been applied 'without due consideration' of the state party's *non-refoulement* obligations under the *CAT*.[93]

6.2.4 Collective Expulsion

The lack of robust screening procedures during Australian and US interdiction and push-back operations may violate the prohibition of collective expulsion. Although not explicitly mentioned in international human rights treaties, the Human Rights Committee has read in an implied prohibition of collective expulsion in art 13 of the *ICCPR*.[94] This prohibition is also enshrined in the *International Convention on Migrant Workers*,[95] and in numerous regional human rights mechanisms.[96] The principle is also arguably now considered to be part of customary international law.[97] The prohibition is a due process right that entitles non-nationals to an individualised assessment of any claims they may have which mitigate against their expulsion. The risk of *refoulement* is one such consideration; however, there may be numerous others. For example, the individual should be able to put forward claims relating to any right of entry or residence, the right to family life or protections resulting from any specific vulnerabilities, such as their status as a minor or trafficked person.[98] There is some debate as to whether the principle as found in the *ICCPR* applies extra-territorially at sea.[99] This is a result of the fact that that art 13 of the *ICCPR* refers to aliens 'lawfully in the territory of a State Party'.[100] The collective expulsion provision in the

---

[93] UN Committee against Torture, Concluding Observations on the Combined Fourth and Fifth Periodic Reports of Australia, UN Doc CAT/C/AUS/CO/4-5 (23 December 2014) [15].

[94] Human Rights Committee, *General Comment No 15: The Position of Aliens under the Covenant*, 27th sess, UN Doc HRI/GEN/1/Rev.9 (Vol I) (11 April 1986) [10].

[95] *International Convention on the Protection of the Rights of All Migrant Workers and Members of Their Families*, opened for signature 18 December 1990, 2220 UNTS 3 (entry into force 1 July 2003) art 22(1).

[96] See *Protocol No 4 to the Convention for the Protection of Human Rights and Fundamental Freedoms, Securing Certain Rights and Freedoms Other Than Those Already Included in the Convention and in the First Protocol Thereto*, opened for signature 16 September 1963, ETS 46 (entry into force 2 May 1968) art 4; European Union, *Charter of Fundamental Rights of the European Union*, 2012/C 326/02 (26 October 2012) art 19(1); *American Convention on Human Rights*, opened for signature 22 November 1969, 1144 UNTS 123 (entry into force 18 July 1978) art 22(9); *Arab Charter on Human Rights*, opened for signature 22 May 2004 (entry into force 15 March 2008) art 26(2); *African Convention on Human and Peoples' Rights*, opened for signature 27 June 1981, 1520 UNTS 217 (entry into force 21 October 1986) art 12(5) (prohibiting mass expulsions aimed at national, racial, ethnic or religious groups).

[97] See Jean-Marie Henckaerts, *Mass Expulsion in Modern International Law and Practice* (Martinus Nijhoff Publishers, 2nd ed, 1995) 32; Massimo Frigo and Róisín Pillay, *Migration and International Human Rights Law: A Practitioners' Guide No 6* (International Commission of Jurists, 2014) 138; Vincent Chetail, 'The Transnational Movement of Persons under General International Law – Mapping the Customary Law Foundations of International Migration Law' in Vincent Chetail and Céline Bauloz (eds) *Research Handbook on International Law and Migration* (Edward Elgar, 2014) 1, 55.

[98] For a detailed list of examples, see Intervener Brief Filed on Behalf of the UNHCR, *Hirsi Jamaa v Italy* (European Court of Human Rights, Grand Chamber, Application No 27765/09, 23 February 2012) ('*Hirsi Jamaa*') [9].

[99] Azadeh Dastyari, 'Out of Sight, Out of Right? The United States' Migrant Interdiction Program in International Waters and in Guantanamo Bay, Cuba' (PhD Thesis, Monash University, 2013) 128–31.

[100] Article 13 is one of only two articles (the other being article 12) that refers to lawful stay in territory. The remainder of the protections set out in the instrument are not bound by any territorial limitations.

European Convention on Human Rights (*'ECHR'*) does not contain any such limitation.[101] Article 4 of Protocol 5 provides simply that '[c]ollective expulsion of aliens is prohibited'. In *Hirsi Jamaa*, the European Court of Rights found that Italy's maritime interdiction and push-back operations violated this provision, even though they were carried out on the high seas and in Libyan territorial waters.[102]

6.2.5 'Place of Safety'

The requirement under international search and rescue protocols that rescuees be disembarked at a 'place of safety' creates additional safeguards prohibiting the taking of asylum seekers to certain locations. As already discussed, the term 'place of safety' is not defined in the key search and rescue treaties.[103] There is some debate as to whether it is limited to safety in an immediate physical sense, or whether it requires states to consider broader protection considerations, such as *non-refoulement*.[104] The IMO Guidelines advocate the broader view, affirming 'the need to avoid disembarkation in territories where the lives and freedoms of those alleging a well-founded fear of persecution would be threatened'.[105] This is also in line with EU regulations, which require that interdicted/rescued persons not 'be disembarked in', nor 'forced to enter, conducted to or otherwise handed over to the authorities of', a country where there are serious risks of being subjected to persecution or inhuman or degrading treatment or punishment, whether directly or by onward removal to another country.[106] This broader reading of the meaning of a 'place of safety' creates a *de facto* obligation to avoid *non-refoulement* in the context of search and rescue operations, even if we were to accept the controversial claim that the *Refugee Convention* does not apply extraterritorially.

6.3 Extraterritorial Processing

Extraterritorial processing practices in the United States have taken many different forms over the years. The legality of extraterritorial processing carried out at sea aboard government vessels was examined in the maritime interdiction section of this chapter. Here, I examine current US and Australian policies which involve carrying out status determination procedures in extraterritorial processing camps. The United States has used its external territory of Guantánamo Bay for this purpose, while Australia has enlisted the cooperation of Papua New Guinea (PNG) and Nauru. The analysis begins with

---

[101] Convention for the Protection of Human Rights and Fundamental Freedoms, opened for signature 4 November 1950, 213 UNTS 222 (entered into force 3 September 1953), as amended by *Protocol No 14bis to the Convention for the Protection of Human Rights and Fundamental Freedoms*, opened for signature 27 May 2009, CETS No 204 (entered into force 1 September 2009).

[102] *Hirsi Jamaa* (European Court of Human Rights, Grand Chamber, Application No 27765/09, 23 February 2012) 76: see Chapter 7, nn 84–8 and accompanying text.

[103] See above nn 52–3 and accompanying text.   [104] See Chapter 4, nn 139–42 and accompanying text.

[105] Resolution MSC.167(78) – Guidelines on the Treatment of Persons Rescued at Sea, IMO Doc MSC 78/26/Add.2 (4 June 2004) annex 34, para 6.17.

[106] Regulation (EU) No 656/2014 of the European Parliament and of the Council of 15 May 2014 Establishing the Rules for the Surveillance of the External Sea Borders in the Context of Operational Cooperation Coordinated by Frontex [2014] OJ L 189/93 art 4(1). Further, art 4(7) states that 'This Article shall apply to all measures taken by Member States or the Agency in accordance with this Regulation', making it clear that this would apply equally in search and rescue situations, and regardless of location. For more discussion on this, see Ghezelbash et al, above n 42.

concerns relating to the conditions of detention and RSD procedures carried out on the extraterritorial camps. I then examine the degree to which any breaches of international refugee and human rights law can be attributed to the United States and Australia. The section concludes with an examination of the legal requirements that must be met before a state can transfer asylum seekers to a third country for processing.

6.3.1 Conditions in Extraterritorial Camps

The issues relating to the arbitrary nature and conditions of detention examined in relation to onshore mandatory detention above, are magnified in remote offshore settings. The degree of restriction placed on the freedom of movement of persons transferred to Guantánamo Bay, Nauru and Manus Island varies depending on the location and status of the individuals. On Guantánamo Bay, the population is divided between: (1) 'undetermined migrants' who are awaiting determination of their protection claims; (2) 'non-protected migrants' who have been assessed and found not to be refugees; and (3) 'protected migrants' who have been found to be refugees and are awaiting resettlement.[107] While the US government admits that the first two categories are detained, it has argued that the 'protected migrant' population are not, as they are free to check out of the facility and move around other parts of Guantánamo Bay.[108]

On both Nauru and Manus Island, there have been recent changes which purport to have transformed detention centres into open reception facilities. In February 2015, a limited release program was introduced at the Regional Processing Centre (RPC) on Nauru, which allowed certain asylum seekers to leave the centre on day release three days a week.[109] In October 2015, further legislative and policy changes were introduced that purported to transform the RPC there to an 'open centre', allowing all asylum seekers to move freely around the island while awaiting status determinations.[110] Those found to be refugees are issued temporary visas which allow them to live and work in Nauru.[111] Following a finding by the Supreme Court of PNG that detention of asylum seekers at the RPC on Manus Island was unconstitutional,[112] changes were introduced allowing those recognised as refugees to leave the centre between the hours of 7am and 4pm each day. While refugees may also apply for a visa that would allow them to move to the Refugee Transit Centre in East Lorengau, many of those recognised as such have not done so because of safety concerns.[113] With the RPC slated for closure in October 2017, the remaining detainees will be forced to move to the Transit Centre or other alternate accommodation.

---

[107] Dastyari, *United States Migrant Interdiction and the Detention of Refugees in Guantánamo Bay*, above n 38, 172–3.
[108] US Department of State, Bureau of Population, Refugees and Migration, *Migrant Operations at Guantanamo Bay, Cuba* (Fact Sheet, September 2015) https://assets.documentcloud.org/documents/2772373/Guantanamo-MOC-Fact-Sheet-as-of-Sept-2015.pdf.
[109] Government of the Republic of Nauru, 'Nauru Commences Open Centre Arrangements' (Media Release, 25 February 2015) www.naurugov.nr/government-information-office/media-release/nauru-commences-open-centre-arrangements.aspx.
[110] Government of the Republic of Nauru, 'No More Detention, Greater Assistance for Nauru Asylum Seekers' (Media Release, 5 October 2015) https://assets.documentcloud.org/documents/2448162/media-release-no-more-detention-greater.pdf.
[111] See Chapter 5, n 160 and accompanying text.
[112] *Namah v Pato* [2016] PGSC 13 (26 April 2016): see Chapter 5, nn 207–11 and accompanying text.
[113] See below nn 126–8 and accompanying text.

Despite the limited freedom of movement afforded to refugees and asylum seekers on Guantánamo Bay, Manus Island and Nauru, it is likely that they can still be characterised as being detained for the purposes of art 9 of the *ICCPR*. The *ICCPR* does not define detention and there remains some debate about what degree of restriction on movement amounts to detention. The observation by the UN Human Rights Committee that 'deprivation of liberty involves more severe restrictions of motion within a narrower space than mere interferences with liberty of movement' does little to address this ambiguity.[114] While the UN Human Rights Committee has found that mere confinement of a person to a small town or neighbourhood does not necessarily amount to deprivation of liberty within the meaning of art 9,[115] the situation facing asylum seekers and refugees on Guantánamo Bay, PNG and Nauru may be distinguished on the basis of the additional constraints imposed on them.[116]

In Guantánamo Bay, 'protected migrants' are subject to strict curfews, must account for their whereabouts at all times and are prohibited from freely accessing many sections of the territory.[117] Those at the Manus Island RPC face more severe restrictions. Effective access to the newly introduced day release program is hampered by the centre's location within a naval base, which precludes asylum seekers and refugees from exiting the centre on foot. All travel to and from town is carried out on buses controlled by centre staff and under heavy guard. Further restrictions on movement result from fears arising from security threats against asylum seekers while on day release.[118] These threats will continue to hamper the movement of refugees and asylum seekers following the closure of the RPC and the transfer of detainees to community-based accommodation. Reports indicate that refugees will be prohibited from leaving Manus to travel to other parts of PNG, effectively turning the island into an open air prison. Despite the move to an 'open centre' on Nauru and claims that asylum seekers are free to move at will, UNHCR has observed that 'key aspects of conditions are indistinguishable from previous detention arrangements. This includes the number of security guards, the configuration of the fences at the perimeters and the sub-compounds and overcrowding in accommodation, including the continued use of communal tents ('marquees') for protracted periods of time. Individuals remain living in a detention-like setting'.[119]

---

[114] Human Rights Committee, *General Comment No 35: Article 9 (Liberty and Security of Person)*, 112th sess, UN Doc CCPR/C/GC/35 (16 December 2014) [5]. Liberty of movement here refers to art 12 of the *ICCPR*, which governs freedom of movement.

[115] Human Rights Committee, *Views: Communication No 456/1991*, 51st sess, UN Doc CCPR/C/51/D/456/1991 (26 July 1994) ('*Celepli v Sweden*'); Human Rights Committee, *Views: Communication No 833/1998*, 70th sess, UN Doc CCPR/C/70/D833/1998 (26 October 2000) ('*Karker v France*').

[116] See Dastyari, *United States Migrant Interdiction and the Detention of Refugees in Guantánamo Bay*, above n 38, 177–84; Azadeh Dastyari, 'Detention of Australia's Asylum Seekers in Nauru: Is Deprivation of Liberty by any Other Name Just as Unlawful?' (2015) 38 *University of New South Wales Law Journal* 669, 679–80; Azadeh Dastyari and Maria O'Sullivan, 'Not for Export: The Failure of Australia's Extraterritorial Processing Regime in Papua New Guinea and the Decision of the PNG Supreme Court in Namah' (2016) 42(2) *Monash Law Review* 308.

[117] Dastyari, *United States Migrant Interdiction and the Detention of Refugees in Guantánamo Bay*, above n 38, 174–7.

[118] Office of the UNHCR, Submission on the Inquiry into the Serious Allegations of Abuse, Self-Harm and Neglect of Asylum-Seekers in Relation to the Nauru Regional Processing Centre, and Any Like Allegations in Relation to the Manus Regional Processing Centre (Submission 43, UNHCR, 12 November 2016) [19] ('Submission on the Inquiry into the Serious Allegations of Abuse, Self-Harm and Neglect of Asylum-Seekers').

[119] Ibid [23].

Similarly, a report by Amnesty International has found that asylum seekers and refugees continue to be held in a 'detention-like environment' and that 'Nauru is to all intents and purposes an open-air prison that people cannot leave, even where they have been officially recognised as refugees'.[120]

Whether on Nauru, Manus Island or Guantánamo Bay, the cumulative impact of the restrictions, combined with the fact that asylum seekers are confined to a small territorial area which they cannot leave, is likely sufficient to reach a conclusion that asylum seekers and refugees are being detained. This cumulative approach is in line with the jurisprudence of the European Court of Human Rights, which has held that the question of whether a person is detained is one of 'degree or intensity and not one of nature or substance'.[121] This approach has also been affirmed by UNHCR.[122]

If we accept the proposition that asylum seekers and refugees are being detained on Guantánamo Bay, Nauru and Manus Island, then a finding that this detention is arbitrary likely follows. In relation to both Nauru and Manus Island, UNHCR has stated that the 'Policy and practice of detaining all asylum-seekers at the closed RPC, on a mandatory open-ended basis, without individualised assessment as to necessity, reasonableness and proportionality of the purpose of such detention amounts to arbitrary detention that is inconsistent with international law'.[123]

The reasons given for such a finding, namely the open-ended basis of detention and its imposition without individualised assessment as to necessity, reasonableness or proportionality, equally apply to the current arrangement in Guantánamo Bay.

In all three locations, asylum seekers and refugees do not know when they may access durable solutions and detention may continue for a potentially indefinite period. In Nauru, those recognised as refugees are given six-month renewable temporary settlement visas.[124] It is unclear how long these will be renewed for, with suggestions that it could be as long as twenty years. The Nauruan government has made it clear that they will not let refugees settle there permanently. While those on Nauru have a standing offer of resettlement in Cambodia, very few have taken up this offer because of the poor conditions in the latter country.[125] Those on Manus Island theoretically have access to permanent visas to settle in the PNG community.[126] In practice, refugees have been reluctant to pursue this option. Many have refused to leave the Manus RPC because of fears for their safety.[127]

---

[120] Amnesty International, 'Island of Despair: Australia's 'Processing' of Refugees on Nauru' (Report, October 2016) 5.
[121] *Amur v France* (1996) 22 Eur Court HR 533, [42]; see also *Guzzardi v Italy* (1981) 3 EHRR 333, [95].
[122] UNHCR, Guidelines on the Applicable Criteria and Standards relating to the Detention of Asylum-Seekers and Alternatives to Detention (2012), above n 4, [6].
[123] See UNHCR, *UNHCR Monitoring Visit to the Republic of Nauru: 7 to 9 October 2013* (Report, UNHCR, 26 November 2013) 2; UNHCR, *UNHCR monitoring visit to Manus Island, Papua New Guinea: 11–13 June 2013* (Report, UNHCR, 26 November 2013) 1. UNHCR affirmed in November 2016 that the findings of these reports were still valid: UNHCR, Submission on the Inquiry into the Serious Allegations of Abuse, Self-Harm and Neglect of Asylum-Seekers, above n 118, [16].
[124] *Immigration Regulations 2013* (Nauru) reg 9A.
[125] See Chapter 5, nn 161–4 and accompanying text.
[126] See Government of Papua New Guinea, 'National Refugee Policy' (Policy Paper, June 2015) www.immigration.gov.pg/images/PNG_National_Refugee_Policy_FINAL_ENDORSED_BY_CABINET.pdf.
[127] Ben Doherty, 'Hundreds of Refugees are Refusing to Settle in PNG's "Land of Opportunities"', *The Guardian* (online), 24 October 2015 www.theguardian.com/australia-news/2015/oct/24/hundreds-of-refugees-are-refusing-to-settle-in-pngs-land-of-opportunities.

Others have refused to engage in the RSD process at all and have not lodged claims for asylum.[128] The resettlement deal with the United States has created the possibility that some of those held on Nauru and Manus Island may be transferred to the United States, but details of this agreement remain unclear.[129] At Guantánamo Bay, refugees are detained until they are offered resettlement in a third country. There is no way for refugees to know if and when such an offer may be found, with reports of the process taking up to four years.[130]

There are also serious concerns about the conditions of detention. The issues discussed in relation to onshore detention are magnified in the remote tropical settings of Guantánamo Bay, Nauru and Manus Island. Of the three locations, the conditions in Guantánamo Bay appear to be the best, with significant reported improvements in recent years. The tent-cities surrounded by barbed wire established in the 1990s have given way to apartment-like complexes,[131] and proximity to the Guantánamo Naval Base means that the asylum seekers have access to adequate medical and dental care, as well as other support services. Nonetheless, the open-ended nature of detention as refugees await resettlement in third countries can have a seriously detrimental impact on mental health.

The situation is markedly worse on Manus Island and Nauru. Concerns have been raised in relation to living conditions in both locations, including problems of overcrowding, lack of privacy, exposure to the elements and lack of sufficient drinking water, sanitation and food.[132] Asylum seekers and refugees have to contend with a range of serious tropical diseases. For example, in April 2017, an outbreak of dengue fever on Nauru infected 10 per cent of the asylum seekers and refugees living in the RPC.[133] Medical services in both locations are also reportedly inadequate, with long waiting times for basic treatment and an absence of specialist doctors.[134] Those with serious medical conditions are generally airlifted to Port Moresby or Australia. However, long delays in organising such transfers are commonplace. Inadequate medical treatment may have contributed to the death of a number of asylum seekers. Hamid Khazaei, an Iranian asylum seeker, died in a Brisbane hospital in September 2014 as the result of severe sepsis from a leg infection acquired on

---

[128] 'Refugee Status Determination on Manus Island, Papua New Guinea' (Fact Sheet, UNSW Kaldor Centre for International Refugee Law, January 2017) 10–11.

[129] See Chapter 5, nn 213–24 and accompanying text.

[130] Dastyari, *United States Migrant Interdiction and the Detention of Refugees in Guantánamo Bay*, above n 38, 174.

[131] Ibid 172.

[132] Amnesty International, 'Australia: This Is Still Breaking People: Update on Human Rights Violations at Australia's Asylum Seeker Processing Centre on Manus Island, Papua New Guinea' (Report, 12 May 2014) 5–8; Amnesty International, 'Island of Despair: Australia's "Processing" of Refugees on Nauru', above n 120, 5; Select Committee on the Recent Allegations relating to the Conditions and Circumstances at the Regional Processing Centre on Nauru, Parliament of Australia, *Taking Responsibility: Conditions and Circumstances at Australia's Regional Processing Centre in Nauru: Final Report* (2015) 59–80.

[133] Michael Koziol, 'Dengue Fever Outbreak in Nauru Hits 10 Per Cent of Asylum Seekers', *Sydney Morning Herald* (online), 27 April 2017 www.smh.com.au/federal-politics/political-news/dengue-fever-outbreak-in-nauru-hits-10-per-cent-of-asylum-seekers-20170427-gvtk2u.html.

[134] Amnesty International, 'Island of Despair: Australia's "Processing" of Refugees on Nauru', above n 120, 23–29; Amnesty International, 'Australia: This Is Still Breaking People: Update on Human Rights Violations at Australia's Asylum Seeker Processing Centre on Manus Island, Papua New Guinea', above n 132, 9.

Manus Island. Mr Khazaei had presented at the medical clinic on Manus Island thirteen days before his death and his transfer to Australia was delayed for a number of days as required approvals were being obtained.[135] In December 2016, Faysal Ishak Ahmed, an asylum seeker from Sudan, suffered a fall and seizure on Manus Island and was transferred to a Brisbane hospital where he subsequently died. Mr Ahmed had reportedly complained about heart problems, headaches and seizures to medical staff at the Manus Island RPC for months, but had not received any treatment.[136]

These poor conditions and a lack of adequate medical care, combined with open-ended mandatory detention and an absence of viable long-term settlement solutions, have resulted in high levels of mental illness among refugees and asylum seekers. During a visit to Manus Island in April 2016, UNHCR reported that 88 per cent of detainees surveyed were suffering from a depressive or anxiety disorder and/or post-traumatic stress disorder.[137] A similar study carried out by UNHCR in Nauru found that 83 per cent of asylum seekers and refugees surveyed suffered from post-traumatic stress disorder and/or depression.[138] Multiple sources have confirmed that incidents of self-harm have become endemic for those living both within and outside the RPCs on Nauru and Manus Island.[139] Leaked incident reports, dubbed the 'Nauru files', written by staff in the Nauru RPC reveal that there were more than 362 incidents of actual or threatened self-harm over an eighteen-month period ending in October 2015.[140] There have been a number of incidents of suicide. Omid Masoumali, an Iranian refugee, died in March 2016 in Nauru after lighting himself on fire in front of visiting officials from UNHCR.[141] A month later, Raqib Khan, a Bangladeshi asylum seeker, died of heart failure after reportedly overdosing on Panadol and other pills.[142] In each of these instances, there were also allegations that inadequate medical care

---

[135] Andrew Kos, 'Hamid Khazaei: Inquest Hears Approvals Process Slowed Medical Transfer from Manus Island', *ABC News* (online), 6 December 2016 www.abc.net.au/news/2016-12-06/khazaei-inquest-hears-medical-transfer-could-have-been-faster/8097376.

[136] 'Asylum Seekers Riot on Manus Island after Refugee Death: Police', *SBS News* (online), 25 December 2016 www.sbs.com.au/news/article/2016/12/25/asylum-seekers-riot-manus-island-after-refugee-death-police.

[137] Office of the UNHCR, Submission on the Inquiry into the Serious Allegations of Abuse, Self-Harm and Neglect of Asylum-Seekers, above n 118, [33]–[40].

[138] Ibid [41]–[50].

[139] Refugee Council of Australia, Submission No 22 to Senate Legal and Constitutional Affairs References Committee, Parliament of Australia, *Conditions and Treatment of Asylum Seekers and Refugees at the Regional Processing Centres in the Republic of Nauru and Papua New Guinea*, 5 May 2016, [1.2]; Amnesty International, 'Island of Despair: Australia's "Processing" of Refugees on Nauru' above n 120, 19–22; Michael Koziol and Nicole Hasham, 'Self-Harm in Detention Centres at Epidemic Levels, Internal Documents Show', *Sydney Morning Herald* (online), 16 January 2016 www.smh.com.au/federal-politics/political-news/selfharm-in-detention-centres-at-epidemic-levels-internal-documents-show-20160115-gm74q3.html#ixzz4DAvN8H5e; *The Nauru Files*, The Guardian (online), August 2016 www.theguardian.com/news/series/nauru-files.

[140] *The Nauru Files*, above n 139.

[141] Michael Edwards and Peter Lloyd, 'Omid Madoumali Set Himself on Fire after UNHCR Told Him He Would Remain on Nauru, Asylum Seekers Say', *ABC News* (online), 2 May 2016 www.abc.net.au/news/2016-05-02/refugee-set-himself-on-fire-after-unhcr-meeting:-asylum-seekers/7377396.

[142] Simone Fox Koob, 'Bangladeshi Asylum Seeker Dies on Manus Island', *The Australian* (online), 11 May 2016 www.theaustralian.com.au/national-affairs/immigration/bangladeshi-asylum-seeker-dies-on-manus-island/news-story/f7516bca922226bfaa3733c3566f7b4f.

on the island may have contributed to the deaths. Accurate statistics are difficult to obtain in relation to self-harm on Manus Island because of an alleged culture of under-reporting, but even the official numbers are alarming, with fifty-five self-harm acts reported in the year to July 2015.[143] There have also been two cases of suspected suicide.[144]

Refugees and asylum seekers have been subject to many reported incidents of abuse and neglect. Numerous Australian government reviews into the conditions in the Nauru and Manus Island RPCs have found evidence of sexual and physical assault, including against minors.[145] A 2015 Senate Inquiry into the Nauru RPC found a culture of secrecy and abuse within the facility fostered by the 'lack of independent avenues of complaint and oversight'.[146] Asylum seekers and refugees at the Manus Island RPC have been the target of violent attacks by staff and members of the local population. The most serious incident occurred in February 2014 and resulted in the murder of Iranian asylum seeker Reza Barati. More than seventy other asylum seekers and refugees were also injured, many seriously.[147] In April 2017, a large group of local men, including personnel from the adjoining naval base, unsuccessfully attempted to storm the RPC. Numerous shots were fired towards the accommodation buildings and at least one asylum seeker was injured.[148]

Refugees and asylum seekers have also been attacked by locals outside the centres.[149] In Nauru, the attacks became so frequent that some refugees living in the community requested they be returned to detention to protect their safety.[150] A similar scenario has played out on Manus Island, with an Iraqi refugee allegedly attempting to break back into a guarded transit centre because of concerns about his safety.[151] Local police on Nauru and Manus Island appear unwilling to protect asylum seekers and refugees or investigate claims

---

[143] Office of the UNHCR, Submission on the Inquiry into the Serious Allegations of Abuse, Self-Harm and Neglect of Asylum-Seekers, above n 118, 12; Koziol and Hasham, above n 139.

[144] An Iranian national, Hamed Shamshirpour, died in August 2017 and Rajeev Rajendran, a Tamil refugee from Sri Lanka, died in October 2017: Eric Tlozek, 'Asylum Seeker Dies on Manus Island, Police Confirm', ABC News (online), 2 October 2017 www.abc.net.au/news/2017-10-02/manus-island-asylum-seeker-dies-police-confirm/9007034.

[145] DIBP, 'Review into Recent Allegations Relating to Conditions and Circumstances at the Regional Processing Centre in Nauru' (Final Report, 6 February 2015) [3.1]–[3.188]; Select Committee on the Recent Allegations relating to the Conditions and Circumstances at the Regional Processing Centre on Nauru, above n 132.

[146] Select Committee on the Recent Allegations relating to the Conditions and Circumstances at the Regional Processing Centre on Nauru, above n 132, 133.

[147] Senate Legal and Constitutional Affairs References Committee, Parliament of Australia, *Incident at the Manus Island Detention Centre from 16 February to 18 February 2014* (2014) [8.1].

[148] 'Shots fired at Manus Island Centre, One Asylum Seeker Injured' SBS News (online), 15 April 2017 www.sbs.com.au/news/article/2017/04/14/shots-fired-manus-island-centre-one-asylum-seeker-injured.

[149] Amnesty International, 'Island of Despair: Australia's "Processing" of Refugees on Nauru', above n 120, 34–7; Amnesty International, 'This is Breaking People: Human Rights Violations at Australia's Asylum Seeker Processing Centre on Manus Island, Papua New Guinea', (Report, December 2013) 48–9.

[150] Karl Mathiesen, 'Refugees Living on Nauru Say They Want to Return to Detention to Flee Violence', *The Guardian* (online), 31 December 2014 www.theguardian.com/australia-news/2014/dec/31/refugees-living-on-nauru-say-they-want-to-return-to-detention-to-flee-violence.

[151] Michael Gordon, 'Desperate Refugees Arrested Trying to Return to Manus Island Centre', *Sydney Morning Herald* (online), 22 April 2016 www.smh.com.au/federal-politics/political-news/desperate-refugees-arrested-trying-to-return-to-manus-island-centre-20160422-gocyg1.html.

of physical or sexual abuse. In fact, there is evidence that the police have been responsible for and/or complicit in a number of physical assaults perpetrated against asylum seekers and refugees.[152] There have also been allegations of arbitrary arrest and intimidation.[153]

It is likely that the conditions outlined here in relation to the treatment of refugees and asylum seekers on Nauru and Manus Island breach the right to humane conditions in detention and amount to cruel, inhuman or degrading treatment, or even torture.[154] The eight confirmed deaths of transferees raise concerns relating to the obligation to protect the right to life,[155] while reports of abuse and endemic mental health problems may violate the right to physical and mental integrity of all persons.[156] The substandard medical facilities and care may be in violation of the right to health.[157]

6.3.2 Quality of RSD and Risk of Refoulement

The inadequacies of the RSD procedures carried out in Guantánamo Bay, Nauru and Manus Island mean that refugees transferred there are at risk of *refoulement*. One of the central rationales of extraterritorial processing is to dispense with the legal protections and safeguards that asylum seekers would have if they were processed onshore. Asylum seekers processed in Guantánamo Bay are not provided with access to legal assistance and there is no avenue to have an adverse determination reviewed by an independent body.[158] The procedures operate completely outside the regular statutory framework governing RSDs on the US mainland. Instead, they are carried out pursuant to a wholly discretionary and non-compellable power to screen for protection claims given to the Secretary of Homeland

---

[152] See, eg, Eric Tlozek, 'Manus Island Asylum Seekers "Bashed by PNG Police" Released from Custody', *ABC News* (online), 2 January 2017 www.abc.net.au/news/2017-01-02/manus-asylum-seekers-bashed-in-png-released-by-police/8157646.

[153] Amnesty International, 'Island of Despair: Australia's "Processing" of Refugees on Nauru', above n 120, 39–42.

[154] *CAT* arts 1(1), 16; *ICCPR* art 7; *CRC* art 37(a); UNHCR, *UNHCR Monitoring Visit to the Republic of Nauru: 7 to 9 October 2013*, above n 123, 2, 13, 16; Amnesty International, 'Nauru Camp: A Human Rights Catastrophe with No End in Sight' (Media Release, 23 November 2012). The Special Rapporteur on torture and other cruel, inhuman and degrading treatment made an explicit finding in this regard in relation to detention on Manus Island: Human Rights Council, *Report of the Special Rapporteur on Torture and Other Cruel, Inhuman or Degrading Treatment or Punishment*, 28th sess, Agenda Item 3, UN Doc A/HRC/28/68/Add.1 (6 March 2015) [30], and Amnesty International has made a similar finding in relation to the treatment of asylum seekers and refugees on Nauru: Amnesty International, 'Island of Despair: Australia's "Processing" of Refugees on Nauru', above n 120, 43.

[155] *ICCPR* art 6(1), *CRC* art 6(1); The Border Crossing Observatory, *Australian Border Deaths Database* (online), 15 August 2017 artsonline.monash.edu.au/thebordercrossingobservatory/publications/australian-border-deaths-database/ (listing the details of seven deaths). One additional death occurred on 2 October 2017: see n 142 above.

[156] *ICCPR* arts 9(1), 12(1); *CRC* art 19(1); Human Rights Committee, *General Comment No 35: Article 9 (Liberty and Security of Person)*, 112th sess, UN Doc CCPR/C/GC/35 (16 December 2014) [19].

[157] International Covenant on Economic, Social and Cultural Rights, opened for signature 16 December 1966, 993 UNTS 3 (entered into force 3 January 1976) art 12(1) ('ICESCR'); *CRC* art 24(1); Convention on the Elimination of all Forms of Discrimination Against Women, opened for signature 18 December 1979, 1249 UNTS 13 (entered into force 3 September 1981) art 12(1) ('CEDAW').

[158] Dastyari, *United States Migrant Interdiction and the Detention of Refugees in Guantánamo Bay*, above n 38, 143.

Security pursuant to an executive order.[159] As discussed in Chapter 5, US courts have found that the First and Fifth Amendment protections of the *US Constitution* do not apply to status determinations in Guantánamo Bay.[160] This means that asylum seekers do not have a right to legal counsel, nor can they challenge RSD outcomes on the basis of substantive or procedural due process grounds.

RSD of asylum seekers transferred to PNG and Nauru is carried out pursuant to the domestic law of those countries.[161] Neither country has much experience in carrying out such a role. Nauru only acceded to the *Refugee Convention* and *Protocol* in 2011, and passed legislation setting up RSD procedures in 2012.[162] While PNG acceded to the *Refugee Convention* and *Protocol* in 1986, it did not introduce laws and processes governing RSD until 2013.[163] This lack of experience has led to criticism that both nations lack the expertise and capacity to carry out fair and effective status determination procedures.[164] In the case of PNG, the legislative framework contains some substantial shortcomings which all raise the risk of *refoulement*. The grounds for exclusion from protection are much broader than what is found in the *Refugee Convention*. Of particular concern is the exclusion on the basis of 'a demeanour incompatible with a person of good character and standing' in relation to behaviour carried out after arrival in PNG.[165] The regulations do not require the consideration of complementary protection grounds in the RSD procedures. As such, there is a risk of breaching the *non-refoulement* provisions of the *CAT*, *ICCPR* and other human rights treaties. There are also concerns relating to effective review of negative determinations. While asylum seekers in PNG have access to merits review before the purportedly independent Refugee Assessment Review Panel, there is little public information as to its composition or function; nor does it appear to have any legislative authority.[166] The scope for judicial review is unclear, with the PNG *Migration Act* expressly stating that any decision relating to the grant of an entry permit or removal from the country is not reviewable or open to challenge 'in any court on any ground'.[167] The legislative framework in Nauru is somewhat more robust, with express provisions relating to the creation of an independent merits review body,[168] and the right of judicial review of merits review tribunal decisions in the Supreme Court of Nauru.[169] Amendments in 2014 also incorporated complementary protection grounds.[170]

The significant variations in RSD outcomes are a red flag in relation to the efficacy of procedures. Approximately 77 per cent of asylum seekers transferred to Nauru have

---

[159] See Exec Order No 13276, 67 Fed Reg 69985 (19 November 2002) as amended by Exec Order No 13286, 68 Fed Reg 10619 (3 May 2003).

[160] See Chapter 5, nn 24–76 and accompanying text.

[161] This can be contrasted to the regime operating under the original 'Pacific Solution' (2001–2007), where RSD was carried out by UNHCR or Australian immigration officials: Chapter 5, nn 92–5 and accompanying text.

[162] *Refugees Convention Act 2012* (Nauru).

[163] *Migration Amendment Regulation 2013* (Papua New Guinea), amending *Migration Regulation 1979* (Papua New Guinea).

[164] UNHCR, UNHCR Monitoring Visit to Manus Island, Papua New Guinea: 11–13 June 2013, above n 123, [33]; UNHCR, UNHCR Monitoring Visit to the Republic of Nauru: 7 to 9 October 2013, above n 123, [32].

[165] *Migration Regulation 1979* (Papua New Guinea) reg 14(2)(h).

[166] 'Refugee Status Determination on Manus Island, Papua New Guinea', above n 128, 9.

[167] *Migration Act 1978* (Papua New Guinea) s 19. [168] *Refugees Convention Act 2012* (Nauru) ss 35–41.

[169] Ibid ss 43–44. [170] *Refugee Convention (Amendment) Act 2014* (Nauru).

been recognised as refugees.[171] The figure is substantially lower on Manus Island, with the recognition rate sitting at around 55 per cent. This raises concerns about the possible differences between processes in the two locations.[172] The situation becomes even more worrying when we compare these figures to the yearly acceptance rates in Australia in the years prior to the re-introduction of extraterritorial processing, which ranged between 88 per cent and 100 per cent between 2008 and 2013.[173] Also of concern is the fact that asylum seekers on Manus Island and Nauru are actively encouraged to abandon their claims for refugee protection and return to their home countries. A total of 262 asylum seekers and refugees were 'voluntarily' repatriated from the Manus Island and Nauru RPCs between July 2014 and December 2016.[174] There are concerns that some of these returns were prompted by uncertainty and harsh conditions in detention and/or pressure from immigration officials, and were, as such, not fully informed and consensual.[175]

6.3.3 *State Responsibility*

The governments of the United States and Australia have argued that they are not responsible for breaches of international human rights or refugee law that may occur in their extraterritorial processing centres. The United States relies on Guantánamo Bay's special legal status, in particular the fact that it is outside its municipally defined territory and that *de jure* sovereignty lies with Cuba. The Australian government has repeatedly expressed the view that it is not responsible for activities carried out within the sovereign borders of Nauru and PNG by the authorities of those governments.[176] However, as already discussed, it is now well established in international jurisprudence that a state can have human rights obligations to persons situated outside their territory, provided the state exercises 'effective control' over that person.[177]

Given the *de facto* sovereignty the United States exercises over Guantánamo Bay, and the complete control it exerts over all aspects of the Migrant Operations Centre, it clearly exercises effective authority and control over asylum seekers and refugees transferred there. As such, the US government is responsible for the breaches of international refugee and human rights law which may occur. This responsibility cannot be abdicated through the special designation given to Guantánamo Bay under municipal US law.

---

[171] 'Refugee Status Determination on Manus Island, Papua New Guinea', above n 128, 3.   [172] Ibid.
[173] DIAC, 'Asylum Trends – Australia: 2012–2013 Annual Publication' (Report, 2013) 27–30 www.border.gov.au/ReportsandPublications/Documents/statistics/asylum-trends-aus-2012-13.pdf (asylum seekers from top five countries of citizenship, taking into account decisions overturned); 'Refugee Status Determination on Manus Island, Papua New Guinea', above n 128.
[174] Madeline Gleeson, 'Transfer Tracker' (UNSW Kaldor Centre for International Refugee Law, 10 March 2017) www.kaldorcentre.unsw.edu.au/publication/transfer-tracker.
[175] UNHCR, *UNHCR Monitoring Visit to the Republic of Nauru: 7 to 9 October 2013*, above n 123, [138]; Amnesty International, 'Island of Despair: Australia's "Processing" of Refugees on Nauru', above n 120, 23.
[176] See, eg, Human Rights Council, *Report of the Working Group on the Universal Periodic Review: Australia*, 31st sess, Agenda Item 6, UN Doc A/HRC/31/14/Add.1 (29 February 2016) [14]; Evidence to Senate Standing Committee for the Scrutiny of Bills, Parliament of Australia, Melbourne, 19 December 2012 (Vicki Parker).
[177] See above n 65–8 and accompanying text.

The situation on Nauru and Manus Island is not as clear-cut, with the governments of those countries ostensibly responsible for managing the RPCs and carrying out RSDs. However, it is well documented that the Australian government has exercised and will continue to exercise a significant degree of control over asylum seekers transferred to Nauru and Manus Island. Australia is solely responsible for funding the processing centres and pays a leasing fee for the sites to the Nauruan and PNG governments.[178] There is a significant presence of Australian staff working at both locations, with UNHCR noting that the officials from the Australian Department of Immigration appeared to be in effective control of the both centres' management.[179] Department of Immigration officials have also been involved in carrying out RSD procedures,[180] and the Australian government is ultimately responsible for facilitating resettlement.[181] In light of these factors, the Parliamentary Joint Committee on Human Rights has concluded that Australia could be viewed as exercising 'effective control' over the treatment of people it had transferred to Nauru and Manus Island.[182] The UN Committee against Torture reached the same conclusion in its 2014 periodic review of Australia's compliance with the *CAT*.[183] In 2015, the Special Rapporteur on Torture and other Cruel, Inhuman and Degrading Treatment went further, by making an explicit finding that Australia's involvement in the Manus Island RPC violated the right of asylum seekers to be free from torture or cruel, inhuman or degrading treatment.[184]

The UN Special Rapporteur on the Human Rights of Migrants, François Crépeau, has been similarly unequivocal in assigning responsibility for human rights abuses on Nauru and Manus Island to the Australian government. In a report released in April 2017, he notes:

> All detention centres and detainees – whether onshore or offshore – fall under the responsibility of the Government of Australia ... All persons who are under the effective control of Australia – because, inter alia, Australia transferred them to regional processing centres, which are funded by Australia, and with the involvement of private

---

[178] Parliamentary Joint Committee on Human Rights, Parliament of Australia, *Examination of the Migration (Regional Processing) Package of Legislation*' (2013) 37–8.

[179] Ibid 39; UNHCR, *UNHCR Mission to the Republic of Nauru: 3–5 December 2012* (Report, December 2012) [31]; Madeline Gleeson, 'Offshore Processing: Australia's Responsibility for Asylum Seekers and Refugees in Nauru and Papua New Guinea' (Fact Sheet, UNSW Kaldor Centre for International Refugee Law, 8 April 2015) 14.

[180] Parliamentary Joint Committee on Human Rights, above n 178, 40–1.

[181] *Memorandum of Understanding between the Republic of Nauru and the Commonwealth of Australia, relating to the Transfer to and Assessment of Persons in Nauru, and Related Issues*, signed 3 August 2013, cl 13. While a similar clause was omitted from the updated MOU with Papua New Guinea (*Regional Resettlement Arrangement between Australia and Papua New Guinea*, signed 19 July 2013), Australia's efforts in negotiating the US resettlement deal illustrate that it retains responsibility for the resettlement of refugees transferred to Papua New Guinea.

[182] Parliamentary Joint Committee on Human Rights, above n 178; A similar conclusion was reached by the Senate Legal and Constitutional Affairs Reference Committee, Parliament of Australia, *Incident at Manus Island Detention Centre from 16 February to 18 February 2014* (11 December 2014) [8.33].

[183] UN Committee against Torture, *Concluding Observations on the Combined Fourth and Fifth Periodic Reports of Australia*, 53rd sess, UN Doc CAT/C/AUS/CO/4-5 (23 December 2014) [17].

[184] Human Rights Council, *Report of the Special Rapporteur on Torture and Other Cruel, Inhuman or Degrading Treatment or Punishment*, 28th sess, Agenda Item 3, UN Doc A/HRC/28/68/Add.1 (6 March 2015) [16]–[31]. Amnesty International has made a similar finding in relation to the treatment of asylum seekers and refugees on Nauru: Amnesty International, 'Island of Despair: Australia's "Processing" of Refugees on Nauru', above n 120, 43.

contractors of Australia's choice – enjoy the same protection from torture and ill-treatment under [CAT] ... The Government of Australia is ultimately accountable for any human rights violations that occur in the regional processing centres based in Nauru and Papua New Guinea. The combination of the harsh conditions in Nauru or on Manus Island, the protracted periods of closed detention and the uncertainty about the future reportedly creates serious physical and mental anguish and suffering. The Special Rapporteur observes that regarding human rights issues, the system cannot be salvaged.[185]

Less than two months later, in June 2017, the Australian government settled a class action made by 1,905 detainees held at the Manus Island RPC between November 2012 and May 2016.[186] The plaintiffs had sought damages on the grounds that the conditions of their detention gave rise to multiple breaches of the government's duty of care. This included substandard medical treatment, and the failure to secure the centre and protect detainees from violence at the hands of locals. The plaintiffs also claimed to have been falsely imprisoned in the period following the PNG Supreme Court decision ruling that their detention was illegal.[187] The settlement, which is reported to be in the vicinity of AUD $70 million plus costs, is being touted as Australia's largest ever human rights-related settlement.[188] While not an admission of liability, the government's decision to settle reflects a lack of confidence that they would be able to successfully argue that they were not responsible for the treatment of the detainees. This was confirmed by the Immigration Minister, Peter Dutton, who cited the fact that the case would have an 'unknown' outcome as one of the reasons why it was prudent to settle.[189]

Even if the Australian government's involvement does not amount to effective control, it may still be responsible for human rights violations which occur in Nauru and PNG under the principle of joint and several liability. This will occur if it can be shown that Australia knowingly aided or assisted, directed or controlled, or coerced Nauru and PNG to commit these violations.[190] UNHCR has expressed the view that at a minimum, such a level of influence exists, and Australia is jointly responsible with PNG and Nauru, under international law, for the care and protection of all asylum seekers transferred to those destinations.[191]

---

[185] Human Rights Council, *Report of the Special Rapporteur on the Human Rights of Migrants on his Mission to Australia and the Regional Processing Centres in Nauru*, 35th sess, Agenda Item 3, UN DOC A/HRC/35/25/Add.3 (24 April 2017) 14.

[186] Supreme Court of Victoria, *Manus Island Detention Centre Class Action* (14 June 2017) www.supremecourt.vic.gov.au/law-and-practice/class-actions/manus-island-detention-centre-class-action. See *Kamasaee v Commonwealth of Australia* [2017] VSC 272 (19 May 2017); Ben Doherty and Calla Wahlquist, 'Government to Pay Damages to 1,905 Manus Island Detainees in Class Action', *The Guardian* (online), 14 June 2017 www.theguardian.com/australia-news/2017/jun/14/government-to-pay-damages-to-manus-island-detainees-in-class-action.

[187] *Namah v Pato* [2016] PJSC 13; see Chapter 5, nn 207–11.

[188] Michael Koziol and Benjamin Preiss, 'Manus Island Class Action: Government to Compensate Former Detainees in Huge Settlement', *Sydney Morning Herald* (online), 14 June 2017 www.smh.com.au/federal-politics/political-news/manus-island-class-action-government-to-compensate-former-detainees-in-huge-settlement-20170613-gwqlu3.html.

[189] Doherty and Wahlquist, above n 186.

[190] *Responsibility of States for Internationally Wrongful Acts*, GA Res 56/83, UN GAOR, 56th sess, 85th plen mtg, Supp No 49, UN Doc A/RES/56/83 (28 January 2002, adopted 12 December 2001) annex ('*Responsibility of States for Internationally Wrongful Acts*') arts 16–18.

[191] Select Committee on the Recent Allegations relating to the Conditions and Circumstances at the Regional Processing Centre on Nauru, above n 132, 121; UNHCR, *UNHCR Mission to Manus Island, Papua New Guinea, 15–17 January 2013* (Report, February 2013) [22].

6.3.4 Transferring Asylum Seekers to Third Countries

In cases where the extraterritorial processing location is a third country, there are additional constraints under international law that apply *before* asylum seekers are transferred. UNHCR has made it clear that the preferred and normal practice for processing asylum claims is to provide access to fair in-country procedures.[192] However, it may be permissible to transfer asylum seekers to third countries if certain strict conditions are met. This is where there is a significant difference between the current Australian and US extraterritorial processing models. Given that the United States exercises complete *de facto* sovereignty and control over Guantánamo Bay, the rules around third country transfers are not directly relevant. However, these clearly apply to Australia's third country transfer arrangements.

UNHCR sets out the minimum standards that any third country transfer arrangement must meet in its *Guidance Note on Bilateral and/or Multilateral Transfer Arrangements of Asylum Seekers*.[193] The guidelines require legally binding undertakings that transferees, among other things,

> will be protected against *refoulement*; will have access to fair and efficient procedures for the determination of refugee status and/or other forms of international protection; will be treated in accordance with accepted international standards (for example, appropriate reception arrangements; access to health, education and basic services; safeguards against arbitrary detention; persons with specific needs are identified and assisted); and if recognised as being in need of international protection, will be able to enjoy asylum and/or access a durable solution.[194]

The MOUs that Australia has concluded with Nauru and PNG do not satisfy these requirements. First, a number of the protections are simply not mentioned. For example, the MOU with Nauru does not include an unqualified obligation to grant asylum or access to durable solutions.[195] Neither MOU contains detailed obligations relating to reception arrangements and access to health, education or basic services, nor safeguards against arbitrary detention.[196] More important, however, is the fact that the MOUs are not legally

---

[192] UNHCR, Maritime Interception Operations and the Processing of International Protection Claims: Legal Standards and Policy Considerations with Respect to Extraterritorial Processing (Protection Policy Paper, November 2010), above n 89, [1]–[2]; UNHCR, 'Guidance Note on Bilateral and/or Multilateral Transfer Arrangements of Asylum-Seekers' (Note, May 2013) [1].

[193] UNHCR, 'Guidance Note on Bilateral and/or Multilateral Transfer Arrangements of Asylum-Seekers', above n 192.

[194] Ibid [3(vi)].

[195] Note that under clause 12, Nauru undertakes to settle some of those found to be in need of international protection in Nauru, but only subject to a separate agreement between Australia and Nauru on arrangements and numbers: *Memorandum of Understanding between the Republic of Nauru and the Commonwealth of Australia, Relating to the Transfer to and Assessment of Persons in Nauru, and Related Issue*, signed 3 August 2013, cl 12.

[196] Although clause 17 of both MOUs sets out a very general obligation that the transferees be treated 'with dignity and respect and in accordance with relevant human rights standards': *Memorandum of Understanding between the Republic of Nauru and the Commonwealth of Australia, Relating to the Transfer to and Assessment of Persons in Nauru, and Related Issues*, signed 3 August 2013, cl 17; *Memorandum of Understanding between the Government of the Independent State of Papua New Guinea and the Government of Australia, Relating to the Transfer to, and Assessment and Settlement in, Papua New Guinea of Certain Persons and Related Issues*, signed 6 August 2013, cl 17.

binding on the parties. As such, there is no legal obligation on either party to honour their commitments under the arrangements, or hold each other accountable for any breaches.

There are serious concerns that persons transferred to PNG and Nauru are at risk of direct and secondary *refoulement*. Direct *refoulement* occurs when a refugee is transferred to a country where they face persecution because of their race, religion, nationality, political opinion or membership of a particular social group.[197] There is some evidence that certain asylum seekers transferred to PNG and Nauru may be persecuted in this fashion. For example, UNHCR has expressed concern for lesbian, gay, bisexual, transgender and intersex individuals transferred to Manus Island, given that homosexuality is criminalised under PNG law.[198] The fact that transferees are the targets of physical violence in the community in both Nauru and PNG because of their status as refugees or asylum seekers may amount to persecution because of membership of a particular social group.[199]

Direct *refoulement* will also occur when asylum seekers are transferred to a territory where they are subject to certain types of serious harm as articulated in the *ICCPR*, *CAT* and *CRC*, including torture or cruel, inhuman or degrading treatment.[200] As examined at length in the preceding section, there is a strong case to be made that the treatment of asylum seekers transferred to Nauru and PNG may amount to such harm. This is particularly the case for vulnerable asylum seekers, such as children, pregnant women and persons with physical or mental health conditions that cannot be properly treated in PNG or Nauru.[201]

States that transfer asylum seekers for processing in third countries are liable not only for persecution or harm that an asylum seeker may face in that country, but also for situations where an asylum seeker may be sent onwards to another country where they would be at risk. This is known as secondary *refoulement*. The shortcomings of the RSD procedures in PNG and Nauru examined above, combined with the pressure placed on asylum seekers to 'voluntarily' return to their home countries, create a serious risk of secondary *refoulement* for refugees transferred to those countries.

6.4 Special Protections for Child Asylum Seekers

Additional concerns arise in relation to asylum-seeker and refugee children subject to mandatory detention, extraterritorial processing and maritime interdiction. The *CRC* requires that the primary consideration in regards to all government decisions that affect children should be the 'best interests of the child'.[202] Placing a minor in immigration

---

[197] *Refugee Convention* art 33(1).
[198] UNHCR, UNHCR Monitoring Visit to Manus Island, Papua New Guinea: 23 to 25 October 2013, above n 123, [123]–[124].
[199] For an examination of the meaning of 'a particular social group' in this context, see T Alexander Aleinikoff, 'Protected Characteristics and Social Perceptions: An Analysis of the Meaning of "Membership of a Particular Social Group"' in Erika Feller, Volker Türk and Frances Nicholson (eds) *Refugee Protection in International Law: UNHCR's Global Consultations on International Protection* (Cambridge University Press, 2003) 263.
[200] See above nn 59–60 and accompanying text.
[201] Madeline Gleeson, 'Offshore Processing: Australia's Responsibility for Asylum Seekers and Refugees in Nauru and Papua New Guinea', above n 179, 7.
[202] *CRC* art 3.

detention could rarely, if ever, be justified as being in the best interests of a child.[203] The *CRC* also imposes strict limitations on detention, requiring that a child should only be detained as a measure of last resort and for the shortest appropriate period of time,[204] and that children in detention are treated with humanity and respect for their inherent dignity.[205] Protection is also afforded by art 24(1) of the *ICCPR*, which provides that 'Every child shall have, without any discrimination as to race, colour, sex, language, religion, national or social origin, property or birth, the right to such measures of protection as are required by his status as a minor, on the part of his family, society and the State'.

In *Bakhtiyari v Australia*,[206] the UN Human Rights Committee held that the best interests of the child test forms an integral part of the protection afforded by art 24(1) of the *ICCPR*. The UN Human Rights Committee found that the immigration detention of a group of children for two years and eight months contravened this provision, given the fact they had suffered demonstrable, documented and ongoing damage as a result of their detention. It also noted that detention was arbitrary and thus violated art 9(1) of the *ICCPR*.

While the long-term mandatory detention of children onshore in Australia is now quite rare, a significant number continue to be held in detention-like conditions in Nauru. Although a policy change in July 2013 meant that the Manus Island RPC should house only adult males, there have been reports of children being sent there by mistake.[207] It is hard to see how the transfer of a child to either Nauru or Manus Island could ever meet the best interests of the child test. Not only are they subject to general harm suffered by all asylum seekers at those destinations (examined in the previous section), but they are also vulnerable to human rights violations particular to their status as minors. The plight of asylum-seeker children in Nauru exemplifies this. The UN Committee on the Rights of the Child's periodic review of Nauru issued in September 2016 found 'persistent discrimination against asylum-seeking and refugee children in all areas',[208] and expressed deep concern about a number of issues, including:

> Inhuman and degrading treatment, including physical, psychological and sexual abuse, against asylum seeking and refugee children living in the Regional Processing Centres ... as well as reports of intimidation, sexual assault, abuse and threats of violence against families living in refugee settlements around the island, all of which has a detrimental impact on the psychological well-being of their children.

The US government continues to detain children on a large scale. UNHCR calculated that more than 100,000 children were being detained in 2015.[209] A number of recent legal

---

[203] Committee on the Rights of the Child, 'Report of the 2012 Day of General Discussion: The Rights of All Children in the Context of International Migration' (Report, United Nations, 28 September 2012) www.ohchr.org/Documents/HRBodies/CRC/Discussions/2012/DGD2012ReportAndRecommendations.pdf.

[204] *CRC* art 37(b).   [205] Ibid art 37(c).

[206] Human Rights Committee, *Views: Communication No 1069/2002*, 79th sess, UN Doc CCPR/C/79/D/1069/2002 (29 October 2003).

[207] Oliver Laughland, '"Every Day I Am Crying": Boys Held on Manus Island Tell of Their Despair', *The Guardian* (online), 7 November 2013 www.theguardian.com/world/2013/nov/07/every-day-i-am-crying-manus.

[208] UN Committee on the Rights of the Child, *Concluding Observations on the Initial Report of Nauru*, 73rd sess, UN Doc CRC/C/NRU/CO/1 (28 October 2016) [22].

[209] 103,140 children were detained in 2015, down from 136,986 in 2014: UNHCR, Beyond Detention: A Global Strategy to Support Governments to End the Detention of Asylum-Seekers and Refugees – 2014–2019, Progress Report mid-2016 (August, 2016) 80.

victories have placed mounting pressure on the government to reduce the reliance on detention and improve the conditions of detention for those who cannot be released.[210] However, children and families continue to be detained in prison-like conditions.[211] Up-to-date figures on the number of children detained at Guantánamo Bay are not available, but reports indicate that the facilities are designed to cater for families and unaccompanied minors.[212]

It is unclear to what extent the particular vulnerabilities of children are taken into account by Australia and the United States in the course of maritime interdiction activities. There is no information available as to whether these factors are considered during RSD procedures carried out at sea. What is clear, however, is that both countries routinely return asylum-seeker children intercepted at sea to their point of departure[213] – an action that is almost always likely not to be in the best interest of the child.

6.5 Non-Discrimination and Non-Penalisation

The *Refugee Convention* prohibits the imposition of penalties on refugees for entering or being present in a state's territory without authorisation.[214] Mandatory detention in both Australia and the United States targets asylum seekers who arrive without authorisation. Further, maritime interdiction and extraterritorial processing only apply to asylum seekers utilising a particular form of unauthorised arrival: namely, travelling by boat. Persons subject to these policies are afforded substantially fewer rights and protections when compared to those processed onshore.

The differential treatment may also violate prohibitions against discrimination under international law. Article 26 of the *ICCPR* affirms the fact that all people are equal before the law and are entitled to the equal protection of the law without discrimination.[215] Accordingly, it prohibits discrimination on any ground, including 'race, colour, sex, language, religion, political or other opinion, national or social origin, property, birth or other status'.[216] James Hathaway has described this provision as 'an extraordinarily robust guarantee of non-discrimination including, in particular, an affirmative duty to prohibit discrimination and effectively to protect all persons from discrimination'.[217] The *Convention on the Elimination of all Forms of Racial Discrimination* ('*CERD*') contains additional

---

[210] See Chapter 3, n 51 and accompanying text.

[211] Eleanor Acer and Jessica Chicco, *U.S. Detention of Asylum Seekers: Seeking Protection, Finding Prison* (Report, Human Rights First, June 2009); Lara Domínguez, Adrienne Lee and Elizabeth Leiserson, *U.S. Detention and Removal of Asylum Seekers: An International Human Rights Law Analysis* (Analysis Paper, Allard K. Lowenstein International Human Rights Clinic, Yale Law School, 20 June 2016) 3–7, 23.

[212] Dastyari, *United States Migrant Interdiction and the Detention of Refugees in Guantánamo Bay*, above n 38, 174.

[213] See details of individual push-back operations under Operation Sovereign Borders in Schloenhardt and Craig, above n 79, 548–58; Jacqueline Bhabha and Mary Crock, *Seeking Asylum Alone: A Comparative Study of Laws, Policy and Practice in Australia, the UK and the US* (Themis Press, 2007) 143–9.

[214] *Refugee Convention* art 31(1). Note that this protection only applies where the refugee has come directly from a territory where they faced persecution, and has presented themselves to authorities without delay. For detailed analysis of the effect of this provision, see Goodwin-Gill, above n 5, 185–252.

[215] *ICCPR* art 26.

[216] Ibid. Additional protections against discrimination are set out in arts 2(1) and 3. Similar protections specifically targeting children are found in art 2 of the *CRC*.

[217] Hathaway, above n 74, 126 (citations omitted).

specific protections against racial discrimination.[218] It prohibits any distinction that has the *purpose* or *effect* of impairing rights and freedoms.[219] Thus, it extends beyond measures that are explicitly discriminatory to encompass measures which are not discriminatory at face value but are discriminatory in fact and effect.[220]

To the extent that the policies of mandatory detention, maritime interdiction and extraterritorial processing in the United States and Australia disproportionately target asylum seekers from particular countries, they amount to effective discrimination. The policies of interdiction and extraterritorial processing have a particularly disproportionate impact. The composition of asylum seekers arriving by boat, both in terms of ethnicity and nationality, is different to that of those who arrive by other means and have their claims processed onshore. The US maritime interdiction program overwhelmingly targets asylum seekers from Cuba and Haiti.[221] Moreover, the US government discriminates in respect of the procedures for screening asylum claims at sea, placing non-Cubans at a serious disadvantage.[222] No exact breakdown of the nationalities of asylum seekers transferred to Nauru and Manus Island is publicly available, but the Department of Immigration has confirmed that the majority are from Iran.[223] However, Iranians made up less than 2 per cent of protection visa applicants processed onshore in the 2015–16 financial year.[224]

It is important to note that not every instance of differential treatment will automatically violate the principles of non-discrimination. For example, the UN Human Rights Committee has made it clear that differential treatment is authorised in circumstances where it is reasonable and objective, has the aim of achieving a legitimate purpose and is consistent with the full set of rights enshrined in the *ICCPR*.[225] Given the extensive human rights breaches examined in this chapter resulting from the use of mandatory detention, maritime interdiction and extraterritorial processing, it is difficult to see how these exceptions for differential treatment could apply.

---

[218] *International Convention on the Elimination of All Forms of Racial Discrimination*, opened for signature 21 December 1965, 660 UNTS 195 (entered into force 4 January 1969) art 1(1) ('*CERD*').
[219] *CERD* art 2(1)(c).
[220] Committee on the Elimination of Racial Discrimination, *Communication No 31/2003*, 66th sess, UN Doc CERD/C/66/D/31/2003 (10 March 2005) [10.4] ('*Ms LR et al v Slovak Republic*').
[221] See *Appendix*, Table A.1.   [222] See above nn 83–4 and accompanying text.
[223] DIBP, Statistics provided to the Senate Legal and Constitutional Affairs References Committee, Parliament of Australia, *Incident at the Manus Island Detention Centre from 16 February to 18 February 2014* (2014); Select Committee on the Recent Allegations relating to the Conditions and Circumstances at the Regional Processing Centre on Nauru, Parliament of Australia, *Taking Responsibility: Conditions and Circumstances at Australia's Regional Processing Centre in Nauru: Final Report* (2015) 7.
[224] DIBP, Onshore Humanitarian Programme 2015–16: Delivery and Outcomes for Non-Illegal Maritime Arrival (Non-IMA) as at 30 April 2016, Australian Government www.border.gov.au/Reportsand Publications/Documents/statistics/ohp-april-16.pdf.
[225] Human Rights Committee, *CCPR General Comment No 18: Non-Discrimination*, 37th sess (10 November 1989) [1].

7

Lessons for Other Jurisdictions

> [W]e do not always practice what we preach. A group of countries cannot pursue regional containment policies while expecting others, due to the sheer coincidence of geography, to have admission policies without meaningful or sustained support. This is a recipe for resentment, non-cooperation, and a race to the bottom. We cannot have two sets of scales for measuring our responses to refugee influxes or long-lasting refugee situations. We cannot hold ourselves to one set of standards and others to another.
>
> Volker Türk, Assistant High Commissioner for Protection,
> UNHCR, March 2017

The policies of mandatory detention, maritime interdiction and extraterritorial processing have spread beyond the United States and Australia. Copycat lawmaking in this area is very much a live issue. European leaders are currently debating whether maritime interdiction, push-backs and extraterritorial processing should be deployed to address the so-called refugee crisis gripping their region. In recent years, mandatory detention laws modelled on the US and Australian systems have been introduced in Canada and New Zealand, and South East Asian governments have carried out maritime interdiction and push-backs in the Andaman Sea. In each of these instances, the policies were identified, and sometimes justified, on the grounds that they are used in Australia and the United States. In this chapter, I examine these recent examples and consider the ramifications of my findings for lawmakers involved in current and future transfers.

7.1 The 'Australian Solution' as a Model for Europe?

Australia's use of interdiction, boat turn-backs and extraterritorial processing has been touted as a possible answer to Europe's refugee crisis. More than one million undocumented migrants travelled by boat across the Mediterranean to Europe from North Africa and Turkey in 2015.[1] A further 356,000 made the journey in 2016.[2] The large number of arrivals has been accompanied by significant loss of life at sea. In one weekend alone in April 2015, more than 1,000 migrants perished in separate incidents across the Mediterranean.[3] These

---

[1] UNHCR, 'Refugees & Migrants Sea Arrivals in Europe: Monthly Data Update' (Bureau for Europe, December 2016) 1 https://data2.unhcr.org/en/documents/download/53447.

[2] Ibid.

[3] Sam Greenhill and Daniel Martin, '"Send Gunboats to the Mediterranean": Australian PM Warns Europe Crisis Will Not Stop until It Copies Tough Stance on People-Smugglers', *Daily Mail Australia* (online), 21 April 2015 www.dailymail.co.uk/news/article-3048375/If-want-stop-migrants-crossing-Mediterranean-don-t-let-asylum-seekers-set-foot-land-Australian-Prime-Minister-urges-EU-adopt-tough-policies-proved-success.html.

deaths were the immediate trigger for calls for Europe to adopt the 'Australian Solution'.[4] Australian Prime Minister, Tony Abbott responded to the tragic incident by urging European countries to use his government's tough asylum-seeker policies to stop people-smuggling, to prevent future loss of life at sea.[5]

Across Europe, and particularly in Germany, Austria and the United Kingdom, newspapers carried stories asking whether Australia's tough border protection regime could serve as a model for Europe.[6] Prime Minister Abbott, as well as *The Australian* newspaper, reported that European immigration officials requested a briefing on the workings of Australia's push-back and extraterritorial processing policies.[7] It appears Australian officials provided such a briefing to senior immigration officials from Europe, North America and New Zealand in the context of the Intergovernmental Consultations on Migration, Asylum and Refugees ('IGC') meeting, which took place in Sydney in May 2015.[8] Abbott used the occasion of the Margaret Thatcher Lecture, delivered in London in October 2015 – shortly after he was deposed as Prime Minister – to again call on European leaders to follow Australia's lead. In his words:

> This means turning boats around for people coming by sea. It means denying entry at the border, for people with no legal right to come; and it means establishing camps for people who currently have nowhere to go. It will require some force; it will require massive logistics and expense; it will gnaw at our consciences – yet it is the only way to prevent a tide of humanity surging through Europe and quite possibly changing it forever.[9]

Some European leaders seemed in favour of such an approach. In March 2016, UK Prime Minister, David Cameron called on the EU to begin turning migrant boats back to Libya.[10] Prime Minister Cameron had reportedly been briefed by Australian officials in the lead-up to making those statements.[11] In June 2016, the Austrian Foreign Minister, Sebastian Kurz, urged the EU to look at the 'Australian example' and adopt a system of offshore processing.[12] In August 2016, a Danish parliamentary delegation made plans to visit Nauru

---

[4] Nikolas Feith Tan, 'Europe Rejects "Australian Solution"' (2015) 25(9) *Eureka Street* 35.

[5] Steven Scott, 'Follow My Lead on Boats: Abbott Tells Europe Turn-Back Model Stops Deaths', *Courier-Mail* (Brisbane), 22 April 2015, 1, 8.

[6] David Wroe, 'Refugee Crisis: Europe Looks to Australia for Answers', *Sydney Morning Herald* (online), 24 April 2015 www.smh.com.au/national/refugee-crisis-europe-looks-to-australia-for-answers-20150424-1ms804.html.

[7] Stefanie Balogh, 'Europe Seeks Asylum Advice from Abbott Government', *The Australian* (online), 6 May 2015 www.theaustralian.com.au/national-affairs/immigration/europe-seeks-asylum-advice-from-abbott-government/story-fn9hm1gu-1227337899105.

[8] Ibid. For analysis of the IGC and the role it plays in facilitating transfers, see Chapter 3, nn 99–104 and accompanying text.

[9] Tony Abbott, 'Second Annual Margaret Thatcher Lecture' (Speech delivered at the Margaret Thatcher Centre, London, 27 October 2015).

[10] Rowena Mason and Patrick Kinsley, 'David Cameron: Send More Patrol Ships to Turn Refugee Boats Back to Libya', *The Guardian* (online), 18 March 2016 www.theguardian.com/world/2016/mar/18/refugee-boats-david-cameron-early-intervention-libya-migrants-mediterranean-eu-leaders.

[11] Ellen Whinnett, 'Secret Talks: European Countries Ask Australia How to Stop Asylum-Seekers', *The Daily Telegraph* (online), 14 January 2017 www.dailytelegraph.com.au/news/world/secret-talks-european-countries-ask-australia-how-to-stop-asylumseekers/news-story/fda3996385509fdeac4bef4f9784b098.

[12] Ibid.

to study the use of offshore processing and its appropriateness for Europe.[13] The visit was aborted after two members of the delegation, who had previously criticised the policy, had their visas cancelled.[14] In November 2016, senior representatives from Australia's Border Force were invited to give a keynote address about Australia's policies at the European Coast Guard Cooperation Network Meeting in Warsaw.[15] The audience included 'more than 40 different national authorities of EU member states, including coast guards, navies, border police, customs and maritime authorities', as well as representatives from various EU agencies and international organisations.[16]

The irony of all this, as I discussed in Chapters 4 and 5, is that Australia's offshore processing and interdiction policies are modelled on US practice. The suite of policies labelled the 'Australian Solution' could just as accurately be called the 'American Solution'. It is important to note that these proposals for interdiction and extraterritorial processing in the EU are not completely novel. What follows is a brief overview of historic and current European proposals and initiatives which include elements of these policies.

7.1.1 Maritime Interdiction

Maritime interdiction operations to combat irregular migration have been carried out by individual European nations, as well as at the EU level. Italy implemented a scheme in 1991 to block boats from Albania attempting to cross the Adriatic sea following the fall of Albania's communist regime.[17] From 1997 onwards, interdicted migrants were returned to Albania pursuant to a bilateral agreement between Albanian and Italian authorities.[18] Italian legal scholar, Tullio Scovazzi justified the legality of these measures with reference to US interdiction practices.[19] Italy began interdicting boats coming from Libya and other North African states in 2006.[20] Initially, these were not push-back operations, with most of the intercepted migrants taken to Italy. However, in 2009, intercepted migrants were returned to Libya pursuant to a bilateral agreement with the Libyan government.[21] Italy carried out nine push-back operations in that year, returning to Libya and Algeria

---

[13] 'Danish Politicians to Visit Nauru to Study Use of Offshore Detention Centres, Government Says', *Australian Broadcasting Corporation News* (online), 25 August 2016 www.abc.net.au/news/2016-08-25/danish-politicians-to-visit-nauru-offshore-detention-centre/7783164.

[14] Nicole Hasham, 'Nauru Bans Unsympathetic Danish MPs from Detention Centre Visit', *The Sydney Morning Herald* (online), 31 August 2016 www.smh.com.au/federal-politics/political-news/nauru-bans-unsympathetic-danish-mps-from-detention-centre-visit-20160830-gr4y8g.html.

[15] Ibid.

[16] Frontex, 'Frontex Hosts 1st European Coast Guard Cooperation Network Meeting' (News Release, 8 November 2016) http://frontex.europa.eu/news/frontex-hosts-1st-european-coast-guard-cooperation-network-meeting-U8iGMu.

[17] Derek Lutterbeck, 'Policing Migration in the Mediterranean' (2006) 11 *Mediterranean Politics* 59, 67.

[18] Ibid 71.

[19] Tullio Scovazzi, 'Le Norme di Diritto Internazionale Sull'immgrazione Illegale via Mare Con Particolare Riferimento Ai Rapporti Tra Albania e Italia', in Andrea de Guttry and Fabrizio Pagani (eds), *La Crisi Albanese Del 1997* (Franco Angeli, 1999) cited in Itamar Mann, 'Dialectic of Transnationalism: Unauthorised Migration and Human Rights, 1993–2013' (2013) 54 *Harvard International Law Journal* 315, 333.

[20] For a detailed overview of Italy's maritime interdiction program see Alessia di Pascale, 'Migrant Control at Sea: The Italian Case' in Bernard Ryan and Valsamis Mitsilegas (eds), *Extraterritorial Immigration Control: Legal Challenges* (Martinus Nijhoff, 2010) 281.

[21] Ibid 297–8.

approximately 850 migrants intercepted on the high seas.[22] Some of these people were the applicants in the *Hirsi Jamaa* case examined in section 7.4.1.[23] Spain has also carried out maritime interdictions, targeting migrants attempting to reach the Canary Islands from North Africa. Like the Italian operations, Spain's program was carried out pursuant to bilateral arrangements with countries of departure. Spain concluded agreements allowing for joint interdiction operations and repatriation of interdictees with Mauritania and Senegal in 2006, Cape Verde in 2007 and Gambia, Guinea and Guinea Bissau in 2008.[24]

At times, Italian and Spanish interdiction activities have been carried out with the support of Frontex, EU's external frontiers agency (renamed the European Border and Coast Guard in 2016).[25] Frontex began operations in 2005 with the mission of improving 'the integrated management' of the EU's external borders. The aim was to ensure 'a uniform and high level of control and surveillance'.[26] Spain's interdiction activities were supported through operations *Hera I, Hera II* and *Hera III*, which took place in 2006 and 2007. These involved joint patrols by up to seven member states targeting migration flows from the West African coast to the Canary Islands.[27] Frontex coordinated similar activities to assist Spain's interdiction activities in subsequent years.[28] Italy's interdiction program was supported by operations codenamed *Nautilus* carried out between 2006 and 2008. Under these arrangements, France, Germany and Greece provided maritime and aerial assistance to the Italian and Maltese interdiction efforts in the Mediterranean.[29] This was followed by a series of operations codenamed *Hermes*, carried out between 2007 and 2013.[30] Operation *Mare Nostrum*, which began in October 2013, represented a change in tack. Rather than earlier operations, which focused on border control, *Mare Nostrum* was a search and rescue operation designed to minimise deaths at sea. Italian Navy vessels would actively search for boats and bring the passengers to Italy. Frontex was not involved, but the European Commission contributed funds for the operation. It was wound down in October 2014, after concerns that it was acting as a pull factor for migrants. It was replaced by the Frontex-led operation *Triton*, which shifted the focus back to border control.

By and large, the Frontex operations that have been carried out since 2006 have involved taking intercepted migrants to Europe. In some instances, push-backs have occurred.[31]

---

[22] Efthymios Papastavridis, *The Interception of Vessels on the High Seas* (Hart Publishing, 2013) 284.
[23] *Hirsi Jamaa v Italy* [2012] II Eur Court HR 1, see below nn 84–7 and accompanying text.
[24] Paula Garcia Andrade, 'Spanish Perspective on Irregular Immigration by Sea' in Bernard Ryan and Valsamis Mitsilegas (eds), *Extraterritorial Immigration Control: Legal Challenges* (Martinus Nijhoff, 2010) 311, 319.
[25] For a detailed examination of Frontex's role in maritime interdiction activities, see Violeta Moreno-Lax, 'Seeking Asylum in the Mediterranean: Against a Fragmentary Reading of EU Member States' Obligations Accruing at Sea' (2011) 23 *International Journal of Refugee Law* 174.
[26] *Council Regulation (EC) No 2007/2004 of 26 October 2004 establishing the European Agency for the Management of Operational Cooperation at the External Borders of the Member States of the European Union* [2004] OJ L 349/1, art 1.
[27] For an overview of these operations, see Frontex, *Archive of Operations* http://frontex.europa.eu/operations/archive-of-operations/.
[28] See, eg, operation *Minerva*, targeting irregular maritime flows from Africa to the southern seaports of Spain, in 2009 and subsequent years until 2012: Frontex, above n 27.
[29] Pascale, above n 20, 292; Frontex, above n 27.   [30] Frontex, above n 27.
[31] See, eg, Operation Hera II, discussed in Violeta Moreno-Lax, 'Seeking Asylum in the Mediterranean: Against a Fragmentary Reading of EU Member States' Obligations Accruing at Sea' (2011) 23 *International Journal of Refugee Law* 174, 181.

These were accompanied by asylum screening procedures at sea. But commentators have raised concerns, claiming that the screenings 'are far from ideal and in many cases are probably of little practical effectiveness in ensuring protection'.[32] The push-back activities carried out by Spain and Italy outside the Frontex framework have generally not included any procedures for screening asylum claims.[33]

Frontex operations are now complemented by an EU military operation called European Union Naval Force Mediterranean ('EUNAVFOR Med') (also known as *Operation Sophia*). Established in May 2015 within the crisis management framework of the EU's Common Security and Defence Policy, the operation has the aim of disrupting the business model of human smuggling and trafficking networks in the Southern Central Mediterranean.[34] Thus far, operations have included conducting boarding, search, seizure and diversion on the high seas.[35] These have been carried out pursuant to authority granted under a UN Security Council Resolution.[36] Intercepted migrants have generally been taken to Italy, with any suspected people smugglers handed over to the Italian authorities for prosecution. The mandate also includes scope for future operations in the territorial waters of coastal states.[37] However, to date, Libya has not provided authorisation for such action.[38] In the absence of such authorisation, in June 2016, the EU extended the mandate of the EUNAVFOR Med operation to include training the Libyan Coast Guard and Navy to 'disrupt smuggling and trafficking'.[39] There have been recent reports of the Libyan Coast Guard intercepting migrant vessels in Libya's territorial sea and international waters and returning them to Libya.[40] In effect, this amounts to the outsourcing of European interception and turn-back operations to Libyan authorities, purportedly acting outside the restrictions imposed by the *European Convention on Human Rights* ('ECHR').

7.1.2 Extraterritorial Processing

Plans for the extraterritorial processing of asylum claims have been discussed in Europe for some time. In 1986, Denmark proposed a draft resolution in the UN General Assembly,

---

[32] Silvia Borelly and Ben Stanford, 'Troubled Waters in the *Mare Nostrum*: Interception and Push-Backs of Migrants in the Mediterranean and the European Convention on Human Rights' (2014) 10 *Review of International Law and Politics* 29, 33.

[33] Violeta Moreno-Lax, '*Hirsi Jamaa and Others v Italy* or the Strasbourg Court versus Extraterritorial Migration Control?' (2012) 12 *Human Rights Law Review* 574, 576.

[34] *Council Decision (CFSP) 2015/778 of 18 May 2015 on a European Union military operation in the Southern Central Mediterranean (EUNAVFOR MED)* [2015] OJ L 122/31, 31.

[35] European External Action Service, 'EUNAVFOR MED Op SOPHIA – Six Monthly Report 22 June–31 December 2015' (28 January 2016) 5453/16.

[36] SC Res 2240, UN Doc S/RES/2240 (9 October 2015).

[37] *Council Decision (CFSP) 2015/778 of 18 May 2015 on a European Union military operation in the Southern Central Mediterranean (EUNAVFOR MED)* [2015] OJ L 122/31, art 2(2)(ii).

[38] European External Action Service, 'EUNAVFOR MED Op SOPHIA – Six Monthly Report 22 June–31 December 2015' (28 January 2016) 5453/16.

[39] General Secretariat of the Council, 'EUNAVFOR MED Operation Sophia: mandate extended by one year, two new tasks added' (Press Release, 365/16, 20 June 2016) www.consilium.europa.eu/en/press/press-releases/2016/06/20/fac-eunavfor-med-sophia/.

[40] Lizzie Dearden, 'Aid Workers "Lucky to Be Alive' after Libyan Coastguard Intercepts Refugee Boat Rescue in Mediterranean', *Independent* (online), 11 May 2017 www.independent.co.uk/news/world/europe/refugee-crisis-libya-migrants-boat-crossings-intercept-sea-watch-lucky-to-be-alive-coastguard-a7731176.html.

which called for the establishment of regional asylum processing centres run by the UN.[41] All asylum seekers who travelled irregularly to third countries outside their region were to be returned to the UN processing centre of their home region to have their claims examined.[42] A similar proposal was put forward by the Netherlands in the IGC in 1993.[43] The idea was revived in a 2003 UK Cabinet Office and Home Office policy paper entitled 'A New Vision for Refugees'.[44] The document outlined plans to create 'transit processing camps' on the non-EU side of Europe's borders. Under the proposal, no asylum claims would be processed within EU territory. Any asylum seekers who managed to enter the EU would be transferred to one of the extraterritorial camps for assessment of their protection claims. The camps were to be run by the International Organization for Migration and screening procedures were to be approved by UNHCR.[45] Countries such as Albania and Croatia were suggested as possible locations for the camps.[46] The proposal was backed by the Danish and Dutch governments,[47] but it was abandoned after it met strong resistance from a number of other European governments, including Germany, which referred to the proposed centres as 'concentration camps'.[48] However, by 2004, Germany had changed tack and, with the support of Italy, revived the proposal for extraterritorial processing. The Baltic States, Slovakia and Ukraine were suggested as possible locations for the camps.[49]

The UK proposal clearly drew inspiration from the US and Australian precedents.[50] This is borne out in IGC policy documents. Gregor Noll explains: 'The Spring 2003 debate reveals that the 'Pacific Solution' constituted a source of inspiration for the British and Danish governments. On the 23 April meeting of the mini-IGC ... the Australian model as well as the Haiti and Cuban interdiction programs implemented by the US were discussed.'[51]

---

[41] UN General Assembly, *International Procedures for the Protection of Refugees: Draft Resolution/Denmark*, UN Doc A/C.3/41/L.51 (12 November 1986).

[42] Ibid.

[43] Dutch State Secretary of Justice Aad Kosto (Speech delivered at the Fifth Conference of European Ministers Responsible for Migration Affairs, Athens, 18–19 November 1993) quoted in Gregor Noll, 'Visions of the Exceptional: Legal and Theoretical Issues Raised by Transit Processing Centres and Protection Zones' (2003) 5 *European Journal of Migration and Law* 303, 312.

[44] UK Home Office, 'New Vision for Refugees' (7 March 2003). This document was originally intended to be confidential, but was leaked to *The Guardian* newspaper and thereafter circulated informally in the NGO sector. The document formed the basis of discussions pursued in the IGC on Asylum, Refugees and Migration; the European Council; and the EU Committee on Immigration and Asylum: Noll, above n 43, 305, 319.

[45] Ibid.

[46] Carl Levy, 'Refugees, Europe, Camps/State of Exception: "Into The Zone", the European Union and Extraterritorial Processing of Migrants, Refugees, and Asylum-seekers (Theories and Practice)' (2010) 29 *Refugee Survey Quarterly* 92, 110.

[47] Noll, above n 43, 304, 309.

[48] Michael Flynn, 'On Its Borders, New Problems' (2006) 62 *Bulletin of Atomic Scientists* 21, 21.

[49] Levy, above n 46, 111.

[50] See, eg, Alexander Betts, 'The International Relations of the "New" Extraterritorial Approaches to Refugee Protection: Explaining the Policy Initiatives of the UK Government and UNHCR' (2004) 22 *Refuge* 58; Alexander Betts, 'Towards a Mediterranean Solution? Implications for the Region of Origin' (2006) 18 *International Journal of Refugee Law* 652, 661; Orla Lynskey, 'Complementing and Completing the Common European Asylum System: A Legal Analysis of the Emerging Extraterritorial Elements of EU Refugee Protection Policy' (2006) 3 *European Law Review* 230, 241; Susan Kneebone, Christopher McDowell and Gareth Morrell, 'A Mediterranean Solution? Chances of Success' (2006) 18 *International Journal of Refugee Law* 492; Noll, above n 43, 313.

[51] Noll, above n 43, 313.

On the role of Australia's policies, Liza Shuster observes that 'developments in Australia were watched very closely ... The Pacific Solution was referred to approvingly by both [Prime Minister] Tony Blair and [Home Secretary] David Blunkett when they first mooted the idea of external camps'.[52] Australia was actively promoting its extraterritorial processing as a best practice model during this period. Graham Thom notes:

> [t]he Australian government appears to have spent a great deal of money from 2000 to 2004, sending officials and consultants to international forums, extolling the virtues of their system and defending their system against criticisms from organisations like Amnesty International ... [T]he UK has quite clearly picked up on the Australian initiatives, as seen in some of the options that the UK has flagged.[53]

The idea of extraterritorial processing has also been explored at the EU level. A feasibility study was carried out on the issue in 2002.[54] It was then flagged in the Commission's 2008 Policy Plan on Asylum and 2009 Communication on the Stockholm Programme.[55] These EU proposals involved utilising extraterritorial processing as a humanitarian tool to enhance access to protection and complement, rather than replace, in-country processing. A French proposal to the EU Presidency in 2009 set out a plan that was more along the lines of the US and Australian use of extraterritorial processing as a tool for minimising access to domestic asylum procedures.[56] Asylum seekers were to be intercepted at sea and returned to the country of embarkation, where they would have their claims assessed by UNHCR. Member states were to offer resettlement opportunities to those recognised as refugees.[57] The idea was again picked up in a 2015 report by the European Commission's European Political Strategy Centre, which recommended a move towards offshore asylum processing and the establishment of 'EU-run facilities in North Africa and key transit countries'.[58]

---

[52] Quoted in Madeleine Byrne, 'Exporting the "Pacific Solution"', *New Matilda* (online), 22 December 2004 https://newmatilda.com/2004/12/22/exporting-pacific-solution.

[53] Quoted in Kazimierz Bem, Nina Field, Nic Maclellan, Sarah Meyer, and Tony Morris, 'A Price Too High: The Cost of Australia's Approach to Asylum seekers' (Report, A Just Australia and Oxfam, August 2007) 49.

[54] Gregory Noll, Jessica Fagerlund and Fabrice Liebaut, 'Study on the Feasibility of Processing Asylum Claims Outside the EU against the Background of the Common European Asylum System and the Goal of a Common Asylum Procedure' (European Commission, 2002) http://www.refworld.org/docid/58ac44504.html.

[55] Policy Plan on Asylum, Commission of the European Communities (2008) 360 final, 17 June 2008, [5.2.3]; and Communication in Preparation of the Stockholm Programme, Commission of the European Communities (2009) 262 final, 10 June 2009, [5.2.3]. These proposals are discussed in Violeta Moreno-Lax, 'Europe in Crisis: Facilitating Access to Protection, (Discarding) Offshore Processing and Mapping Alternatives for the Way Forward' (Study prepared for the Red Cross EU Office) (December 2015) 17–18.

[56] *Migration Situation in the Mediterranean: Establishing a Partnership with Migrants' Countries of Origin and of Transit, Enhancing Member States' Joint Maritime Operations and Finding Innovative Solutions for Access to Asylum Procedures*, Council Doc 13205/09, 11 September 2009.

[57] This proposal is examined in detail in Violeta Moreno-Lax, 'External Dimension' in Steve Peers, Violeta Moreno-Lax, Madeline Garlick and Elspeth Guild, *EU Immigration and Asylum Law*, vol 3 (Brill, 2nd ed, 2015) 654–6.

[58] European Political Strategy Centre, 'Legal Migration in the EU: From Stop-Gap Solutions to a Future-Proof Policy' (EPSC Strategic Notes, Issue 2/2015, European Commission, 30 April 2015) 4 http://ec.europa.eu/epsc/pdf/publications/strategic_note_issue_2.pdf. However, this has not yet been formally adopted as EU policy.

While the proposals for a full-fledged offshore asylum processing system are yet to see the light of day, a number of current EU initiatives do contain external processing elements. The most notable is the EU–Turkey agreement announced in March 2016.[59] The deal provides for the return of certain asylum seekers and irregular migrants from Greece to Turkey. For every migrant returned, the EU is to resettle one Syrian refugee from Turkey. The processing and selection of these refugees is being carried out in Turkey by UNHCR, which makes recommendations for resettlement. The plan is reminiscent of the agreement reached between Australia and Malaysia in 2011, which provided for the transfer of 800 asylum seekers who arrived by boat in Australia, in return for Australia resettling 4,000 UNHCR-recognised refugees from camps in Malaysia.[60]

7.2 Interdiction and Push-Back Operations in Thailand, Malaysia and Indonesia

In recent years, a number of South East Asian governments have engaged in maritime interdiction activities against asylum-seeker vessels. The Thai Navy intercepted and pushed back vessels carrying Rohingya asylum seekers fleeing Myanmar in early 2013.[61] In May 2015, the Thai, Malaysian and Indonesian governments all carried out push-back operations against Rohingya and Bangladeshi asylum seekers in the Andaman Sea. These activities resulted in a temporary humanitarian disaster, with approximately 8,000 asylum seekers stranded at sea on decrepit vessels.[62] The purported justification for the interdiction activities echoed that used by Australian authorities. The operations were promoted as necessary to save lives at sea by deterring future asylum seekers from making the dangerous journey. Australia's then Prime Minister, Tony Abbott, publicly supported the actions of Thailand, Malaysia and Indonesia on these grounds, stating: 'I don't apologise in any way for the action that Australia has taken to preserve safety at sea by turning boats around where necessary. And if other countries choose to do that, frankly that is almost certainly absolutely necessary if the scourge of people smuggling is to be beaten.'[63]

---

[59] European Council, 'EU–Turkey Statement' (Press Release, 144/16, 18 March 2016). For a discussion of other recent EU initiatives with potential extraterritorial processing components, see Violeta Moreno-Lax, 'Europe in Crisis: Facilitating Access to Protection, (Discarding) Offshore Processing and Mapping Alternatives for the Way Forward' (Study prepared for the Red Cross EU Office) (December 2015) 18–20.

[60] See Chapter 5, nn 120–147 and accompanying text.

[61] 'Thailand Pushes 200 Rohingya Back to Sea', *The Australian* (online), 30 January 2013 www.theaustralian.com.au/news/latest-news/thailand-pushes-200-rohingya-back-to-sea/story-fn3dxix6-1226565278697.

[62] Kate Lamb, '"They Hit Us, with Hammers, by Knife": Rohingya Migrants Tell of Horror at Sea', *The Guardian* (online), 18 May 2015 www.theguardian.com/world/2015/may/17/they-hit-us-with-hammers-by-knife-rohingya-migrants-tell-of-horror-at-sea.

[63] 'Tony Abbott Defends Other Countries Turning Back Asylum-Seeker Boats', *The Guardian* (online), 17 May 2015 www.theguardian.com/australia-news/2015/may/17/tony-abbott-backs-other-countries-turning-back-asylum-seeker-boats.

After a two-week stand-off, Indonesian and Malaysian authorities reached an agreement to allow the asylum seekers to temporarily land on their territories.[64] The agreement came too late for some – dozens of deaths were reported as a consequence of the operations.[65]

7.3 Mandatory Detention in Canada and New Zealand

Canada and New Zealand have introduced mandatory detention laws targeting certain classes of asylum seekers. The Canadian laws appear to have been modelled on US and Australian mandatory detention measures.[66] In turn, New Zealand's mandatory detention model draws heavily from the Canadian approach. Canada's laws were introduced in response to the arrival of just two asylum-seeker boats. The *Ocean Lady* arrived on Canada's shores in October 2009, carrying seventy-six Tamil passengers. This was followed by the *Sun Sea*, which was intercepted off the west coast of Canada in August 2010 with 490 Tamil passengers on board. Jason Kenny, then Canadian Minister for Citizenship, Immigration and Multiculturalism, travelled to Australia on a fact-finding mission to assist in formulating his government's response to these arrivals.[67]

After a two-year legislative process, the *Protecting Canada's Immigration Act* (or 'Bill C-31') was enacted in June 2012.[68] The Act amended the *Immigration and Refugee Protection Act* to give the Canadian Minister of Citizenship, Immigration and Multiculturalism authority to label groups of non-citizens 'designated foreign nationals'.[69] The designation process is triggered when non-citizens enter Canada in violation of immigration law, with the assistance of a smuggler motivated by profit, or when the Minister believes the non-citizens, as a group, cannot be examined and dealt with 'in a timely manner'.[70] One ramification of being a 'designated foreign national' is detention for a period of up to one year for the purpose of determining identity, inadmissibility and illegal activity.[71] The original legislative proposal provided that detainees would not have their detention reviewed for a minimum of twelve months, and thereafter every six months. In a concession to refugee advocates and opposition parties, an amendment was introduced that provides for the review of mandatory detention within fourteen days, and thereafter every

---

[64] Euan McKirdy, 'Indonesia, Malaysia Agree to Take in Migrant Ships, Report Says', *CNN* (online), 21 May 2015 http://edition.cnn.com/2015/05/20/asia/asian-countries-migrant-ships/.
[65] '"Desperate" Rohingya Migrants Send SOS as Indonesia, Malaysia Refuse Entry', *Al Jazeera America* (online), 12 May 2015 http://america.aljazeera.com/articles/2015/5/12/up-to-6000-rohingya-bangladeshi-migrants-stranded-at-sea.html.
[66] For a detailed account of this purported transfer, see Mary Crock and Daniel Ghezelbash, 'Secret Immigration Business: Policy Transfers and the Tyranny of Deterrence Theory' in Satvinder S Juss (ed), *The Ashgate Research Companion to Migration Theory and Policy* (Ashgate, 2013) 617.
[67] Citizenship and Immigration Canada ('CIC'), 'Governments of Canada and Australia Working to Combat Human Smuggling' (News Release, 19 September 2010); CIC, 'Meeting with Senior Officials from Australia at Parliament House to Discuss Effective Solutions to Combat the Global Problems of Migrant Smuggling and Human Trafficking' (News Release, 20 September 2010).
[68] *Protecting Canada's Immigration Act*, SC 2012, c 12. The measures were initially introduced in Bill C-49, 'An Act to amend the Immigration and Refugee Protection Act, the Balanced Refugee Reform Act and the Marine Transportation Security Act', Third Session, Fortieth Parliament, 59 Elizabeth II, 2010.
[69] *Immigration and Refugee Protection Act*, SC 2001, c 27, s 20.1(1).   [70] Ibid s 20.1(1).
[71] Ibid s 55(3.1). The second major ramification is disqualification from eligibility for permanent visa if found to be a genuine refugee: see s 24(5). This measure is itself modelled on the Australian Temporary Protection visa regime that operated from 1999–2007.

six months.[72] Even with this concession, the changes represent a major departure from existing detention provisions (which continue to apply to persons not designated by the Minister). These only allow for detention in clearly defined, exceptional circumstances, such as where there are reasonable grounds to believe that the person in question is unlikely to appear at their next hearing or interview, is considered a danger to public safety, is inadmissible on security grounds or for violating human or international rights, or cannot provide adequate identification to satisfy the officer of their identity.[73] A decision to detain under these provisions must be reviewed within forty-eight hours, again after seven days, and then every thirty days after that.[74]

In New Zealand, the *Immigration Amendment Act 2013* (NZ) introduced provisions for the detention of irregular migrants who reach New Zealand as part of a 'mass arrival group'.[75] This is defined as thirty people or more. Such arrivals can be subject to detention for an initial period of up to six months.[76] While the New Zealand laws draw heavily from the Canadian and Australian systems, they include an important additional safeguard. The group warrant for detention can only be issued by a District Court judge, who must be satisfied that detention is necessary based on certain stipulated grounds.[77] This judicial oversight is absent in Australia, the United States and Canada. In Australia and the United States, detention is automatic for *all* unauthorised arrivals. In Canada, the decision to designate a group as subject to mandatory detention is made by the Minister for Citizenship, Immigration and Multiculturalism.

While detention laws in the United States, Australia and Canada were all introduced in response to specific boat arrivals, New Zealand has never actually had an asylum-seeker vessel reach its shores. The need for the proposed measures is based on a claim of an 'ongoing threat' of mass arrivals. In justifying this statement, then New Zealand Prime Minister John Key pointed to the arrival of Tamil asylum seekers in Canada, stating: 'if they can get to Canada they can get to New Zealand'.[78] He also cited a number of cases in which asylum seekers arriving in Australia had declared that their intended destination was New Zealand as it did not have mandatory detention laws.[79]

In this regard, the introduction of New Zealand's mandatory detention regime is a clear example of a transfer motivated by *competition to deter*. However, the fact that no asylum-seeker boats have ever reached New Zealand indicates that this 'competition' can be just as much about reassuring a domestic audience as about sending a signal to potential irregular entrants. The logic behind this move is that some New Zealanders may fear that their nation's relaxed detention policy (particularly when compared to Australia or Canada) will make them a target for future boat arrivals. The policy is aimed, at least in part, at addressing this fear so as to gain political mileage for the conservative government. Neither the unnecessary nature of the proposed changes nor their resemblance to the Australian

---

[72] Ibid s 57.1(1). [73] Ibid s 55. [74] Ibid s 57. [75] *Immigration Amendment Act 2013* (NZ).
[76] *Immigration Act 2009* (NZ), s 317A.
[77] The judge must determine that the warrant is necessary to effectively manage the mass arrival group; or to manage any threat or risk to security or to the public arising from, one or more members of the mass arrival group; or to uphold the integrity or efficiency of the immigration system; or to avoid disrupting the efficient functioning of the District Court: ibid, ss 317A(1)(a), 317B.
[78] Andrea Vance, 'Key Says No to Refugee Detention Centre', *stuff.co.nz* (online), 29 October 2010 www.stuff.co.nz/national/politics/4287400/Key-says-no-to-refugee-detention-centre.
[79] Michael Flynn, *Immigration Detention in New Zealand* (Global Detention Project, February 2014) 4 www.globaldetentionproject.org/fileadmin/docs/NZ_report_v2.pdf.

and Canadian precedents went unnoticed by New Zealand's Labour opposition. In 2012, Darien Fenton, then the party's Spokesperson for Immigration Issues, quipped that 'the Minister of Immigration has been carried away by spending too much time with the big boys in Australia and Canada instead of focusing on the real issues in New Zealand'.[80]

New Zealand has also made arrangements that allow for the potential extraterritorial processing of asylum seekers who arrive in New Zealand as part of a 'mass arrival group'. In February 2013, New Zealand negotiated an agreement with Australia pursuant to which New Zealand would resettle 150 refugees per year from Australia's extraterritorial processing facilities in Nauru and Papua New Guinea ('PNG'). In return, New Zealand was given the option of transferring future 'mass arrival groups' to those facilities.[81] To date, no asylum seekers have been transferred by either side under the deal.

7.4 Lessons for Lawmakers

As these examples illustrate, the transfers of restrictive asylum and border control measures between the United States and Australia are not isolated incidents. Rather, they represent examples of a much broader global process of diffusion. What can lawmakers considering engaging in future transfers learn from the US and Australian experience? I examine the ramifications of my findings in relation to four distinct dimensions of success against which an imported law may be measured: *legal, programmatic, process* and *political*.[82]

7.4.1 Legal Success

Mandatory long-term detention, interdiction and extraterritorial processing push the boundaries of what is acceptable under both international and domestic law. In Chapter 6, I outlined the concerns which the policies raise under international law. The issue will again be taken up in the concluding section of this chapter, where I examine the future viability of the international protection regime. My concern here is with domestic law and the possibility of *legal failure*, which occurs when an imported law or policy is rejected by the legal system of the receiving state. This may take the form of a judicial finding that the measures are unlawful, or an interpretation of the law that frustrates the policy's underlying purpose of maximising government control over asylum seekers and irregular migrants. So, what factors do lawmakers need to take into account to avoid such a failure?

The comparative analysis of the Australian and US case law in Chapters 3–5 suggests that in those jurisdictions, this question cannot be answered solely by reference to compatibility (or incompatibility) of domestic legal structures. Factors such as the existence of a constitutional bill of rights in the United States and the absence of any equivalent protections in Australia, did not play a determinative role in explaining judicial approaches in each jurisdiction. This is due to the exceptional position given to unauthorised arrivals in both US and Australian law. In the United States, this is the result of the long-standing plenary power doctrine, which holds that the arriving aliens have very limited recourse to

---

[80] Darien Fenton, *No Justification for Mass Detention Bill* (28 August 2012) NZ Labour Party http://web.archive.org/web/*/www.labour.org.nz/news/no-justification-for-mass-detention-bill.
[81] Kate Chapman, 'NZ May Put Refugees in Aust Camps: Move May Deter "Boat People" – PM', *Timaru Herald* (Timaru), 12 February 2013, 4.
[82] See Chapter 1, nn 54–82 and accompanying text.

constitutional protections.[83] In Australia, the courts have not been as explicit in spelling out an equivalent principle. However, the exceptional treatment of unauthorised arrivals is clearly discernible in judicial decision-making. This is evident in the judiciary's approach to statutory interpretation and determining the scope of the aliens power, executive power and constitutional immunity from executive detention. In both jurisdictions, the special status given to unauthorised arrivals has created a great deal of ambiguity in relation to the rights that ought to be afforded to such persons. This in turn has given significant leeway to individual judicial discretion when determining the leading cases challenging the case-study policies.

This means that compatibility of legal structures and domestic legal protections in the sending and receiving jurisdictions may not be enough to ensure legal success. Further, incompatibility of legal structures and domestic legal protections will not necessarily lead to legal failure. My findings suggest that lawmakers ought to adopt a more holistic approach to comparing the compatibility of the exporting and importing jurisdiction by taking into account wider political and social forces. Identifying and measuring the impact of such factors on judicial decision-making is beyond the scope of the present study. Future research could explore how, in the face of interpretive leeway created by ambiguous legal principles, factors such as changes in public opinion, asylum flows, irregular migrant flows, economic prosperity or the national security climate may influence judicial decision-making in relation to the rights of unauthorised arrivals.

It is important to note that my findings downplaying the role of legal structures in determining legal success or failure may not necessarily hold true across other jurisdictions. In the United States and Australia, the result flows from the exceptional legal status of arriving non-citizens. In jurisdictions with rights protection mechanisms that do not discriminate in this way, transfers of harsh deterrent measures are likely to end in legal failure. This is evident when one examines the approach of the European Court of Human Rights ('ECtHR') to maritime interdiction and push-back operations. In the 2012 case of *Hirsi Jamaa v Italy*,[84] the Grand Chamber of the ECtHR found that the *ECHR* applies extraterritorially and provides extensive protections for asylum seekers interdicted on the high seas by member nations.[85] The case was brought on behalf of a group of Somali and Eritrean asylum seekers who were intercepted at sea by Italian authorities in 2009 and forcibly returned to Libya. The Court grounded its jurisdiction to review these actions on the fact that the Italian authorities exercised continuous and exclusive *de jure* and *de facto* control over the applicants.[86] The findings of the Court in relation to the rights of interdicted asylum seekers are summarised by Violeta Moreno-Lax:

> extraterritoriality does not preclude the application of the ECHR in the context of border surveillance and migration control operations. The interdiction of migrants on the high seas without consideration of the particular case of each individual concerned is prohibited by the Convention. Information on the procedure to be followed to oppose

---

[83] Stephen Legomsky, 'Immigration Law and the Principle of Plenary Congressional Power' [1984] *Supreme Court Review* 255.

[84] *Hirsi Jamaa v Italy* [2012] II Eur Court HR 1.

[85] For a detailed analysis of this case see Moreno-Lax, '*Hirsi Jamaa*', above n 33; Maarten Den Heijer, 'Reflections on *Refoulement* and Collective Expulsion in the *Hirsi* Case' (2013) 25 *International Journal of Refugee Law* 265.

[86] *Hirsi Jamaa v Italy* [2012] II Eur Court HR 1, 133 [81].

removal to a third country as well as access to legal assistance and linguistic interpretation must be guaranteed. There must also be an opportunity to suspend the removal before it is implemented. In addition, the safety of the receiving State cannot be presumed in absolute terms. Public information on the prevailing situation must be taken into account. These conditions must be respected regardless of whether asylum has been explicitly requested.[87]

This expansive view of state responsibility is a far cry from the restrictive approaches taken by Australian and US courts in cases challenging interdiction practices in those jurisdictions.[88] The difference appears to be a direct result of the different legal structures which operate in Europe – namely the binding supranational human rights protection instrument in the form of the *ECHR*. Importantly, this regime was held to apply extraterritorially and to non-citizens regardless of their immigration status. This can be contrasted with the territorial limitations of statutory and constitutional protections and the broader exceptional treatment of unauthorised non-citizens in Australia and the United States.

Transfers initially rejected by the courts can be modified through legislative reform to survive subsequent judicial challenges. In this regard, what starts out as a legal failure can turn into a legal success with a little tweaking. Itamar Mann notes that '[w]hen courts review policy and enforcement directed towards unauthorised migrants, they provide guidelines to policymaking and enforcement networks on how to push policies beyond the courts' jurisdiction'.[89] The Australian government's reaction to *Plaintiff M70/2011 v MIAC* ('*Malaysian Solution Case*') is an example of such responsive lawmaking.[90] The High Court's decision that Malaysia did not meet the statutory safeguards for third country transfers provided the blueprint for the amendments creating the current offshore processing regime. These new provisions survived judicial challenge in *Plaintiff S156/2013 v MIBP*.[91]

But protection instruments may not always be so easily modified. For example, a decision grounded in the *US Constitution* or in the *ECHR* cannot be circumvented via a simple process of legislative amendment. States may still be able to get around such decisions by amending the operation of the policy itself. We may see this course of action emerge in Europe in response to *Hirsi*. By saying that states cannot turn back asylum seekers with boats under their *de jure* or *de facto* control, the Court left the door open for interdiction policies conducted with no such control. As such, it may be possible to ensure the legal success of interdiction polices within the context of the *ECHR* if European nations outsource interdiction and return activities to foreign-flagged boats.[92] The recent expansion of the EUNAVFOR Med's mandate to include training the Libyan Coast Guard and Navy to carry out interdiction and disruption operations in Libyan waters appears to be an attempt to outsource responsibility in precisely this manner.[93] However, measures that involve third countries in this way may face additional hurdles. Such policies are vulnerable

---

[87] Moreno-Lax, '*Hirsi Jamaa*', above n 33, 595. [88] See Chapter 4. [89] Mann, above n 19, 369.
[90] (2011) 244 CLR 144. [91] (2014) 254 CLR 28. [92] Mann, above n 19, 367.
[93] See above nn 39–40 and accompanying text. Note that even with this outsourcing, European nations may still be liable for their complicity with, and direction and/or control of, internationally wrongful acts committed by the Libyan coast guard: see Violeta Moreno-Lax and Mariagiulia Giuffré, 'The Rise of Consensual Containment: From "Contactless Control" to "Contactless Responsibility" for Migratory Flows', in Satvinder Juss (ed), *Research Handbook on International Refugee Law* (Elgar, 2017) (forthcoming).

to *legal failure* resulting from an adverse decision in the courts of the third country. The fate of extraterritorial processing on Manus Island in PNG is instructive in this regard. After withstanding judicial scrutiny in Australian courts, it was ultimately a decision of the Supreme Court of PNG which led to the policy's demise.[94] Given the current state of lawlessness in Libya, it is unlikely that we will see a similar outcome in relation to Libyan interdiction activities.

7.4.2 Programmatic Success

Programmatic success is assessed with reference to whether a policy achieved its intended outcomes, and whether the benefits of these outcomes outweigh any negative consequences (intentional or unintentional). The focus of my analysis in this book has been on *legal success*. Evaluating programmatic success raises complex methodological considerations that make such a task beyond the scope of the present study.[95] What follows is a discussion of some considerations that future studies on this issue would need to address. The first hurdle is the inherently subjective nature of success. Different stakeholders have varying views as to what constitutes success or failure, and success is always going to be contested to some degree. A useful starting point for a benchmark to measure programmatic success is whether it met the goals of the actors involved in the transfer process. This can be achieved with reference to the typology of motivations driving transfer which I set out in Chapter 2. We can ask questions such as: did the efficiency-driven transfer lead to an efficient policy outcome? Did the transfer driven by considerations of prestige result in authority and legitimacy for the imported law or policy? Did the cooperative transfer succeed in its aim of mutually beneficial harmonisation for the state parties involved? Did the competitive transfer lead to an advantage for the importing jurisdiction vis-à-vis competitor jurisdictions?

Even when we are clear as to what outcomes constitute success, measuring whether a policy achieved these outcomes poses significant challenges. Isolating the causal effect of a policy compared to other independent variables is a very difficult task. Currently, there is a lack of evidence-based research measuring the impact of restrictive asylum and border control measures.[96] Simple questions such as whether deterrent measures have been successful in reducing irregular migration flows remain unanswered. There needs to be more robust research carried out in this area. Studies examining this question will need to isolate the influence of policy changes from push factors, such as changing conditions in the migrant source countries, as well as pull factors, such as community ties and the availability of people-smuggling services. Isolating these factors is close to impossible when dealing with a small sample group of jurisdictions. However, a well-designed large-*n* study comparing changes in immigration policies and shifts in flow data across multiple countries could control for and isolate the effect of these various factors.[97]

Any analysis of programmatic success must also take into account the negative consequences of transfers of restrictive immigration measures. In this regard, I am concerned that

---

[94] See Chapter 5, nn 207–12.   [95] See Chapter 1, nn 71–80 and accompanying text.
[96] For a notable exception in the European context, see Eiko Thielemann, 'How Effective Are National and EU Policies in the Area of Forced Migration' (2012) 31 *Refugee Survey Quarterly* 21.
[97] The International Migration Policy and Law Analysis (IMPALA) Database is currently compiling a data set that could facilitate such analysis: see Michel Beine et al, 'Comparing Immigration Policies: An Overview from the IMPALA Database' (2016) 50 *International Migration Review* 827.

insufficient attention has been paid to the damage caused by such policies. Australia provides an instructive example of the harm that can be caused by measures such as mandatory detention, maritime interdiction and extraterritorial processing.[98] These policies have had a devastating impact on the welfare of the vulnerable asylum seekers they target. Numerous studies have demonstrated the adverse impact of mandatory detention on physical and mental health.[99] These problems are only compounded when detention occurs in remote extraterritorial processing facilities.[100] On top of these mental health issues, asylum seekers held in offshore processing facilities in Nauru and PNG have to contend with a range of tropical diseases and substandard medical assistance, as well as hostile local populations. These issues were examined at length in Chapter 6. What has not yet been noted is the harm these policies have done to the host communities in Nauru and Manus Island. This includes damage to social cohesion, rising tensions between locals and their governments and public unrest resulting from the development of a two-tiered economy benefiting foreign companies and workers rather than the local population.[101]

Australia's maritime interdiction activities have put both asylum seekers and Navy personnel at serious risk. Vice Admiral Ray Griggs provided the following warning, in regard to his experience with interdiction activities, to a Senate Estimates Hearing in 2011:

> There are risks involved in this whole endeavor. As I said, there were incidents during these activities [in 2001], as there have been incidents subsequently, which have been risky. There have been fires lit ... attempts to storm the engine compartment ... people jumping in the water and that sort of thing.[102]

A number of asylum-seeker deaths can be directly linked to Australia's push-back operations. An asylum-seeker vessel returned to Indonesia by the Australian Navy in 2001 ran aground a few hundred metres from the Indonesian shore and three passengers reportedly drowned while trying to reach the shore.[103] A further five asylum seekers died in 2009 as a

---

[98] For a more detailed look at these harms, see Mary Crock and Daniel Ghezelbash, 'Do Loose Lips Bring Ships? The Role of Policy, Politics and Human Rights in Managing Unauthorised Boat Arrivals' (2010) 19 *Griffith Law Review* 238; Daniel Ghezelbash and Mary Crock, 'Out of Sight, Out of Mind? The Myths and Realities of Mandatory Immigration Detention' in Diego Acosta and Anja Wiesbrock (eds), *Global Migration Issues: Myths and Realities* (Praeger International, 2015) vol 2, 23.

[99] Janette Green and Kathy Eagar, 'The Health of People in Australian Immigration Detention Centres' (2010) 192 *Medical Journal of Australia* 65; Derrick Silove, Zachary Steel and Charles Watters, 'Policies of Deterrence and the Mental Health of Asylum Seekers' (2000) 284 *Journal of the American Medical Association* 604; and Zachary Steel and Derrick Silove, 'The Mental Health Implications of Detaining Asylum Seekers' (2001) 175 *Medical Journal of Australia* 596.

[100] A 2014 report by International Health and Medical Services ('IHMS'), the organisation contracted by the Australian government to provide medical services in detention centres, indicated that the rate of mental health disorders is substantially higher in offshore detention centres than in detention centres in Australia: 'Rate of Mental Health Disorders Higher in Offshore Detention Centres, Report Reveals', *ABC News* (online), 26 May 2014 www.abc.net.au/news/2014-05-26/asylum-seekers-in-offshore-detention-suffering-mental-health/5477392.

[101] Brian Opeskin and Daniel Ghezelbash, 'Australian Refugee Policy and Its Impacts on the Pacific' (2016) 36 *Journal of Pacific Studies* 73–90.

[102] Evidence to Senate Foreign Affairs, Defence and Trade Legislation Committee, Parliament of Australia, Canberra, 19 October 2011, quoted in Tony Kevin, 'Abbott's Asylum Seeker Turn-Back Policy Is a Bad Joke' (2012) 22(14) *Eureka Street* 1, 2.

[103] ABC TV, 'To Deter and Deny', *Four Corners*, 15 April 2002.

result of an explosion on an asylum-seeker vessel under the control of the Australian Navy. The fire was reportedly lit deliberately by some of the asylum seekers in an apparent bid to prevent their return to Indonesia.[104]

These policies have come at a massive financial cost. The exact amount is difficult to establish as the expenditure is spread across ten government agencies. Analysis of government budgetary documents by Save the Children and UNICEF revealed that offshore processing, boat turn-backs and onshore mandatory detention cost Australian taxpayers at least $9.6 billion between 2013 and 2016.[105] This expenditure comes at a time when Australia is purportedly experiencing a budgetary crisis. Any evaluation of programmatic success must take into account these hefty outlays and consider whether these funds would be better spent on other government programs.

By pushing the boundaries of what is acceptable under international human rights law and the *Refugee Convention*, these policies have undermined Australia's international reputation and moral authority to call out human rights abuses carried out by other nations. For example, Chinese representatives have used Australia's treatment of asylum seekers to deflect Australian criticism of their government's crackdown on dissidents and academics.[106]

Finally, by demonising so-called 'boat people', the policies of mandatory detention, interdiction and extraterritorial processing have damaged the general health of Australia's multicultural society. This demonisation has created and exacerbated divisions within emergent ethnic communities and between migrant and traditional Anglo-Saxon communities. Writing in 2010, when the Australian government was considering the reintroduction of interdiction and offshore processing, Mary Crock and I cautioned: 'It is more than a passing coincidence that the years of extraordinarily harsh border control policies under the Howard government [1996–2007] culminated in, first, an unprecedented number of wrongful arrests, detention and removals of citizens and lawful permanent residents and, second, in inter-racial rioting that made headlines all over the world.'[107]

Itamar Mann describes the fundamental political challenge facing states in this context: 'For governments with ostensible human rights commitments, the dilemma has ultimately been between treating people as humans and risking changing who "we" are (in terms of the composition of our population), or giving up human rights and risking changing who "we" are (in terms of our constitutive commitments).'[108]

The damage caused in Australia by the decision to adopt the latter option should be taken as a warning for other nations considering going down this path.

---

[104] 'Coroner Says SIEV 36 Fire was Deliberate', *Sydney Morning Herald* (online), 17 March 2010 http://news.smh.com.au/breaking-news-national/coroner-says-siev-36-fire-was-deliberate-20100317-qe2u.html.

[105] Save the Children and UNICEF Australia, 'At What Cost? The Human, Economic and Strategic Cost of Australia's Asylum Seeker Policies and the Alternatives' (Report, September 2016) www.unicef.org.au/Upload/UNICEF/Media/Documents/At-What-Cost-Report.pdf.

[106] Stephen McDonell, 'China Criticises Australia's Asylum Seeker Policies during Human Rights Talks', *ABC News* (online), 20 February 2014 www.abc.net.au/news/2014-02-20/china-criticises-australia-human-rights-record/5273478.

[107] Crock and Ghezelbash, 'Do Loose Lips Bring Ships?', above n 98, 276.

[108] Itamar Mann, *Humanity at Sea: Maritime Migration and the Foundations of International Law* (Cambridge University Press, 2016) 11.

7.4.3 Process Success

The process dimension of success relates to the legitimacy of the way in which lawmakers go about carrying out legal or policy transfer. In relation to the transfers between the United States and Australia, my research raised concerns about the *quality* of the information relied upon when deciding to emulate a foreign practice and the *transparency* of the process generally. Policy and legal transfer can only be an effective policymaking tool when it is informed by reliable and independent information about the operation and effect of the policy in the source country. As discussed already, there exists a relative dearth of hard research on the real effects and effectiveness of migration control measures in influencing irregular migrant flows.[109] The discourse on immigration and border control in many countries seems to be characterised by assertion and assumption rather than by reasoned and evidence-based exposition. The unreliability of the information relied upon is compounded by the closed and exclusionary nature of the forums in which governments share information about migration control policies. As discussed in Chapters 4 and 5, the main forums for the sharing of policy ideas between Australia and the United States were various regional consultative processes ('RCPs') (in particular the Five Country Conferences) and informal bilateral discussions. These forums all took place behind closed doors and the information shared at such meetings was generally not open to public scrutiny.

I make two suggestions for improving the quality of the transfer process. First and foremost, there is a need for robust research into the effects of restrictive asylum and border control measures on irregular migration flows of the type described in this chapter. Second, there needs to be more transparency in the transfer process and a greater degree of public scrutiny of the policy choices being considered. In particular, academics, immigration practitioners and civil society actors should be afforded an opportunity to scrutinise and comment on the evidence being relied upon to justify a transfer. The first step to achieving this would be for policymakers to be more open about the fact that they are engaging in transfers in the first place. As borne out in my interviews examined in Chapters 3, 4 and 5, policymakers involved in importing policies are generally reluctant to admit that they have done so. Without disclosing that transfers are occurring, independent scrutiny of the process becomes very difficult. Further, the evidence relied upon for transfers should be made public, either by the inclusion of a wider range of participants, such as academics and NGO representatives in RCPs and bilateral discussions, or through the release of policy documents which explicitly set out the evidence relied upon to justify the transfer.

In the absence of such measures, academics, civil society and migration lawyers must work hard to recognise potential transfers and influence the policy debate. This can only be achieved by these parties taking an active role in sharing and discussing policy developments in their respective countries. These non-government actors need to share their experience about the practical implications and impacts of policy developments with their overseas counterparts. By engaging with developments abroad, these actors will not only be in a position to react appropriately to poor transfer proposals, but can also play an active role in lobbying for and facilitating sound transfers based on solid evidence.

---

[109] See above nn 96–7 and accompanying text.

7.4.4 Political Dimension

Transfer of restrictive immigration control measures may at times be driven by political rather than programmatic considerations. This is based on a belief that tough border control policies are popular with the electorate. As John Pilger notes, the barbarity of Australia's border control policies is 'considered a vote-winner' by both of Australia's major parties.[110] The introduction of mandatory detention by former Prime Minister Paul Keating has been explained by Ben Eltham as a 'knee-jerk policy prescription designed to appease xenophobic Labor voters in marginal seats, dressed up in the language of deterring people smugglers'.[111] In a similar vein, former Prime Minister John Howard's decision to interdict and deflect the asylum seekers aboard the *MV Tampa* has often been recognised as a decisive factor in his come-from-behind victory in the 2001 federal election.[112] This is not an issue that is unique to Australia. Ruud Lubbers, the United Nations High Commissioner for Refugees, warned in 2001:

> [a]sylum seekers have become a campaign issue in various recent and upcoming election battles, with governments and opposition parties vying to appear toughest on the 'bogus' asylum seekers 'flooding' into their countries. In some nations – Australia, Austria, Denmark, Italy and Britain, for example, individual politicians and media appear at times to be deliberately inflating the issue. Statistics are frequently manipulated, facts are taken out of context, and the character of the asylum seekers as a group is often distorted in order to present them as a terrible threat – a threat their detractors can then pledge to crush. Politicians taking this line used to belong to small extremist parties. But nowadays the issue is able to steer the agenda of bigger parties ... Genuine refugees should not become victims yet again. Surely, there are other ways to win elections.[113]

In the fifteen years that have elapsed since this statement was made, the politicisation of asylum has only intensified. Regardless of whether the underlying assumption that harsh deterrent measures win votes holds true, transfers in the immigration control policy sphere should never be driven by such considerations. Given the substantial human, social and financial damage caused by these policies, their use as tools for scoring cheap political points is beyond reckless.

7.4.5 Ramifications for the International Refugee Protection Regime

The final, and perhaps most important, issue that should be considered by lawmakers considering engaging in the transfer of restrictive asylum and border control policies is the impact of such moves on the viability of the international refugee protection regime. As

---

[110] John Pilger, 'Australia's "Stop the Boats" Policy Is Cynical and Lawless', *The Guardian* (online), 30 July 2013 www.theguardian.com/commentisfree/2013/jul/29/australia-gulag-votes-aboriginal-concentration-camps.

[111] Ben Eltham, 'Asylum Seekers a Wicked Problem', *New Matilda* (online), 26 June 2012 https://newmatilda.com/2012/06/26/asylum-seekers-wicked-problem.

[112] See, eg, Peter Mares, 'Comment: Ten Years after Tampa', *The Monthly* (online), August 2011 www.themonthly.com.au/issue/2011/august/1316394350/peter-mares/comment-ten-years-after-tampa; Robert Manne, 'How Tampa Sailed into 2002' *The Age* (online), 30 December 2002 www.theage.com.au/articles/2002/12/29/1040511254630.html.

[113] Ruud Lubbers, 'Don't Kick Refugees Just to Score Points: Politicians Who Demonise Asylum Seekers are Playing with Peoples Lives', *The Australian*, 20 June 2001, 13.

states compete to deter irregular migrants, the result is the dissemination of progressively harsher and more punitive measures. In Chapter 2, I explained this behaviour by drawing an analogy with regulatory theory. The interdependence of governments' migration policy decisions and the resulting transfers resemble the 'competitive interdependence' observed in the context of economic regulation. In the same way that the decision of one government to reduce corporate taxes to attract investment may place pressure on other governments to do the same, the introduction of certain immigration policies by one government can create externalities for other governments.

In this policy paradigm, the adoption of harsh deterrent measures targeting asylum-seeker flows places pressure on comparator jurisdictions to follow suit or face a possible increase in the number of asylum seekers attempting to enter their territory. The assumption is that asylum seekers choose countries in which to seek refuge according to ease of access and what might loosely be termed immigration and settlement outcomes. This competitive approach creates a vicious cycle which leads to a race to the bottom in which governments seek to outdo each other by implementing progressively more restrictive policies. In this context, the policy imperative becomes deflecting irregular arrivals to alternative destinations and reassuring the public that the government is in control of the nation's borders. States are essentially being called upon to weigh up their competitiveness in *deterring* unwanted immigration against the value of abiding by their obligations under the *Refugee Convention*. As more states opt for deterrence over protection, this places pressure on other states to follow suit. This scenario has, and will continue to have, a devastating impact on the institution of asylum and international human rights more generally.

Harsh deterrent measures such as mandatory detention, interdiction and extraterritorial processing raise serious concerns under international law.[114] The diffusion of these measures is resulting in repeated non-compliance with the *Refugee Convention* and international human rights norms. This has the potential to completely unravel the international protection regime. There are a number of different theories which seek to explain why nations conform to international human rights norms.[115] Goodman and Jinks aggregate these into three broad categories: coercion, persuasion and acculturation. Compliance through coercion occurs when states and institutions influence the behaviour of other states by creating benefits for conformity and/or imposing costs on non-conformity.[116] Persuasion theory explains the influence of international law on state behaviour as resulting from 'processes of social "learning" and other forms of information conveyance'.[117] According to this approach, actors need to be consciously convinced of the appropriateness of a norm. Acculturation explains conformance with international norms through a 'general process by which actors adopt the beliefs and behaviour patterns of the surrounding culture'.[118] This is the result of pressures to assimilate, both self-imposed and emanating from external actors. It is unnecessary for our current purposes to engage in the debate about which of

---

[114] See Chapter 6.
[115] See, eg, Ryan Goodman and Derek Jinks, 'How to Influence States: Socialization and International Human Rights Law' (2004) 54 *Duke Law Journal* 621; Harold Hongju Koh, 'Why Do Nations Obey International Law?' (1997) 106 *Yale Law Journal* 2599; Oona Hathaway, 'Between Power and Principle: An Integrated Theory of International Law' (2005) 72 *University of Chicago Law Review* 469; Andrew Guzman, 'A Compliance-Based Theory of International Law' (2002) 90 *California Law Review* 1823.
[116] Goodman and Jinks, above n 115, 633.   [117] Ibid 635.   [118] Ibid 626.

these models best reflects the empirical reality. Under all three models, derogations from the *Refugee Convention* or international human rights norms, particularly by liberal democracies, have the potential to seriously undermine the international protection regime. States that violate international refugee or human rights laws would leave themselves open to charges of hypocrisy if they attempted to *coerce* other states to conform to those very same principles. Moreover, such hypocrisy would completely undermine their moral authority to *persuade* other states to conform to such norms. On the acculturation model, non-compliance may itself spread through a process of *acculturation* as states adopt the beliefs and behaviours of the surrounding culture.

We saw a number of these issues play out in May 2015 in the way Thai, Malaysian and Indonesian officials responded to the boats carrying Rohingya and Bangladeshi asylum seekers. The decision of each of these governments to undertake push-back operations was fuelled at least in part by competitive interdependence. This was based on a view that if one jurisdiction was to grant entry to the asylum seekers while the others continued to deny such access, then this would act as a pull factor for future arrivals. The resulting stalemate saw thousands of asylum seekers adrift at sea with nowhere to go. The fact that a liberal democracy like Australia has engaged in push-backs provides legitimacy to operations which in reality raise serious concerns under international law. As Human Rights Watch Deputy Director in Asia, Phil Robertson noted:

> Australia's shameful actions on boat people seeking asylum in Australia has given the green light to other countries in the region to believe that they can get away with pushing boats back. It's undermined humanitarian protection and refugee protection throughout the region. The Abbott Government should be ashamed of themselves and their example is part of the reason that these governments are going ahead with this kind of policy.[119]

The protections set out in the *Refugee Convention* and other human rights treaties are only words. Their effectiveness in the real world is shaped by state practice. The implementation of international law into state practice requires leadership – it needs states to lead by example to induce, persuade and acculturate other states to adhere to protection norms. This role has traditionally been carried out by wealthy liberal democracies, which have had the resources and ideological legitimacy required for the task. The restrictive policies introduced in the United States and Australia examined in this book mean that these nations now lack the credibility to take on this leadership role. All eyes are now on European states. While the recent adoption of restrictive measures has eroded some of Europe's credibility, much of the world still looks towards the EU and its member states as among the last bastions of rights protection. We are at a tipping point. If Europe goes down the same path as the United States and Australia, it will be inflicting a mortal wound on the universal principle of asylum and the international refugee protection regime more broadly.

---

[119] ABC TV, 'Saving People "Key Right Now" as Migrants Adrift and in Limbo on Boats off Thailand', *7:30*, 15 May 2015 www.abc.net.au/7.30/content/2015/s4236809.htm.

APPENDIX: US AND AUSTRALIAN BOAT MIGRANT STATISTICS

Table A.1 US Coast Guard migrant interdiction, 1982–2016

Fiscal Year	Haitian	Dominican	Chinese	Cuban	Mexican	Ecuadorian	Other	Total
2016								6,346
2015	561	257	10	2,927	27	3	43	3,828
2014	949	293	0	2,059	48	0	29	3,378
2013	508	110	5	1,357	31	1	82	2,094
2012	977	456	23	1,275	79	7	138	2,955
2011	1,137	222	11	985	68	1	50	2,474
2010	1,377	140	0	422	61	0	88	2,088
2009	1,782	727	35	799	77	6	41	3,467
2008	1,583	688	1	2,216	47	220	70	4,825
2007	1,610	1,469	73	2,868	26	125	167	6,338
2006	1,198	3,011	31	2,810	52	693	91	7,886
2005	1,850	3,612	32	2,712	55	1,149	45	9,455
2004	3,229	5,014	68	1,225	86	1,189	88	10,899
2003	2,013	1,748	15	1,555	0	703	34	6,068
2002	1,486	177	80	666	32	1,608	55	4,104
2001	1,391	659	53	777	17	1,020	31	3,948
2000	1,113	499	261	1,000	49	1,244	44	4,210
1999	1,039	583	1,092	1,619	171	298	24	4,826
1998	1,369	1,097	212	903	30	0	37	3,648
1997	288	1,200	240	421	0	0	45	2,194
1996	2,295	6,273	61	411	0	2	38	9,080
1995	909	3,388	509	525	0	0	36	5,367
1994	25,302	232	291	38,560	0	0	58	64,443
1993	4,270	873	2,511	2,882	0	0	48	10,584
1992	37,618	588	181	2,066	0	0	174	40,627
1991	2,065	1,007	138	1,722	0	0	58	4,990
1990	871	1,426	0	443	1	0	95	2,836
1989	4,902	664	5	257	30	0	5	5,863
1988	4,262	254	0	60	11	0	13	4,600
1987	2,866	40	0	46	1	0	38	2,991
1986	3,422	189	11	28	1	0	74	3,725
1985	3,721	113	12	51	0	0	177	4,074
1984	1,581	181	0	7	2	0	37	1,808

Table A.1 (*cont.*)

Fiscal Year	Haitian	Dominican	Chinese	Cuban	Mexican	Ecuadorian	Other	Total
1983	511	6	0	44	0	0	5	566
1982	171	0	0	0	0	0	0	171

Source: US Coast Guard, *Alien Migrant Interdiction: Total Interdictions – Fiscal Year 1982 to Present* (19 January 2016). At the time of writing in June 2017, this website was no longer accessible. The author retains a copy on file. The total number of Coast Guard migrant interdictions for 2016 was obtained through a *Freedom of Information Act* (FOIA) request: Letter from Zsatique L Ferrell, US Coast Guard to Niels Frenzen, 15 June 2017. A breakdown by nationality was not provided.

Table A.2 Asylum-seeker boat arrivals in Australia, 1991–2016

Calendar year	Number of arrivals
2016	0
2015	0
2014	160
2013	20,587
2012	17,202
2011	4,565
2010	6,555
2009	2,726
2008	161
2007	148
2006	60
2005	11
2004	15
2003	53
2002	1
2001	5,516
2000	2,939
1999	3,721
1998	200
1997	339
1996	660
1995	237
1994	953
1993	81
1992	216
1991	214

Source: Janet Phillips, 'Boat Arrivals and Boat "Turnbacks" in Australia since 1976: A Quick Guide to the Statistics' (Research Paper, Parliamentary Library, 17 January 2017). Note that these exclude the passengers of boats which are turned back at sea. See Table A.3.

Table A.3 Known boat 'turnbacks' carried out by the Australian government, 2001–2016

Calendar year	Boats	Number of people
2016	6	55
2015	9	234
2014	11	296
2013	3	104
2012	0	0
2011	0	0
2010	0	0
2009	0	0
2008	0	0
2007	0	0
2006	0	0
2005	0	0
2004	0	0
2003	1	14
2002	0	0
2001	4	600

Source: Janet Phillips, 'Boat Arrivals and Boat "Turnbacks" in Australia since 1976: A Quick Guide to the Statistics' (Research Paper, Parliamentary Library, 16 November 2017).

INDEX

Abbott, Tony
    and European refugee crisis, 1, 167–8
    and maritime interdiction, 74, 174–5, 186
    and Operation Sovereign Borders, 84
acculturation, 185–6
Administrative Decisions (Judicial Review) Act 1977 (Cth), 33, 86n
admission
    and *Chinese Exclusion Acts*, 33n
    defined, 55n
    and entry fiction, 36
    and habeas review, 39n
    and *Lim*, 70
    and mandatory detention, 35–7, 59–60, 62, 64–5, 70–2
    and parole of aliens, 37, 64–5
    and US deportation proceedings, 55–6, 58
Aleinikoff, Alexander, 30, 55–6
aliens. *see also* asylum seekers; parole of aliens
    and *Australian Constitution*, 56
    and *Chinese Exclusion Acts*, 28–9
    and collective expulsion, 149–50
    defined, 17–18
    and entry fiction, 113
    excludable, 64–5
    and Guantánamo Bay, 104–5, 107–8, 130–1
    and IIRIRA, 38–9
    and indefinite detention, 62–4, 64–5n, 65–6, 69–70
    limited parole of, 134n
    and mandatory detention, 41–3, 45, 58–9, 58n, 67–8, 71–2
    and maritime interdiction, 77–8, 80, 95, 142
    and *non-refoulement* obligations, 77–80
    and plenary power doctrine, 55, 57–8, 177–8
    and separation of powers doctrine, 62
    and sovereignty, 30, 53–4
    and third country processing, 124–6
    and US removal procedure, 55–6
aliens power (Australia)
    and administrative detention, 71–2
    and Australian case law, 62, 67, 177–8
    and mandatory detention, 61–2
    and plenary power, 57–8
    and third country processing, 123–4
Al-Kateb v Godwin, 57n, 62–3, 66–8, 70–3, 116, 131

alternatives to detention ('ATD')
    based in community, 40–1, 135
    and legal and policy transfer, 46, 50–3
    and proportionality, 133–4
Amnesty International, 153, 173
Aristide, Jean-Bertrand, 75
Ashcroft, John, 40–1
Ashmore Reef, 111–12
asylum claims
    and differential treatment, 166
    and Dublin System, 25
    extraterritorial processing of, 1–3, 46, 100–1, 129–30, 171–4
    and Frontex, 170–1
    and Guantánamo Bay, 106–7
    by Haitian boat migrants, 75
    and maritime interdiction, 74, 146–7
    and *non-refoulement*, 102
    and Operation Relex, 83
    and UNHCR processing guidelines, 162–3
asylum policy
    and border control, 1
    goals of, 21
    and interdependence, 2, 20
    international context of, 19
    and legal and policy transfer, 2–3, 7, 13–14, 22–5
    and RCPs, 25–6
    success of, 14–15
asylum seekers. *see also* aliens; *boat migrants; specific nationalities*
    and Australian detention, 45
    and Christmas Island, 113n, 113–14
    and competitive policy transfers, 23
    and cooperative policy transfers, 22–3
    and credible fear, 41–3
    deaths of, 181–2
    and economic migrants, 1–2
    extraterritorial processing of, 172–4
    and forum shopping, 25, 27
    and international competition, 26–8
    and mandatory detention, 35–43
    and maritime interdiction, 74, 77
    and *non-refoulement*, 31–2, 146
    and plenary power doctrine, 59–60
    and processing at sea, 129–30
    and refugee status determination, 158–9
    and Temporary Protection visa, 116–17n
    and third country processing, 162–3
    and US-Australia resettlement deals, 128–9
ATD. *see* alternatives to detention
Australia
    and child asylum seekers, 164
    and detention conditions, 151–7
    and differential treatment, 165–6
    and extraterritorial processing, 100–1, 131–2
    and Five Country Conferences, 25–6
    government structure of, 18–19, 56–8

INDEX

Australia (*cont.*)
    and indefinite detention, 68
    and independent judiciary, 32–4
    and legal and policy transfer to Europe, 167–9, 172–3
    and legal similarities to United States, 16–17
    and mandatory detention, 43–6, 73, 81, 135–8
    and maritime interdiction, 81–94, 140
    and *non-refoulement*, 146–9
    and political dimension of harsh policies, 184
    and processing at sea, 129–30
    and programmatic failure, 181–2
    and public opinion on immigration, 29
    and *Refugee Convention* and *Protocol*, 24, 32
    and refugee status determination, 158–9
    and state responsibility, 159–61
    and third country processing, 162–3
    and *US Constitution*, 56
    and xenophobia, 30–1
Australian Border Force, 18–19
Australian case law. *see specific cases*
Australian Constitution
    and aliens power. *see* aliens power
    and executive power. *see* executive power
    and immigration law, 56–8
    and individual rights protection, 33
    and separation of powers doctrine, 70
    and *US Constitution*, 56
Australian Department of Immigration
    and extraterritorial processing, 148–9, 160
    and legal and policy transfer, 49–50, 83
    and refugee status assessment, 114
    structure of, 18–19
Australian High Court. *see specific cases*
Australian Human Rights Commission, 137
Australian Labor Party
    and bridging visas, 45–6
    and extraterritorial processing, 127–8
    and mandatory detention, 43–4
    and maritime interdiction, 84
    and Pacific Solution, 113–14
    and Pacific Solution Mark II, 120–2
Australian Liberal/National Coalition government, 45–6, 84
Australian Liberal Party, 43–4
Austria, 1, 167–8
A v Australia, 136–7, 136n

Bahamas, 110, 140
Bakhtiyari v Australia, 164
Belize, 75, 110–11
Bill of Rights (United States), 54
Blair, Tony, 173
boat migrants
    and Australian detention, 43–4, 46
    defined, 17–18
    and extraterritorial processing, 101–3
    and maritime interdiction, 74, 77, 81–2

and Operation Relex, 82–4
and parole of aliens, 37
and xenophobia, 30–1
Boochani, Behrouz, 100
border control
   and asylum flows, 2, 28, 32
   and conditionality, 22
   and damage to multiculturalism, 182
   and European refugee crisis, 170
   and extraterritorial processing, 74
   and international refugee protection regime, 1–2, 184–6
   and legal and policy transfer, 1, 19, 175–7
   and people smuggling routes, 27
   political dimension of, 184
   and programmatic success, 180
   and public opinion, 29–31
   and transfer process, 183
Border Protection Legislation Amendment Act 1999 (Cth), 82
Boumediene v Bush, 107–10, 130–1
bridging visas (Australia), 45–7, 121
Brubaker, Rogers, 2
Budapest Process, 26
Bush, George HW administration, 75–8, 104
Bush, George W administration, 77, 107, 110

Cameron, David, 168
Canada
   and Five Country Conferences, 25–6
   and Intergovernmental Consultations on Migration, Asylum and Refugees ('IGC'), 47–8
   and legal and policy transfer, 167
   and mandatory detention, 175–6, 177–85
carrier sanctions, 26–8
Castro, Fidel, 37
Castro v DHS, 59–60
Central American migrants, 41, 41n, 128
Central Europe, 22
Chae Chan Ping v United States, 28–30, 53–5
children
   and ATD programs, 50–3
   and Australian detention, 45–6
   and mandatory detention, 41n, 164n
   and maritime interdiction, 163–5
   and parole of aliens, 41
Chinese Exclusion Acts, 28–9, 33, 55, 57–8
Christmas Island
   and extraterritorial processing, 111, 113–17
   and maritime interdiction, 84
   and *Offshore Processing Case*, 131
   and Pacific Solution, 111–12
   and *Ruddock v Vadarlis*, 86–9
Chu Kheng Lim v MILGEA
   and *Al-Kateb*, 67
   and *CPCF v MIBP*, 90–1, 94
   and detention duration, 71–2, 91–2
   and extraterritorial detention, 98, 125–6
   and mandatory detention, 60–2

Chu Kheng Lim v MILGEA (cont.)
  and *Plaintiff S156*, 123–4
  and proportionality, 62
  and *Ruddock v Vadarlis*, 87–8
  and separation of powers doctrine, 61–2, 70
Clark v Martinez, 65–6, 69–70
Clinton administration, 76, 110–11
Cocos (Keeling) Island, 89–90, 111–12
coercion, 20, 22
collective expulsion, 138–9, 149–50
Common European Asylum System (CEAS), 25
competition
  and asylum policy, 26–8
  and danger to refugee protection regime, 3, 184–6
  and New Zealand's mandatory detention policy, 176–7
  as transfer mechanism, 20, 23
conditionality, 22
Convention against Torture and Other Cruel, Inhuman and Degrading Treatment or Punishment ('CAT'), 31n, 137, 144–6
Convention on the Elimination of all Forms of Racial Discrimination ('CERD'), 165–6
Convention on the Rights of the Child ('CRC'), 31n, 144, 163–4
cooperation, 20, 22–6, 110–11, 150–1
Costa Rica, 128
Cotterrell, Roger, 11, 15
CPCF v MIBP, 86, 89–94, 95–6n, 95–9
credible fear (United States)
  and asylum eligibility, 39n
  and maritime interdiction, 75
  and parole of aliens, 38–9, 39n, 41–3
  and status determination, 40
Crépeau, François, 160–1
Crock, Mary, 62, 182
Cuban Adjustment Act of 1966, 37n
Cuban American Bar Association v Christopher ('CABA'), 106–8, 130–1
Cuban asylum seekers
  and credible fear, 102–3
  and differential treatment, 166
  and indefinite detention, 65–6, 138
  and mandatory detention, 37
  and maritime interdiction, 77
  and *non-refoulement*, 147–8
  and safe haven, 106–7, 110–11
culture
  and legal and policy transfer, 11–13, 15–16, 185–6
  and xenophobia, 30n, 30–1
C v Australia (2002), 137

Deakin, Alfred, 56
Demore v Kim, 58–60, 62
Denmark, 168–9, 171–2
Department of Homeland Security ('DHS'), 19, 135n, 157–8
deportation. *see also* expulsion
  and admission to United States, 55–6
  and aliens power, 123–4
  and Australian judicial review, 33
  and detention, 35–6, 43, 60n, 61–8, 72–3

and due process, 55, 55n
and indefinite detention, 53
and *Lim*, 70
and *non-refoulement*, 78–9
and sovereignty, 53–4
and third country processing, 125–6
detention. *see* indefinite detention; mandatory detention
deterrence
   and custody determinations, 41n
   and danger to refugee protection regime, 184–6
   and international competition, 28
   and mandatory detention, 37–8, 40, 41n, 135n, 135–6
   and maritime interdiction, 74
   and state sovereignty, 28–31
diffusion
   and conditionality, 22
   and legal scholars, 4n
   mechanisms of, 20
   versus policy transfer, 6–7
   and prestige, 21–2
   quantitative nature of study, 7
   scholarship on, 6–7
distress, and duty to render assistance, 140–1, 141n
Dolowitz, David, 18
Dominican Republic, 110, 140
dualist jurisdictions, 24
Dublin System, 25
due process. *see also* Due Process Clause
   and collective expulsion, 149
   and deportable aliens, 55n
   and Guantánamo Bay, 105–6, 130–1, 157–8
   and indefinite detention, 60, 62–8
   and mandatory detention, 58–60
   and plenary power doctrine, 55
Due Process Clause (United States). *see also* due process
   and indefinite detention, 64–5, 68–70
   and mandatory detention, 62
   and plenary power doctrine, 54, 59–60
   and *US Constitution*, 102
Dutton, Peter, 128–9, 161

Eastern Europe, 22
economic migrants, 1–2
economic regulation, 22–3, 27, 185
efficiency as a transfer mechanism, 20–1
entry fiction
   and Australian detention, 43, 45
   and legal and policy transfer, 113
   and US detention, 36
Europe
   and Australian model, 167–9
   and extraterritorial processing, 171–4
   and legal and policy transfer, 167
   and maritime interdiction, 169–71
European Convention on Human Rights ('*ECHR*'), 149–50, 171, 178–80
European Court of Human Rights ('ECtHR'), 178–9

European Union
    and Australian model, 168–9
    and coercion, 22
    and extraterritorial processing, 173–4
    as last bastion of rights protection, 186
    and legal and policy transfer, 6
    and maritime interdiction, 169–71
    and transit processing camp plans, 172
European Union Naval Force Mediterranean ('EUNAVFOR Med'), 171, 179–80
Evans, Chris, 45–6, 52
excision policy (Australia), 113–17
Executive Order 13276, 77, 109–10
Executive Order 13286, 102–3, 109–10
Executive Order 13780, 129
executive power (Australia)
    and *Australian Constitution*, 87–8
    and Australian High Court, 89n
    and detention, 93n
    and maritime interdiction, 88–90, 93–5
    and *Migration Act 1958* (Cth), 88
    and *Ruddock v Vadarlis*, 88n
expedited removal (United States), 38–9, 41–3, 49–50
expulsion. *see also* deportation
    and Nauru, 126
    and non-statutory prerogative power, 87
    and Papua New Guinea, 126–7
    prohibition of by international treaties, 31n, 79, 138–9, 144, 149–50, 149n
    and separation of powers doctrine, 72–3
extraterritorial processing
    by Australia, 111
    and case law of Australia and United States, 130–2
    and coercion, 22
    defined, 17–18, 100–1
    and differential treatment, 165–6
    and Europe, 171–4
    and international law, 150–1
    and legal and policy transfer, 167
    and maritime interdiction, 74n, 82–5
    and programmatic failure, 181–2
    by the United States, 101–3

failures of legal or policy transfer
    difficulty in predicting, 73, 132
    dimensions of, 15–16, 21
    and domestic law, 177–80
    factors contributing to, 11, 180–2
    frameworks for testing, 7–8
    and process improvement, 183
    varying degrees of, 14–15
Family Case Management program, 51–2
Ferrer-Mazorra et al v United States, 138
Five Country Conferences, 25–6, 47–8, 183
forced displacement, 1–2, 20, 23–5
forum shopping, 25, 27
France, 24, 170
Frontex, 170–1

INDEX

Gammeltoft-Hansen, Thomas, 32
Germany, 1, 167–8, 170, 172
Gillard, Julia, 117–21
globalisation, 5–6, 20, 26–7
Guantánamo Bay
   and child asylum seekers, 164–5
   and Cuban asylum seekers, 77
   and detention, 110n
   and detention conditions, 151–4
   and extraterritorial processing, 100–3
   and extraterritorial processing case law, 130–1
   and Haitian asylum seekers, 76
   and maritime interdiction, 77
   and refugee resettlement, 112–13
   and refugee status determination, 157–8
   and safe haven, 110–11
   and state responsibility, 159
   and US-Australia resettlement deals, 127–8
Guterres, António, 1

habeas corpus
   and Australian courts, 87n
   and Guantánamo Bay, 107–10
   and IIRIRA, 38–9, 39n
   and *Ruddock v Vadarlis*, 86–9
Habeas Suspension Clause (United States), 59–60
Haitian asylum seekers
   and differential treatment, 166
   and extraterritorial processing, 101–3
   and maritime interdiction, 75–7
   and parole regulations, 37–8, 49–50
   and refugee resettlement, 112–13
   and third country processing, 110–11
Haitian Centers Council v McNary, 105
Haitian Centers Council v Sale ('Haitian HIV case'), 105–6
Haitian Refugee Center v Baker, 104, 107–8, 130–1
Haitian Refugee Center v Gracey, 102
Hand, Gerry, 44
Hathaway, James, 32, 165
Hawke, Bob, 44
Hirsi Jamaa v Italy, 169–70, 178–80
Honduras
   asylum seekers from, 41
   and Haitian asylum seekers, 75
   and safe haven, 110–11
   and third country processing, 110
   and US pre-screening, 128
Howard, John, 29, 81–2, 184
human rights treaties. *see also* international law; *specific treaties*
   and asylum policy, 3, 21
   and Australian third country processing, 158–9
   and Australia's reputation, 182
   and child asylum seekers, 163–5
   and collective expulsion, 149–50
   and differential treatment, 165–6
   and *non-refoulement*, 31n, 31–2, 92–3, 143–9

human rights treaties (*cont.*)
    and real world practice, 186
    and state responsibility, 159
    violations of, 159–61, 185–6

Illegal Immigration Reform and Immigrant Responsibility Act of 1996 ('*IIRIRA*'), 38–9, 58, 58n
immigration
    Australian and US judicial approaches to, 53
    and *Australian Constitution*, 56
    and history of Australia and United States, 16–17
    and legal and policy transfer, 47–53
    and plenary power doctrine, 54–6
    and politics, 34
    and sovereignty, 32, 53–4
    and xenophobia, 30n
Immigration Act of 1891, 36
Immigration Act of 1893, 36
Immigration and Customs Enforcement ('ICE'), 135n
Immigration and Nationality Act ('*INA*')
    and credible fear, 39n
    and extraterritorial processing, 102, 104, 107
    language of, 17–18
    and mandatory detention, 36–7, 58, 59n
    and maritime interdiction, 95
    and *non-refoulement*, 77–9, 81, 105
    and parole of aliens, 39n, 58n
immigration law. *see specific laws*
Immigration Restriction Act 1901 (Cth), 43
IMO Guidelines on the Treatment of Persons Rescued at Sea, 142–3
indefinite detention
    alternatives to, 45–6
    and Australian High Court, 66–8, 70–1
    and extraterritorial processing, 124
    and inadmissible aliens, 65n
    and international law, 137–8
    legal challenges to, 53, 66–8
    and US Supreme Court, 62–6, 68–70
Independent Merits Review ('IMR'), 114–15
Indonesia
    and Australian interdiction, 83–5, 129–30, 146–7, 181–2
    and maritime interdiction, 174–5, 186
    and Pacific Solution, 82–3
    and Syrian asylum seekers, 26–7
    and UNHCR asylum claims processing, 121
Informal Thematic Debate on International Migration and Development, 47
innocent passage, 139n, 139
Intensive Supervision Appearance Program ('ISAP'), 51–2
Intensive Supervision Appearance Program II ('ISAP II'), 51–2
Inter-American Commission on Human Rights, 81, 137–8
Intergovernmental Consultations on Migration, Asylum and Refugees ('IGC')
    and European extraterritorial processing plans, 171–2, 172n
    and European refugee crisis, 167–8
    as forum for transfer, 47–8
    and RCPs, 26
International Convention for the Safety of Life at Sea ('*SOLAS*'), 140–3
International Convention on Migrant Workers, 149–50

International Covenant on Civil and Political Rights ('ICCPR')
    and child asylum seekers, 164
    and collective expulsion, 31n, 149–50
    and detention conditions, 137–8, 152
    and differential treatment, 165–6
    on mandatory detention, 133–4
    and *non-refoulement*, 144–6
    on right to challenge detention, 136–7
    and right to life, 141n
International Dialogue on Migration in Southern Africa, 26
International Dialogue on Migration in West Africa, 26
international law. *see also* human rights treaties; *specific treaties*
    and asylum policy, 3, 133
    Australian and US response to, 138
    Australian versus US reception of, 17
    and Australia's reputation, 182
    derogations from by liberal democracies, 185–6
    and legal and policy transfer, 23
    and self-executing treaties (United States), 96n
    and state practice, 186
    statute law's precedence over (Australia), 117n
International Organisation for Migration ('IOM'), 26, 47, 128, 172
Italy
    and asylum screening, 171
    and extraterritorial processing, 172
    and maritime interdiction, 149–50, 169–71, 178–9
    and politics of border control, 184

Jamaica, 110–11
Jennings v Rodriguez, 60
Johnson v Eisentrager, 107
judicial review, 15–16, 18, 32–4

Kahn-Freund, Otto, 12–13
Keating, Paul, 184
Kennebunkport Order, 76–8, 102–3, 110–11
Kiyemba v Obama, 109–10

Latin America, 24
legal and policy transfer, defined, 18
legal failure, 21
'Legal Irritants' thesis, 12–13
legal success
    defined, 15–16
    difficulty in predicting, 73, 132
    and domestic law, 177–80
    factors contributing to, 7, 19
    and programmatic success, 180
legal transfers. *see also* transfers
    between Australia and United States, 2–3, 10
    and comparative analysis, 9
    ease of, 12
    evidence for, 9–10
    identification of, 8
    and international cooperation, 23–6
    and maritime interdiction, 83

legal transfers (*cont.*)
  mechanisms of, 20
  motive for, 8–9
  naïve model of, 7–8
  political dimension of, 184
  and process success, 183
  qualitative nature of study, 7
  study of, 4–6, 13
  success of, 11–16, 177–80
Legomsky, Stephen, 102
Legrand, Pierre, 11–13
Libya, 171
Lubbers, Ruud, 184

Malaysia
  and asylum seekers, 186
  and extraterritorial processing, 111, 131–2
  and maritime interdiction, 174–5
  and third country processing, 117–20
mandatory detention
  and Australia, 43–6
  and Australian and US case law, 58–60, 62
  and community supervision, 135
  conditions of, 137
  defined, 35–6
  and deterrence, 41n, 135n
  and differential treatment, 166
  duration of, 137–8
  and international law, 32, 133–4, 136n, 136
  and legal and policy transfer, 46–50, 167, 175–7
  and programmatic failure, 181–2
  and proportionality, 134–5
  right to challenge, 136–7
  and separation of powers doctrine, 56–8
  and third country processing, 123, 125–6
  and US policy, 1, 36–43
Manila Process, 26
Mann, Itamar, 179, 182
Manus Island. *see also* Papua New Guinea
  and child asylum seekers, 164
  and detention conditions, 151–7, 161
  and differential treatment, 166
  and extraterritorial processing, 100, 111, 111n
  and legal failure, 179–80
  and Operation Relex, 83–4
  and Pacific Solution, 82–3, 112
  and Pacific Solution Mark II, 120–2
  and programmatic failure, 181–2
  and refugee status determination, 158–9
  and US-Australia resettlement deals, 128–9
Mare Nostrum, 170
Mariel Boatlift, 37, 37n, 65–6
maritime interdiction
  as Australian and US policy, 2–3
  Australian legislative framework for, 89–90
  defined, 74

   and detention, 86n
   and differential treatment, 165–6
   and Europe, 169–71
   and international law, 32, 85, 138–41
   and legal and policy transfer, 167
   and programmatic failure, 181–2
   in South East Asia, 174–5
Maritime Powers Act 2013 (Cth), 85–6, 89–95
Marsh, David, 18
Mediterranean 5 + 5 Dialogue, 26
mental health
   and Guantánamo Bay, 153–4
   and mandatory detention, 45–6, 50–3, 181–2
   and Manus Island and Nauru, 157, 162–3, 181n
Migrant Smuggling Protocol, 140, 142
Migration Act 1958 (Cth), 24, 43–4, 61n, 82
   and ATD programs, 50–3
   and executive power, 88–9
   and extraterritorial processing, 114
   and indefinite detention, 66
   and *Lim* test, 72
   and Malaysian Solution, 119–20
   and *Malaysian Solution Case*, 122–3
   and mandatory detention, 44–6, 60–2, 66n
   and maritime interdiction, 86–9, 93–4
   and *Maritime Powers Act 2013* (Cth), 85–6
   and non-statutory review, 114–15
   and OEPs, 113n, 117–21
   and *Offshore Processing Case*, 131
   and *Refugee Convention*, 95–6n
   and regional processing arrangements, 124–5
Migration and Maritime Powers Legislation Amendment (Resolving the Asylum Legacy Caseload) Act 2014 (Cth), 86n, 86
migration flows
   and deterrence, 180
   and European interdiction, 170–1
   and Guantánamo Bay, 109
   and international policy, 2
   and policy goals, 21
   and transfer process, 183
Migration Legislation Amendment (Regional Processing and Other Measures) Act 2012 (Cth), 117n, 122–3
Migration Regulations 1994 (Cth), 114
MIMIA v QAAH, 116–17
Mitchell, Grant, 11n, 53
monist jurisdictions, 24
MV Tampa, 81–2, 86–7n, 86–9, 184
Myanmar, 174–5

nativism, 30–1
Nauru, 82–4
   and Australian detention, 46
   and child asylum seekers, 164
   and Danish study of Australian model, 168–9
   and detention conditions, 151–7
   and differential treatment, 166
   and extraterritorial processing, 111, 111n

Nauru (*cont.*)
    and OEPs, 118
    and Pacific Solution, 112
    and Pacific Solution Mark II, 120–2
    and programmatic failure, 181–2
    and refugee status determination, 158–9
    and state responsibility, 159–61
    and third country processing, 124–6
    and US-Australia resettlement deals, 127–9
Nelken, David, 11, 14
Netherlands, 24
New Zealand
    and Five Country Conferences, 25–6
    and Intergovernmental Consultations on Migration, Asylum and Refugees ('IGC'), 168
    and legal and policy transfer, 167
    and mandatory detention, 176–7
    and *MV Tampa*, 81–2, 88, 96
    and Regional Consultative Processes, 47–8
Nishimura Eiku v United States, 55
non-citizens. *see* aliens
non-refoulement obligations
    and collective expulsion, 149
    and extraterritorial processing, 100–1
    and international law, 31–2, 143–9
    and maritime interdiction, 74, 76–81, 86, 92–3, 95–8, 138–9
    and place of safety, 150
    and *Refugee Convention*, 96n, 133
    and third country processing, 162–3
    and US extraterritorial processing, 102

Obama administration
    and detention reform, 40–1, 53
    and Guantánamo Bay, 109–10
    and immigration reform debate, 29
    and Leaders' Summit on Refugees, 47
    and number of refugees resettled, 129
    and parole of aliens, 42, 59–60
    and private contractors, 51–2
    and US-Australia resettlement deals, 128–9
offshore processing, defined, 17–18
Offshore Processing Case, 114–17, 119–20, 124, 131
'Operation Liberty Shield,' 40
Operation Relex, 82–4
Operation Sovereign Borders, 84, 129–30
Örücü, Esin, 6

Pacific Solution
    and European extraterritorial processing plans, 172
    and extraterritorial processing, 100–1, 111–13
    and maritime interdiction, 83–4
    and OEPs, 113n
    and US influence, 83
Pacific Solution Mark II, 120–7
Panama, 110–11
Papua New Guinea. *see also* Manus Island
    and detention conditions, 151–7

   and Pacific Solution, 112
   and Pacific Solution Mark II, 120–2
   and refugee status determination, 158–9
   and state responsibility, 159–61
   and third country processing, 126–7
parallel path development, 9
parole of aliens. *see also* aliens
   and Attorney General's discretion, 39n
   and Australian bridging visa system, 45
   Australia's avoidance of, 48–9
   and Central American women and children, 41n
   and credible fear, 38–9, 39n
   exclusion of Haitians from, 40
   and IIRIRA, 58n
   and legal and policy transfer, 46–7
   and Mariel Boatlift, 37n
   regulation of, 37–8
   and Trump Administration, 41–3
   and US adoption of Australian policy, 49–50
people smuggling
   and European refugee crisis, 167–8
   and international competition, 26–7
   and international law, 142, 142n
   and maritime interdiction, 174–5
   and policy outcomes, 180
   proliferation of, 2
   of refugees and economic migrants, 2
Pilger, John, 184
place of safety
   and international law, 133, 142–3, 150
   and *Maritime Powers Act 2013* (Cth), 95
Plaintiff M47/2012 v Director-General Security, 70–1
Plaintiff M68/2015 v MIBP, 93n, 98, 124–6
Plaintiff M70/2011 v MIAC ('*Malaysian Solution Case*'), 118–20, 122–4, 131–2, 179
Plaintiff M76/2013 v MIMAC, 70–1
Plaintiff S4/2014 v MIBP, 72n, 72–3, 91–2
Plaintiff S156/2013 v MIBP, 123–4, 179
plenary power doctrine (United States)
   and admission to United States, 59–60
   and *Chinese Exclusion Acts*, 33, 55
   and due process, 54–6, 177–8
   and inadmissible aliens, 64–5, 68–70
   and maritime interdiction, 98
   and US courts, 32
policy transfers. *see also* transfers
   between Australia and United States, 2–3
   and bounded rationality, 21
   and danger to refugee protection regime, 184–6
   defined, 18
   and extraterritorial processing, 111
   and identifying transfers, 8
   and legal scholars, 4n
   and maritime interdiction, 83
   mechanisms of, 20
   political dimension of, 184
   and prestige, 21–2

policy transfers (*cont.*)
    and process success, 183
    qualitative nature of study, 7
    scholarship on, 6–7
prestige, 20–2
privatisation, 51–2
process success, 183
programmatic success, 21, 180–2
proportionality, 134–5
Puebla Process, 26

racism, 30–1
Rasul v Bush, 107–8
Reagan, Ronald, 30, 37–8
Refugee Act of 1980, 24
Refugee Convention and *Protocol*. *see also* refugees
    and asylum policy, 3, 21, 133
    and Australia's reputation, 182
    and cooperation mechanisms, 24–5
    definition of refugee in, 31n
    derogations from by liberal democracies, 185–6
    and differential treatment, 165
    and domestic violence, 97n
    and extraterritorial processing, 114, 131
    and international cooperation, 23–5
    and Malaysian Solution, 119–20
    and mandatory detention, 133–4
    and maritime interdiction, 74, 76–81, 95–8
    and *Migration Act 1958* (Cth), 95–6n
    and *non-refoulement*, 78–80, 86, 92–3, 96n, 143–9
    obligations created by, 31–2, 34
    and *Offshore Processing Case*, 131
    and place of safety, 150
    and *Plaintiff S4*, 72
    and refugee protection regime, 184–6
    and state practice, 186
    and United States' obligations, 77n
    and US extraterritorial processing, 102, 104, 107
    and US Supreme Court, 96n
    and vertical legal and policy transfer, 6
Refugee Review Tribunal, 113n
refugees, 20, 112, 167–9. *see also Refugee Convention* and *Protocol*
refugee status determination ('RSD')
    and child asylum seekers, 164–5
    and extraterritorial processing, 148, 150–1
    and *Migration Act 1958* (Cth), 114–15
    and *non-refoulement*, 157–9
    and *Refugee Convention*, 114
    and state responsibility, 160
Regional Consultative Processes ('RCPs'), 25–6, 47–8, 183
regulatory theory, 20
Re Woolley; Ex parte M276/2003 ('*Woolley*'), 71
right to life, 141n
Robtelmes v Brenan, 57–8
Rose, Richard, 18
Royingya asylum seekers, 174–5, 186

Rudd, Kevin, 113n
Ruddock, Phillip, 29, 34
Ruddock v Vadarlis
   and *CPCF v MIBP*, 89–90
   and executive power, 82, 86–9, 88n, 93–6
   and mandatory detention, 86–7n
   and *Migration Act 1958* (Cth), 95n, 95–6n
   and *Refugee Convention*, 96n
   and refugee status assessment, 115
   and writ of habeas corpus, 87n

Sadiqi litigation, 118–20, 118n, 131–2
safe haven, 77, 106–7, 110–11
Sale v Haitian Centers Council, 76–81, 88, 95–9, 144
search and rescue, 140–3, 141n
Search and Rescue Convention, 142–3
separation of powers doctrine (Australia), 56–8, 62, 67, 70
Shaughnessy v United States ex rel Mezei, 60, 64–5
Sophia. *see* European Union Naval Force Mediterranean ('EUNAVFOR Med')
South East Asia, 174–5, 186
Spain, 170–1, 170n
Sri Lankan asylum seekers, 84n, 84–5, 89–90
statelessness, 142
state responsibility, 159–61
stopping boats. *see* maritime interdiction
strategic adjustment, 22–3
Suriname, 110–11
Switzerland, 24
Syrian refugees, 26–7

Temporary Protection visa, 116–17n
territorial sea, 139–42
Teubner, Gunther, 12–13
Thailand, 174–5, 186
third country transfers, 100–3, 123, 162–3
transfers. *see also* legal transfers; policy transfers
   between Australia and United States, 48–53
   and coercion, 22
   cooperative versus competitive, 22–3
   failures of, 21
   and globalisation, 20
   interdisciplinary approach to, 4, 7
   and legal success, 177–80
   and maritime interdiction, 83
   opportunity for, 47–8
   phases of, 46–7
   political dimension of, 184
   and prestige, 21–2
   and process success, 183
   and programmatic failure, 180–2
   success of, 177
transit processing camps, 172
Trinidad and Tobago, 75, 110
Trump administration
   and ATD programs, 51–2
   on border control, 30

Trump administration (*cont.*)
    and mandatory detention, 41–3, 46–7
    and travel ban, 1, 41–2n
    and US-Australia resettlement deals, 128–9
Türk, Volker, 20, 167
Turkey, 22
Turks and Caicos, 110–11
Turnbull, Malcolm, 128
Twining, William, 5, 7–8

UN Committee on the Rights of the Child, 164
undocumented migrants, 28, 35–6
UNHCR
    on Australia's detention practices, 152
    and detention conditions, 153
    and European extraterritorial processing plans, 172
    Executive Committee (ExCom) meetings of, 24–5
    and extraterritorial processing, 100–1, 112–13
    as forum for transfer, 47
    on mandatory detention, 133–4
    and refugee status determination, 148
    on *Sale*, 80
    and state responsibility, 160–1
    and third country processing, 110–11, 162–3
    2012 Revised Detention Guidelines, 135
UN High-Level Dialogue on International Migration and Development ('HLD'), 47
UN Human Rights Committee
    on Australia's detention practices, 136–8, 136n
    and collective expulsion, 149–50
    and differential treatment, 166
    on mandatory detention, 133–4
    and *non-refoulement*, 145–6
    on right to life, 141n
UNICEF, 182
United Kingdom
    and Australian model, 1, 167–8
    and extraterritorial processing plans, 172
    and Five Country Conferences, 25–6
United Nations Convention of the Law of the Sea ('*UNCLOS*'), 139n, 139–41
United States
    and border control, 1–3, 30, 34
    and child asylum seekers, 164–5
    and detention conditions, 151, 153–4
    and deterrence through mandatory detention, 135–6
    and differential treatment, 165–6
    and European extraterritorial processing plans, 172
    and exclusion laws, 28–9
    and extraterritorial processing, 100–3, 131
    and extraterritorial processing case law, 130–1
    and Five Country Conferences, 25–6
    and Guantánamo Bay, 103–10
    immigration administration structure of, 19
    and indefinite detention, 68–70
    influence of on Pacific Solution, 112–13
    and legal similarities to Australia, 16–17
    and mandatory detention, 36–43, 73, 137–8

and maritime interdiction, 75–81, 85, 140
and *non-refoulement*, 144–9
and public opinion on immigration, 29
and *Refugee Convention* and *Protocol*, 24, 32
and refugee status determination, 157–8
and state responsibility, 159–61
and third country processing, 110–11
and xenophobia, 30–1
US-Australia resettlement deals, 127–9
US case law. *see specific cases*
US Citizenship and Immigration Services ('USCIS'), 19
US Coast Guard, 74–6
US Congress, 53–4
US Constitution
   and extraterritorial processing, 104
   and Guantánamo Bay, 107–8
   and immigration law, 53–6
   and legal success, 179–80
   and refugee status determination, 157–8
US Customs and Border Protection ('CBP'), 19
US Immigration and Customs Enforcement ('ICE'), 19, 40–3, 52
US Immigration and Naturalization Service ('INS'), 19, 37, 38–9n, 38–9, 101–3
US Supreme Court. *see specific cases*

Venezuela, 75
vertical transfer, 6

Watson, Alan, 4, 12
Wilsher, Daniel, 36
Wong Wing v United States, 53–4

xenophobia, 30–1

Yamataya v Fisher, 55

Zadvydas v Davis, 62–70